INTERSUBJECTIVITY IN ECONOMICS

Belief in the nineteenth-century neoclassical vision of atomistic economic agency, the foundation of twentienth-century economics, is now fast disappearing. This collection of lively essays responds to the emerging consensus that understanding the economic realities of today and of tomorrow requires theoretical approaches that recognize the intersubjective nature of economic reality.

It is now self-evident that interdependencies between the tastes, preferences, demands, goals, ethics, perceptions and decisions of economic actors are pervasive. Intersubjective economic phenomena can no longer be sensibly treated as inconsequential exceptions to an atomistic neoclassical rule. Economists today face the challenge of developing conceptual frameworks and analytical systems for comprehending the economic realities structured by intersubjectivity.

The essays in this volume, many of them outstanding and some likely to become classics, survey the foundational steps in this project. This international collection brings together theorists of note from Europe and America who, from a variety of perspectives, explore the possibilities for a non-atomistic economic theory. Each essay is both an independent exploration and a starting point for work by others.

Edward Fullbrook is the author of numerous academic works – books, chapters in books and journal articles – in economics, philosophy and social theory.

ECONOMICS AS SOCIAL THEORY
Edited by Tony Lawson
University of Cambridge

Social theory is experiencing something of a revival within economics. Critical analyses of the particular nature of the subject matter of social studies and of the types of method, categories and modes of explanation that can legitimately be endorsed for the scientific study of social objects, are re-emerging. Economists are again addressing such issues as the relationship between agency and structure, between economy and the rest of society, and between the enquirer and the object of enquiry. There is a renewed interest in elaborating basic categories such as causation, competition, culture, discrimination, evolution, money, need, order, organization, power probability, process, rationality, technology, time, truth, uncertainty, value, etc.

The objective for this series is to facilitate this revival further. In contemporary economics the label 'theory' has been appropriated by a group that confines itself to largely asocial, ahistorical, mathematical 'modeling'. *Economics as Social Theory* thus reclaims the 'theory' label, offering a platform for alternative rigorous, but broader and more critical conceptions of theorizing.

Other titles in this series include:

ECONOMICS AND LANGUAGE
Edited by Willie Henderson

RATIONALITY, INSTITUTIONS AND
ECONOMIC METHODOLOGY
Edited by Uskali Mäki, Bo Gustafsson, and Christian Knudsen

NEW DIRECTIONS IN ECONOMIC METHODOLOGY
Edited by Roger Backhouse

WHO PAYS FOR THE KIDS?
Nancy Folbre

RULES AND CHOICE IN ECONOMICS
Viktor Vanberg

BEYOND RHETORIC AND REALISM IN ECONOMICS
Thomas A. Boylan and Paschal F. O'Gorman

INTERSUBJECTIVITY IN ECONOMICS

Agents and structures

Edited by
Edward Fullbrook

London and New York

First published 2002
by Routledge
11 New Fetter Lane, London EC4P 4EE

Simultaneously published in the USA and Canada
by Routledge
29 West 35th Street, New York, NY 10001

Routledge is an imprint of the
Taylor & Francis Group

Typeset in 10/12 Palatino by Newgen Imaging Systems (P) Ltd.
Printed and bound in Great Britain by St Edmundsbury Press,
Bury St Edmunds, Suffolk

British Library Cataloguing in Publication Data
A catalogue record for this book is available
from the British Library

Library of Congress Cataloging in Publication Data
Intersubjectivity in economics: agents and structures/[edited by]
Edward Fullbrook
p. cm.—(Economics as social theory)
Includes bibliographical references and index.
ISBN 0-415-26697-1 (alk. paper)—ISBN 0-415-26698-X (pbk.: alk. paper)
1. Economics—Psychological aspects. I. Fullbrook, Edward. II. Series.

ISBN 0-415-26697-1 (hbk)
ISBN 0-415-26698-X (pbk)

CONTENTS

CONTENTS

ILLUSTRATIONS

Figures

Tables

CONTRIBUTORS

Frank Ackerman is Research Director of the Global Development and Environment Institute at Tufts University. He has written widely on environmental economics, and on alternative approaches to economic theory. His most recent books are *The Changing Nature of Work*, 1998, (for which he was lead editor) and *Why Do We Recycle? Markets, Values and Public Policy*, 1997, both available from Island Press. He received his PhD in economics from Harvard University, and has taught at the University of Massachusetts and at Tufts University.

John B. Davis, Professor of Economics and International Business, PhD in Philosophy (University of Illinois, 1993) and PhD in Economics (Michigan State University, 1985), teaches International Trade and International Economics at Marquette University. He is the author of *Keynes's Philosophical Development* (Cambridge, 1994), editor of *New Economics and Its History* (Duke 1998), and co-editor of *The Handbook of Economic Methodology* (Elgar 1998). Among the journals he has published in are *Cambridge Journal of Economics*, *Economic Journal*, *Review of Political Economy*, *Economics and Philosophy*, *The European Journal of the History of Economic Thought*, and *Journal of Economic Methodology*. He has been a visiting scholar at Cambridge University and Duke University. He is President-Elect of the History of Economics Society, and has been the editor of the *Review of Social Economy* since 1987. Currently, he is working on a book to be published by Routledge on theories of the individual in economics.

Jean-Pierre Dupuy is Professor of Social and Political Philosophy at the Ecole Polytechnique (Paris), the founder-director of Centre de Recherche en Epistémologie Appliquée (CREA) and Professor of Political Science at Stanford University. His most recent books are *La Sacrifice et l'envie, Le libéralisme aux prises avec la justice sociale*, Calmann-Lévy, Paris, 1992 (a critical analysis of Anglo-American moral and political philosophy, from Adam Smith and the Utilitarians to John Rawls, Robert Nozick and Friedrich Hayek); *Understanding Origin* (with F. Varela), Kluwer, Boston, 1992 (a philosophical study of the concept of "origin" in biology, cultural studies, artificial intelligence and anthropology); *La Panique*, Delagrange, Paris, 1992 (a philosophical analysis of the most elusive collective phenomenon in human affairs: panic); *Introduction aux sciences sociales, Logique des phénomènes collectifs*, Ellipses, Paris, 1992; *Aux origines des sciences cognitives*, La Découverted, Paris, 1994 and English translation forthcoming Princeton University Press (an intellectual history of cybernetics from 1943 to 1954); editor of *Self-Deception and Paradoxes of Rationality*, Stanford University Press, 1998 (a confrontation of continental and analytical philosophy on the phenomenon of self-deception). His current research is focused on the paradoxes of rationality, especially the antinomies of reason in the age of rational choice theory, analytic philosophy and cognitive science.

Armin Falk is Assistant Professor and Researcher at the Institute for Empirical Research in Economics at the University of Zurich. He has published papers in *Journal of Political Economy* and *Journal of Economic Psychology*.

Ernst Fehr is Professor in Economics at the University of Zurich. He is best known for his recent papers on the economics of reciprocity and cooperation, which have appeared in the *American Economic Review, Quarterly Journal of Economics, European Economic Review, Journal of Political Economy*, and *Quarterly Journal of Economics*.

Edward Fullbrook researches in phenomenological philosophy and social theory, as well as in economics. His current fields include analysis of market price/quantity phenomena from the point of view of a measurement rather than an equilibrating process and development of approaches to economics ruled by neither atomistic nor holistic metaphysics. His most recent book is *Simone de Beauvoir: A Critical Introduction* (with Kate Fullbrook), Polity Press, UK and Blackwell, US, 1998. He has published numerous articles in academic journals and collections. He is editor of the *post-autistic economics newsletter*.

Shaun P. Hargreaves Heap is Professor of Economics at the University of East Anglia and the author of several monographs and numerous articles.

Geoffrey M. Hodgson is a Research Professor in Business Studies at the University of Hertfordshire. He was formerly a Reader in Economics at the University of Cambridge. His books include: *How Economics Forgot History* (2001), *Economics and Utopia* (1999), *Evolution and Institutions* (1999), *Economics and Evolution* (1993) and *Economics and Institutions* (1988). He has published widely in the academic journals and he is listed in *Who's Who in Economics* (3rd edn).

Frédéric Lebaron is a member of the Centre de Sociologie européenne and "maître de conférences" at the University of Picardie. He specializes in economic sociology and the sociology of economic rhetoric. His book *The Production of Economic Beliefs* was recently published by Le Seuil.

Thierry Levy is *Professeur-Agrégé* at the French Institute for Advanced Mechanics and at the department of Management of the Institute of Technology at University Jean-Monnet. He also is a researcher at the Entrepreneurship and Management Research Center of the University of Grenoble-II. His current research interests include: epistemology, value theory, theories of the firm, international economics, industrial organization, quality economics, and entrepreneurship.

Paul Lewis was educated at Peterhouse, Cambridge and Christ Church, Oxford. He was a Research Fellow of Emmanuel College, Cambridge, before becoming Director of Studies in Economics, and also in Social and Political Sciences, at Newnham College, Cambridge. His research lies in the philosophy of the social sciences, especially the relationship between social structure and human agency, and the methodology of economics.

Roger Mason is Professor of Consumer Theory at the University of Salford and author of *The Economics of Conspicuous Consumption* (1998). His teaching and research interests are in consumer economics and the history of economic thought. Previous publications include *Conspicuous Consumption: A Study of Exceptional Consumer Behaviour* (1981) *Robert Giffen and The Giffen Paradox* (1989) and numerous articles on consumer theory, economics and related subjects.

Anne Mayhew is Professor of History and Associate Dean for Academic Programs in the College of Arts & Sciences at the University of Tennessee. She has been editor of the *Journal of Economic Issues*. Her research has been in U.S. economic history and in the history and current development of American Institutionalist Theory, with particular emphasis on the work of Thorstein Veblen and his anthropological perspective.

Paul Ormerod is the author of *The Death of Economics* (1994) and *Butterfly Economics: A New General Theory of Social and Economic Behaviour* (Faber, 1999).

Ralph William Pfouts is Professor Emeritus of Economics at the University of North Carolina at Chapel Hill. He has published over 70 articles in academic journals and collections.

Jochen Runde is University Lecturer in Economics at the University of Cambridge. His main research area is the methodology of economics, especially as concerns probability, uncertainty and decision theory, idealisation and abstraction, causality and causal explanation, and rational choice theory.

S. Abu Turab Rizvi received his PhD from the New School for Social Research in 1990, and now is Associate Professor and Chair of Economics at the University of Vermont. His research interests include preference formation, the concept of utility, and the limitations of game theory and of general equilibrium theory.

Laurent Thévenot is Professor at the Ecole des Hautes Etudes en Science Sociales (Paris) where he teaches Social Theory and Institutional Economics. His research agenda covers issues concerning both disciplines: theory of action, cognition and coordination; forms of evaluation (not restricted to market price) and processes of critique and justification. He co-authored, with Luc Boltanski, *De la Justification* (forthcoming, Harvard University Press) which analyzes the most legitimate forms of evaluation governing political, economic and social relationships. Other publications in the so-called "Economie des conventions" include *Conventions économiques* and *Le travail: marchés, règles, conventions* (this last book was co-edited with Robert Salais). He recently edited two books concerning new approaches to action, the practical engagement of objects and social cognition: *Les objets dans l'action* (With Bernard Conein and Nicolas Dodier); *Cognition et information en société* (with Bernard Conein). A co-edited book with Michèle Lamont presenting the results of four years of comparative research is forthcoming from Cambridge University Press: *Polities and Repertoires of Evaluation in France and the United States*.

Peter Wynarczyk is Head of Economics at the University of Northumbria. His research interests include macroeconomics, economics of crime, and political economy. He is the author (with B. Snowdon and H. Vane) of *A Modern Guide to Macroeconomics: An Introduction to Competing Schools of Thought* (1994) with translations in French, Italian, Polish and Chinese, and of the forthcoming *The Dynamics of Capitalism: A Comparative Analysis of Schumpeter and Hirshman* (Edward Elgar, 2001/2).

ACKNOWLEDGEMENTS

A few years ago, while presenting a paper in a session on mathematical economics at a conference in Brussels, I noticed the most improbable thing. In the third row a very young man was sitting on the edge of his chair, apparently rigid with interest. The discussion that followed confirmed this unlikelihood, so after the session I approached him. He said his name was Thierry Levy, that he was a graduate student in Paris, and that he knew some French economists who would be interested in my paper.

So I sent copies of that and another paper to Levy. He wrote back saying he had sent them on to his contacts and was now sending me something that he had written. A few days later my heart sank when a 40,000 word typescript arrived. Titled "Conventions et Fondements de l'Echange marchand et de la Monnaie", it had no apparent connection with anything in which I was interested. But for honor's sake, I decided to give it an hour. That was the beginning of this collection.

As editor of the series *Economics as Social Theory*, Tony Lawson generously gave me both his moral support and a free hand for this project. Jean-Pierre Dupuy's encouragement, advice and practical assistance were essential for getting it started. Likewise André Orléan. I am also grateful to Geoffrey Hodgson and Ralph William Pfouts for their encouragement and early support. Thanks also are owed to Marc Lavoie, Peter Earl, Robert Lane and Pierre Bourdieu for assistance in lining up contributors. But most of all this collection is indebted to the many-faceted and wise assistance of my partner, Kate Fullbrook.

INTRODUCTION
Why intersubjectivity?

Edward Fullbrook

Science and anti-science

"It often happens," observed John Stuart Mill, "that the universal belief of one age of mankind ... becomes to a subsequent age so palpable an absurdity, that the only difficulty then is to imagine how such a thing can ever have appeared credible" (*Principles of Political Economy*, "Preliminary Remarks"). Although the belief that neoclassical economics' concept of an atomistic economic man suffices as a conceptualization of economic agency never quite gained universality among economists, it was long compulsory for them to profess allegiance to it. Such compliance is evidenced by the fact that the terms "economic man" and *"homo economicus"* were, until recently, used without qualification to refer to their neoclassical or atomistic construction. Likewise "economic rationality". Today, however, many of the former verities of economic orthodoxy are increasingly subjected to critique as the spirit of scientific inquiry recrudesces. All around us, belief in the sufficiency of the nineteenth-century neoclassical vision of economic agency is now disappearing like snow at the end of winter. In response, this collection of papers is about conceptualizing *non*-atomistic economic agents and the interactive structures to which they give rise.

The neoclassical atomistic *homo economicus* is a conceptual Frankenstein. The idea was fabricated in the late nineteenth century to serve the dream of constructing models of the economic universe in the image of Newtonian mechanics. Such models treat economic agents as if they were particles obeying mechanical laws whose behavior could, in principle, be described by a solvable system of equations. Determinate models of economic behavior, even when not reified as a belief in a determinate economic universe, require "economic agents" possessing properties formally corresponding to those of Newton's particles. Above all, economic subjects must be declared atomic. Application of atomism to the economic realm means treating human desires and proclivities as fundamental data, which, like the masses of physical bodies in classical mechanics, are not affected by the relations being modeled.

1

Application of the doctrine of atomism implicitly divides interactions between entities, be they inanimate or not, into two primary categories. Some interactions result in a change only in the *behavior* of the individuals, whereas the rest – and this is the set that atomistic conceptualisation excludes – result in a change in the *properties* of the individuals. In the human realm, this is the distinction between *intra*subjective and *inter*subjective relations. A purely intrasubjective interaction between two human subjects or between a human subject and socio-cultural-economic structures (for example, markets), is one that leaves the subjects, like Newton's atoms, unchanged as entities. An intersubjective interaction is one that does not.

In terms of economic model building, the difference between intra and intersubjective relations is fundamental. Neoclassical economics' two basic functional concepts, supply and demand, are predicated on the assumption that no intersubjective relations enter into the determination of market supply and demand. They are conceived as simple additive aggregations of the supplies and demands of the individual subjects. These conceptions preclude any intersubjective relations between economic agents influencing the determination of their supplies and demands, because such interdependencies would void the definition of market demand and supply. This formalistic imperative has meant that, for more than a century, intersubjectivity has been taboo in mainstream economics.

From the vantage point of a high-tech, instantaneous mass communication consumer society, the notion that economic agents are autonomous subjectivities and that, therefore, economic phenomena are exclusively *intra*subjective appears as a palpable absurdity. In our age we all know that what we think, desire and decide as economic actors depends a great deal on what other actors are seen to think, desire and decide. But this was not always so much the case. When neoclassical economics was in its formative stages (1870–1890), economic activity was primarily about satisfying material needs in a pre-electronic world. Prior to the last century, most people in the West lived at or near subsistence level. Inter-subjectivity does not enter directly into the determination of the biological requirements of sustaining a human life and of providing it with basic physical comfort. So at the time of economics' founding and through much of the nineteenth century, basing the concept of *homo economicus* on atomistic individualism and sensationalist psychology, although limiting the scope of its inquiry, left it with a wide field to cover. In other words, it was an age when *intrasubjective economics* could arguably claim as its domain the greater part of economic phenomena. But in our age, outside of the poorest countries, the economic realm to which intrasubjective economics pertains grows smaller and smaller every year.

Indeed, for a long time now it has been impossible for neoclassicalism to offer justifications of its lingering hegemony by appealing to economic reality. That has increased the difficulty of concealing the fact that formalist expediency, rather than scientific curiosity, accounts for neoclassical economics' atomist metaphysic. Supporters of this metaphysic, especially in economics textbooks, have proceeded as if the atomist framework of classical mechanics characterizes the physical sciences in general. This is very far from the truth. Scientists settled upon the concept of immutable units for this particular field of inquiry, not for ideological or philosophical reasons, but because it fits this particular class of physical phenomena. For other modes of physical interaction and other classes of physical entities, natural science has not and does not always proceed from the presupposition of immutable units. Chemistry is the most obvious example, its primary focus being the property changes in units of matter resulting from their interactions. If, instead of being pragmatic and pluralistic, natural science had taken a dogmatic approach to its metaphysics, insisting upon the same set of presuppositions for every class of physical phenomena, then very little of modern science would exist.

As noted, something like this did happen in economics. This collection of essays is about changing that, about accelerating the breakdown of the anti-scientific ethos that blocks critical inquiry, about creating, in addition to the intrasubjective economics of neoclassicalism, an *intersubjective economics*. This is a project for a century. Initially, it requires conceptual ground-work. That is the business of this collection. Each chapter is an independent exploration, each a possible starting point for work by others.

Ideally, the concept development required for this undertaking falls into two categories. First, concepts of non-atomistic agents must be formed, concepts subtle enough to capture the ambiguity and complexity of the intersubjective agent. Second, social, cultural and economic structures created by such agents must be identified and analyzed in terms of the way they in turn shape and reshape the agents. Hence, the division of this collection's chapters into two parts: agents and structures. But of course intersubjectivity means that agents and agents, and agents and socio-economic structures are interdependent, so that conceptualizing one level inevitably involves concepts relating to the other. In all the chapters, therefore, you will find considerations of both kinds of concepts.

Intersubjective agents

Theories of human behavior tend to divide between the extremes of free-will atomism and social determinacy. The causal monism of these polar opposites makes their conceptualization relatively unproblematic and therefore attractive to theorists. Intersubjectivity, the third possibility, presents a much stiffer challenge, as it falls in the tangled and recursive middle ground. The first chapter, by John Davis, seeks to conceptualize the interface between the individual and society, with the aim of creating a framework for treating economic agents as socially embedded. He does so by drawing on the relatively new philosophical concept of collective intentionality. This is the idea that the intentions of agents are mediated by the intentions that they attribute to the groups to which they belong. Davis uses these "we-intentions" to show how socially embedded agents influence the institutions and social values that have shaped them. He also demonstrates that the individual behavior of socially embedded agents cannot be explained solely in terms of instrumental rationality.

In Chapter 2 Ernst Fehr and Armin Falk arrive at conclusions similar to those of Davis, but by radically different means. Fehr and Falk belong to the small but growing number of experimental economists. In their Zurich laboratories they attempt to unravel the enigmas of economic agency. One such is that, despite the ubiquity of material incentives for cheating, most economic actors most of the time do not cheat other actors. Some of these choices to forgo rewards are explainable by game theory models of repeated interaction. But most are not. For these Fehr and Falk hypothesize that, given favorable social conditions, there exists a proclivity for agents to be willing to sacrifice resources to be kind to those who are being kind and to punish those who are being unkind. They call their hypothesis, which is confirmed in laboratory experiments, *reciprocal fairness*. Fehr and Falk review the empirical evidence. They also explore the relationship between reciprocal fairness and socio-economic cooperation and explain how social structures aimed at deterring cheating may have the opposite effect, so much so as to induce the majority of people to cheat.

In Chapter 3 Anne Mayhew challenges a foundational idea, not just of neoclassical economics, but also of the classical and Marxian traditions. She argues that an agent's subsistence needs, beyond basic nutritional and shelter requirements, are socially constructed. In all societies, she writes, "what is 'surplus' and what is needed for survival is defined socially." Neoclassical theorists, she argues, have had to deny, ignore or play down the social determination of consumption patterns and the significance of advertising in order to continue with their definition of the rational consumer. Mayhew notes that economists are the only social scientists who treat the social role of consumption as trivial. She then takes apart the two arguments that mainstream economists have used to justify their eccentric position.

In the late 1970s a succession of papers that have become known as the "SMD results" threw the General Equilibrium Theory into radical crises. They showed that the equilibrium of GET is necessarily neither unique nor stable. In Chapter 4 Frank Ackerman builds the case that this disaster for neoclassical theory at the aggregate level stems from its micro-model of individual agents as uncoordinated, unchanging and asocial. In an analytical *tour de force*, Ackerman traces the breakdown of the general theory back to the underlying model of economic agency, especially as it relates to consumers, arriving at the conclusion that "the assumption of asocial individualism in neoclassical economics guarantees that the aggregation problem is insurmountable."

In Chapter 5 Ralph Pfouts conducts a dialogue between his neoclassical roots and the ideas of Tony Lawson's *Economics and Reality*. Taking the ontology of the agent as consumer as his focus, Pfouts provides an exemplary essay of intellectual give and take, mixing stiff criticism with sympathy and respect for Lawson's project. Pfouts, against Lawson, argues that event regularities exist and can be discovered in the economic realm. He concedes that economics' corpus has been shaved too closely by Occam's razor, but cautions against taking economics into a quagmire of psychological theories. In his conclusion Pfouts writes:

> Too often economic theorists have not adopted logical methods appropriate for investigating the economic world, but instead have assumed an imaginary economic world that submits to the logical methods they want to use. They have preferred to abandon the world in favor of their preferences in mathematics rather than using mathematical and other methods that are effective in analyzing the real world.

These sentences, written before the onset of the recent events in France, would be at home in the French students' manifesto that launched the Post-Autistic Economics Movement.

Conspicuous consumption has long been the most salient example of intersubjectivity entering significantly into the determination of economic outcomes. Roger Mason, in Chapter 6, provides an historical overview of economics' fear, avoidance and occasional fascination with real-life consumerism. Beginning with Mandeville's *The Fable of the Bees*, Mason traces economics' moral concerns with intersubjectively-inspired consumption in the classical period and then surveys Veblen's notorious violations of the neoclassical taboo on acknowledging the intersubjective dimension of economic agents. But Mason gives most space to a needed survey of post-World-War-II literature on intersubjective consumption, including Morgenstern, Leibenstein, Duesenberry, the Friedmans, Modigliani, Lancaster and Hirsch.

In the 1960s and 1970s, neoclassical theory, *à la* Chicago, developed what has come to be called the economics of criminal participation. Windy-city orthodoxy initially had this field all to itself, but more recently economists with Austrian and intersubjective frameworks have entered this politically charged area of inquiry. In Chapter 7 Peter Wynarczyk, putting politics to the side, compares these approaches for their ability to account for crime statistics, and critiques the adequacy, plausibility and heuristic value of their concepts. Wynarczyk shows that the Chicago approach neither explains why there has been such an increase in crime in the West in recent decades nor why it is not experiencing much more. Explanation of criminal participation, he argues, requires "a conceptually richer model of human agency", one that includes temporal and intersubjective dimensions. Drawing on very recent literature, Wynarczyk considers the possibilities.

The conversation value of a television program approaches nil for the viewer when no one else watches it. In the television industry everyone knows that a prime reason for choosing to regularly watch a particular program is that other people, especially people one knows, are watching it. This hypothesis, that an agent's demand for a product may depend positively on the number of other people demanding it, though uncontested throughout the media industries, remains out of bounds for neoclassical, that is, intrasubjective theory. In Chapter 8 Hargreaves Heap, beginning with the case of television, argues that this variety of demand interdependence operates also in non-media industries, but that because the origin of the interdependence may be different in those industries, it is for them not necessarily a common cause of market failure. Hargreaves Heap, therefore, seeks to develop an understanding of the various ways in which demand is intersubjectively constituted.

Intersubjective structures

Both Keynes and Hayek developed conceptions of the role of imitation in markets, Keynes in *The General Theory* (1936) and Hayek much later in his final book. In Chapter 9 Jean-Pierre Dupuy compares and critiques Keynes's and Hayek's approaches, leading us to new levels of understanding of intersubjective market structures. The literature of economics includes very few papers as acute, subtle and elegant as this one.

Geoffrey Hodgson's ambitious essay, which comprises Chapter 10, develops the concept of "reconstitutive downward causation" in the context of individual agency. It, in fact, addresses the agency–structure problem head on. Reconstitutive downward causation involves the proposition that individuals are formed as well as constrained by their situation. Hodgson briefly discusses the genealogy and basis of this idea, and argues that this concept or one very like it is necessary if social science is to avoid inconsistent or incomplete arguments. He also contrasts reconstitutive downward causation with other approaches found in the social sciences.

In Chapter 11 Laurent Thévenot investigates what he calls "critical situations", in which there is no single rationale, e.g. neoclassical rationality, for behavior that applies to everyone in all their varying circumstances. In such situations agents may be torn between incommensurable rationales, thereby revealing to themselves and to researchers that no form of justification is "natural" or uniquely objective. Thévenot identifies various decision-making structures in addition to neoclassical rationality that enter into behavior choices in economic situations. He then explores the possibility of developing an analytical framework that accounts for critical situations while remaining compatible with traditional intrasubjective economic analysis.

In Chapter 12 Paul Lewis and Jochen Runde compare and evaluate the project of Critical Realism in economics in relation to "the phenomenological approach to the investigation of the socio-economic world, promoted in economic methodology by Edward Fullbrook and employed in substantive economic theory by members of the French intersubjectivist school." Lewis and Runde, two of Critical Realism's most engaging and incisive interpreters, bring Lawson's *Economics and Reality* to the fore. Their stylish essay considers the ins and outs of conceptualizing intersubjectivity and the socio-economic realm, especially interpersonal social structures, and concludes that Critical Realism wins the highest marks.

Are the structures of intersubjective relations amenable to mathematical analysis? In Chapter 13 Paul Ormerod makes the case that they are and that formal modeling has an important role to play in the study of economic intersubjectivity, especially as a means of developing alternatives to orthodoxy. Ormerod believes that the atomist assumptions of neoclassical economics were designed to make the math tractable, but that today computing power enables the construction of more realistic models. To prove his point, he first adumbrates a model that, relaxing just two of the assumptions of the perfect competition model, leads to an industry outcome in which, as in reality, oligopoly rather than perfect competition is the norm. To further illustrate his point, Ormerod sketches a second model which shows unemployment rates to be a function of the presence and shape of social networks.

Given the French tradition of locating intellectual vacuums, it comes as no surprise that French sociologists have recently undertaken a "sociological reconstruction of the economic sciences". In this project, Pierre Bourdieu figures large, and in Chapter 14 Frédéric Lebaron surveys his contribution. This includes probing various presuppositions that haunt traditionalist economics, especially its fantasy that market systems, capitalist institutions and "rationality" are natural phenomenon rather than socially constructed. Lebaron's essay overflows with ideas that economists need to think about immediately, none more so than the fact that economics itself, by imposing certain visions of economic reality, is a key player in the social construction of economic reality.

S. Abu Turab Rizvi makes the case in Chapter 15 that normative economics fails to thrive because it lacks a framework broad enough to accommodate the many questions and issues that the very idea of such an economics raises. For help, Rizvi turns to Adam Smith's theory in *The Theory of Moral Sentiments*, especially its intersubjective dimension. Rizvi wants to identify what features of theories impede progress and what features make normative theory workable. To this end he brings together in conversation with Smith a disparate but intriguing collection of theorists, including Nussbaum, Stanley Fish, Milton Friedman, Derrida, Arrow and Benhabib. In the end it is Smith's development of the idea that our normative intuitions have their origins in society that Rizvi identifies as the way out of the morass.

If it is absurd to exclude intersubjectivity from the theory of markets, arguably it is even more so to exclude it from the theory of the firm. As a first step toward overcoming the latter deficiency, Thierry Levy in Chapter 16 develops a theory of quality control in organizations. To do so, he draws heavily on the work of Thévenot and Boltanski. Levy's paper begins with a devastating critique of the neoclassical theory of quality, including Lancaster's reworking of it. It also includes a cogent survey of recent attempts to get beyond the neoclassical axioms. But the real and intriguing heart of Levy's essay is its application of the French theory of conventions to "the" concept of quality. He identifies several different concepts of quality, some internally defined and others externally, as typically operating within the same firm. He then, with case history examples, explores the interactions that take place in these complex webs of intersubjectivity.

Chapter 17, my own, offers a radical critique of one of economics' most basic foundational structures. It has always been regarded as self-evident that the algebraic properties of exchange value are Euclidean. But no one, it seems, has bothered previously (because it is essential to intrasubjective economics) to look at the evidence for or against this usually tacit but most fundamental of all propositions of economics. Chapter 17 considers various widely observed market phenomena (e.g. inflation and inelastic demand) from the standpoint of what they tell us about the algebraic structure of exchange value. The evidence reveals that the truth is rather different from the traditional belief. Some consequences of this for economic theory, past, present and future, are examined.

Part 1

INTERSUBJECTIVE AGENTS

1

COLLECTIVE INTENTIONALITY AND INDIVIDUAL BEHAVIOR

John B. Davis

In this paper I develop a heterodox economics account of how individuals influence institutions and social values. In contemporary economics there are two opposed ways of characterizing this influence. Mainstream economics treats institutions and social values as the products of *atomistic* individual activity, meaning that when individuals act, they act free of any significant social attachments. In contrast, heterodox economics treats institutions and social values as the product of *socially embedded* individual activity, meaning that when individuals act, they act socially or as members of various kinds of groups. The atomistic view has dominated economics for a half century or more. Thus, to make sense of this difference from a heterodox perspective, we need to show how individuals in groups act differently from groups of atomistic individuals, or how individuals acting in an organized way behave differently from unorganized collections of individuals. I understand the difference to be essentially a matter of explaining how individuals acting in groups have "shared" intentions about the groups of which they are members.

This distinction between "shared" intentions and ordinary individual intentions may seem relatively straightforward in everyday language, since people use "we" language in an intentional manner when they focus on their membership in groups ("what we want," "what our department decided," "what the community has chosen to do," etc.), and use "I" language when they see themselves as acting independently of others ("what I want," "what I believe," etc.). Yet, until recently the philosophical explanation of intentionality has been almost entirely associated with the explanation of individual intentions associated with the use of "I" language. Moreover, proponents of individualist explanations in the social sciences and especially in economics argue that it makes no sense to ascribe intentions to groups of individuals, because only individuals can have intentions. For them, our ordinary ways of speaking are at best an ill-founded expedient, and a proper analysis of "we" language should reduce such expressions to sets of "I" expressions.

Here, my strategy is to develop an account of "shared" intention that answers these objections by drawing on a more recent philosophical literature on the subject of collective intentionality. In this literature, when we speak of individuals as being socially embedded, we mean that they have *we-intentions*, that is, intentions that they attribute – and believe that others attribute – to the group of which they are members. Though these we-intentions are often said to be "shared" in this literature, caution needs to be shown in using this term. Collective intentionality analysis is non-holistic, meaning that only individuals have intentions, not groups. Individuals attribute intentions to the groups of which they are members, and participate in this attribution by using "we" language. In this sense we-intentions are shared. But this does not imply that a group has an intention over and above the intentions of the individuals that make it up. We-intentions are individually expressed intentions, though of a special kind in making the group rather than the individual their subject. In what follows, then, only individuals exist in regard to intentional expression. The issue then becomes whether the relationships between individuals expressing we-intentions are compatible with characterizing individuals atomistically, or whether individuals' use of "we" language requires that we characterize individuals as being socially embedded.

This issue, however, cannot be kept separate from another. As I will argue, the most important consequence of treating individuals as being socially embedded in groups is that their behavior can no longer be explained solely in instrumentally rational terms. That is, when individuals are seen to be socially embedded in groups, the requirements upon them as members of those groups dictate that their behavior be explained as what I label a *deontologically rational* behavior or as *"principled" rational* behavior. Thus, if a collective intentionality analysis of individuals' use of "we" language implies that individuals cannot be conceived of atomistically, but must be thought to be socially embedded in groups, then it also implies that their behavior needs to be reconceptualized as well, with instrumental rationality taking a back seat to a deontologically rational or "principled" rational type of behavior.

In this chapter, I thus address the question of how individuals influence institutions and social values in terms of a conception of the individual as socially embedded, explaining this conception in terms of we-intentions, and drawing out the implications all this has for how we understand individual behavior. Section 1 introduces the concept of collective intentionality, relying on the thinking of the leading contributor to the subject, Finnish philosopher, Raimo Tuomela. Section 2 applies the collective intentionality concept to the agency-structure model as drawn from Tony Lawson (1997) to explain how individuals socially embedded in groups can be thought to influence institutions and social values through their ability to form we-intentions. Section 3 addresses how our understanding of individual economic behavior needs to be revised to include deontologically or "principled" rational behavior when we consider the socially embedded individual. Section 4 briefly comments on individuals' capacity to form we-intentions in terms of the idea of seeing things from others' points of view, and then summarizes the argument of the paper.

1. Collective intentionality and individuals' influence on institutions and social values

Until recently, analytic philosophers have explained the concept of intentionality – the idea that mental states have an "aboutness" to them – in terms of the actions and intentions of individuals (e.g. Anscombe 1963; Davidson 1980).[1] Having an intention involves settling on a course of action, either by deciding to act in some way or even by simply excluding considerations that favor alternative courses of action. Having an intention involves forming a commitment to action, and intentional action only occurs when an agent aims to bring something about by acting in a purposive way. But if a collection of individuals performs some set of actions as a group or team, and each individual acts intentionally, does this mean that the group acts intentionally as well, settling on a group course of action and making a commitment to action as a group?

In the atomist tradition, individuals form intentions and act, groups do not. Individuals may act as members of groups, but they still form their intentions individually, because only individual minds exist. Thus Hayek held that supra-individual entities such as groups, classes, etc. should be thought of as theoretical concepts rather than real things (e.g. Hayek 1955), and Arrow's assertion that "society" "is just a convenient label for the totality of individuals" (Arrow 1984: 80). From their perspective, because all intentionality is individual, collective intentionality must be a theoretical concept rather than a really existing thing. The alternative is to imagine some fanciful sort of Hegelian super-mind floating above and about individual minds. Yet, the dilemma this poses is a false one. We can say that all mental life occurs within individual minds, but this does not imply that all intentions are individual and must be expressed in first person singular terms. It is not incoherent for an individual to refer to a group of which that individual is a member, and say, "we intend," or to use first person plural expressions in a variety of circumstances to indicate what a group's intentions might be. Nor does the use of "we-intentions" presuppose the existence of any sort of super-mind or other type of supra-individual entity. Indeed, since "we-intentions" language is as common in everyday life as "I intentions" language, there is every reason to investigate the implications of collective intentionality for economic behavior.

In the current philosophical literature on the subject, collective intentionality and we-intentions are explained as a structure of reciprocal attitudes shared by individuals. The main contributions may be found in Bratman (1993; 1999), Gilbert (1989), Searle (1990; 1995), Tuomela and Miller (1988) and Tuomela (1991; 1995). In the discussion that follows I rely on Tuomela's work, which is the most extensive and well-developed. Tuomela's analysis is conservative, in that though it sometimes makes reference to intentions as being shared, this is not meant to imply that there is any actual sharing of intentions, beliefs, desires, or other we-intentions by individuals using "we" language. Rather, a we-intention is an individual's attribution of an intention to a group that the individual believes is reciprocally held by other individuals in that same group. Indeed, an individual may have a we-intention that no other individuals actually have if that individual is mistaken about others having that we-intention. Thus, a we-intention is not a supra-individual group intention separate from the attributions of individuals. Rather, a we-intention is an individual's expression of a group intention based on a sense of there being like attributions on the part of others in the group to which the individual belongs. Thus, the expression "the intentions of the group" is really shorthand for a set of individual we-intentions on the part of a collection of individuals in the group.

Two characteristics of we-intentions are accordingly emphasized in Tuomela's analysis. First, the individual expressing a we-intention believes that this intention is widely if not universally held by other group members, and secondly, the individual believes this intention is mutually held by members of the group. (In the limiting case above both of these beliefs are mistaken.) Consider the case in which an individual's we-intention is rooted in an attitude ("fear") that the individual believes group members also attribute to the group. For an individual A who is a member of a group G, "A we-fears that X if A fears that X and believes that it is feared in G that X and that it is mutually believed in G that X is feared in G" (Tuomela 1995: 38). On this basis A might suppose that G has some intention reflecting the fear of X. This we-intention would have the same structure as the attitude A ascribes to the group. Of course, A can only surmise that others in G have the same fear and that the fear of X is mutually believed by members of the group. Ideally, the idea that X is "mutually believed" would involve saying that the fear that X is believed by everyone, but Tuomela allows that "mutual" can have strong and weak interpretations, because groups themselves have strong and weak criteria for supposing their members share a belief, attitude, or intention. The main point is that we-attitudes are a group attitude, not in the sense that a group apart from its members has an attitude towards something, but in the sense that individuals "generally" in a group have some such attitude expressible in "we" terms. Thus, saying that they "generally" have a we-attitude depends not just on the mutual belief condition, but on both conditions, which if combined, provide us with reason to suppose that individual members of a group are justified in saying what they ("we") intend.[2]

Note that this very basic understanding of collective intentionality already takes us some way towards understanding how individuals can be thought to influence institutions and social values. From an atomist point of view, the main difficulty in understanding how individual behavior influences institutions and social values lies in showing how something fundamentally individual in nature gets translated into something that is fundamentally social in nature. Thus, game theory accounts that attempt to explain how social conventions and institutions emerge from the choices of atomistic individuals are either forced to rely on *ad hoc* assumptions not explainable in terms of individual choice to get the job done, or they simply fail to get the job done (cf. Hargreaves Heap and Varoufakis 1995; Rizvi 1994). In contrast, when we suppose that individuals are socially embedded in groups and form we-intentions about those groups' activities, we have already assumed that individuals are engaged in social activity. Institutions and social values are products of social activity. What Tuomela's analysis adds to this basic idea is an explanation of social activity in terms of structures of reciprocally related we-intentions possessing a mutually reinforcing character. These structures of interaction, as it were, function as the skeletons of social activity and therefore of the institutions and social values that are the products of social activity. Thus, change and evolution in structures of we-intentions in groups bring about change and evolution in institutions and social values, and individuals influence institutions and social values as they continually form new and different we-intentions about the groups of which they are members.

Tuomela's analysis also provides a basis for distinguishing how individuals influence institutions as compared to how they influence social values. Using his distinction between *rules* and *norms*, we-attitudes and we-intentions associated with rules underlie institutions, and we-attitudes associated with norms underlie social values. With rules, an explicit or implicit agreement brought into existence by some authority determines a distribution of tasks and activities to individuals. Rules may be formal and written, such as laws, statutes, regulations, charters, by-laws, etc., or they may be informal agreements between individuals, sometimes orally established and sometimes silently agreed to. With norms, mutual beliefs substitute for actual agreements between individuals in determining distributions of tasks and activities across individuals. As with we-intentions generally, mutual beliefs are beliefs reciprocally established between individuals, such that each believes that others have the same belief, and each also believes that others think the same about the others, and so on in a structure of reinforcing, mutually held beliefs.

Rules and norms are both understood to have motivational force, meaning that they constitute reasons for action on the part of the individuals who accept them. Indeed, rules and norms are typically framed as "ought" principles, and impose requirements on individuals as members of groups in the form of specific prescriptions for individual action. Formally, individual A feels obliged to do X, because A is a member of the group with a we-intention representable in terms of a rule or norm to the effect, "we believe members of the group should do X." But rules and norms are different in virtue of the different means by which they enforce a distribution of tasks and activities among individuals (Tuomela 1995: 22–24). The prescriptive force of rules derives from there being sanctions that apply, whether formal/legal or informal, to those individuals who do not observe them. In contrast to rules, sanctioning with norms takes the form of approval or disapproval on the part of others. Because norms are internalized by individuals in that they themselves accept them as reasons for acting, individuals apply others' potential disapproval to themselves, as when feeling shame or embarrassment.

In Tuomela's collective intentionality analysis, then, rules are the basis for institutions, and norms are the basis for social values. While it is true that many institutions also involve norms, as relatively settled social arrangements institutions generally place greater reliance on rules. Social values, in contrast, are rarely rooted in agreements, even informally, and thus place little weight on rules. Rather, social values reflect systems of mutual belief about individuals' interaction with one another. Thus, when individuals create and/or change institutions, they adopt new rules, and produce new we-attitudes that define group action within an institutional framework characterizable in terms of agreements and corresponding sanctions. When individuals develop and/or influence social values, they adopt new norms, and produce new we-attitudes that define group action within a social value framework based on their mutual beliefs and systems of (dis)approval. In both frameworks, rules/institutions and norms/social values, we-intentions are the foundation for understanding group action. Individuals thus influence institutions and social values as members of groups, and group action is the intermediate link between individual action and supra-individual institutions and social values missing from mainstream accounts of individuals' influence on institutions and social values.

To complete this picture, we need to briefly consider how rules and norms create obligations for individuals in terms of how different tasks, rights, and positions apply to different individuals in groups. Tuomela characterizes an individual's *position within a particular group* in terms of that individual's *tasks* and *rights* within that group. An individual's tasks and rights are then further distinguished according to whether they flow from rules or norms operating within the group, that is, whether they are rule-based tasks and rights or norm-based tasks and rights. Across groups, individuals' *social positions* are understood in terms of the whole

16

array of actions individuals are required and permitted to do across various economic settings. These social positions assign individuals a variety of different tasks whose performance is, in each instance, protected by rights, where these tasks–rights combinations may themselves exist within established modes of implementation that are also understood in tasks–rights terms. The overall framework thus explains individual rights and duties within and across groups in terms of tasks–rights pairs that ultimately have we-attitudes in groups as their foundation. Individuals influence institutions and social values by acting within this framework.

2. The agency-structure model with collective intentionality

I focus on the agency-structure model, first, because it describes human agency as an "*embedded* intentional causality" and human rationality as a situated rationality (Lawson 1997: 63, 187), and, second, because it describes not only how individuals are influenced by institutions and social values, but also how they influence institutions and social values. A precursory formulation of the model is Anthony Giddens' influential "structuration theory," which treats individuals and social structures as interdependent, or as a duality, such that each may be said to help constitute the other, especially through recurrent social practices (1976; 1984). Roy Bhaskar (1979 [1989]) and Margaret Archer (1995) revised and extended Giddens' thinking, principally by seeing reality as stratified and multi-layered with emergent properties differentiating one layer or level from another (cf. Hodgson 2000: 5–13; also Collier 1994). Lawson developed this latter, critical realist conception of the agency-structure relationship specifically for economics in Part III of his *Economics and Reality* (1997), and used it primarily to critique the methodological posture of mainstream economics. An important aspect of Lawson's analysis is that individuals engage in routinized forms of activity, rely on tacit knowledge and skills, and observe rules, norms and conventions. What, then, does the concept of collective or group intentionality add to this account?

In the first place, the concept of collective intentionality permits us to develop a more concrete understanding of individuals' embeddedness and situated rationality in terms of the ways in which groups of individuals are organized. Groups, in virtue of their complexity, are organized so as to assign power and responsibility differently to individuals in different positions, yet, in virtue of their having "shared" intentions, still in a manner that aims at consistency in overall action across these assignments. Focusing on individuals' involvement in groups allows us to explain why individuals engage in particular types of routinized activity, what particular tacit knowledge and skills they need to rely upon, and what particular rules, norms, and conventions they need to observe based on the way that the group as a whole organizes a set of positions in a relatively coherent structure. Simply referring to individuals' reliance on routines, tacit abilities, and so forth fails to account for why different individuals act in different ways, and therefore, ultimately, how changes in the ways that individuals act in concert with one another influences institutions and social values. Individuals act in the ways that they do, because they occupy particular positions in groups organized in terms of collections of positions (cf. Lawson 1997: 163 ff).

But more is involved than simply adding new detail to our analysis of individual embeddedness and to the account of the influence of individuals on institutions and social values. When individuals act under rationales involving we-intentions, groups become agents over and above the collection of individuals that make them up. Individuals' actions still have effects, but specifically as a particular pattern of effects that can be identified as the effects that the group has as a distinguishable agent in its own right. Tuomela's account of collective intentionality, in explaining collective intentionality and "shared" intention as a structure of individual intentions, at once combines the causal effectivity of individual action with the fact of individuals' organization in groups to justify treating groups as cohesive, single agents. Thus the fact that individuals follow routines, adopt norms, etc. is not just evidence that human agency involves an "*embedded* intentional causality" and a situated rationality, but it is evidence that individuals influence institutions and social values by way of the group structures in which individuals are embedded.

But one point needs clarification. We saw above that mainstream economics lacks an account of how groups mediate between individuals and institutions and social values, and that this tends to produce a reliance on *ad hoc* assumptions in efforts to explain how individuals influence institutions and social values. Given that such explanations enjoy limited success at best, it does not come as a surprise that the language of "unintended consequences" strongly underlies 'mainstream economics' accounts of the relation of individuals to institutions and social values. But this reliance should not be thought to imply that, when we turn to collective intentionality analysis of groups, that institutions and social values are fully intended consequences of the activities of individuals in groups. In the first place, in the agency-structure model, structure, or institutions and social values also influence individuals (just as they are influenced by individuals), and this causal process makes the evolution and development of institutions and social values an open-ended process with unintended consequences. But there are other reasons specific to the operation of groups which lead us to the same conclusion.

First, the number and variety of kinds of groups which exist in human society is truly staggering, ranging from more tightly organized groups such as firms, governments, and households (March and Simon 1956) to more loosely formed ones such as social movements or even just two individuals "going for a walk together" (Gilbert 1989). Indeed, if we add to groups in this more "objective" rule-governed sense all those collections of individuals who constitute groups in the more "subjective" sense of adhering to shared social values, then the number of groups is even larger. Second, membership in and across groups is obviously cross-cutting, overlapping, and often conflicting. Add to this the fact that membership in groups is continually changing, and we have further reason to expect considerable "unintended consequences" in our analysis. Third, groups however defined, do not make up the entire universe of economic agents. Individual action that is relatively autonomous (if not atomistic) also contributes to the evolution of institutions and social values. For these reasons, the activity of groups of individuals ought only be said to influence rather than fully explain or determine the evolution of institutions and social values.

What general methodological strategy does the collective intentionality account of individuals as socially embedded thus add to the agency-structure model? First, we begin by surveying and identifying particular groups of individuals acting as economic agents, where the selection of those groups that are of interest to us is driven by our current cause-and-effect concerns presented to us in the form of "why" questions regarding the way things happen in the economic world (Runde 1998). Second, our characterization of these groups involves our explaining their position–task–right structures, which accounts for their internal organization and their capacity to coherently organize the different activities of different individuals. Third, we attempt to explain interaction between groups, where this involves institutions or social values with across-group rules and norms. This broader framework is no less a domain of collective intentionality, though it stretches the idea of a group to think of institutions and social values being groups.

3. A revised view of individual economic behavior

I now turn to why our understanding of individual economic behavior needs to be revised when we make use of the concept of collective intentionality. The behavior of atomistic individuals is understood in instrumentally rational terms, because individual objective functions are defined solely in terms of individuals' own preferences. With no basis for action other than their own preferences, and assuming that they do not act out of habit or behave irrationally, atomistic individuals can do nothing other than attempt to realize their own preferences as efficiently as possible. When we treat individuals as socially embedded, however, we can no longer say that individuals act only on their own preferences, because socially embedded individuals generally act in accordance with those rules and norms associated with their membership in groups. These rules and norms, we saw, function as "ought" principles or social requirements, and as such generally lead socially embedded individuals to behave in ways different from the ways that atomistic individuals behave. It is this emphasis on "ought" principles and the social requirements of group membership, then, that is at odds with explaining the behavior of socially embedded individuals in instrumentally rational terms, and suggests that socially embedded individuals are fundamentally different from atomistic individuals.

Those who defend the atomistic conception of the individual and instrumental rationality would likely first reject these arguments for the following reason. Explaining individual behavior in terms of group requirements is ultimately equivalent to explaining individual behavior as instrumentally rational though now subject to constraints additional to those usually assumed in standard constrained optimization analysis, namely, constraints associated with observing the rules and norms of group membership. These additional "social" constraints further narrow individuals' choice sets, but individuals still ought to be thought to maximize their preferences within this additionally delimited space. Even socially embedded individuals, that is, ultimately behave in an instrumentally rational fashion, and it thus follows that socially embedded individuals are not different in any substantive sense from atomistic individuals.

This response, however, overlooks what is different about individual behavior in groups in which individuals express we-intentions. On the understanding developed by Tuomela and others, since we-intentions are the intentions of individuals and not the intentions of groups, whatever these intentions imply in the way of individual behavior – say, that one ought to observe group rules and norms – must be thought of as having been intended by the individuals who have them. That is, intentional behavior, whatever its nature, reflects what the individual chooses to do, not what the individual is limited to doing. In the language of mainstream rationality theory, we-intentions derive from individuals' objective functions no less than do those individual intentions standard theory would associate with individuals acting on own preferences. Thus, acting in accordance with rules and norms is not evidence of acting under an additional set of constraints ("social" constraints). And since rules and norms impose requirements on individuals, supposing we-intentions derive from socially embedded individuals' objective functions, it gives us good reason to think individual behavior cannot be explained in instrumentally rational terms.

But might not defenders of the atomistic conception of the individual and instrumental rationality use this reply for one further defense of the standard conception? If we-intentions enter individuals' objective function, they might argue, then they must be produced by we-preferences, just as ordinary individual intentions are produced by own preferences (or I-preferences). If this is so, thus might not the behavior of socially embedded individuals still be explained in instrumentally rational terms? Indeed we-preferences have recently been analyzed along these lines by Robert Sugden in the form of team preferences (Sugden 2000). Sugden explicitly rejects collective intentionality analysis as carried out by Tuomela and others, precisely because it introduces the idea that individuals are bound by social obligations (or group requirements) which he regards as being inconsistent with an account of instrumentally rational behavior. To preserve the latter, then, the former has to go. This, in turn, would imply that rules and norms are things teams prefer to observe rather than believe their members are compelled to observe. Moreover, if this is all true, then it is hard to see why, with a team preferences analysis of rules and norms, individuals should be treated as socially embedded. If their we-intentions derive from we-preferences, and consequently impose no obligations or requirements upon them, it seems that their relationship to others is incidental to their behavior. Indeed, Sudgen effectively takes this position when he argues that the "existence" question regarding whether teams and other groups exist is independent of the theory of (instrumental) rationality enlarged to include we-preferences. In the final analysis, Sugden's view is that the conception of the individual as an atomistic being is sufficient for any discussion of we-preferences, we-intentions, and action in accord with rules and norms.

Clearly, Sugden's analysis turns on the idea that we-preferences do not impose "ought" principles or social requirements upon individuals. Why is it, then, that Tuomela and other proponents of collective intentionality see this as an essential dimension of we-intentions? The answer lies in their specific understanding of we-intentions. Individual we-intentions are what individuals think are the intentions of individuals in a group generally. They are not what individuals think ought to be the intentions of the group, nor are they the intentions of the group from any individual's own particular point of view. Since successfully expressing we-intentions requires that an individual believe that other individuals have that same we-intention and also believe that this we-intention is mutually believed, an individual's expression of a we-intention basically involves the individual's best guess regarding a structure of intentions on the part of different individuals regarding what they all think everyone else believes is the intention of the group. But this means that there is a tension of some kind within the individual between this best guess view and whatever might be this individual's own view of what the group intends. This tension is a product of the fact that one does not use "we" language properly unless one makes a best effort to get at what everyone else means in using "we." In effect, an individual using "we" language must make a commitment to a group's view of its intentions irrespective of whether the individual personally agrees about this use of "we." For this reason, using "we" language and expressing we-intentions in the collective intentionality sense imposes obligations on individuals associated with standing by whatever the group's intention involves. Moreover, an obligation in this sense is not just something that binds an individual, but also a binding that the individual embraces. One only feels a genuine obligation, that is, when one has embraced that obligation oneself.

Sugden's treatment of we-preferences as preferences of instrumentally rational atomistic individuals consequently does not really get at what is involved in we-intentions. We-intentions do not derive from we-preferences, but rather from individual commitment to a use of "we" language that (self-) imposes obligations on the individual. But atomistic individuals do not act out of any such sense of obligation but only on the basis of what they prefer. Moreover, in Sugden's we-preference analysis, the individual's relation to others is an incidental one. We-preferences are held in essentially the same way by all team members, and there is no difference between the way we-preferences properly represent the team and the way an individual might understand the team's we-preferences. In contrast, we-intentions require the individual's commitment to the use of a shared we-language that goes beyond individual perspective. This, and the obligation it brings, socially embeds the individual in the group, and brings about a non-incidental relationship between the individual and others.

As said above, acting out of a sense of obligation or the requirements upon oneself may be characterized as being deontologically rational rather than instrumentally rational. Philosophers have traditionally seen the difference as being a matter of doing what one thinks one ought to do as opposed to doing what one wants to do. This may well suggest that what is meant here is that being deontologically rational is equivalent to acting morally, and that, therefore, the behavior of socially embedded individuals needs to be explained in terms of the categories of ethics. It is true that philosophers of ethics have used the term "deontology" to refer to a particular (non-consequentialist) approach to moral behavior. But clearly, many, if not most, of the obligations and requirements that groups impose upon individuals have little to do with acting morally. The term "ought," of course, is also used in a non-normative, pragmatic sense. It is this sense of the term that I generally mean to refer to when I characterize socially embedded individuals as acting in a deontologically rational way. Indeed, the second expression used above to characterize acting out of a sense of obligation or in terms of group requirements – acting in a "principled" rational way – is probably the better one to employ. Individual action in groups is guided by a variety of principles, whose observance can be thought rational in a broad sense. For example, accepting the tasks assigned to one in an agreed-upon division of labor would be thought by most people to involve acting on a rational principle. Nor would it be said that a principle of this nature has any special moral content. Such principles simply constitute working principles in the operation of many groups. I thus characterize their observation by individuals as a "principled" type of rational behavior, and leave it to another occasion to investigate the extent to which such behavior also raises questions of morality.

My general argument, it should also be emphasized, is not that socially embedded individuals behave only in a "principled" rational fashion. Individuals who express we-intentions and are members of groups clearly also have their own preferences, and may seek to realize them in an instrumentally rational manner, either when they find themselves at odds with what is expected of them in groups, or even when they see themselves as acting in conformity with what the group expects of them. Indeed, in the organization of many groups, individuals are expected to act in an instrumentally rational way in order to best fulfill the requirements of group membership. Consider an employee in a business assigned a set of rule and norm-based tasks associated with doing a particular job. If one rule is to invoice customers by the end of the month, and the norm for how this is to be done is to include in the invoice a complete description of all purchases made by those customers, the individual assigned these tasks is likely still free to perform them in a variety of ways (inquire as to customer satisfaction, pursue follow-up orders, institute new record-keeping practices, etc.). How well individuals do their assigned jobs, then, can be a matter of the extent to which they also act on their own preferences regarding the way a job is best done. They consequently act in an instrumentally rational way when already behaving in a "principled" rational manner.

Individuals, it thus seems fair to say, engage in both instrumentally rational and "principled" rational kinds of behavior, and that the balance or mix of these depends upon the circumstances and the setting. Abstractly, one might begin by imagining a spectrum. At one extreme, there exists a set of activities in which individuals operate free of significant group attachments, and can be described as behaving solely in an instrumentally rational manner. This is the case that mainstream economists have treated as universal. At the opposite extreme, there exists a set of activities in which individuals act solely according to the dictates of the group, and their behavior is fully explained by group membership. Heterodox economists have on occasion seen this as the universal case (for example, in some Marxist accounts when class is said to determine individual behavior). But between these two extremes lies a variety of activities and what is probably the great majority of types of economic behavior. This behavior is complex in involving both instrumentally rational and "principled" rational behavior in some overall structure, and developing explanations of this large range of cases seems to be a matter of explaining how these two forms are integrated and organized with respect to one another.[3] My view is that explaining these types of cases should be the first goal of economists trying to describe individual behavior.

4. The capacity to express we-intentions; summary

I close with a brief discussion of why we should suppose that individuals are socially embedded in the sense of having a capacity to form we-intentions. The capacity to express we-intentions is a capacity to remove oneself from one's own particular case and circumstances, and adopt a point of view held by others. When an individual uses "we" language correctly, that individual successfully grasps how a structure of we-attitudes on the part of individuals in a group justifies that individual saying what the group's intentions are. The closest mainstream economists come to this sort of explanation is in their treatment of sympathy as a possible argument in the atomistic individual's own objective function. Individuals who are sympathetic towards others are sometimes said to be "altruistic" in having preferences regarding others' well-being. But this conception involves an understanding of altruism at odds with what most people associate with the concept, since the "good" acts that these "altruistic" individuals engage in are only undertaken because they raise these individuals' own utility. Most people, rather, see altruistic behavior as a kind of selfless behavior. Sympathy explained in this way does not really involve individuals removing themselves from their own circumstances, or becoming selfless. It consequently does not get at what is involved in being able to express we-intentions which take individuals beyond their own cases.

One way of explaining this capacity to remove oneself from one's own particular case and circumstances lies in terms of Philippe Fontaine's recent treatment of the concept of empathy in early and later history of economics (Fontaine 1997; 2001). Fontaine distinguishes between sympathy and empathy, where sympathy is having an own preference regarding another's well-being, and empathy involves imagining oneself being in the place of another. If one is empathetic towards another person, one somehow grasps what the other's situation involves (an imagined transposition of places), and then acts in one's own capacity with that understanding in mind. Empathetic individuals, however, need not have other individuals' well-being in mind when they act. They may simply register how others look at the world, in order to make better decisions on their own.[4] But empathy, in the sense of imagining another's circumstances, would also allow for altruistic behavior in the strong sense, in that one could behave sympathetically toward another having grasped what the other's situation involved. Thus, Fontaine distinguishes between imagining oneself in the place of others by intellectually appreciating their circumstances as compared to imagining oneself in the place of others by embracing their feelings and attitudes. That latter transposition could give rise to altruistic behavior when one was sympathetic toward those feelings and attitudes, though of course it could also give rise to quite the opposite type of behavior were those feelings and attitudes not thought admirable.

Fontaine's account of how individuals may remove themselves from their own circumstances is quite like the capacity Tuomela and others interested in collective intentionality attribute to individuals who have we-intentions. There is a difference, however. Fontaine's transposition of places involves an individual imagining the situation of another individual. But the capacity to form we-intentions is more abstract than this. When individuals successfully express we-intentions, they grasp how a reciprocal use of "we" language, backed up by a mutual belief condition across many individuals, entitles them to say what a group's intentions are. Thus, the business of removing oneself from one's own circumstances is less a matter of seeing things from someone else's point of view, and rather more a matter of grasping how a structure of we-intentions emerges across many individuals. Nonetheless, there is a clear point of contact between the two conceptions. While collective intentionality analysis attributes a capacity to individuals to grasp a structure of we-intentions within a group, being able to do this could be argued to presuppose that individuals are able to place themselves in the shoes of one individual after another in a group to produce that sense of what the structure of we-intentions in the group is. That is, individuals arguably engage in a sampling of other's views, removing themselves from their own individual circumstances in doing so, as they develop an understanding of the correct use of "we" language in the group. Fontaine's individual-to-individual transposition of places analysis, then, might be thought to underlie collective intentionality's assumption of a capacity on the part of individuals to form we-intentions.

To summarize, what the discussion in this paper attempts to do is provide an account of individuals as socially embedded so as to be able to explain how individuals influence the development and evolution of institutions and social values. Individuals are characterized as being socially embedded when they are members of groups in which "we" language is used. Collective intentionality analysis, as recently developed in philosophy, is employed to explain individuals' use of "we" language, and then this conception of the socially embedded economic agent is introduced into agency-structure thinking about how individuals and institutions/social values influence one another. A key implication of the discussion is that individual behavior cannot be understood solely in instrumentally rational terms, but needs to be enlarged and modified to accommodate individuals' deontologically rational or "principled" rational behavior in groups. Whether or not such behavior actually occurs, and thus whether individuals can indeed be characterized as socially embedded, ultimately depends on whether one believes individuals can form we-intentions in the sense explained here. That they do have this capacity is suggested by the idea that individuals can imagine and place themselves in one another's places.

Notes

1 The analytic conception follows an earlier continental philosophy understanding of intentionality that began with the work of Franz Brentano, and was further developed in the phenomenological work of Edmund Husserl. My focus on the literature from analytic philosophy is motivated by this tradition's emphasis on the conditions of individuality.
2 Tuomela draws on an account of mutual belief that has become fairly standard among philosophers which relies on the idea of a hierarchical set of beliefs iterated across individuals (Tuomela 1995: 41ff). See Lewis (1969: 52ff) for a parallel account in terms of common knowledge that has played a role in game theory.
3 For one example of how such an explanation might be produced, see Minkler (1999), where a "commitment function" is added to a standard utility function representation of individual behavior. The individual is said to engage in a two-step iterative procedure with the first step corresponding to a response to group requirements and the second step corresponding to an instrumentally rational maximization of utility.
4 I use this understanding of empathy in my discussion of Keynes's treatment of investment in the stock market as like a newspaper beauty contest (Davis 1994: 130ff).

References

Anscombe, G. E. M. (1963) *Intention*, Oxford: Basil Blackwell.

Archer, M. (1995) *Realist Social Theory: The Morphogenetic Approach*, Cambridge: Cambridge University Press.

Arrow, K. J. (1984) *The Economics of Information*, Cambridge, MA: Belknap Press of Harvard University.

Bhaskar, R. (1979 [1989]) *The Possibility of Naturalism: A Philosophic Critique of the Contemporary Human Sciences*, 2nd edn. Brighton: Harvester.

Bratman, M. (1993) "Shared intention," *Ethics* 104, 97–113.

Bratman, M. (1999) *Faces of Intention*, Cambridge: Cambridge University Press.

Collier, A. (1994) *Critical Realism: An Introduction to Roy Bhaskar's Philosophy*, London: Verso.

Davidson, D. (1980) *Essays on Actions and Events*, Oxford: Clarendon Press.

Davis, J. (1994) *Keynes's Philosophical Development*, Cambridge: Cambridge University Press.

Fontaine, P. (1997) "Identification and economic behavior: Sympathy and empathy in historical perspective," *Economics and Philosophy* 12(2), 261–80.

Fontaine, P. (2001) *History of Political Economy*, forthcoming.

Giddens, A. (1976) *Central Problems in Social Theory*, Berkeley: University of California Press.

Giddens, A. (1984) *The Constitution of Society*, Cambridge: Policy Press.

Gilbert, M. (1989) *On Social Facts*, London: Routledge.

Hargreaves Heap, S. and Varoufakis, Y. (1995) *Game Theory: A Critical Introduction*, London: Routledge.

Hayek, F. (1979) *The Counter-revolution in Science: Studies on the Abuse of Reason*, Indianapolis, Indiana: Liberty Press.

Hodgson, G. (2000) "Structures and Institutions: Reflections on Institutionalism, Structuration Theory and Critical Realism," (unpublished).

Lawson, T. (1997) *Economics and Reality*, London: Routledge.

Lewis, D. (1969) *Convention: A Philosophical Study*, Cambridge, Mass.: Harvard University Press.

March, J. and Simon, H. (1956) *Organizations*, New York: Wiley.

Minkler, L. (1999) "The problem with utility: Toward a non-consequentialist/utility theory synthesis," *Review of Social Economy* 52(1): 4–24.

Rizvi, S. A. T. (1994) "Game Theory to the Rescue?" *Contributions to Political Economy* 13: 1–28.

Runde, J. (1998) "Assessing causal economic explanations," *Oxford Economic Papers* 50: 151–72.

Searle, J. (1990) "Collective intentions and actions," P. Cohen, J. Morgan and M. E. Pollack (eds) in *Intentions in Communication*, Cambridge, Mass.: MIT Press.

Searle, J. (1995) *The Construction of Social Reality*, New York: Free Press.

Sugden, R. (2000) "Team preferences," *Economics and Philosophy* 16(2): 175–204.

Tuomela, R. (1991) "We will do it: An analysis of group intentions," *Philosophy and Phenomenological Research* 51: 249–77.

Tuomela, R. (1995) *The Importance of Us: A Philosophical Study of Basic Social Notions*, Stanford: Stanford University Press.

Tuomela, R. and Miller, K. (1988) "We-intentions," *Philosophical Studies* 53: 367–89.

2

RECIPROCAL FAIRNESS, COOPERATION AND LIMITS TO COMPETITION[1]

Ernst Fehr and Armin Falk

1. Introduction

A key fact about human society is the ubiquity of material incentives to cheat on implicit or explicit cooperative agreements. In any kind of social or economic exchange situation between two or more individuals in which not all aspects of the exchange are determined by enforceable contracts, there are material incentives to cheat the exchange partners. Even in modern human societies with a large cooperative infrastructure in the form of laws, courts and the police, the material incentive to cheat on cooperative agreements is probably the rule rather than the exception. This is so because, in general, not all obligations that arise in various contingencies of exchange situations can be unambiguously formulated and subjected to a binding contract.[2] Therefore, by reneging on implicit or unenforceable obligations a party can always improve their material payoff relative to a situation where they meet its obligations. Of course, in premodern societies which lack a cooperative infrastructure, cheating incentives are even more prevalent.

Another key fact about human society is that, despite these incentives to cheat, many non-binding agreements occur and are kept. Since cooperation regularly also takes place among non-kin, genetical kinship theory[3] cannot account for this fact. One possibility to account for the manifest cooperation among non-kin is to recognise that many social interactions take place repeatedly. Evolutionary theorists, for example, have shown that natural selection can favour reciprocally cooperative behaviour when the chances to interact repeatedly with the same individual in the future are sufficiently high.[4] Since cheating, i.e. not reciprocating a cooperative act, can be deterred by the withdrawal of future cooperation, it is in the long-term interest of organisms not to cheat. Therefore, in repeated interactions reciprocal cooperation can be an evolutionary stable outcome. In a similar spirit, game theorists have shown that, when the chances for repeated interactions are sufficiently high, rational egoists, i.e. rational actors that are solely interested in their own material well-being, can establish an equilibrium with full cooperation despite the existence of short-run cheating incentives.[5] The reason for this is that cheating has not only short run benefits but also long run costs. The implicit or explicit threat to withdraw future cooperation from the cheaters deters cheating and, as a consequence, cooperation can be sustained by self-interested rational actors.

We have no doubt that the expectation of future returns in repeated interactions provides a powerful force against the short run incentives to cheat. However, we will argue, and provide strong evidence, in favour of another force that has so far been largely neglected. We call this force 'reciprocal fairness'. A person is reciprocally fair if she is willing (i) to sacrifice resources to be kind to those who are being kind (= positive reciprocal fairness) and (ii) to sacrifice resources to punish those who are being unkind (= negative reciprocal fairness). The essential feature of reciprocal fairness is thus a willingness to sacrifice resources for rewarding fair and punishing unfair behaviour. Whether an action is perceived as fair or unfair depends on the distributional consequences of the action relative to a neutral reference action and the intentions that led to the action.[6] We will show that there exist many people who are willing to forgo substantial material gains in favour of reciprocal rewards or reciprocal punishments. Reciprocally fair behaviour can be observed in laboratory experiments in which the monetary gains that are at stake reach the level of three months' income for the subjects.[7] Moreover, reciprocal fairness is present even among experimental subjects who know that they will never be informed about the identity of their interaction partners. We show further that the existence of reciprocally fair people greatly improves the prospects for cooperation. We provide evidence that reciprocal fairness can give rise to almost maximal cooperation in circumstances in which the standard repeated interaction approach predicts no cooperation at all. However, we also provide evidence indicating that there are social structures in which the interaction between reciprocally fair persons and purely selfish persons induces the majority of people to cheat. This highlights the importance of social structures for the achievement of stable cooperation. In addition, we show that explicit material incentives that aim at the deterrence of cheating, may reduce positive reciprocal fairness, that is, the willingness to voluntarily cooperate in response to kind behaviour. Finally, our results also indicate that the cooperation-enhancing property of reciprocal fairness constitutes a powerful competition-limiting force.

It is important to distinguish reciprocal fairness from terms like 'reciprocal altruism' and 'altruism'. The distinction between these terms can most easily be illustrated in the context of a *sequential* Prisoner's Dilemma (PD)

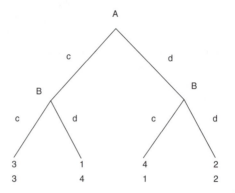

Figure 2.1 The Prisoner's Dilemma Game.

that is played *exactly once*. In a sequential PD player A first decides whether to cooperate (c) or to defect (d) (compare Fig. 2.1). Then player B observes player A's action after which she decides to cooperate or to defect. To be specific, let the material payoffs for players A and B (π_A, π_B) be (3, 3) if both cooperate, (2, 2) if both defect, (1, 4) if A cooperates and B defects and (4, 1) if A defects and B cooperates.

If player B is an altruist she never defects even if player A defected. Altruism, as we define it here, is thus tantamount to *unconditional* kindness. In contrast, a reciprocally fair player B defects if A defected and cooperates if A cooperated because she is willing to sacrifice resources to reward a behaviour that is perceived as kind. A cooperative act by player A, despite the material incentive to cheat, is a prime example of such kindness. The kindness of a reciprocally fair person is thus *conditional* on the perceived kindness of the other player. The term 'reciprocal altruism' as it is frequently used in evolutionary biology differs fundamentally from reciprocal fairness because a reciprocal altruist only cooperates if there are future returns from cooperation. Thus, a reciprocally altruistic player B will always defect in a sequential *one-shot* PD. Since a reciprocal altruist performs altruistic actions only if the total material returns exceed the total material costs we do not use this term in the rest of the paper. Instead, we use the term 'selfish' for this motivation.

2. Enforcement of 'nonbinding' agreements

In many bilateral one-shot encounters in real life people behave in a reciprocally fair way. People return gifts, invitations and favours and punish others for being unfair, mean, e.g. because they cheated or lied. In addition to real world examples, there is strong evidence for reciprocal fairness that comes from well controlled laboratory experiments.[8] In these experiments, subjects could earn real money according to their decisions and to the rules of the experiment. This means that reciprocally fair behaviour had real costs for the experimental subjects because it implied that they had to give up monetary returns in favour of a reciprocal action. Moreover, subjects were never informed about the identity of their exchange partner – neither before nor after the experiment. In addition, experimental procedures also ensured that no individual subject could ever gain a reputation for being, for example, cooperative. Exchange partners were located in different rooms. These features of the experiment ensured that the exchange really took place between anonymous strangers. In all experiments discussed in this paper completely anonymous strangers, who never learn the identities of their interaction partners, interact with each other. In the pages that follow we illustrate the regularities of reciprocally fair behaviour on the basis of one of these experiments conducted at the University of Zurich (for details compare E. Fehr, S. Gächter and G. Kirchsteiger (1997)).

In the experiment, a subject, in the role of an employer, can make a job offer to the group of subjects in the role of workers. Each worker can potentially accept the offer. There are more workers than employers in order to induce competition among the workers. A job offer consists of a *binding* wage offer w and a *nonbinding* 'desired effort level' $\hat{e}$. If one of the workers accepts an offer $(w, \hat{e})$ she has to determine the *actual* effort level e. The desired and the actual effort levels have to be in the interval $[e_{min}, e_{max}] \equiv [0.1, 1]$. The higher the e the larger is the material payoff for the employer but the higher are also the costs $c(e)$ of providing e for the worker. Material payoffs from an exchange are given by $\pi_f = 100e - w$ for the employer and $\pi_w = w - c(e)$ for the worker. A party who does not manage to trade earns zero. Note, that since $\hat{e}$ is non-binding, the worker can choose any $e \in [0.1, 1]$, i.e. in particular $e < \hat{e}$, without being sanctioned. It is obvious that, since $c(e)$ is strictly increasing in e, a selfish worker will always choose $e = e_{min}$. Therefore, a rational and selfish employer, who believes that there are only selfish workers, will never offer a wage above $w_{min} \equiv c(e_{min}) + 1$. At w_{min} the trading worker earns $\pi_w = 1$ which is more than if the worker does not trade.

In sharp contrast to the predictions based on the selfishness assumption we observe the following regularities: The vast majority of contract offers imply, if accepted and met, a much larger profit than $\pi_w = 1$ for the worker. On average, the profit implied by the offer, which is defined by $w - c(\hat{e})$, is 35 units. Moreover, the higher the desired effort level $\hat{e}$ the higher is the profit $w - c(\hat{e})$ offered to the worker (see Fig. 2.2). This indicates that employers appeal to the reciprocal fairness of the workers by being more generous the more costly the desired effort choice for the worker is. Workers, in turn, exhibit a considerable amount of reciprocal fairness (see Fig. 2.2). Although the actual average effort is below the

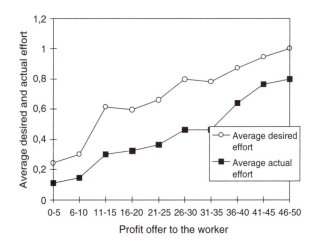

Figure 2.2 Relation of desired effort and actual effort to the profit offered to the worker ($N = 141$).

Source: E. Fehr, S. Gächter and G. Kirchsteiger (1997).

desired average effort, it is, in general, clearly above e_{min}. Moreover, there is a strong positive correlation between the generosity of the offer, i.e. the level of $w - c(\hat{e})$, and the actual average effort.

In an extension of the above experiment we examined the impact of giving the employers the option of responding reciprocally to the worker's effort choice e. This is done by giving the employer the opportunity to reward or punish the worker after she observes the actual effort. Employers can choose a reward/punishment variable r in the interval $[-1, +1]$ where $r < 0$ denotes a punishment and $r > 0$ represents a reward. Yet, both punishing and rewarding is costly for the employer; her costs $c(r)$ are given by $c(r) = -10r$ if $r \in [-1, 0]$ and $c(r) = 10r$ if $r \in [0, 1]$. In the extended design material payoffs from an exchange are given by $\pi_f = 100e - w - c(r)$ for the employer and $\pi_w = w - c(e) + 25r$ for the worker. The important feature of this design is that, if there are only selfish employers, they will never reward or punish a worker because this is costly. Therefore, in case there are only selfish employers there is no reason why the opportunity for rewarding/punishing workers should affect workers' choice of effort relative to the situation where no such opportunity exists. However, if a worker expects her employer to behave reciprocally fairly it is likely that workers will provide higher effort levels in the presence of a reward/punishment opportunity. This is so because reciprocally fair employers are likely to reward the provision ($e = \hat{e}$) or the overprovision ($e > \hat{e}$) of effort and to punish the underprovision ($e < \hat{e}$). This is exactly what one observes. If there is underprovision of effort employers punish in 68 percent of the cases with an average punishment of $r = -0.7$. If there is overprovision employers reward in 70 percent of these cases with an average reward of $r = 0.7$. If workers exactly meet the desired effort employers still reward in 41 percent of the cases with an average reward of $r = 0.45$.

We also elicited workers' expectations about the r-choice of their employers so that we are able to check whether they anticipate employers' reciprocal fairness. It turns out that, in case of underprovision, workers expect to be punished in 54 percent of the cases with an average expectation of $r = -0.4$, while in case of overprovision, they expect to receive a reward in 98 percent of the cases with an average expectation of $r = 0.65$. As a result of these expectations workers choose much higher effort levels when employers have a reward/punishment opportunity. The presence of this opportunity decreases underprovision from 83 percent to 26 percent of the trades, increases exact provision of $\hat{e}$ from 14 to 36 percent and increases overprovision from 3 to 38 percent of the trades (see Table 2.1). The average quality level is increased from $e = 0.37$ to $e = 0.65$ so that the gap between desired and actual effort levels almost vanishes. An important consequence of this increase in average effort is that the aggregate monetary payoff increases by 40 percent – even if one takes the payoff reductions that result from actual punishments into account.

The evidence presented above confirms that reciprocal fairness substantially contributes to the enforcement of cooperative agreements in bilateral sequential exchanges. The power of reciprocal fairness derives from the fact that it provides incentives for the potential cheaters to behave cooperatively or at least to limit their degree of noncooperation. In the above experiments, for example, even purely selfish employers have an incentive to make a cooperative first move, i.e. to make a generous job offer, if they expect sufficiently many workers to behave in a reciprocally fair manner. Similarly, even purely selfish workers have an incentive to

Table 2.1 Effort choices with and without reward/punishment opportunities

	Underprovision (percent)	Exact provision (percent)	Overprovision (percent)	Actual effort (mean)
Employers have *no* reward/ punishment opportunity	83	14	3	0.37
Employers have a reward/ punishment opportunity	26	36	38	0.65

provide a high effort in case of a reward/punishment opportunity if they expect that sufficiently many employers are reciprocally fair.

3. Explicit versus implicit punishment threats

In the previously discussed extension of the employer–worker game employers cannot explicitly announce a punishment threat. However, in the presence of reciprocally fair employers the opportunity to punish *ex post* constitutes a kind of implicit threat. The fact that the majority of subperforming workers expect to be punished confirms this. The advantage of the existence of an implicit threat like this is that it constrains the opportunistic inclinations of the selfish or insufficiently reciprocal types while it allows – at the same time – the maintenance of a friendly and trustful atmosphere. This is different in the presence of explicit *ex ante* threats. Such threats are likely to generate an atmosphere of hostility and distrust which in turn may destroy the willingness of reciprocally fair types to respond reciprocally. By making a generous contract offer the employer implicitly tries to elicit the *voluntary* cooperation of workers who are, in principle, willing to respond reciprocally. If, however, the message is 'please respond reciprocally, but if you don't I punish you' it is easily conceivable that the propensity to respond reciprocally is strongly weakened. It seems, therefore, that an explicit *ex ante* punishment threat psychologically contradicts an appeal to behave reciprocally.

To test the impact of *ex ante* threats on the propensity to behave reciprocally fairly we implemented the following control condition for the simple employer–worker game discussed above (for details compare Fehr and Gächter 1998a). Instead of opportunities for *ex post* punishments and rewards, employers have the opportunity to stipulate *ex ante* binding threats. In addition to $(w, \hat{e})$ the contract contains a potential fine f, $0 \leqslant f \leqslant f_{max}$. This fine has to be paid by the worker to the employer in case of verifiable subperformance $(e < \hat{e})$. The probability of verification is given by $1/3$. The maximum feasible fine f_{max} is chosen such that it is in the interest of a purely selfish and risk neutral worker to choose $e = 0.4 > e_{min}$ if $f = f_{max}$. Interestingly, in almost all contract offers experimental employers stipulate a positive fine and in the majority of cases the fine is maximal.

The effect of these *ex ante* threats on workers' propensity to respond reciprocally is quite dramatic. In case employers have no opportunity to stipulate a fine there is a strong reciprocal relation between the generosity of the offer and the effort response that is similar to the relation in Fig. 2.2. In the presence of explicit *ex ante* threats, however, this reciprocal relation is almost absent. This is consistent with our conjecture that explicit *ex ante* threats may destroy reciprocity and shows that there may be a conflict between reciprocity-based incentives and explicit material incentives based on explicit threats. The data also show that the aggregate material payoff is higher in the absence of explicit fines because the average effort is higher in this condition. This leads to the striking conclusion that explicit performance incentives, when they take the form of binding *ex ante* threats, may be inferior in efficiency terms relative to incentives that try to elicit only *voluntary* cooperation. Moreover, if the appeal to voluntary cooperation is combined with the opportunity to punish or reward performance *ex post* the efficiency advantage of reciprocity-based incentives becomes even greater.

4. Cooperation and punishment opportunities

The above experimental evidence indicates the widespread existence of reciprocal behaviour among anonymously interacting strangers in one-shot situations. Roughly speaking, the fraction of subjects exhibiting some degree of reciprocal fairness is almost never below 40 and sometimes well above 60 percent.[9] However, there can also be little doubt that there is a non-negligible fraction of subjects who do not reciprocate and behave completely selfishly.[10] Since there is a non-trivial fraction of selfish subjects the question arises under which circumstances which type dominates the aggregate outcome. Or put differently: What are the interaction structures which enable the selfish types to induce the reciprocally fair types to behave noncooperatively and what are the structures that enable the reciprocally fair types to force or induce the selfish types to behave cooperatively? In view of the fact that reciprocally fair types are willing to punish unfair behaviour it seems likely that the presence or absence of punishment opportunities is crucial here. To see why, consider the example of a *simultaneously* played *one-shot* PD, in which a purely selfish subject is matched with a reciprocally fair subject. If the reciprocal subject knows that she faces a selfish subject, she will defect because she knows that the selfish subject will *always* defect. Consider now a slightly different game in which both players have the opportunity to punish the other player after they could observe the other player's action. Assume further that the *punishment is costly for the punisher*, which ensures that a purely selfish subject will never punish. A cooperating reciprocally fair subject is, however, willing to punish a defecting subject because the defection is likely to be viewed as unfair. Therefore, if the selfish subject anticipates that a defection will be punished, she has an incentive to cooperate. This suggests that in the presence of punishment opportunities reciprocally fair types can force the selfish types to cooperate, whereas in the absence of punishment opportunities the selfish types induce the reciprocal types to defect, too.[11]

The following generalised PD has been used to examine the empirical validity of this conjecture.[12] In a group of four anonymously interacting subjects, each subject is endowed with twenty tokens. Subjects decide *simultaneously* how many tokens to keep for themselves and how many tokens to invest in a common project. For each token that is privately kept a subject earns exactly one token. Yet, for each token a subject invests into the project each of the four subjects earns 0.4 tokens. This means that, irrespective of how much the other three subjects contribute to the project, it is always better for a subject to keep all tokens privately. Therefore, if all subjects are purely selfish they will all keep all their tokens. Yet, if all fully defect, i.e. keep all their tokens privately, each earns only twenty tokens while if – for example – all invest their total token endowment each subjects earns 0.4 * 80 = 32 tokens. As in the prisoner's dilemma in Fig. 2.1 it is collectively better if all cooperate. However, individually, everybody has an incentive not to invest at all.

In the *no-punishment condition* the same group of subjects[13] plays this game for ten periods where, at the end of each period, they are informed about the average contributions of the other three group members. In the *punishment condition* subjects also play the above game for ten periods. In addition to their investment decision, they can also assign punishment points to each of the other group members at the end of each period after they are informed about the others' contributions. The costs of punishment for the punisher are higher when more punishment points are assigned to the others. For each *received* punishment point the monetary income of the punished subject is reduced by ten percent. The experiment ensures that group members cannot trace the history of individual investments or individual punishments of a particular subject in a group. It is, therefore impossible to gain an individual reputation for being (non)cooperative or for being a punisher.

It is important to notice that the ten-fold repetition of the generalised PD does not change the predictions relative to a pure one-shot experiment if it is *common knowledge that all subjects are rational and selfish money maximisers*. In fact, under this assumption, we should observe exactly the same investment behaviour in both the punishment and the no-punishment condition, namely, *no investment at all in all periods*. The no-investment prediction is most transparent for period ten. Since all subjects know that the experiment ends in period ten, their best private choice in the *no-punishment* condition is to invest nothing. In the punishment condition, their best choice at the punishment stage in period ten is to not punish at all, because punishment is costly. Yet, since rational egoists anticipate that nobody will punish, the presence of the punishment stage does not change the behavioural incentives at the investment stage of period ten. Therefore, in the *punishment condition* as well nobody will invest in period ten. Since rational egoists will anticipate this outcome for period ten, they know that their actions in period nine do not affect the decisions in period ten. Therefore, punishing in period nine makes no sense for selfish players and, as a consequence, full defection at the investment stage of period nine is again their best choice. This backward induction argument can be repeated so that full defection and no punishment is predicted to occur for all ten periods of the punishment treatment. The same backward induction logic also predicts, of course, defection in all periods of the no-punishment treatment.[14]

In sharp contrast to the prediction of zero punishment, subjects punish very often. Moreover, punishment follows a clear pattern. The large majority of punishments are imposed by the cooperators on the defectors. The punishment a subject receives is the higher the more their contribution falls short of the average contribution of the other three group members (see Fig. 2.3). Figure 2.3 shows, for example, that if a subject contributes between fourteen and seventeen tokens less than the other group members, it gets punished so that its income from the investment stage is reduced by roughly 70 percent. The positive relation between received punishment and the negative deviation from others' contributions is highly significant while there is no relation between positive deviations and the received punishment. Punishment of sub-average investments also prevails in period ten.

What is the impact of this punishment pattern on investment behaviour? It turns out that contribution rates dramatically differ between the two conditions. Already in period one contribution rates are significantly higher in the punishment condition. Then they quickly converge towards almost full cooperation in the punishment condition whereas in the absence of a punishment opportunity they steadily decrease to rather low

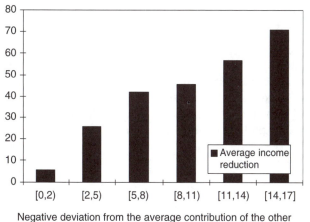

Negative deviation from the average contribution of the other group members

Figure 2.3 Income reduction due to punishment in relation to the deviation from others' contributions to the project ($N = 400$).

Source: E. Fehr and S. Gächter (2000).

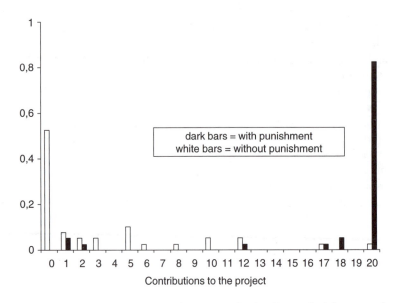

Figure 2.4 Distribution of contributions in the final period of the generalized
PD with and without punishment (relative frequencies) ($N = 80$).

Source: E. Fehr and S. Gächter (2000).

levels. In the final period of the punishment condition 82.5 percent of all
subjects cooperate fully. In the final period of the no-punishment condition
almost nobody cooperates fully and 53 percent defect fully (see Fig. 2.4).

The very high cooperation in the punishment condition represents an
unambiguous rejection of the standard economic approach while it is consistent with the reciprocal fairness approach. Moreover, the big difference
in cooperation rates across conditions indeed suggests that in the presence of punishment opportunities the reciprocally fair types can force the
selfish types to cooperate, while in the absence of such opportunities the
selfish types induce the reciprocally fair types to defect, too. Thus, interaction structures that have theoretically identical implications, if there are
only selfish types, generate fundamentally different behavioural patterns
in the presence of reciprocally fair types.

5. Reciprocal fairness as a limit to competition

The importance of reciprocal fairness derives to a significant extent from
the fact that it changes the incentives for the selfish types. This became
transparent in the previous discussion of the simultaneous PD with punishment opportunities where the reciprocally fair types constrained the
cheating inclinations of the selfish types. This change in incentives can also

be illustrated in the context of a sequentially played one-shot PD (without punishment) in which a selfish player A faces a reciprocally fair player B. Since player B defects in response to defection and cooperates in response to cooperation, the selfish player A has an incentive to cooperate, too. We will show now that this incentive change has important consequences for the impact of competition on wage or price formation. We will, in particular, show that, when there is an effort elicitation problem, experimental employers are willing to pay voluntarily much higher wages compared to a situation where they do not face an effort elicitation problem.

To show this consider a simple variant of the employer–worker game mentioned above.[15] In this experiment there are seven experimental employers each of which can make wage offers w to the group of 11 workers. If a worker accepts w she has to make a costly effort choice $e \in [0.1, 1]$. After the effort choice no rewarding or punishing of workers is possible and there are also no fines. Each employer can only employ one worker so that there is an excess supply of 4 workers. Employers are, therefore, in a very strong position that allows them to pay rather low wages. In a control condition we removed workers' effort choice and enforced, instead, an exogenously given effort level. Everything else was kept identical in the control condition. The important difference between the effort–choice condition and the control condition is that, in the former, workers can respond reciprocally to generous wage offers by choosing a high effort level while this is not possible in the control condition. In the presence of reciprocally fair workers, employers face, therefore, very different wage setting incentives in the two conditions. In the effort–choice condition, employers have a material incentive to elicit workers' reciprocity by paying generous wages, while in the control condition this incentive is absent. As a consequence, the reciprocal fairness approach predicts that in the effort–choice condition workers' reciprocal responses will constrain the employers' desire to pay low wages.

The experimental data strongly support this hypothesis. The correlation between wages and effort is significantly positive and sufficiently steep to render a high wage policy profitable. This induces employers to pay considerably higher wages in the effort–choice condition (see the first two columns of Table 2.2). In the control condition many employers actively exploit the excess supply of workers by offering extremely low

Table 2.2 Reciprocal fairness limits competition

	Effort choice condition with competition	Exogenous effort with competition (control condition)	Effort choice condition without competition
Average wage	61	35	61
Number of observations	280	140	300

wages. In contrast, in the effort–choice condition employers 'voluntarily' refrain from offering low wages.

In a further variation of the effort–choice condition we removed the excess supply of workers so that there were exactly as many employers as workers. Moreover, employers and workers were matched by the experimenter and employers could make a wage offer only to the matched worker. Thus, this condition *completely removes competition* among the workers. By comparing the effort–choice condition with and without competition we can examine whether competition has a wage-decreasing effect. Contrary to what most economists probably – and perhaps even most social scientists – believe, it turns out that *competition has no impact at all on wage formation in the effort–choice condition*. As columns 1 and 3 in Table 2.1 reveal, wages in the effort–choice conditions are very close to each other.

6. Conclusions

The empirical evidence shows that many people have inclinations to behave in a reciprocally fair manner. This deviation from purely self-interested behaviour constitutes a powerful constraint for potential cheaters that can generate almost universal cooperation in situations in which purely selfish behaviour would cause a complete breakdown of cooperation. In sequential interactions reciprocal fairness constitutes also an important cooperation incentive for purely self-interested first movers. However, we also have uncovered interaction structures in which the selfish types induce the reciprocally fair types to behave in a very noncooperative manner. In general, our experimental results show that the existence of reciprocally fair types greatly improves the prospects for cooperation and limits the impact of competition. The existence of reciprocally fair behaviour can, however, not be taken for granted because the willingness to cooperate voluntarily can be destroyed by explicit threats to punish cheating.

Notes

1 Financial support by the Swiss National Science Foundation (1214-051000.97/1) and the EU-TMR Research Network ENDEAR (FMRX-CT98-0238) is gratefully acknowledged.
2 There is a large economic literature that tries to provide microfoundations for the existence of incomplete contracts. The empirical fact that many agreements contain an element of incompleteness is, however, undisputed. A prominent example is, of course, the labour contract.
3 W. D. Hamilton (1964).
4 R. Trivers (1971); R. Axelrod and W. D. Hamilton (1981).
5 D. Fudenberg and E. Maskin (1986).
6 For this definition of reciprocal fairness see M. Rabin (1993) and A. Falk and U. Fischbacher (1999).

7 L. Cameron (1995) and Fehr and Tougareva (1995) conducted experiments that show this. In Cameron (1995) subjects could earn the income of three months in a one-shot experiment that lasted 15 minutes. In Fehr and Tougareva (1995) subjects earned three months' monetary income in an experiment that lasted for two hours.

8 Besides our experiments discussed in this paper compare, e.g. J. Berg, J. Dickhaut and K. McCabe (1995) and W. Güth (1995).

9 E. Fehr and A. Falk (1999); E. Fehr, G. Kirchsteiger and A. Riedl (1998).

10 In E. Fehr and A. Falk (1999) and in E. Fehr, G. Kirchsteiger and A. Riedl (1998) between 20 and 30 percent of the subjects behaved in a completely selfish manner. Subjects who are unconditionally altruistic are virtually non-existent in these studies.

11 For a rigorous proof of this statement see E. Fehr and K. Schmidt (1999). They show that in a generalised one-shot PD with a heterogeneous population of players, full defection by everybody can be the unique equilibrium in the PD without punishment while full cooperation can be an equilibrium in the PD with punishment.

12 E. Fehr and S. Gächter (2000).

13 We also conducted experiments in which the group composition was randomly changed in each of the ten periods. Due to space constraints and because the results are qualitatively similar we concentrate here on the results with a constant group composition.

14 If rationality and selfishness are not common knowledge there exist other equilibria in which there is cooperation and punishment during the early periods. However, for the final periods the no cooperation – no punishment prediction still holds.

15 E. Fehr and A. Falk (1999). The main difference to the employer–worker experiment considered above is that employers cannot stipulate a 'desired effort level' $\hat{e}$. Effort costs $c(\hat{e})$ are, however, the same as before.

References

Axelrod, R. and W. D. Hamilton (1981) 'The Evolution of Cooperation', *Science* **211**, 1390–1396.

Berg, J., J. Dickhaut and K. McCabe (1995) 'Trust, Reciprocity and Social History', *Games and Economic Behaviour* **10**, 122–142.

Cameron, L. (1995) 'Raising the Stakes in the Ultimatum Game: Experimental Evidence form Indonesia', *Discussion paper, Princeton University*.

Falk, A. and U. Fischbacher (1999) 'A Theory of Reciprocity', *Discussion paper, University of Zurich*.

Fehr, E. and A. Falk (1999) 'Wage Rigidities in a Competitive Incomplete Contract Market', *Journal of Political Economy* **107**, 106–134.

Fehr, E. and S. Gächter (1998a) 'Do Incentive Contracts Destroy Voluntary Cooperation?', *Discussion paper, University of Zurich*.

Fehr, E. and S. Gächter (2000) 'Cooperation and Punishment in Public Good Experiments – An Experimental Analysis of Norm Formational and Norm Enforcement', *American Economic Review* **90**, 980–994.

Fehr, E., S. Gächter and G. Kirchsteiger (1997) 'Reciprocity as a Contract Enforcement Device: Experimental Evidence', *Econometrica* **65**, 833–860.

Fehr, E., G. Kirchsteiger and A. Riedl (1998) 'Gift Exchange and Reciprocity in Competitive Experimental Markets', *European Economic Review* **42**, 1–34.

Fehr, E. and K. Schmidt (1999) 'A Theory of Fairness, Competition and Cooperation', *Quarterly Journal of Economics* **114**, 817–851.

Fehr, E. and E. Tougareva (1995) 'Do High Stakes Remove Reciprocal Fairness – Evidence from Russia', *Discussion paper, University of Zurich.*

Fudenberg, D. and E. Maskin (1986) 'The Folk Theorem in Repeated Games with Discounting and with Incomplete Information', *Econometrica* **54**, 533–554.

Güth, W. (1995) 'On Ultimatum Bargaining Experiments – A Personal Review', *Journal of Economic Behavior and Organization* **27**, 329–344.

Hamilton, W. D. (1964) 'The Genetic Evolution of Social Behaviour', *Journal of Theoretical Biology* **7**, 1–52.

Rabin, M. (1993) 'Incorporating Fairness into Game Theory and Economics', *American Economic Review* **83**, 1281–1302.

Trivers, R. (1971) 'The Evolution of Reciprocal Altruism', *Quarterly Review of Biology* **46**, 35–57.

3

ALL CONSUMPTION IS CONSPICUOUS

Anne Mayhew

Harvey Leibenstein, in an effort to incorporate the concept of "conspicuous consumption" into neoclassical demand theory, classified demand for consumer goods and services into two general categories: functional and non-functional. "By functional demand," Leibenstein wrote, "is meant that part of the demand for a commodity which is due to the qualities inherent in the commodity itself" (1950: 188–9). "Non-functional demand," as Leibenstein defined it, included demand "due to external effects on utility": a "bandwagon" effect because others are consuming the same product and a "snob" effect resulting from reduction of demand because others are buying it.[1] In this paper I contrast Leibenstein's argument with the quite different anthropological and institutionalist interpretation of consumption, and consider evidence for and against both perspectives.

1. The two perspectives

Leibenstein's unquestioning assumption that there is some large part of consumer demand that is independent of the effects of the consumption of others is, of course, standard in mainstream economics, but contrasts sharply with the treatment of consumption among other social scientists, including institutional economists, most notably Thorstein Veblen. For Veblen, for anthropologists, and for others who work in the broad traditions of sociology and anthropology, *all* consumption is conspicuous in that it serves to reaffirm the consumer's role as part of a group or to mark the outsider. A simple illustration of the importance of consumption as a way of belonging is that, throughout the world, refusal to consume that which is regarded as normal, or consumption of that which is abnormal, is a major marker of the outsider. The hermit who lives in a cave, the recluse who fills her house with "junk", the "bag lady" with the odd attire, the crazy who eats bugs, the heretic who violates dietary prohibitions, are all standard examples of the person who does not belong. It is equally well recognized that people of different cultures consume different things, so much so that food consumption is often used as a standard marker of cultural identity, as is clothing and style of housing.

The proposition that consumption is culturally patterned, and that it serves to mark identity, is integral to anthropological thought and plays an important role in allowing anthropologists to understand the processes by which cultural patterns are formed and reaffirmed. As Marshall Sahlins (quoting Baudrillard) puts it, consumption is an "exchange of meanings, a discourse – to which practical virtues are attached only post facto" (1976: 177). In this anthropological approach, there is no "functional demand" as Leibenstein defines it, no demand that is attributable solely to the "qualities inherent" in the product itself.

Sahlins uses American food preferences and tabus to illustrate his point.

> ... the productive relation of American society to its own and the world environment is organized by specific valuations of edibility and inedibility, themselves qualitative and in no way justifiable by biological, ecological, or economic advantage... The exploitation of the American environment... depends on the model of a meal that includes a central meat element .... Hence also a corresponding structure of agricultural production of feed grains, and in turn a specific articulation to world markets – *all of which would change overnight if we ate dogs*.... The "opportunity costs" of our economic rationality are a secondary formation, an expression of relationships already given by another kind of thought, figured a posteriori within the constraints of a logic of meaningful order. The tabu on horses and dogs thus renders unthinkable the consumption of a set of animals whose production is practically feasible and which are nutritionally not to be despised.
>
> (Sahlins 1976: 171, italics added)

The logic of meaningful order is the cultural logic that people inherit and modify, if slowly, but which is fundamental, in the anthropological view, to determination of consumption patterns. The choice of beef or pork at the meat counter may be based upon price and individual preference: dog is not in the realm of possibility – most Americans would gag at the very thought of eating dog – and would certainly shun, or worse, those who confessed to doing so.

In early editions of his introductory text, Paul Samuelson came close to the anthropological view when he observed that Americans could obtain adequate nutrition (as understood at the time) by consuming a diet of "wheat flour, cabbage, lima beans, kidneys, and not much else" (1958: 167). Samuelson went on to say that "Most of us would bitterly resent such an unpalatable and monotonous diet – just as dogs, if conditioned to eat fish alone, will almost starve before touching the best steak" (167). Even more remarkably Samuelson wrote "… what people consider to be absolute necessities consist to a large degree not of *physiological necessities,* but of *conventional social desirabilities*" (167, italics added).

Samuelson avoided the need to explore the ramifications that this reasoning has for neoclassical consumer demand theory (which he explored in a later chapter) by labeling the section from which the cited passages come "The Backward Art of Spending Money" (a phrase borrowed from Wesley C. Mitchell, who used it to very different purpose). It is clear that the student is meant to understand that a failure to recognize choice of consumer goods as guided by convention rather than "physiological necessity" is "backward" (non-functional in Leibenstein's words). Samuelson lumps this understandable but backward behavior with allowing oneself to be persuaded by advertising, but concludes the section with the reassuring (to economists) thought: "Actually, there are some signs that the American consumer is becoming pretty professional these days," a conclusion buttressed by casual observation of the growing (in 1958) importance of discount houses, "do-it-yourself", and time spent on buying "high-fidelity phonograph sets" (168). Samuelson was reassured that time spent on consumption could be taken as indication of reduction in backwardness and non-functionality of consumption, and could, thereby, ignore the implications of the importance of "conventional social desirabilities".

Samuelson, like Leibenstein, needed to dismiss social determination of consumption patterns and the importance of advertising in order to retain the rational consumer of neoclassical theory. This was made easier for Samuelson by the strongly ethnocentric approach that allowed him to avoid any mention of the possibility that some people might prefer a diet of wheat flour, cabbage, lima beans, and kidneys to steak and potatoes. The question that I want to pose is this: why and how have economists remained so apart from other social scientists in continuing to treat a portion of consumption – the portion defined as non-functional or backward – as relatively trivial and thereby to downplay the social roles of consumption?

What Samuelson did in suggesting a "rational" diet of cabbage, lima beans, and kidneys was to take a small step toward the anthropological view that all consumption signals membership in a particular group. However, as a good economist he does not appear to have been seriously tempted by the thought that most if not all consumption is so patterned. It is probably true to say that economists who have been tempted have often rejected this view because it would undermine the welfare conclusions derived from consumer sovereignty. It is not too difficult to see what would be sacrificed if the anthropological view of consumption were accepted; it is harder to understand how economists have suppressed the evidence in favor of this view.

Thorstein Veblen did see consumption as socially patterned. In *The Theory of the Leisure Class* (1899) he argued that consumption was based on emulation and the desire to impress others. Rather than emphasizing, as Sahlins does, that consumption is a way of signaling solidarity with one's group, Veblen emphasized the use of "conspicuous consumption" to signal superiority and to emulate the superiority established by others. However, the point is the same. The desirability of goods consumed is socially determined and cannot be said to be inherent in the goods themselves. Since Veblen wrote, the growth of advertising and marketing, as well as the arguments of such as Duesenberry (1949), Hamilton (1962), Galbraith (1976) and others have provided further evidence of a truth that has nevertheless been steadfastly ignored in the core of mainstream economic theory, just as Samuelson did in his text.

Though it has been accepted by economists that there may be *some* portion of consumption that is "conspicuous" or non-functional, consumer demand theory has continued to be based upon the assumption that it is the individual who determines what to consume. In the remainder of this essay I consider two arguments that might seem to support the mainstream economic view. Both arguments are to be taken seriously, but both should be rejected, as I shall argue.

2. Theory and evidence

One possible argument in favor of the standard view of neoclassical economists is that consumption theorists, such as Veblen and the anthropologists, have confused the long-term and fundamental functionality of consumption patterns with the faddishness and non-functionality allowed by modern affluence. Thus it *can* be argued that Veblen, with his emphasis on waste and leisure among the newly rich of late nineteenth-century America, was dealing with marginal consumption and not with the more fundamental consumption patterns of the great majority.

It could, however, be argued that the "the logic of meaningful order" that gives rise to fundamental, culturally specific preferences such as the consumption of beef but not of dog, of beef but not pork, are rational adaptations to long-ago practical and functional choices. This is the argument that has been advanced by Marvin Harris, an anthropologist who writes from what he calls a "cultural materialist" perspective (Harris 1979).

Harris rejects the "emic" explanations of anthropology, in which native explanations and behaviors are taken to be sufficient material for analysis in favor of an "etic" explanation in which observers use their own explanatory categories and processes to "explain" native patterns. In the case of food taboos (which have played a large role in debates among anthropologists over the adequacy of emic and etic approaches), Harris rejects the efforts of Mary Douglas and others to explain the Israelite taboo on eating pork by use of Israelite classifications. The adequacy of the emic explanations offered by Douglas are of no importance here. What is of importance is Harris's conclusion that the prohibition against consumption of pork was a consequence of a sharp decline, after about 7000 BC, in forest land where pigs could forage, with the consequence that the pigs would have to be fed grain that would otherwise be consumed by people and would require the special provision of artificial shade and moisture. This would make them more costly although they remained "a tempting source of protein and fat" (1979: 193). From this arose the taboo against their consumption. Israelite society chose the economically rational pattern of consumption and placed religious taboos on the tempting but costly, and therefore irrational, consumption of pork.

Harris's approach allows us to place the economists' rational consumer in an anthropological context of culturally patterned consumption by restating Leibenstein's classifications: "functional demand" is demand for goods whose "inherent qualities" have been manifest at some time in the past in the specific technological and ecological context of a people. Inherited patterns of consumption continue to reflect those realities. "Nonfunctional" demand then becomes the variation on deep cultural, but nevertheless highly rational, patterns of consumption.

Is Harris's etic interpretation superior to Douglas's emic explanation of the taboo on pork? No absolute answer can be given. Harris's story of the taboo on consumption of pork is internally consistent, as is Douglas's emic account. It should trouble the analyst that Harris's account is so consistent with the emic explanations of consumption in his own culture, but beyond the doubt introduced by concern on that score, there is no way to prove Harris right or wrong. The historical record tells us only that eating of pork was tabooed and that the Israeli culture survived. Orthodox Jews do not eat pork, whatever the price relative to beef. Speculation about how those patterns emerged may be intellectually rewarding, but must ultimately be frustrated by the proposition that "rational" choice is always conditioned by some prior cultural patterning. Why was pork considered so attractive that it had to be tabooed when ecological conditions changed? Why was it consumed before it became "too costly?" A reasonable response to Harris, and to neoclassical economists, is that, as a matter of practical social science, all consumption had best be seen as conspicuous, which is to say, as social. Leibenstein's "inherent" qualities of goods are always in the eye of the encultured individual.

The importance of cultural patterning is supported by anthropological observations of modern people who live close to the margin of survival, people who might be thought to eat any and all things that would support and sustain life. Although it is a mistake to think that modern hunters and gatherers are good models of our long-ago ancestors (DeGregori 1998; Lee 1976) we can learn some things from them about people who have a very primitive technology. We learn that cultural patterning even among the most geographically and technologically confined people is apparent. Under normal non-starvation conditions choices are made among possible foodstuffs, choices that are not dictated simply by technology or geography. Richard B. Lee did a survey of food consumed in the early 1960s by the !Kung Bushmen of the Kalahari Desert and concluded that 90 percent of the vegetable diet by weight came from only twenty-three of the eighty-five edible species of plants available. There were 223 local species of animals known and named by the Bushmen, with fifty-four classified as edible, but only seventeen species were regularly hunted (1968: 35).[2] The Bushmen have been found by others to be victims of malnutrition. Whatever the truth may be, or may have been when Lee did his survey in the early 1960s, the fact remains that cultural patterning of consumption was apparent even among these people.

What is even more interesting for our purposes is that among the !Kung Bushmen, as among other hunters and gatherers, seasonal and cyclical drought results in travel over a larger area in order to maintain existing patterns of consumption.

> For the greater part of the year, food is locally abundant and easily collected. It is only during the end of dry season in September and October, when desirable foods have been eaten out in the immediate vicinity of the waterholes that the people have to plan longer hikes of 10–15 miles and carry their own water…. The important point is that food is a constant, but distance required to reach food is a variable….
>
> (Lee 1968: 33)

Lee does say that the diet becomes "more eclectic" during the dry season with some roots, bulbs and edible resins being consumed, but the !Kung maintain the preferred diet even though other foodstuffs are more easily available.

This last observation suggests the impracticality of tracing consumption patterns back to a completely "functional" beginning. While it is almost certainly true that some foodstuffs and other goods may have become less easily available as ecological conditions changed, and that people will change their cultural "tastes" in response, it is also true that people have had culturally patterned "meaningful orders" to food and other materials since well before any recorded history.

The conclusion that there is no known time when all consumption was "functional" is relevant to a second argument in justification of the neoclassical and individualistic approach. This second argument posits that, until very recently, say in the past century or so, roles in production and other social markers rather than consumption served to define social status and belonging. For example, Grant McCracken, an anthropologist, has argued that "culture and consumption have an unprecedented relationship in the modern world" (1988: xi). He argues that "consumption booms" in the sixteenth and eighteenth century in parts of Europe gave consumption a new variety of cultural roles and meanings. For example, in sixteenth-century Elizabethan England, consumption was used to provide theatrical proof of importance and legitimacy. By the nineteenth century "a permanent and continual dynamic relationship between social and consumer changes" had developed (22) and remains a feature of modern Western society. By the twentieth century, consumption had become a primary way of indicating group allegiance and identity.

McCracken's dating and the details of his argument are not important for this paper. What is important is that McCracken sees conspicuous consumption, playing a social marking role, as something new in human history. So too do a number of other writers who, somewhat ironically, have criticized Veblen as well as neoclassical economists for failing to recognize the complex social meaning that consumption has come to have. In this view (well reviewed by Ramstad 1998), Veblen, being among the early observers of the importance of consumption as social marker, and writing when advertising had not achieved its modern pervasiveness, saw only "pecuniary prowess" when he viewed the social meaning of consumption. He did not appreciate, and could not have done so late in the nineteenth and very early in the twentieth century, the full range of cultural meaning carried by consumer goods today.[3]

Modern affluence, the growth of advertising and the influence of TV, movies and the internet have obviously caused an enormous expansion in the use of consumer goods as ways to identify with a wide variety of social groups. "Gourmets" in America, after reading the magazines that instruct in "good eating," go in search of arugula, fiddlehead ferns, or Thai basil in a process that allows them to know themselves to be eating the very best in a process that allows group identity around the sophisticated table or in the shops where the foraging takes place. Teenagers throughout almost all parts of the world listen to the latest pop artists and know themselves to be "with it," and are known by their peers to be so. It is even possible through visible (and highly conspicuous) consumption to reveal oneself to be scornful of modern conspicuous consumption. Stores with names like "Green Earth" offer large varieties of "back to nature natural products," the purchase of which signals awareness that modern consumption has become excessive.

Clearly, groups to which one signals belonging by consumption are no longer defined or confined by locality or kinship. One can signal identity with a group of strangers by choices of clothing, food, music, presence or absence of tattoos, and so on and on.

While the current complexity of consumption and of group identity is much greater than in the past, it is not the case that those wedded to neo-classical analysis of consumption should take comfort in knowing that they are only slightly behind the times and were once correct. As Veblen made clear in his critiques of the neoclassical approach, it has always been wrong to see consumers as isolated "calculators of pleasure and pain". Even before advertising became widespread, and even before some con-sumers had time and money to spend on socially complex modern consumption, consumers consumed what they did primarily because of the groups of which they were part. Whether we use modern ethno-graphic records as an imperfect mirror to reflect patterns among our tech-nologically primitive ancestors, or make use of written historical records, it is apparent that clothing, food consumption, housing styles, art styles, pottery patterns and the like varied culturally rather than individually. Groups were more tightly defined by geographic place and by kinship than they are today when choice of exotic food, new music, fashion in clothing, and other translocal and even transnational patterns have become more important. Nevertheless, the human process of eating, adorn-ing, and protecting in a patterned manner remains constant.

In short, the evidence is overwhelming that all consumption has been conspicuous as far back as we can trace it and that takes us back to the central question of the paper. How have economists continued to deny this? Samuelson made a tentative approach but backed off by finding evi-dence that consumers were becoming more professional and thus more like the advertising-immune individual utility maximizing choosers of neoclassical theory. Leibenstein acknowledged that Veblen had a point, but made it relevant only to a relatively trivial part of consumption. How has this orthodoxy retained its power?

3. An emic explanation

There are a number of ways of answering this question. The one that I will pursue in the remainder of this paper is an emic explanation; an explana-tion that makes sense not because of correspondence with reality as des-cribed by non-economists (and some heterodox economists) but because it is consistent with classical, neoclassical, and Marxian patterns of thought. Leibenstein made Veblen (and those who argued as Veblen did) a minor contributor to neoclassical theory, and thereby diverted the threat that Veblen's argument posed by embedding his contribution in one of the most basic, but often unexamined, ideas in the shared traditions of classical, Marxian, and neoclassical economics. Leibenstein made a micro proposition of the macro proposition that economies satisfy basic needs *before* a surplus can add luxury and complexity to human society (where *before* has both logical and historical meaning).

The commonplace idea that economics is a study of human reaction to natural scarcity, and that such scarcity is a stark fact that has faced all of mankind, is closely related to another idea: "… the appearance of a 'surplus' over bare subsistence needs [is] the critical determinant in the evolution of complex social and economic institutions… ." (Pearson 1957: 321). At first blush the truth of this idea seems so obvious as to make a challenge ludicrous. How could populations that eke out a living with primitive agricultural equipment build the cities, the laboratories, the transportation networks of complex modern societies? The problem is, however, that in all societies what is "surplus" and what is needed for survival is defined socially. There are clearly caloric levels too low for human survival and reproduction, and there are temperatures below which humans cannot survive without protective clothing and shelter, but, as the anthropologists have told us, in all societies the acceptable range of actual items consumed is socially determined. It follows that subsistence needs, except insofar as they are defined extraculturally by scientists in terms of caloric and basic nutritional needs, can only be defined in a relative sense. Pearson put it this way:

> If the concept of surplus is to be employed … at all, it must be in a relative or constructive sense. In brief: A given quantity of goods or services would be surplus only if the society in some manner set these quantities aside and declared them to be available for a specific purpose. Into this category might then fall such things as food set aside for ceremonial feasts or in anticipation of future dearth, war chests, budgetary surpluses, or savings for whatever purpose… . [R]elative surpluses are initiated by the society in question. It is true that such surpluses may be made to appear along with a windfall increase of material means, or a more permanent rise in productive capacity; but they may also be created with no change whatever in the quantity of subsistence means by re-allocating goods or services from one use to another. The Biblical story of the grain storage by Joseph in Egypt is one illustration of the latter. More important than the natural conditions associated with the creation of relative surpluses is thus an attitude towards resources, and the institutional means of counting out, setting aside, and making available (p. 323).

Veblen made a related point about conspicuous waste/consumption:

> In strict accuracy nothing should be included under the head of conspicuous waste, but such expenditure as is incurred on the ground of an invidious pecuniary comparison. But in order to

bring any given item or element in under this head it is not necessary that it should be recognized as waste in this sense by the person incurring the expenditure. It frequently happens that an element of the standard of living which set out with being primarily wasteful, ends with becoming, in the apprehension of the consumer, a necessary of life; and it may in this way become as indispensable as any other item of the consumer's habitual expenditure (1899: 99).

Surpluses, necessities, and consumption that show the consumer capable of wasteful expenditure are all socially defined; they can be given meaning only within the context of a particular culture.

However, modern western economic thought has been founded on the idea of absolute surplus. The Physiocrats found the source of the surplus in agriculture; Smith and the classical economists found it in the ability of labor to produce more than required to sustain the laborers. Although Marx adopted and changed the same idea to argue that the surplus was taken from labor, he also said that the surplus was "... a gift, not of nature, but of a history embracing thousands of centuries" (as quoted in Pearson: 333). But, in spite of Marx's redefinition of the surplus as a social (historical) creation rather than a natural phenomenon, the idea that a surplus drove history was retained. The subtle distinction between viewing this surplus as derived from human definition of the appropriate uses of total output as opposed to a natural occurrence has had relatively little impact on the use of Marx's ideas. While it is true that some analysts have talked of the "socially necessary wage" as socially constructed, Marxian scholars appear to have spent little time considering the social and changing nature of consumption, probably because the surplus, however defined, has been the crucial element in explication and denunciation of exploitation and in use of the idea of accumulation as the driving force in socio-economic evolution.

With the shift from class analysis to focus on the individual that marked the neoclassical revolution in economic thought, the idea of a subsistence wage, of the "socially necessary wage," and the importance of an "iron law of wages" faded in importance. It did not totally disappear; the idea that there is indeed an absolute surplus makes periodic appearances in a variety of areas of economic analysis. As Pearson observed, the idea of a social surplus as the explanation of differential rates of economic development has been commonplace in the literature of economic development. Surplus in the form of capital accumulation is fundamental both to neoclassical and to Marxian explanations of growth (see Mokyr 1990, for a review and critique of the neoclassical, and Perelman 2000, for a recent example of the Marxian). The informed reader will undoubtedly be able to provide many other examples of ways in which the idea of economic surplus plays an important role in economic analysis. A concomitant idea is that there is a level of subsistence that is naturally defined and this idea has led to efforts to develop a theoretically derived definition of basic needs (Hodgson 1993).

As fundamental as the idea of surplus (at Leibenstein's micro level, non-functional demand) and basic needs or subsistence (at Leibenstein's micro level, functional demand) are, John Adams has suggested that they are part of an even more fundamental thought process that is deeply embedded in all economic analysis. In an article written to extend Harry Pearson's critique of the concept of surplus, Adams notes that use of the idea of an absolute surplus always entails use of a simple equation of the following form:

$$A - B = C$$

> For a firm or farm, for example, A is total revenue, B is total cost, and C is net income. In rough terms, C is what Marx calls "surplus value" or what Alfred Marshall would call "profit"
> (Adams 1991: 192).

Adams goes on to point out that, in macroeconomic and growth theory,[4] A represents income or output, B consumption, and C becomes savings or investment; in mercantile thought (which still influences international trade accounting), exports are A, imports are B, and C becomes the movements of specie – or, in modern terms, the balance of payments. In development economics "surplus labor" was described as the result of subtracting the necessary agricultural labor from total labor and the surplus was then available for industrialization and modernization; the classic welfare triangle gives a "spatial C". Other examples are provided by Adams but his treatment of the basic idea of unlimited wants and scarcity is of particular relevance here:

> The first idea taught to economics students in introductory courses is that all economies are characterized by "scarcity" – the mirror opposite of "surplus." Human wants and social needs are said to be infinite while resources and product are not. The operant equation converts the A term to infinite wants, the B term to finite productive capacity, and the C term, once again to infinity… . Thus from the very beginning does training in the wonderful logic of economics begin with a special case of The Subtractive Principle. Something minus something else yields a residual of great meaning – and something that deflects attention from the major terms from which it is derived. Student focus is directed towards the

abstract putative condition of scarcity rather than towards the substance of the economy: How do individual and social wants arise and of what do they consist? Are they reasonable or can they be deflated? Is some level of production, B, enough to satisfy when wants, A, are limited? What are the direct and indirect costs – especially environmental burdens – of different levels of B? (p. 195).

My argument in this paper is that allegiance to this fundamental Subtractive Principle allowed Leibenstein, and continues to allow economists who may never have read Leibenstein, to ignore the strong evidence that all of consumption is indeed conspicuous.

4. Conclusion

All consumption is visible and made visible to mark the consumers as members of their group, to mark the status of each, and to inform outsiders that each is a member, not an outsider. Thus is all consumption conspicuous. Of course, people enjoy many traits inherent in the goods and services that they consume: the taste, sound, feel, smell, and use of goods are important. But non-functional and functional demands are all functional in establishing group identity; all demand is intersubjective.

Notes

1 Leibenstein says his article resulted from Oskar Morgenstern's observation that "the market demand curve is not the lateral summation of the individual demand curve" because of the non-additivity that results from intersubjective demand.
2 There has been considerable controversy over the adequacy of diet among these Bushmen. Described by some as "affluent" because of the ease with which they obtained their food, the Bushmen have been found by others to be victims of malnutrition. Whatever the truth may be, or may have been when Lee did his survey in the early 1960s, the fact remains that cultural patterning of consumption was apparent even among these people.
3 It should be noted that Leibenstein also offered a very narrow interpretation of what Veblen said, by describing the "Veblen effect" as the result of a larger quantity of demand at higher prices, a smaller quantity at lower prices, with the "snob" and "bandwagon" effects attributed to others. It is difficult to understand how this narrow interpretation of Veblen's argument can be reached if the whole of *The Theory of the Leisure Class* is read.
4 I was once told by a young PhD who was a recent product of a prestigious US economics program that the intersection of the aggregate demand curve with the vertical axis in the once-standard diagram that showed aggregate demand as a positively sloped line drawn with total income on the horizontal axis, represented the subsistence or minimal possible level of consumption expenditure for that society. When I suggested that the point of intersection was a statistical artifact rather than a measure of any social reality, he observed that I obviously

did not understand modern consumption theory very well. Thus, had the idea of subsistence and surplus crept into Keynesian economics.

References

Adams, J. (1991) "Surplus, Surplus, Who's Got the Surplus? The Subtractivist Fallacy in orthodox economics," *Journal of Economic Issues* 15: 187–97.

DeGregori (1998) "Back to the future: A review article," *Journal of Economic Issues* 32: 1153–61.

Duesenberry, J. (1949) *Income, Saving and the Theory of Consumer Behavior,* Cambridge, Mass: Harvard University Press.

Galbraith, J. (1976) *The Affluent Society,* Boston: Houghton Mifflin.

Hamilton, D. (1962) *The Consumer in Our Economy,* Boston: Houghton Mifflin.

Harris, M. (1979) *Cultural Materialism: The Struggle for a Science of Culture,* New York: Random House.

Hodgson, G. (1993) *Economics and Evolution,* Ann Arbor: University of Michigan Press.

Lee, R. and Irven DeVore (eds) (1976) *Kalahari Hunter-Gatherers: Studies of the !Kung San and Their Neighbors,* Cambridge, Mass: Harvard University Press.

Leibenstein, H. (1950) "Bandwagon, Snob, and Veblen Effects in the Theory of Consumers' demand," *Quarterly Journal of Economics* 64: 183–207.

Mokyr, J. (1990) *The Lever of Riches: Technological Creativity and Economic Progress,* New York: Oxford University Press.

Perelman, M. (2000) *The Invention of Capitalism: Classical Political Economy and the Secret History of Primitive Accumulation,* Durham, North Carolina: Duke University Press.

Pearson, H. (1957) "The Economy has no Surplus: Critique of a Theory of Development," in Karl Polanyi, Conrad M. Arensberg, and Harry W. Pearson (eds) *Trade and Market in the Early Empire, Economies in History and Theory,* Glencoe, Ill: The Free Press.

Ramstad, Y. (1998) "Veblen's Propensity for Emulation: Is It Passé," in Doug Brown (ed.) *Thorstein Veblen In the Twenty-First Century,* Cheltenham, UK: Edward Elgar.

Sahlins, M. (1976) *Culture and Practical Reason,* Chicago, Ill: The University of Chicago Press.

Samuelson, P. (1958) *Economics,* New York: McGraw-Hill.

Veblen, T. [1899] (1975) *The Theory of the Leisure Class: An Economic Study of Institutions,* New York: Augustus M. Kelley.

4

FLAWS IN THE FOUNDATION

Consumer behavior and general equilibrium theory

Frank Ackerman

Economists, pursuing the rigor and respectability of "hard sciences," are fond of observing that a good theory can be built on unrealistic or implausible assumptions, so long as it leads to realistic predictions or other useful results. This idea dates back at least to Milton Friedman (1953) in economics, and more importantly, draws on powerful, well-known examples in physics. Nothing could be more intuitively implausible than quantum mechanics, yet its predictions have been confirmed in great detail.

The same is true of neoclassical economics – except for the part about the predictions. What if implausible assumptions lead only to implausible conclusions and empty predictions? When grand theories are built up from a model of economic actors as uncoordinated, unchanging, asocial individuals, the flaws in the foundation show up as cracks in the super-structure. For this reason, there is a connection between two seemingly separate areas of economic theory, namely the simple stories of consumer decision-making and the intricate theoretical conclusions of general equilibrium analysis. Simple problems in the former lead directly to complex problems in the latter.

Consider one of the classic individuals described in economic theory. All students of economics are familiar with the textbook model of the consumer. She is an individual with a unique and methodical approach to shopping. She may not literally draw budget lines and indifference curves to study their tangencies (though a casual reading of an introductory text might create that impression). But she does have well-defined, insatiable desires, and she certainly knows how to make marginal adjustments in her purchasing plans to reach the absolute maximum of attainable bliss. Indeed, she is continually making such adjustments whenever the market provides her with new information. She resembles a mutual fund portfolio manager, except that she is better informed about the future value of her purchases, and hence less often disappointed. Her resemblance to actual consumers is more tenuous.

Now consider the theoretical structure built on the behavior of individuals like her. General equilibrium theory, the complete model of individuals interacting through a system of markets, represents the capstone of the conventional economic edifice. In the standard image, the existence and Pareto optimality of an equilibrium point are the ultimate mathematical expression of the metaphor of the invisible hand.

However, theorists have known for some time that the equilibrium of a general equilibrium model is not necessarily either unique or stable. There may be multiple sets of prices, and associated allocations of resources, that are all equilibrium points. Moreover, an equilibrium may be unstable, meaning that small market fluctuations can lead farther away from the equilibrium rather than back toward it. There is no economically plausible dynamic process that always leads toward an equilibrium point. The Pareto optimality of general equilibrium is thus only a mathematical curiosity, devoid of economic significance even if the theory's numerous simplifying assumptions are granted.

A closer look will reveal the connection between the two distinct, problematical theories of consumer behavior and general equilibrium. After presenting the two separate sets of problems, and then discussing their connection, I will turn to more realistic analyses of consumer behavior, and conclude with the implications of these analyses for an overall framework that might replace general equilibrium.

1. Theorizing the consumer

A wave of new interdisciplinary research on consumption has swept through most of the social sciences – except for economics (Miller 1995). Yet, despite the central role that consumers play in economic theory, economics has been almost unaffected by new ideas about consumption of any variety (Goodwin *et al.* 1997). A review of innovations in neoclassical economic theory, written in the early 1990s, simply asserts that "the microeconomic theory of consumer choice under conditions of certainty is well developed, and has not been the subject of any significant advances in recent years" (Darnell 1992).

That "well developed" theory, of course, assumes that consumers come to the market with well-defined, insatiable desires for private goods and services. Those desires are not affected by social interactions, culture, economic institutions, or the consumption choices or well-being of others. Only prices, incomes, and personal tastes affect consumption – and since tastes are exogenous to neoclassical economics, there is little point in talking about anything but prices and incomes.

More precisely, there are three fundamental assumptions of the neoclassical theory of consumption; these assumptions may be called asocial individualism, insatiability, and commodity-based utility (Ackerman 1997):

1 *Asocial individualism.* Consumer desires and preferences are exogenous; they are not affected by social or economic institutions, interactions with others, or observation of the behavior of others. In the language of this volume, the existence or at least the economic significance of intersubjectivity is denied by assumption.
2 *Insatiability.* It is human nature to have a multiplicity of insatiable material desires. No matter what you already have, more is always better than less; there is no such thing as "enough."
3 *Commodity-based utility.* Consumer preferences consist of well-informed desires for specific goods and services available on the market. The only economically meaningful forms of individual satisfaction result from more consumption (or less work, a related point that will not be addressed here).

The first two assumptions are at times explicit; frequently, however, all three are implicit in the basic formulation of the theory. The first assumption, the lack of social interaction, is built into the theory when indifference curves or preference relations are defined solely as functions of the consumer's own commodities. By definition, therefore, institutions, culture, and social forces do not affect a consumer's choices. The second assumption, insatiability, implicitly enters simple versions of the theory in the familiar sketch of a nested series of indifference curves, rising to higher and higher levels of utility as the quantity of commodities increases. In more formal, mathematical versions of the theory, insatiability is explicitly assumed (see, for example, Mas-Colell *et al.* 1995). The third assumption, commodity-based utility, is, like the first, a result of defining utility or preference relations solely as functions of the consumer's commodity bundle.

It is easy to reject all three assumptions as descriptions of real consumer behavior. First, consumers are not asocial individualists. Social influences such as advertising and peer group pressure clearly affect our consumption choices. From cars to clothes to computers, we buy many things, in part, because others are buying them, or because others will observe our purchases of them. Intersubjectivity is the norm, not the exception.

Second, consumer desires are satiable. That is to say, it is possible to have enough of many things. People typically stop eating before the refrigerator is empty. Some people even start to save money or make gifts to charities or relatives, rather than spending it all, as their incomes rise.

Finally, our desires do not always take the shape of well-informed, well-defined preferences for specific commodities. Many consumers do not know exactly what they want to buy. Often people want things that are not marketed commodities. This is why advertising does not merely offer technical information about products and prices, but claims that particular brand names can deliver adventure, romance, athletic prowess, and other non-material feelings and experiences.

In short, common knowledge about consumer behavior is repeatedly at odds with the traditional model assumed in economic theory. This alone does not necessarily refute the theory; for some, it may even add to the esoteric allure of the discipline. However, a theory with unrealistic assumptions depends heavily on the validity and usefulness of its results. Where are the successful, non-trivial predictions that derive from the economic theory of the consumer?

The theory of consumer behavior is not typically used to make direct predictions, at least beyond the obvious responses to price and income changes. Rather, it is a foundation for much more elaborate theories. In particular, it is the basis for general equilibrium theory – and the basis, as well, for the mathematical difficulties which have undermined the promise of general equilibrium.

2. Beyond stability[1]

General equilibrium theory was one of the great theoretical advances of mid-twentieth-century economics. The theory asks whether there is always a set of prices at which supply equals demand for every commodity (an equilibrium point), and explores the characteristics of such points. In the 1950s Kenneth Arrow and Gerard Debreu proved that, under standard assumptions defining an idealized competitive market economy, any market equilibrium is a Pareto optimum. Moreover, under slightly more restrictive assumptions, an equilibrium point is guaranteed to exist, and any Pareto optimum is a market equilibrium for some set of initial conditions.

There is a longstanding debate about the interpretation of the Arrow–Debreu results, in light of the obvious lack of realism of some of their assumptions. For example, non-convexities, such as increasing returns to scale in production, are common in reality. If they are allowed into the theory then the existence of an equilibrium is no longer certain, and a Pareto optimum need not be a market equilibrium.

Yet, despite awareness of this and other qualifications, economists frequently talk as if deductions from general equilibrium theory are applicable to reality. For example, it is often suggested that any efficient allocation of resources – for instance, one based on a preferred distribution of income – could be achieved by market competition, after an appropriate lump-sum redistribution of initial endowments.

59

This interpretation is a mistaken one. Even if the conditions assumed in the proofs applied in real life (which they clearly do not), meaningful application of the Arrow–Debreu theorems would require dynamic stability. Consider the process of redistributing initial resources and then letting the market achieve a new equilibrium. Implicitly, this image assumes that the desired new equilibrium is both unique and stable. If the equilibrium is not unique, one of the possible equilibrium points might be more socially desirable than another, and the market might converge toward the wrong one. If the equilibrium is unstable, the market might never reach it, or might not stay there when shaken by small, random events.

In the 1970s theorists (including Debreu) reached quite strong, and almost entirely negative, conclusions about both the uniqueness and the stability of general equilibrium. There is no hope of proving uniqueness in general, since examples can be constructed of economies with multiple equilibria. At best, there is a persuasive argument that the number of equilibrium points is virtually always finite. There are certain restrictions on the nature of aggregate demand that ensure uniqueness of equilibrium, but no compelling case has been made for the economic realism of these restrictions. This means that for some initial conditions, there are multiple possible outcomes of market competition, i.e. multiple sets of prices at which supply equals demand for every commodity.

For stability the results are, if anything, even worse. There are examples of three-person, three-commodity economies with permanently unstable price dynamics (Scarf 1960), showing that there is no hope of proving the stability of general equilibrium in all cases. The basic finding about instability – known as the "SMD theorem" because it was presented in a limited form by Sonnenschein (1972) and generalized by Mantel (1974) and Debreu (1974) – is that almost any continuous pattern of price movements can occur in a general equilibrium model, so long as the number of consumers is at least as great as the number of commodities. Cycles of any length, chaotic price changes, or anything else you can describe, will arise in a general equilibrium model for some set of consumer preferences and initial endowments. Not only does general equilibrium fail to be reliably stable; its dynamics can be as bad as you want them to be. Further investigation has confirmed the generality of the SMD result, showing that the potential for instability in general equilibrium cannot be attributed to a specific pattern of individuals' preferences, nor to a particular distribution of income. In a sweeping generalization of the SMD theorem, Kirman and Koch (1986) proved that the full range of instability can result – i.e. virtually any continuous price dynamics can occur – even if all consumers have identical preferences, and any arbitrarily chosen income distribution is used, as long as the number of different income levels is at least as great as the number of commodities.

This means that the SMD theorem can be established even for a population of nearly identical consumers – with identical preferences and almost, but not quite, equal incomes (Kirman 1992).

Another important generalization shows that "SMD instability" can affect an n-commodity economy, even if every subset of the economy with $n-1$ or fewer commodities satisfies conditions that guarantee stability of equilibrium (Saari 1992). This means, among other things, that the addition of one more commodity could be sufficient to destabilize a formerly stable general equilibrium model. More broadly, this means that dynamic results that are proved for small models need not apply to bigger ones – a finding that should be troubling to users of applied general equilibrium models with small numbers of composite commodities and sectors.

Might instability be a result of the unrealistic method of price adjustment assumed in general equilibrium theory? Again, the answer is no. In Walrasian general equilibrium, prices are adjusted through a *tâtonnement* ("groping") process: the rate of change for any commodity's price is proportional to the excess demand for the commodity, and no trades take place until equilibrium prices have been reached. This is not realistic, but it is mathematically tractable: it makes price movements for each commodity depend only on information about that commodity. Yet as the SMD theorem shows, *tâtonnement* does not always lead to convergence to equilibrium.

Alternatives to *tâtonnement* have been explored, but they are neither simple nor realistic. There is an iterative mathematical procedure that always leads to a market equilibrium, starting from any set of initial conditions (Smale 1976). However, there is no economic justification for this procedure, and it requires overwhelming amounts of information about the effects of prices of some goods on the demand for other goods. In fact, any price adjustment process that always converges to an equilibrium has essentially infinite information requirements (Saari 1985).

3. Interpretations of the fall

The failure of general equilibrium theory, as revealed in the SMD theorem and related research, is little known and even less widely understood. The key results are typically presented at a staggeringly difficult level of mathematics. However, the persistence of instability under many changes in assumptions, as discussed in the previous section, suggests that basic features of the underlying model are involved, rather than esoteric twists of mathematical analysis.

At its root, the instability demonstrated in the SMD theorem can be traced back to the unrealistic and underspecified neoclassical model of consumer behavior.[2] Two of the leading analysts in this area, Alan Kirman and Donald Saari, have published thoughtful reflections on the subject.

Kirman, in a dramatically titled article ("The Intrinsic Limits of Modern Economic Theory: The Emperor Has No Clothes"), argues that

The problem seems to be embodied in what is an essential feature of a centuries-long tradition in economics, that of treating individuals as acting independently of each other... This independence of individuals' behavior plays an essential role in the construction of economies generating arbitrary excess demand functions [the source of instability in the SMD theorem].

(Kirman 1989, pp. 137–38)

Saari considers the problem from a mathematician's perspective. Examining the "Mathematical Complexity of Simple Economics" (Saari's title), he explores the SMD theorem and related results, and concludes that

[T]he source of the difficulty – which is common across the social sciences – is that the social sciences are based on aggregation procedures... One way to envision the aggregation difficulties is to recognize that even a simple mapping can admit a complex image should its domain have a larger dimension than its image space... [T]he complexity of the social sciences derives from the unlimited variety in individual preferences; preferences that define a sufficiently large dimensional domain that, when aggregated, can generate all imaginable forms of pathological behavior.

(Saari 1995, pp. 228–29)

There are two separate points here: one involves the methodology of aggregation, and the other concerns the behavioral model of the individual. Both are basic causes of the instability of general equilibrium.

Instability arises in part because aggregate demand is not as well-behaved as individual demand. If the aggregate demand function looked like an individual demand function – that is, if the popular theoretical fiction of a "representative individual" could be used to represent market behavior – then there would be no problem. Unfortunately, though, the aggregation problem is intrinsic and inescapable. There is no representative individual whose demand function generates the instability found in the SMD theorem (Kirman 1992). Groups of people can display patterns and structures of behavior that are not present in the behavior of the individual members; this is an idea with obvious importance throughout the social sciences.

For contemporary economics, this shows that the pursuit of microfoundations for macroeconomics is futile. Even if the model of individual behavior were perfectly appropriate, it would be impossible to draw useful conclusions about macroeconomics directly from that model, due to the aggregation problem (Martel 1996; Rizvi 1994).

The microeconomic model of behavior contributes to instability because it says too little about what individuals want or do. From a mathematical standpoint, as Saari suggests, there are too many dimensions of possible variation, too many degrees of freedom, to allow results at a useful level of specificity. The consumer is free to roam over the vast expanse of available commodities, subject only to a budget constraint and the thinnest possible conception of rationality: anything you can afford is acceptable, so long as you avoid blatant inconsistency in your preferences.

Physics, a science which mathematical economists often seek to emulate, is actually more modest in its modeling efforts, and imposes much more definite structure on its analyses (Ackerman 2000). All physical particles are subject to the same forces, and all react to those forces in a predictable manner. For such similar and well-behaved objects, the aggregation problem can sometimes (not always) be solved: useful statements can often be made about the aggregate behavior of a cloud of particles in physics, unlike a crowd of consumers in economics.

If consumers were modeled as having predictable responses to social forces, it might be possible to describe their aggregate behavior in more interesting detail. Instead, the assumption of asocial individualism in neoclassical economics guarantees that the aggregation problem is insurmountable.

Physics also develops mathematical models involving many dimensions – but here economic theory goes even farther. Some of the latest work in theoretical physics analyzes elementary particles as moving in a ten-dimensional space, which leads to mathematical models of great subtlety and complexity. Economic theory effectively treats consumers as particles moving in a space with one dimension per commodity – in other words, a space with thousands, if not millions, of dimensions. As Saari observes in the passage quoted above, this extremely high-dimensional model allows all manner of mathematical pathology, such as the SMD theorem. If nothing imaginable is excluded by mathematical analysis (which is what the SMD theorem says), then the model has no economically significant content.

In this case, the problematical assumption is commodity-based utility. The fateful step occurs when utility, or revealed preference, is defined as a function of the consumer's commodity bundle. This seemingly innocuous assumption means that representation of the utility or preference function requires a mathematical space with one dimension per commodity. The SMD problem suggests that this framework itself is unproductive. Useful mathematical analysis of consumer behavior requires a more compact and manageable structure. In particular, it requires a low-dimensional representation, which cannot be defined in terms of individual commodities.

4. Blasts from the past: Broader views of consumers

So far we have seen that flaws in the standard model of consumer behavior lead to critical problems in general equilibrium theory. A better model of consumption, therefore, is an essential step toward better economic theory in general. Fortunately, there is a long history of broader analysis of consumer behavior. The essential components of a more adequate theory of consumption can be found in the economics literature in decades past – often in works that have since drifted into obscurity. The discussion can again be organized in terms of alternatives to the three basic assumptions of asocial individualism, insatiability, and commodity-based utility.

First, no consumer is an island. The powerful social influences on consumption, from the pursuit of status to the impact of advertising, were the subject of eloquent, well-known analyses by Thorstein Veblen at the opening of the twentieth century, and John Kenneth Galbraith at mid-century. Provocative mathematical models of social interactions in consumption were proposed by James Duesenberry (1949) and Harvey Leibenstein (1950). Unfortunately, Duesenberry's "demonstration effect" of contact with higher-income consumption patterns, and Leibenstein's "bandwagon, snob, and Veblen effects" were soon treated as mere classroom curiosities, and ultimately were forgotten. In the 1970s Robert Pollak made heroic attempts to develop formal models of social interactions in consumption (Pollak 1970; 1976; 1977; 1978), but had little impact on other economists. Among economists engaged in social criticism, such as Fred Hirsch (1976) or Robert Frank (1985), the interactive nature of consumption is taken as a starting point. But such works – even when, as in Frank's case, the criticism is combined with a mathematical model – have remained outside the mainstream of the profession.

Turning to the second assumption, the view of human nature as an ensemble of insatiable desires for private consumption is as standard as it is silly. Many great economists of the past have known better. Adam Smith emphasized the importance of motivations such as self-respect. Alfred Marshall believed that it was possible to make a distinction between higher and lower desires; the resulting hierarchy of more and less urgent wants is one basis for the declining marginal utility of consumption. Dissent from the neoclassical caricature of human nature was also shared by John Maynard Keynes. His "Economic Possibilities for our Grandchildren" (Keynes 1963 [1930]) was a utopian speculation based on the premise that material wants must be satiable – and must be destined to reach the point of satiation within the 100 years after he wrote, i.e. by 2030.

Tibor Scitovsky offered an extensive examination of human nature and its implications for economic behavior (Scitovsky 1976). An exploration of research in psychology provided him with a much richer and more specific theory of human wants than is normally seen in economics.

This led him to ask two questions: Which desires are insatiable? And which satisfactions are necessarily obtained through purchases in the marketplace? Scitovsky's answers in brief were that many basic necessities and comforts are satiable, in contrast to pleasures and novelties; and that many of life's most important satisfactions come from non-market activities or from the process of work, rather than from consumption of purchased goods and services.

Other authors have raised alternative perspectives on human nature, questioning the notion of insatiable desire. Feminist economists (see for example England 1993, among many others) have suggested that the conventional, endlessly acquisitive image of *homo economicus* reflects the male biases of the field; a theory with roots in and respect for women's roles might make very different assumptions. The existence of "downshifters" who choose to lead lives of voluntary simplicity provides further evidence against the hypothesis of material insatiability (Schor 1998).

The third assumption, commodity-based utility, is routinely questioned in other social sciences. The value of commodities and the satisfaction they produce cannot be traced directly to their physical characteristics. Goods may have ritual, social, or emotional meanings that transcend their original utilitarian purpose – an idea that has occurred to advertisers as well as anthropologists.

Economists have also considered alternatives to the assumption of commodity-based utility, in what was, for a time, a prominent theoretical innovation. Almost simultaneously, Kelvin Lancaster (1966a, b), Richard Muth (1966) and Gary Becker (1965) proposed similar rethinkings of the theory of consumer behavior. Rather than knowing in advance exactly how much they will enjoy each potential purchase, the new approach held that consumers want experiences, satisfactions, or characteristics of goods that result from purchases – e.g. flavors, textures, and nutrition from food, or fuel-efficient transportation, comfortable seating, and visible status from cars. (Similarly, discussion of energy conservation often assumes that what consumers want is not fuel per se, but rather "energy services" such as comfortable room temperatures – which can be produced by many different combinations of energy and insulation).

Lancaster assumed that consumer demand for characteristics resembles the conventional picture of demand for goods – consumers know exactly which characteristics they want, and they always want more. The relationship of characteristics to goods is strictly linear and determined by technology: twice as much of a good always produces twice as much of each of its characteristics. In contrast, Muth and Becker dropped the assumption of a linear relationship between goods and characteristics, and used the language of a household production process: the household combines purchased inputs (groceries, cooking utensils, fuels) and household labor to produce desired outputs (meals).

Neither variant is free from problems (Ackerman 1997). Lancaster's linear structure and insatiable demand for characteristics is too rigid for many situations. In contrast, Becker's household production model, the only one of the new theories to receive extensive development, imposes no structure at all. With enough creativity in hypothesizing the desired characteristics or experiences that are produced by households, Becker and his colleagues are able to explain everything and nothing: following ever-changing fashions produces stylish "distinction"; drug addiction is a new household technology for producing "euphoria"; and so on.

Today, aside from Becker's embarrassingly overwrought enthusiasms, there is little to be seen for decades of innovative alternative analysis of the economics of consumer behavior. In textbooks, classrooms, and journal articles, the neoclassical consumer is still asocial, insatiable, and fixated on specific commodities. She still shops till she drops.

5. Building a better theory

We have seen, on the one hand, that the flaws in the neoclassical theory of the consumer are reflected in the problems of general equilibrium theory. On the other hand, the components of a better theory of consumer behavior are readily available. If we began with a broader view of the consumption process as the foundation, what kind of global theory of equilibrium or disequilibrium would we end up building? Changing each of the three standard assumptions about consumer behavior has distinct implications for the big picture in economic theory.

First, recognition of the social influences on consumption undermines both the optimality and the uniqueness of market outcomes. Since consumption patterns are socially determined, the desirability of those patterns depends on what we think of the social forces that cause them. As Galbraith observed years ago, there is no great moral urgency to fulfilling consumer desires that have been newly created by the manufacturer's advertising.

The general point – some social forces are less worthy than others – extends beyond advertising. Social pressure helps some people to stop smoking; social pressure also encourages other people to start smoking. It is hard to view these opposite pressures, and the resulting consumer preferences, as equally desirable. More generally, the optimality of an economic system cannot be guaranteed by satisfaction of individual preferences, unless we are satisfied that those preferences result from reasonable social forces. Difficult ethical judgments, of the sort that economists have long tried to avoid, turn out to be inescapable.

The social nature of consumer preferences also implies that market outcomes are not unique. Small, virtually random events can determine which fashion becomes dominant, or which technology becomes entrenched. Because our preferences depend on what other people have already bought, there is positive feedback in the economic system, and market outcomes are path-dependent. In the extreme, if most consumers are more influenced by the behavior of others than by their own preferences (as occurs, for example, in computer purchases), it is possible for a few initial purchases to start a market "cascade" based on very little information about the new product (Bikhchandi *et al.* 1998). Thus history, as well as ethical judgment, is essential for an understanding of market outcomes.

Changing the assumption of insatiability would have profound effects on economic theory. Since the birth of the subject centuries ago, "the economic problem" has been overcoming scarcity and producing as much as possible from the limited available inputs. From a global perspective, this is still a paramount problem for most of humanity. At low income levels it is obvious that consuming more goods and services leads to longer and healthier lives.

Theoretical objections to output maximization thus far have arisen primarily in the environmental arena, where it is necessary or desirable to protect certain natural resources that might otherwise be used or degraded in production. This converts the economic problem of scarcity into one of maximization of output subject to additional constraints.

The recognition of satiability poses an even more fundamental challenge to the economics of scarcity, entirely rejecting the logic of output maximization. Perhaps the optimum economic outcome is not the point of maximum output, from the point of view of the consumer as well as the environment. In the US, there are still important minorities that face material deprivation. However, a growing number of Americans – perhaps a majority – would live longer and healthier lives if they had less constant access to processed foods and beverages, motorized transportation, and other mechanized, energy-saving "conveniences." The optimum outcome can no longer be identified with maximization of consumption, with or without constraints.

Many people realize this on some level, as shown by the popularity of diets, health clubs, and exercise regimes. Social pressures on consumers, not least from advertisers, make it difficult for most people to wholeheartedly recognize and embrace the fact that they have enough. Yet, on the fringes of society, growing participation in religious and other groups preaching voluntary simplicity suggests a desire to escape the economics of insatiability.

Rejection of the third assumption, commodity-based utility, would call for a different kind of rethinking of economic theory. Unlike other social scientists or advertisers, economists have traditionally assumed an unmediated relationship between consumers and lists of individual commodities. The assumption is built in when utility functions or preference relations are defined as functions of commodity bundles. The disappointing limitations of general equilibrium theory, as revealed in the SMD theorem, show that analysis of consumption at the level of individual commodities is not mathematically manageable or useful. Consumer behavior needs to be reconceptualized in terms of other fundamental variables.

On this point, economic theory came to the brink of a breakthrough in the 1960s, and then blinked. Lancaster, Muth, and Becker began to develop innovative analyses of consumer choice based on characteristics of goods, or non-material experiences. Yet, they quickly reached two dead ends, one of which has now been explored at length. Lancaster's linear relationship between goods and characteristics, and insatiability of demand for characteristics, posed a number of problems that limited the value of his initial approach. Muth, and particularly Becker, assumed no fixed structure at all, allowing the theory to drift into an unhelpful story-telling mode in which a new, unobservable experience is hypothesized as the goal of each new consumer behavior.

On this point, progress in economic theory involves going back to the future – returning to the initial insights of Lancaster, Muth, and Becker, while seeking a way around the two original dead ends. To obtain any benefit from the theory, it will be necessary to impose some structure and limits on the list of desired characteristics or experiences. Yet, that structure will have to look different from Lancaster's early attempt, perhaps departing even farther than he did from the established patterns of neoclassical theory.

If all of the recommendations proposed here were incorporated into a new economic theory, what would it look like? While it might still involve mathematical analysis, the variables would be different, representing human needs, desires, and experiences rather than commodities. Abstract proof of the optimality of any particular market outcome would be unlikely. Instead, evaluation of economic systems would involve history, path-dependence, and institutional analysis. It would draw on sociology, politics, and recognition of the intersubjective nature of human behavior. It would inevitably make ethical judgments about what our society has achieved, and what else it could have done.

In short, many contemporary economists would conclude that such a theory was not really economics. Yet, the alternative theory would be more secure than the wobbly and unwieldy neoclassical edifice, for it would have repaired the flaws in the foundation, deep in the theory of consumer behavior.

Notes

1 The discussion of general equilibrium presented here draws heavily on the more extended treatment in Ackerman (2000).

2 Recent work in general equilibrium theory has typically assumed a pure exchange economy, without production. The obstacles to proving uniqueness or stability seem to arise on the consumption side of the market; including production would make the mathematics more complicated, but would not change the problematical results. Thus, the limitations revealed in the SMD theorem and subsequent analyses, as discussed in the last section, are closely connected to the model of the consumer.

References

Ackerman, Frank (2000) "Still Dead After All These Years: Interpreting the Failure of General Equilibrium Theory," Working Paper 00–01, Tufts University / Global Development and Environment Institute (G-DAE) *http://ase.tufts.edu/gdae*.

Ackerman, Frank (1997) "Consumed in Theory: Alternative Perspectives on the Economics of Consumption," *Journal of Economic Issues* 31: 651–64.

Becker, Gary (1965) "A Theory of the Allocation of Time," *Economic Journal* 75: 493–517.

Bikhchandani, Sushil, David, Hirshleifer and Ivo, Welch (1998) "Learning From the Behavior of Others: Conformity, Fads, and Informational Cascades," *Journal of Economic Perspectives* 12: 151–70.

Colander, David (ed.) (1996) *Beyond Microfoundations: Post-Walrasian Macroeconomics*, New York: Cambridge University Press.

Darnell, Adrian (1992) "Decision-making under Uncertainty," in J. Maloney (ed.) *What's New in Economics?*, New York: Manchester University Press.

Debreu, Gerard (1974) "Excess Demand Functions," *Journal of Mathematical Economics* 1: 15–21.

Duesenberry, James S. (1949) *Income, Saving and the Theory of Consumer Behavior*. Cambridge: Harvard University Press.

England, Paula (1993) "The separative self: Androcentric bias in neoclassical assumptions," in M. A. Ferber and J. A. Nelson (eds) *Beyond Economic Man: Feminist Theory and Economics*, Chicago: University of Chicago Press.

Friedman, Milton (1953) *Essays in Positive Economics*, Chicago: University of Chicago Press.

Frank, Robert, H. (1985) "The Demand for Unobservable and Other Nonpositional Goods," *American Economic Review* 75: 101–16.

Goodwin, Neva, Frank, Ackerman and David, Kiron (eds) (1997) *The Consumer Society*, Washington: Island Press.

Hirsch, Fred (1976) *Social Limits to Growth*, Cambridge: Harvard University Press.

Keynes, John Maynard (1963) [1930]. "Economic Possibilities for Our Grandchildren," in J. M. Keynes (ed.) *Essays in Persuasion*, New York: W.W. Norton.

Kirman, Alan (1992) "Whom or What Does the Representative Individual Represent?," *Journal of Economic Perspectives* 6(2): 117–36.

Kirman, Alan (1989) "The Intrinsic Limits of Modern Economic Theory: The Emperor Has No Clothes," *Economic Journal* 99: 126–39.

Kirman, Alan and Koch, K. J. (1986) "Market Excess Demand in Exchange Economies with Identical Preferences and Collinear Endowments," *Review of Economic Studies* 53: 457–63.

Lancaster, Kelvin (1996a) "Change and Innovation in the Technology of Consumption," *American Economic Review* 56: 14–23.

Lancaster, Kelvin (1966b) "A New Approach to Consumer Theory," *Journal of Political Economy* 74: 132–57.

Leibenstein, Harvey (1950) "Bandwagon, Snob, and Veblen Effects in the Theory of Consumers' Demand," *Quarterly Journal of Economics* 64: 198–207.

Mantel, R. (1974) "On the Characterization of Aggregate Excess Demand," *Journal of Economic Theory* 7(3): 348–53.

Martel, Robert (1996) "Heterogeneity, Aggregation, and a Meaningful Macroeconomics," in Colander 1996. David Colander (ed.) *Beyond Microfoundations: Post-Walrasian Macroeconomics*, New York: Cambridge University Press.

Mas-Colell, Andreu, Michael, Whinston and Jerry, Green (1995) *Microeconomic Theory*, New York: Oxford University Press.

Miller, Daniel (ed.) (1995) *Acknowledging Consumption*, London: Routledge.

Muth, Richard (1966) "Household Production and Consumer Demand Functions," *Econometrica* 34: 281–302.

Pollak, Robert (1978) "Endogenous Tastes in Demand and Welfare Analysis," *American Economic Review* 68: 374–9.

Pollak, Robert (1977) "Price Dependent Preferences," *American Economic Review* 67: 64–75.

Pollak, Robert (1976) "Interdependent Preferences," *American Economic Review* 66: 309–20.

Pollak, Robert (1970) "Habit Formation and Dynamic Demand Functions," *Journal of Political Economy* 78: 745–63.

Rizvi, S. Abu Turab (1994) "The Microfoundations Project in General Equilibrium Theory," *Cambridge Journal of Economics* 18: 357–77.

Saari, Donald (1995) "Mathematical Complexity of Simple Economics," *Notices of the American Mathematical Society* 42(2): 222–30.

Saari, Donald (1992) "The Aggregated Excess Demand Function and Other Aggregation Procedures," *Economic Theory* 2(3): 359–88.

Saari, Donald (1985) "Iterative Price Mechanisms," *Econometrica* 53: 1117–31.

Scarf, Herbert (1960) "Some Examples of the Global Instability of the Competitive Equilibrium," *International Economic Review* 1(3): 157–72.

Schor, Juliet B. (1998) *The Overspent American: Upscaling, Downshifting, and the New Consumer*, New York: Basic Books.

Scitovsky, Tibor (1976) *The Joyless Economy*, New York: Oxford University Press.

Smale, Steven (1976) "A Convergent Process of Price Adjustment and Global Newton Methods," *Journal of Mathematical Economics* 3: 107–20.

Sonnenschein, H. (1972) "Market Excess Demand Functions," *Econometrica* 40: 549–63.

5

ON THE NEED FOR A MORE COMPLETE ONTOLOGY OF THE CONSUMER

Ralph W. Pfouts

> ... I do now believe that anything that confuses reality and
> unreality, or that attempts to equate the two, is the devil's
> own work.
>
> (Alan Judd, *The Devil's Own Work*)

1. Introduction

The word "ontology" has entered economic literature recently. It refers, one may recall, to the branch of metaphysics that deals with the nature of being or existence. The charge that introduced the subject into economics is that economics, especially economic theory as it is now done in the mainstream, does not give sufficient attention to ontology. It does not, in other words, give proper regard to the nature of economic institutions, structures, and actors.

This accusation comes from two separate sources. Tony Lawson in his book *Economics and Reality* contends, on the basis of a lengthy methodological argument, that economic theory, econometrics, and perhaps other parts of economics cannot as now understood be done successfully, and any attempts are doomed to failure. (Lawson 1997) While most economic theorists probably will reject Lawson's conclusion, believing it to be based on a faulty empirical premise, it should be emphasized that the book is a serious, scholarly and well thought-through work. It should not be dismissed lightly because it makes some criticisms of economic theory that many fair-minded economists will admit should be used as an incentive for reconsideration of certain parts of economic theory.

One of Lawson's criticisms is that ontology is given insufficient attention and indeed sometimes totally ignored. This in turn leads to the "epistemic fallacy" which is the error of believing that statements about being can always be considered, stated, or analyzed in terms of knowledge. Thus, ontology can always be stated in epistemological terms. In spite of the philosophical language, this contains a warning based on common sense which economists should heed: the structures, institutions and actors of the economy cannot be ignored and treated as if they had no existence except as predictable functions or operations in the scientific train of thought.

The second source of accusations comes from a group of economists that have become known as the Intersubjectivists. The school originated in France with Jean-Pierre Dupuy and André Orléan being among the leaders. (Dupuy 1989; 1991; 1992ab; Orléan 1988; 1989; 1990; 1992) Their views have been taken up by some English economists with Edward Fullbrook being one of the leaders. (Fullbrook 1996ab, 1998) This group claims that interactions among individuals have been largely, or perhaps entirely, ignored by mainstream economics. They have concentrated their attention, in large part, on the theory of demand and on financial matters as represented by Chapter 12 of *The General Theory*. (Keynes 1936) Their views on demand theory claim that interactions among individuals are specifically ignored. To support this claim they cite the work of economists of the late nineteenth and early twentieth centuries. In this context the claim may be true but they have remained silent, so far as I know, about the demand theory based on the Slutsky and Hicks and Allen approach. Most present day theorists would point out that in interactions between persons, envy, imitation, advertising and so on play an important part in forming the utility or preference function and thus are taken into account. Consequently, their chief charge fails. But they also emphasize the need for an ontology of the consumer. Thus, their views are in some degree compatible with Lawson's.

The stress on ontology seems to me to have merit even though the chief arguments of both Lawson and the Intersubjectivists are incorrect. I will attempt to show the need of a more complete ontology in the case of demand theory.

2. A brief restatement of demand theory and its ontology

The mainstream theory of demand requires the presence of a utility or preference function which shows the relative utility or satisfaction of various sets or vectors or bills of goods. The function must be differentiable and have positive first derivatives. It must also have the proper concavity to permit optimization subject to a budget constraint.

On the basis of this overly simple sketch let us ask what the theory implies about the consumer. Among the things implied are (1) consumers have preferences among goods and services, (2) they are sensitive to small changes in quantities of goods, (3) they are consistent in their choices, (4) they respond to changes in prices and income and (5) they maximize their satisfactions. Clearly, (1) and (3) follow from the presence of the preference function, while (2) follows from its continuity and differentiability, and (4) and (5) from the requirements of optimization.

Suppose that one wants to evaluate the realism of the theory. One might first point out that it permits us to abandon measurable utility; it can easily be shown that this assumption is no longer needed. It also, through the development of the income and substitution effects, enables us to explain inferior goods and Giffen goods. In addition, it enables us to deduce the existence of individual demand function, thus providing a logical basis for market demand equations. These are not merely theoretical but also empirical successes.

But judging a theory entirely by its empirical success is passé in the post-positivist age, so let us invoke ontology and look directly at the inferences about the consumer that we drew from the theory. We first noted that the theory assumes that individuals have preferences among goods and services and we might add that those preferences vary from person to person. This would seem to be obviously true and hence requires no supporting argument. But there are those who question the existence and/or effectiveness of consumers' preferences. (Rosenberg 1992) It is hard to credit this questioning because introspection, belief and experience suggest otherwise. The history of the Soviet Union, for example, suggests that consumers' preferences not only exist but are very strong motivations.

The second of the inferences is sensitivity to small changes in quantities of goods on the part of the consumer. This arises from the continuity of the preference function and from the desire to apply infinitesimal calculus. Consequently, it is a very dubious basis for a theory since it enters the structure, not because it has been observed empirically, but to accommodate the logical methods that will be employed. Carried to its extreme it implies that increasing a consumer's food intake by one green pea per week would be sensed and appreciated. It will be argued below that mainstream theory can be restated in discrete form without the use of calculus and thus the extreme sensitivity of consumers disappears.

The third point is consistent behavior on the part of consumers. Certainly, since a consumer's purchases are not random, some consistency is present. But the mainstream theory places rather stringent conditions on the actions of the individual. The appropriate determinants must take a particular form and so on. In the discrete form reviewed below consistent behavior is assured by the transitivity axiom. This is a much weaker requirement but it also should be questioned on empirical grounds. This will also be discussed below.

The fourth point, response to changes in prices and incomes, is probably generally accepted as realistic. There is a mountain of evidence ranging from the anecdotal to very formal studies that support this view.

The fifth point is utility maximization. Probably, most people agree that individuals and families try to spend their money in a way that will give them as much satisfaction as possible, but many people, including some economists, do not accept the term maximization. It implies pushing toward some goal in an extreme way. Further, it is related to the word equilibrium which suggests some physical system whose parts interact to bring about a condition of rest, a sequence of events whose purity of action is not, it is often contended, replicated by a consumer. It will be suggested below that a restatement of the theory can be made that is free of these overtones and associations.

3. An alternative approach to the mainstream theory

Suppose that we consider a family of four: parents, daughter and son. How will they make decisions about how to spend their monthly income? We first note that some decisions have already been made. The mortgage payment or rent must be paid, the contribution to the tax sheltered savings plan must be met, both reflecting decisions in the past, perhaps years in the past. The gas, electricity and water bills must be paid because of decisions made during the past month, how warm to keep the house and so on.

But some decisions have not been made. What kinds and qualities of food should be purchased. Can mother join a health club? Can father buy a new suit? Can sister get a computer? Can brother have a basketball goal in the backyard? If all of these wants cannot be satisfied this month, which ones should be? Who decides which should be? Presumably, mother or father or the two of them jointly. But our immediate interest is not how the decisions will be made, but how this process fits into the mainstream theory.

To examine this we think of the various possible goods that might be purchased as sets or collections or vectors of goods. Any set that requires an expenditure larger than the money available cannot be purchased. Thus, there are different vectors of goods the family decision-makers will consider and in effect rank in order of desirability. This ranking replaces the preference function of the conventional theory. The highest ranked vector whose cost does not exceed the amount of money available to the family will be chosen. This equilibrium replaces the equilibrium of conventional theory.

Can the income and substitution effect be deduced? They can, if one adds the assumption that the rankings of its vectors of goods are transitive. In this context a simple but rather lengthy mathematical argument can demonstrate their presence. (Pfouts 1977)

To summarize this alternative formulation let us compare it to the five assumptions about the mainstream view of the consumer that were listed above.

The first of these is that consumers have preferences among goods and services. This is clearly present in the reformulated theory. But the second, that they are sensitive to small changes in the quantities of goods and

74

services is not required. This, it is suggested, is an improvement because it removes a fictitious aspect of the theory.

The third point is that preferences are consistent. This is induced in the present formulation by assuming transitivity. While this is a weaker requirement than the mathematical structure of the usual formulation, it is a restriction that should be subjected to demanding empirical testing. The fourth point, that consumers respond to change in prices and income, is present in both formulations.

The fifth point, that consumers maximize their satisfaction, is present in both formulations but in quite different forms. The picture of precise judging of the satisfaction derived from each good is not present in the second formulation. This also means that the concept of equilibrium is different in the two formulations. The analogy to the equilibrium of a physical system is lessened, indeed, removed in the second formulation.

These five, or in the case of the second formulation, four points about the consumer seem to be a meager characterization, certainly not an extensive ontology. Yet, economic theorists have insisted that they are enough in the sense of being sufficient to explain consumer behavior. It will be argued below that this view is too narrow and has played an unfortunate role in the theory of demand.

4. Occam's razor: Too keen an edge? Too dull a barber? Too fragile a throat?

The view that the characteristics listed above are all that is necessary to explain consumer behavior is often defended by invoking Occam's razor, the parsimony principle. Occam's razor was first introduced into economic theory by Hicks (1938). But Hicks was specifically referring to the exclusion of measurable utility, clearly a justified use of Occam's razor. It does not follow that no further characteristics of the consumer need to be considered.

To clarify this point consider the difference between a logical proposition or a mathematical theorem on one hand, and an empirical proposition on the other. In the case of a theorem, assume that a mathematician using hypotheses A and B proves a theorem and shows also that A and B are necessary and sufficient to establish the theorem. Suppose, further, that he now considers a third hypothesis C and shows that A and C are also necessary and sufficient to establish the theorem. Is he now justified in believing that B and C must have some important characteristic in common?

The answer surely must be that they should be so regarded. For, if they did not, the necessity part of the proof would be incorrect. But the mathematician might try to refine the theorem by seeking the common characteristic of B and C. It may be obvious or it may be fiendishly difficult to find. If he succeeds in finding it he can then use the common characteristic as hypothesis D which replaces B or C and abandon their contents other than the common characteristic. The role of Occam in this process is clear and essential.

But an empirical proposition is not a mathematical theorem or a logical proposition. Economic theory must be logical but it must also explain or clarify something in the economic world. This makes the use of Occam much more delicate than in the case of mathematical theorems. Suppose that we consider the consumer again. If we were to show that the four or five conditions discussed above were necessary and sufficient to explain consumer demand, would that end discussion of the entire subject? Surely it would not because there may be additional variables that affect a consumer's decisions and introducing new variables into the discussion, in effect, creates a new universe of discourse in which the old arguments may no longer be enough or may no longer hold.

Against this it might be contended that if the theory were tested empirically the tests would show that something was missing, like the planets Neptune, Uranus and Pluto before their discoveries. The test would show that the model was incomplete. Perhaps in more precise sciences like physics and astronomy this is sometimes true, but measurement is not sufficiently precise in economic data to permit us to believe that it would happen, except perhaps infrequently.

Precision is always a relative term. Because of their gravitational calculations, astronomers had anticipated the existence of additional planets in the solar system before the discoveries of Neptune, Uranus and Pluto. Thus, observations showed that something was missing from the known model of the solar system.

But astronomical thought, observation and calculations were not sufficiently precise to suggest that the path of light was influenced by gravitation. Indeed, when Einstein's theory appeared, many scientists opposed it vigorously, and could have cited Occam in support of their arguments.

The famous eclipse date of 1919 showed that Einstein was correct. But even here the precision was not perfect. Einstein had predicted a deflection of 1.75 seconds of arc, while calculations based on the data showed a deflection of 1.64 seconds.

Consequently, we cannot rely on empirical testing alone to show the absence or presence of additional explanatory variables in economic theory. And we cannot rely on Occam to excuse us from further searching for explanatory variables, or indeed any facts that may be relevant to the theory. To summarize the view taken on Occam, we argue that it applies simply and clearly in the case of a mathematical theorem or purely logical proposition because the playing field or universe of discourse is clearly defined and limited. But in the case of an empirical proposition the confines may not be known and are seldom known with finality, and, consequentially, the playing field is subject to change as empirical evidence accumulates. Occam is still a sound principle, but it may be difficult to use.

5. Is the psychology of the consumer simplistic?

If the ontology of the consumer appears to be deficient how may we find possible improvements? A suggestion commonly made is to turn to psychology. This is often suggested by persons who know little about economics or psychology. It is an old idea, going back at least as far as Veblen, who frequently referred to the absence of "modern psychology" from economics. So far as is known to me, he never specified what modern psychology is or was. Thus, we are uncertain about the exact nature of his charge.

But suppose we consider the psychological motivations of the consumer. Why does a consumer buy food? Nutrition and enjoyment, conspicuous consumption perhaps. Does this tell us anything of use in the theory of demand? Or we could look for some deeper motive. Does she buy bananas and tapers because they are phallic symbols? And what does she do with them? Slices them up and eats them in one case and burns them in the other. Good heavens! Does she save an unusually large portion of her income because she is fixated in the anal retentive stage of the psycho-sexual genesis? Beyond question, such matters are of moment in the psychology of the individual, but they are of no known help in the theory of demand. To suggest that they are might be called the vulgar or Veblenian error.

For psychology to be useful in economics it must be aimed at the problems of economics. When this is done, psychology is potentially of great use and importance. The work of Herbert Simon in economics demonstrates that this is true and suggests very strongly that further benefits may be gained by following this path, (e.g. 1955; 1979; 1996). Another example is the work of Kahneman and Tversky (1982) who conducted experiments which jeopardize the independence axiom of the von Neumann–Morgenstern utility index.

In a similar fashion it should be possible to test the transitivity axiom of mainstream demand theory to determine whether it should be replaced or modified in some way. It is significant to note that this cannot be done by introspection.

Economic motivation is almost always simple and straightforward. Economic actors are seeking gain in some form. Satisfaction and pleasure in the case of consumers. Benefits for members in the case of unions and perhaps political power to be used in obtaining further gains. Profits, perhaps market share and market power and continued existence and growth in the case of firms and so on for other economic actors.

Even though the motivations of economic actors are usually clear, the means of realizing their goals may or may not be clear. In the case of consumers it is quite clear. Consumers seek the set of goods, among those known to them, that they believe will provide the greatest satisfaction without exceeding their budget. In the case of the firm, the means of gaining profit or market status may not be completely clear in the short run, and long run considerations of how to make the firm grow are much more opaque and so on.

But our concern here is with the consumer and the conclusion being argued is that the functioning of the consumer is simple in theory because it is actually simple. It is not simplistic in the sense of evading existing complications.

6. The confines of the playing field

Do purely economic considerations offer promise in developing an ontology of the consumer? To answer this we notice that the existing theory has the consumer res-ponding to prices and income. Might there not be other variables to which she responds. If so what might they be?

One possibility was suggested by Keynes in *The General Theory* (1936) and is sometimes called the "wealth effect." Keynes was referring to aggregate consumption, but, at points, phrased the discussion in terms of an individual. He noted that if the interest rate falls, the portfolio of a bondholder increases in value. This may lead her to spend more on consumption even though her interest income is unchanged.

Similarly, anecdotal evidence suggests that in the United States a sustained rise in the Dow Jones Industrial Average causes purveyors of luxury goods to rub their hands and prepare for increased sales. Indeed a segment of the financial press has expressed concern that at the present time, late summer 2000, a stock market crash would cause a sharp contraction in consumption expenditure and thus induce a recession. With an increasingly large proportion of the population owning securities, wealth effects may be increasingly strong.

Of course the wealth effect is not restricted to securities. It is no doubt true of real estate, collectibles, indeed of anything that is liquid or that may serve as collateral. A friend of mine, a former chef with an expert knowledge of wines, collected and stored wines for several years while the prices of wines increased markedly. Being a teetotaler, he held the wine. Eventually, he sold it and used the proceeds to build a luxurious house which he now occupies.

Thus, there seems to be enough evidence to suggest that changes in wealth may affect consumption. This in turn suggests that a possible relationship should be explored carefully, not only for its effect on aggregate consumption, but also for its effect as a determinant of individual or family consumption. In considering this it should be observed that wealth is ordinarily held with a view to preserving and increasing its total amount. Thus, an increase of wealth may be used in part for consumption and in part for reinvestment. Also, the increase of wealth may not be repeated immediately, in which case the consumption from increased wealth may vanish. In any event, perhaps wealth, in some form, should be included along with prices and income in formulating the theory of consumer choice and demand.

Another element that might be considered in examining market demand is the distribution of income. This arises naturally in the conventional theory of demand.

The individual demand equations show the income of the individual as an argument in the demand functions. Thus, when the individual demand functions are totaled, conceptually, to obtain the market demand function, a distribution of income among the buyers appears in the theoretical market demand equation. But in the statistical market demand equation a total income variable is used instead of a distribution of income, it being argued that using an income distribution is impractical.

The suggestion of impracticality is not trivial. Clearly it is impossible to use a distribution of income for all individuals or families, but it might be possible to use a condensed or summarized version of income distribution similar to those that are published showing income distribution by groups of percentiles or deciles or some similar arrangement.

It is also argued that the distribution of income changes slowly and that data showing income distribution is not always available. Still, income distribution does change and data can be made available. Experimenting with income distribution data might show whether it is of practical importance in statistical demand equations.

Obviously, the motivation for this suggestion is that the goods purchased vary a good deal depending on income level. Those in the lower income groups seldom buy Beluga caviar or Hermés accessories. Consequently, an increase of income in this group will show little effect on such expensive goods. Similarly, a decline of income in the high income groups will not affect the sale of stale bakery products or wilted vegetables. The supermarket sales of goods that have been on the shelf or in the refrigerator too long will not be lessened. These are rather extreme examples, but the same principle applies to cheap automobiles versus expensive and so on.

There is little point in speculating about ontological matters; they should be settled by careful observation. But speculation about new borders for the universe of discourse is a necessary preliminary for establishing or rejecting them.

7. Is economic theory an illusion?

Lawson concludes that economic theory, at least mainstream economic theory, cannot be an empirical science. It, consequently, must be an illusion. Thus the theory of demand is a fiction. Lawson's basis for this conclusion is carefully reasoned and must be considered seriously. To do this, Lawson's view of methodology will be summarized.

He is concerned with regularities of the type if x then y. Often, in scientific work, such regularities are exposed and examined in experiments in which countervailing forces can be excluded. This poses a problem for methodology. If regularities can prevail only in experiments, how can scientific knowledge be applied (or depicted) in the real world?

One could claim that the real world is a symphony of carefully orchestrated regularities that somehow blend together and do not interfere with each other. In short, they are not countervailing. But this is clearly unsatisfactory. Lawson uses the familiar example of a falling autumn leaf. As it falls it is subjected to gravitational, aerodynamic, thermal and other forces. Nobody can predict its ultimate resting place, nor will its resting place necessarily remain fixed.

But if the ontology is considered as Lawson urges, there is no mystery about how the regularities operate in the real world. The fabric, structure, shape and weight of the leaf interacting with gravity and aerodynamics determine the path of its fall. Ontology dissolves the mystery. There is a very strong and much needed lesson for economic theory in this example, a point that will be considered later.

With this background in mind, we now turn to Lawson's reasons for denying the validity of mainstream economic theory or the "economic theory project," or just the "project" as he variously calls it. I will use Lawson's words in stating a summary of his views.

Why does economic theory encounter so many difficulties? "Specifically because the project rests upon an implicit commitment to identifying or formulating regularities of the form whenever event x then event y (albeit perhaps in an a priori or introspective fashion), its legitimate application is restricted to those very special situations in which scientifically significant event regularities are (or might be expected to be) forthcoming – which in the economic sphere, may be hardly any situation at all." (pp. 92–93) This is clear enough. Regularities, event regularities or strict regularities, as Lawson variously calls them, seldom, if ever, occur in economics. But this raises a question as to why they do not occur.

To answer this we can also use Lawson's words in which he summarizes his reasons, saying there are two sets of reasons.

> First, the environment in which any mechanism acts need not be sufficiently homogeneous. In the social realm, indeed, there will usually be a potentially very large number of countervailing factors acting at any one time and/or sporadically over time, and possibly each with varying strength. This means not only that where mechanisms "shine through" they are unlikely to do so in a continuous, unimpeded, clear-cut fashion, but equally that

operative mechanisms need not always "shine through" in any recognizable manner at all. The implication of the latter situation, as we have also previously noted, is that the usual starting point for research into the nature of social mechanisms will invariably be conditions where the effect of mechanisms have in some way *already* been detected. We start from situations where, fortuitously, relatively stable tendencies are revealed. In this sense social scientific explanation is inherently backward looking.

The second reason for the absence of strict regularities is that the mechanism or processes which are being identified are themselves likely to be unstable to a degree over time and space. I see no *a priori* reason to suppose that any relatively enduring, transfactually acting social mechanism need be particularly constant in the way it operates over time and space; nor am I aware of any evidence which indicates that any are. Indeed, given the fact of the dependence of social mechanisms upon inherently transformative human agency, where human beings *choose* their course of action (and so could always have acted otherwise), strict constancy seems a quite unlikely eventuality. Just as there is always some continuity in social change, so there is usually some (and often quite substantial) change in social continuity.

(pp. 218–19, Lawson's emphasis)

These statements summarize Lawson's reasons for believing that economic theory as it is presently done must lead to emptiness and confusion. The required regularities are not present. Because of countervailing "mechanisms" and "factors" they cannot be effective as they are continuously but unevenly offset, and, thus, are impossible to observe except perhaps very briefly and unclearly. If one should break through and become visible it will, like part of a fireworks display, quickly die before our eyes, perhaps leaving a fading image on our retinas impossible to examine or measure. To make matters worse, the process of change is constantly changing.

This suggests an image of the economic and social world in which numerous mechanisms and factors oppose each other, struggling in a constant war that produces no victors except in brief skirmishes. With no clear winners nothing is settled. Over this, disconcertingly, lingers the odor of chaos, not in the mathematical but in the biblical meaning.

Others are less pessimistic, believing that regularities do exist in the economic sphere. To advance this view let me suggest a few examples.

First, the principle of increasing and decreasing returns. It is not possible to satisfy all of the world's need for flour from a single acre of wheat land no matter how much seed, fertilizer and cultivation is applied. Nor can all the world's automobiles be produced in a single factory. I will not repeat the textbook descriptions of increasing, maximum and decreasing returns.

What are the countervailing mechanisms and factors that obscure this principle? Whatever they are, they failed to prevent the principle from emerging quite clearly. Second, consider the mainstream theory of demand which requires that the quantity of a goods sold responds negatively to its own price changes and positively to income changes. This has been confirmed by empirical data many times. Further, it is accepted by industrialists, financiers and others of practical and realistic mind and temperament.

There is, of course, the possibility of a negative income effect. This has been verified many times by statistical studies and there is also the more remote possibility that the perverse income effect may offset the substitution effect. So far as is known to me this has never been verified empirically except in unusual, perhaps undependable, anecdotal ways. But these exceptions, being part of the theory, cannot be countervailing.

Most demand patterns seem to be reasonably stable. They change but certainly do not change from moment to moment. There are goods that come into existence and sell momentarily as a fad or part of a fad and these probably lie outside the scope of the mainstream theory.

As a third example, visualize a country with a fractional reserve banking system overseen by a central bank. The central bank, by selling securities in the open market, can reduce the reserves of the banking system, thus reducing its lending capability, and putting upward pressure on short-term interest rates. The holders of securities certainly believe that this regularity exists because they respond by adjusting their portfolios whenever a central bank announces a change in interest rate goals. Many other regularities could be mentioned. Indeed any branch of economics could furnish examples; there is no need to go on citing them.

Controlled experiments or closed experiments are, of course, excellent ways of testing suspected regularities. These are no doubt the best ways when they are possible. But regularities may be discovered by other methods – principally by observation in different guises. Astronomy, cosmology, geology, seismology and meteorology all depend on observations rather than experiments to a greater or lesser extent. Yet, it would be hard to deny that regularities exist in these fields of inquiry.

It may also be noted incidentally that a new branch of economics, experimental economics, has come into existence in recent years. Not surprisingly, a considerable part of the work is related to psychological experimentation. Lawson does not take note of this development.

9. The importance of Lawson's book

Although many economists probably reject Lawson's claim that regularities do not exist, or at least cannot be discovered, in the economic sphere, the book contains a most important message: ontology cannot be neglected. Further, this message is the consequence of a powerful philosophical argument.

In what ways has ontology been neglected in economic theory? These would seem to fall under two headings: making overly simplistic assumptions and making assumptions that have no empirical counterpart and may even be physically impossible. Examples of both kinds abound in economic theory: assuming all parties to a market have perfect knowledge of the market; assuming all competing firms in a market will follow a simple pricing strategy (perhaps all following the same strategy); assuming instantaneous adjustment; assuming an individual knows his life span, income each year of his life and his future utility functions, and perhaps has the same knowledge for his children; assuming a probability distribution that does not exist so that a model can be completed or mixed strategies employed. The list could go on and on.

Too often economic theorists have not adopted logical methods appropriate for investigating the economic world, but instead have assumed an imaginary economic world that submits to the logical methods they want to use. They have preferred to abandon the world in favor of their preferences in mathematics rather than using mathematical and other methods that are effective in analyzing the real world.

In condemning this approach Lawson is reinforcing statements made by Herbert Simon over many years (e.g. 1959; 1979; 1996). It is significant that the two differ on the proper remedy. Lawson believes any economic theory which purports to represent regularities should be abandoned as an empty exercise, but Simon believes its foundations should be reworked making use of psychological and other empirical research, including experiments as well as new logical methods. Although most economists will reject Lawson's "biggest" conclusion, the book is still an excellent piece of work which, among other things, shows that methodology is important in economics. It contains a great deal of systematic wisdom.

References

Dupuy, J. P. (1989) "Convention et Common Knowledge," *Revue économique* 2: 361–400.

Dupuy, J. P. (1991) *La panique*, Paris, Les empêcheurs de penser en round.

Dupuy, J. P. (1992a) *Introduction aux Sciences Sociales: Logique des Pfenomenes Collectife*, Paris: Ellipses.

Dupuy, J. P. (1992b) *Le Sacrifice et l'envie: Le libéralisme aux prises avec le justice sociale*, Paris: Carlmann-Levy.

Fullbrook, E. (1996a) "The Metaphysics of Consumer Desire and the French Intersubjectivists," *International Advances in Economic Research* 2: 287–94.

Fullbrook, E. (1996b) "Consumer Metaphysics: The Neoclassicists Versus the Intersubjectivists," *Archives of Economic History* 7: 53–74.

Fullbrook, E. (1998) "Caroline Foley and the Theory of Intersubjective Demand," *Journal of Economic Issues* XXXII, 3: 709–31.

Hicks, J. R. (1938) *Value and Capital,* Oxford: Oxford University Press.

Kahnemann, D. and A. Tversky, (1982) "Prospect Theory: An Analysis of Decision Under Risk," *Econometrica* 50: 178–91.

Keynes, J. M. (1936) *The General Theory of Employment, Interest and Money,* New York.

Lawson, T. (1997) *Economics and Reality,* London: Routledge.

Orlean, A. (1988) "L'auto-reference dans la theorie Keynesiense de la speculation," *Cahier du Crea* 120–44.

Orlean, A. (1989) "Pour une approche cognitive des conventions économiques," *Revue économique* 2: 241–72.

Orlean, A. (1990) "Le role des influences interpersonelles dans la formatión des cours boursiurs," *Revue économique* 5.

Orlean, A. (1992) "Contagion des opinions et founctionnement des marchés financiers," *Revue économique* 4: 685–98.

Pfouts, R. W. (1977) "Directional Modeling," *Proceedings of the First International Conference of Mathematical Modeling,* 2313–22.

Rosenberg, A. (1992) *Economics – Mathematical Politics or Science of Diminishing Returns,* Chicago.

Simon, H. A. (1955) "A Behavioral Model of Rational Choice," *Quarterly Journal of Economics* 69: 98–118.

Simon, H. A. (1979) *Models of Thought,* Yale.

Simon, H. A. (1996) *The Sciences of the Artificial,* 3rd ed., Cambridge, Mass: M.I.T. Press.

6

CONSPICUOUS CONSUMPTION IN ECONOMIC THEORY AND THOUGHT

Roger Mason

1. Introduction

Conspicuous consumption is no recent phenomenon. Preoccupations with status-seeking consumption on the part of the rich and powerful are found in the earliest societies, and the extravagances and excesses of ruling élites have been well documented. Sumptuary laws were often introduced to suppress excessive ostentatious display (Hunt 1966: 17–39), but, for the most part, the conspicuous display of aristocracies in the early modern period was tolerated by Church and State alike as a necessary part of the marriage between ascribed status and economic power.

In Europe, social, economic and political changes after 1600 were to transform the nature and importance of conspicuous consumption. The new consumer societies which emerged in the seventeenth and eighteenth centuries brought about a significant redistribution of income and wealth which allowed newly-rich merchant classes to seek status and prestige through ostentatious consumption. The Mercantilists, who had dominated economic thought since 1500, and who continued to see a clear connection between thrift and prosperity, were quick to warn against the evils of excessive luxury expenditure. By the end of the seventeenth century, however, a small but influential group of political economists recognised that consumer preoccupations with status and social position were generating significant levels of economic activity which, if properly managed, could in fact add both to national wealth and to public well-being (Barbon 1690: 6; Locke 1692: 93–4; North 1691: 14–15). As the eighteenth century began, these arguments were given greater public exposure in a controversial defence of luxury consumption.

In 1714, Bernard Mandeville, a Dutch émigré living in London, argued in his book *The Fable of the Bees: or, Private Vices, Publick Benefits* that the much-vaunted economic success of The Netherlands in the seventeenth

85

century owed as much to the conspicuous, luxury consumption of the merchant classes and their emulators as to the country's productive efficiency and international trade ([1714] 1966: I, 188–9). Luxury expenditure, he claimed, could and did work in the wider public interest ([1714] 1966: I, 107–19). His views scandalised the economic and clerical establishments of the day and the book was declared a 'public nuisance' by a grand jury in Middlesex, England, in 1723. Nevertheless, Mandeville, with some style, had raised an issue which demanded a response from contemporary political economists, and had, unknowingly, identified a 'problem' for economic theorists which has refused to go away. The following pages chart the attempts of economists to come to terms with a form of consumer behaviour with which they felt instinctively uneasy.

2. Conspicuous consumption in the classical period

Although others were prepared to concede that the trickle-down effects of ostentatious consumption on the part of the rich could indirectly bring some benefit to society in general, critics argued that Mandeville had failed to draw a necessary moral distinction between traditional and nouveaux riches forms of conspicuous display. David Hume ([1739] 1967: 357–65) believed that the extravagances of ascribed-status élites was 'innocent luxury', driven only by pride in ownership and possession. In contrast, the conspicuous consumption of the emerging merchant classes was seen to be motivated by a desire to impress and to secure social status: it therefore lacked any moral authority and had to be seen as 'vicious luxury' which had no place in securing either economic or social progress ([1751] 1975: 265–6).

While Hume's views found a receptive audience, in France the Physiocrats took a far more pragmatic view of the benefits of luxury consumption, conscious of the importance of the manufacture and sale of luxury products to the French economy (Butel-Dumont 1771). This more liberal interpretation, however, found no response in Britain, and in his *Theory of Moral Sentiments* ([1759] 1976: 308–13) Adam Smith joined Hume in attacking the perceived moral bankruptcy of Mandeville's analysis of vice, consumption and the public good. Smith did not condemn the luxury expenditure of the very rich, arguing that they could legitimately reveal wealth through consumption to confirm their social and economic status. However, he believed that 'Mandeville's notions are in almost every respect erroneous' ([1759] 1976: 308). As for ostentatious display, it could serve a useful purpose by encouraging others to work harder in order to join the ranks of the rich and successful. If, however, the fruits of this hard work were used in the shorter term to seek an improved social status not yet fully earned, then society needed to condemn such vanity without reservation.

Later, in *The Wealth of Nations* (1776), Smith was to concede that not all striving after status among the 'lower orders' could, in Hume's terminology, be considered 'vicious'. Concern for the opinion of others, expressed through the consumption of socially visible goods and services, could be justified at any social level if the intention was only to conform to established rules of decency and to protect social status among one's peers ([1776] 1976: 869–70). Smith, in short, was prepared to condone within-group but not between-group conspicuous display, a view implicitly endorsed by Jeremy Bentham ([1801] 1954: 87).

The early nineteenth century produced no great interest in conspicuous consumption among economists, and there was no suggestion that status-directed luxury expenditure needed to be made a part of a more inclusive theory of consumer demand. What interest there was centred around whether such consumer behaviour could be considered 'good' or 'bad' for society, and, as the century progressed, argument began to divide sharply along ethical and economic lines. First, there were those who continued to reject the idea of conspicuous consumption on moral and religious grounds – most notably, John Rae, a Scots émigré living in Canada, whose book on the principles of political economy (Rae [1834] 1965: II) not only looked at the nature of capital accumulation and at the process of economic development but, more unusually, also explored the nature of luxury consumption in some detail.

To Rae, a highly religious man and a leading member of the Scottish Kirk in Canada, Mandeville's argument that individual self-interest and the national interest could be one and the same was not sustainable. Luxury ostentatious consumption was driven only by man's vanity – a vanity which inevitably corroded the fabric of society and led eventually to social and economic degeneration ([1834] 1965: II, 265–6). Only through a greater commitment to religious values and better education could such pernicious behaviour be eliminated in order to secure the proper ordering of society.

Rae's rejection of vanity-driven consumption was shared by others, but sometimes a more pragmatic view of such behaviour was evident. Nassau Senior ([1836] 1863: 12) held that the desire for social distinction expressed through possession and the display of wealth was the most powerful of human passions, affecting all men at all times – '... it comes with us from the cradle and never leaves us till we go into the grave'. John Stuart Mill, similarly, believed that it was not possible to remove all morally questionable conspicuous consumption from society, but argued that such indulgences could be made to serve the public interest through the taxation system (1848 V vi, 869). Nonetheless, he was clear that, in an ideal world, the pursuit of vanity could have no place in a civilised society.

In contrast to those who rejected conspicuous consumption on moral and ethical grounds, there were others who, like Mandeville, believed that the economic benefits deriving from such behaviour could not be ignored. Friedrich List ([1841] 1974: 381) argued that luxury consumption and the emulation it generated were acceptable engines for sustainable economic growth. Wilhelm Roscher ([1854] 1878: 241) also claimed that, in modern, affluent societies, a more equitable distribution of income and wealth produced what he described as an 'equalising tendency' in the consumption of luxuries which not only generated increased economic activity but was also morally defensible. Only in declining nations did he see dangers in unfettered luxury consumption.

For the most part, mainstream economists continued to marginalise the issue of status-driven consumption. Augustin Cournot ([1838] 1960: 46), anxious to promote a more mathematical treatment of economics, acknowledged that, while products were purchased largely for the purpose of ostentatious display, such behaviour played so unimportant a role in overall economic terms that it could safely be ignored. Others, notably Dupuit in France and Gossen in Germany, supported this view. Later, in the 1870s, William Stanley Jevons, an admirer of both Cournot and Gossen, continued to promote a more mathematical interpretation of utility theory and, together with Carl Menger and Leon Walras, laid the foundations for a neoclassical theory in which any supposed interpersonal effects on demand were hardly recognised or discussed. Their work was subsequently further developed by Alfred Marshall, whose *Principles of Economics* first appeared in 1890, and whose views were to dominate the economic agenda for many years to come.

3. The neoclassical view and its dissenters

Marshall continued a tradition of largely disregarding events and outcomes which seemed only to illustrate the perversity of human behaviour. Certainly, he recognised the existence of status-directed conspicuous consumption, especially in 'new countries' – a clear reference to the United States, where the Gilded Age excesses of the nouveaux riches could hardly be ignored. At the same time, he considered such behaviour to be both tasteless and frivolous, the indulgence of a small minority, and implied that it needed no special treatment within, or incorporation into, theories of consumption.

Marshall's dismissal of the significance of interpersonal effects on consumer demand was not without its critics. Cunynghame (1892: 37–8), Foley (1893: 459–60) and, most significantly, A. C. Pigou (1903: 60–2; 1910: 361; 1913: 19–24), all argued that the degree to which individual consumption decisions could be influenced by the opinions of others had been greatly underestimated. When it was given greater weight, it was not at all possible to derive an aggregate demand curve, as Marshall had assumed, by the simple addition of supposedly independent demand schedules. Marshall, nonetheless, held to his view that conspicuous consumption was of little consequence, and could safely be ignored in developing general theories of consumer demand. Later revisions to *Principles* made no real concessions to his critics on the issue, and the Marshallian view persisted within mainstream economics. Across the Atlantic, however, the subject of status-directed consumption was receiving far greater attention by the turn of the century.

In the first edition of *Principles*, Marshall had recognised the scale of Gilded Age conspicuous consumption in the United States, but had been reluctant to invest such behaviour with any real significance for economic theory. A greater emphasis on the social prestige of philanthropic expenditure and a better sense of chivalry could and would remove such unacceptable, if largely trivial, behaviour in the medium term (Marshall 1907: 25–9). To others, however, the excesses of the American nouveaux riches were symptomatic of a more widespread desire to consume for prestige and social standing. This alternative view was articulated most persuasively by Thorstein Veblen, then an economics lecturer at the University of Chicago.

Veblen had never been happy with the neoclassical approach to consumer theory, and between 1898 and 1900 published a series of articles in the *Quarterly Journal of Economics* (1898; 1899a, b; 1900) attacking many of the assumptions and perceived lack of realism implicit in much neoclassical theory. It was not acceptable, in Veblen's view, for economists to declare that they could only concern themselves with outcomes and not with the underlying motives of consumption, and he pressed for greater interest to be shown in the intersubjectivity of consumer demand as a means to a better understanding of consumer behaviour. Veblen was particularly concerned with the importance of interpersonal effects on consumer preference formation, and in his *The Theory of the Leisure Class* ([1899c] 1957: 22–34; 68–101) he explored the nature of pecuniary emulation and of conspicuous consumption in both sociological and economic terms. His analysis extended far beyond the Gilded Age excesses of the United States towards a more generalised theory of conspicuous economic display ([1899c] 1957, passim).Only by adopting interdisciplinary approaches to economic analysis, Veblen believed, would any real progress be made in developing a consumer theory which could properly describe real-world market behaviour.

For the most part, Veblen's appeals fell on deaf ears. Mainstream economists, particularly those who had embraced the now fashionable mathematical school of economic analysis, rejected his 'sociology' out of hand as misguided and irrelevant. Even orthodox, yet literary (as opposed to mathematical) scholars were not persuaded to change their views on value, utility and consumption (Clark 1898). In short, Veblen's immediate impact on economic thought was minimal and his work, though popular and controversial with a wider readership at the time, stimulated no great debate within economics. He continued to attack what he saw as the limitations of marginal utility analysis (Veblen 1909) but had made no real impression on conventional economic theory and thought by the time of his death in 1929. Only later was his work to be given some greater recognition by economists (few in number) working to secure a better understanding of status-motivated consumption within consumer theory.

Veblen's failure to persuade others of the need to look again at some of the central tenets of conventional consumer theory was, in a sense, predictable. First, while he had argued for a more interdisciplinary approach, in the eyes of many he had failed to translate what was a heavily sociological interpretation of demand into a parallel economic theory which allowed for the measurement of utility. While the inadequacies of orthodox neoclassical theory had, to some, been revealed to good effect, there was no replacement theory on offer which could be used to take economics forward. Second, and more generally, economics as a discipline was, at this time, moving away from sociology and psychology in its attempts to establish itself as a mathematical science and, notwithstanding the protests of a minority who subsequently pressed for a better accommodation of the behavioural sciences within economics (Clark 1918; Downey 1910; Knight 1925a, b; Mitchell 1910; 1914; Schumpeter 1909), this trend was to continue.

By the early 1930s, the gulf between economists and other social scientists was becoming wider, but within economics itself there was now a growing unease with marginal utility theory. This unease, however, stemmed not from any greater recognition of so-called behavioural economics or of the importance of interpersonal effects and interdependent preferences in highly complex consumer goods markets, but from a desire to see all sociology and 'indeterminate psychology' removed from consumer theory. Hicks and Allen (1934a: 53–76; 1934b: 196–219) soon developed an alternative approach to consumer demand based on an indifference curve analysis which moved from cardinal to ordinal measures of utility and which replaced marginal utility with marginal rates of substitution between products. In essence, the new approach represented an attempt to remove what social psychology there was in marginal utility theory by promoting a far stronger mathematical interpretation of consumer behaviour to allow for easier 'measurement'. Keynes (1936: 307–27) took issue with this approach, arguing that many behavioural factors determined the overall propensity to consume and that these factors (defined as enjoyment, short-sightedness, generosity, miscalculation, and [significantly] ostentation and extravagance (1936: 109)) did not lend themselves to a purely mathematical treatment. However, he did not press the issue, being more concerned at that time with macroeconomic rather than with microeconomic analysis (1936: 109–19). Subsequently, Samuelson (1938: 61–71) took the Hicks and Allen work further, developing a theory of consumer behaviour 'freed from all vestigial traces of the utility concept' (1938: 61–2), and later (1947: 90–117) proposed a new theory of 'revealed preference' which, he claimed, was clear of any 'psychology' whatsoever. This extended mathematical purity was a development from which Hicks, himself a committed mathematical economist, felt obliged to distance himself:

> It may well be that for econometric work a theory of Professor Samuelson's type is all we need; it gives a superb model for statistical fitting. But for the understanding of the economic system we need something more, something which does refer back, in the last resort, to the behaviour of people and the motives of their conduct

> (Hicks 1946: 337)

4. External effects and the relative income hypothesis

In the years following the Second World War, the United States experienced a major improvement in living standards and in consumption, fuelled by a significant increase in individual and family incomes after taxes. As discretionary incomes and spending rose, so a desire to emulate others in their consumption behaviour became increasingly evident, a development which generated a major increase in levels of recognisably conspicuous consumption. By 1950, Hicks' reservations over attempts to establish purely econometric treatments of consumer behaviour – treatments which effectively ignored all subjective and intersubjective influences on consumer preference formation – seemed increasingly well-founded. The gap between the new theoretical orthodoxy and the realities of the marketplace was widening as status-directed conspicuous display became a commonplace in the world's largest mass market.

A part of the refusal to recognise the degree to which consumer behaviour was now heavily influenced by intersubjective factors grew from a determination to protect the assumption of 'additivity' in the construction of aggregate demand curves (then a *sine qua non* of econometric analysis). By the later 1940s, however, some eminent mainstream economists were beginning to question such assumptions. Morgenstern (1948: 175) pointed out that the problem of non-additivity 'does not even seem to have been put', although the larger part of demand was, in his opinion, by now demonstrably non-additive. Morgenstern believed that this omission constituted the most serious limitation of current demand theory (1948: 191). Similarly, Stigler (1950: 151–2) attacked economists who were still refusing to include the consumption of other individuals in the consumer's utility function, observing that their faithful adherence for so long to the additive utility function showed not only a lack of enterprise but also of imagination, given that 'no economic problem has only one (mathematical) avenue of approach'.

Disquiet with a theory of demand which was demonstrably unable to accommodate significant levels of socially-inspired consumption led to some greater interest being shown in the consequences of intersubjective effects on consumer behaviour. Prompted by Morgenstern's (1948) paper, Leibenstein (1950) explored the nature of bandwagon, snob and Veblen effects on preference formation, and took tentative steps towards incorporating these effects into current consumer theory. He conceded, however, that his analysis offered only a static explanation of such consumer behaviour, and he imposed other analytical restrictions which were considered necessary 'in order to take care of some of the difficulties raised by Professor Morgenstern' (1950: 188n). In truth, Leibenstein assumed away many of the problems which Morgenstern had identified as major stumbling blocks to further progress in the development of demand theory. As a result, his attempt at integration was of limited value (something which Leibenstein himself acknowledged (1950: 206) but nevertheless did offer new thinking with respect to so-called external effects on consumer behaviour. By the time his paper had been published, however, a more significant contribution to the debate over intersubjectivity and consumer demand had appeared.

In a footnote to his 1950 paper, Leibenstein had referred to the other work which was then being carried out into external effects but which had come to his attention 'too late to be given the detailed consideration it deserves' (1950: 186n). This was a reference to James Duesenberry's *Income, Saving and the Theory of Consumer Behavior* (1949), a book which took a radically different approach to the phenomenon of interpersonal effects on demand, but which was to have a more significant impact on economic theory and thought in the following decade.

Unlike Leibenstein, Duesenberry's analysis of socially inspired consumption was macroeconomic rather than microeconomic and was intended first and foremost as a critique of the Keynesian consumption function. Most significantly, Duesenberry held two fundamental assumptions of aggregate demand theory to be invalid – first, that every individual's consumption behaviour could be taken as independent of every other individual; second, that consumption levels were reversible over time (1949: 1).

On the first point, Duesenberry believed that, for any individual or family, social status was no trivial preoccupation but a key factor influencing the process of choice and the purchase of goods. Consumers, he argued, measured status by comparing the amount and pattern of consumption with that of others with whom they compared themselves socially (1949: 28–32). As some changed and improved their overall consumption rating, so others broke habit patterns in order to emulate them, and these breaks could, significantly, be independent of changes in income and prices. For any given group or family, therefore, the frequency of contact with superior goods increased primarily as the consumption of others with whom they came into contact increased. Duesenberry called this phenomenon the 'demonstration effect' (1949: 27).

In a society in which improvements in the standard of living were a social goal, this drive to maintain self-esteem expressed itself in a drive to acquire goods and services. However, the 'quality' of such purchases need not relate to any measure of practical value in use – indeed, the goods could be expensive yet largely useless items, reflecting a high degree of conspicuous waste. To Duesenberry, this impulse to consume conspicuously came from three principal sources. First, individuals could be seeking to maintain or improve their social status among those perceived as social equals (the 'keeping up with the Joneses' phenomenon); second, they could be determined to keep a suitable distance between themselves and those perceived as being their social inferiors; finally, they themselves could be aspiring to join higher social groups (1949: 25–32). Whatever the intention, the conspicuous consumption of goods and services was seen to be central to their ambitions. In all three cases, moreover, a 'ratchet effect' operated to ensure that consumption standards were not reversible: the pressure to consume either to consolidate or to improve status was, therefore, always positive (1949: 115).

Duesenberry saw such preoccupations with social standing and prestige as a major determinant of consumer behaviour. Importantly, he argued that, as a consequence of such preoccupations, patterns of consumption were decided not by absolute levels of income, as the Keynesian consumption function suggested, but by individual or family income relative to that of 'relevant others' in their immediate social environment. Duesenberry then proposed a 'relative income hypothesis' which claimed that consumption patterns were a function of the consumer's position in the income distribution, and that much expenditure was determined by social rather than by economic motives (1949, passim).

Duesenberry's analysis was, by any measure, an original if controversial contribution to consumer theory and was given greater weight by the fact that he had used empirical evidence of budget studies in the United States to lend support to his thesis (1949: 47–68). Other researchers had independently reported what appeared to be a relative income effect on consumption (Brady and [Rose] Friedman 1947; Modigliani 1949), and this, too, gave some greater credibility to Duesenberry's arguments. Clower (1951: 76) concluded that the practical validity of [Duesenberry's] general interdependence postulate 'can not seriously be questioned'. Such endorsements notwithstanding, Duesenberry's ideas took no great hold within the economic mainstream.

By 1954, Modigliani, heavily influenced by the sight of an unpublished paper by Margaret Reid on permanent income effects on consumer expenditures, had been persuaded that consumption was, indeed, a function of permanent income (Modigliani 1975: 4), and had collaborated with Blumberg to develop a 'life cycle hypothesis' of saving and consumption (Modigliani and Blumberg 1954). Some three years later, [Milton] Friedman (1957) published his seminal *A Theory of the Consumption Function*, building on Modigliani and Blumberg's work and proposing a 'permanent income hypothesis' which effectively removed any considerations of social psychology from consumer theory. Subsequent widespread support among economists for this hypothesis had the effect of marginalising Duesenberry's attempts to introduce social and psychological elements into current economic debates on consumer demand and, after 1960, his work was quickly relegated to the status of an historical footnote or *curiosum* in most economic texts (Frank 1985: 157; Pollak 1978: 376n).

5. Developments since 1960

The marked lack of interest in Duesenberry's treatment of consumption reflected, in part, the increasing mathematicisation of economics and economic theory which had been in evidence for some twenty years. Certainly, Hicks, Samuelson and Friedman had developed consumer theories which explicitly discounted or rejected social interpretations of consumer demand, and which lent themselves to purely mathematical and econometric analysis. Those few economists who continued throughout the 1950s to promote a more intersubjective and sociological explanation of consumer behaviour (Galbraith 1958; Katona 1951; 1953) did so from outside the economic mainstream, and their appeals for some greater recognition of status-directed conspicuous consumption went largely ignored. At the same time, it was becoming increasingly difficult to ignore the high levels of socially inspired consumption, actively encouraged by manufacturers, retailers and their advertising agencies, which were now evident in America and in Europe and for which exclusively 'mathematical' explanations were clearly inadequate and inappropriate.

The general neglect of status-linked consumption within mainstream economics continued in the early 1960s. Some (Houthakker 1961: 733–4) showed mild interest in the degree to which consumers and markets could become occupied with matters of status and prestige, but concluded that these social effects on demand were relatively unimportant and gave no real cause for concern. This was certainly the prevailing view, but, within a few years, the prospects for some better accommodation of status-motivated consumption within demand theory looked more encouraging.

In a radical new approach to consumer theory, Lancaster (1966) argued that Hicksian concepts of value and utility were outdated and sterile, primarily because the traditional view of goods was that they were the direct objects of utility. When utility was seen to derive from the properties or characteristics of goods, then far more progress could be made in understanding the nature and preferences of consumer demand. As any particular good clearly possessed more than one characteristic, so consumption was characterised by joint outputs, and consumers chose their purchases on the basis of the 'bundle' of characteristics offered by any particular product in comparison to others (1966: 132–5).

This 'characteristics of goods' approach could potentially embrace status-seeking consumer behaviour more comfortably than traditional models of consumer demand. In 1971, however, drawing his work together, Lancaster argued that it was better to avoid any speculation concerning the social characteristics of goods and to refrain from explicit 'psychologising' about products and services. Such psychologising was unnecessary and 'when such speculation is removed, so non-additivity presents no particular problem' (Lancaster 1971: 107). In support, Lancaster claimed that his analysis of the United States automobile market 'suggests that [the market] is readily amenable to rational analysis in terms of straightforward physical characteristics of cars, without using such imponderables as "style" or any sex at all' (1971: 174). In short, his perspective on consumer preference formation, in a market already widely seen as particularly susceptible to social engineering and to product symbolism, was that demand was both 'rational' and decided by purely economic considerations, so that any so-called social psychology of consumption could be safely ignored. With Lancaster himself not at all interested in applying his model to accommodate the social characteristics of goods, an immediate opportunity to secure some greater research into interpersonal effects on consumer preference formation was lost. However, by the early 1970s, the degree to which such effects were influencing and shaping patterns of market demand, particularly for high-status, socially visible goods and services, began to generate some renewed interest within economics.

The continuing inability of conventional utility theory to recognise any significant mutual interdependence of consumer preferences prompted Krelle (1972) to propose a theory of social interdependence of consumer evaluations which argued that interpersonal effects on demand now had to be recognised, and which attempted to reconnect economic theories of utility with the social psychology which had been largely removed from mainstream economic analysis since the 1930s. Krelle's work was taken further by Gaertner (1973), who constructed a more detailed model of consumer and consumption interdependence. Becker (1974) independently attempted to develop a more sensitive theoretical framework for the analysis of consumer demand, outlining a theory of social interactions which explored demand for a single commodity described as 'distinction'. This approach was subsequently refined and developed by Stigler and Becker

(1977) in a paper which acknowledged the potential importance of social effects on consumption but which, nonetheless, attempted to distil and explain status-motivated consumption in purely economic terms. In the United States also, Pollak (1976), who had earlier (1970) looked at Duesenberry's work on the importance of habit formation, developed a short-run model of interdependent preferences, commenting that 'the lead provided by James Duesenberry was never systematically explored' (1976: 310). This was complemented by work into price dependent preferences (1977), which examined, in particular, the behaviour of conspicuous consumers when a higher price enhances the 'snob appeal' of a good.

At the same time, Lancaster's 'characteristics of goods' model was being revisited, notably by Hayakawa and Venieris (1977) who attempted to rework and adapt the model specifically in order to accommodate consumer interdependence, and by Douglas and Isherwood (1978) who explored ways in which Lancaster's consumer theory could be given greater application and relevance to status-seeking behaviour (1978: 110–3).

There was now a greater willingness to explore elements of socially-determined conspicuous consumption within the economic mainstream, and the need to accommodate status-seeking consumption within demand theory was made more compelling with the arrival of the 1980s and 1990s, decades characterised by high levels of conspicuous consumption fuelled by consumer preoccupations with image, identity and social standing. After 1980, the term 'Veblen effects', seen for many years by economists as a sociological concept of dubious merit or interest, entered the economic literature to a far greater extent, and the economic consequences of socially-inspired consumption were examined in more detail. Basmann, Molina and Slottje (1985; 1988) and Creedy and Slottje (1991) were able to demonstrate that conventional microeconomic analysis was, indeed, capable of identifying and measuring Veblen effects, provided that the necessary data was available and accessible. Bagwell and Bernheim (1991; 1992) then incorporated Veblen effects into a new theory of conspicuous consumption which was subsequently drawn together and published in the *American Economic Review* (1996: 349–73). By the turn of the century, the literature on status-seeking consumption, while still too small, had noticeably increased.

6. Policies and prescriptions

While recent initiatives exploring the economics of status-directed consumer behaviour have been welcome, a majority of economists interested in consumer issues continue to resist efforts to integrate what is still seen as 'the sociology of consumption' into mainstream economic thought. This reluctance perpetuates the traditional view that the discipline must concern itself only with the measurable outcomes of consumption decisions and not with any underlying motives to consume, whether rational or seemingly irrational. Perversely, however, economists have never denied that consumption can be status-seeking and, while rejecting attempts to develop theoretical explanations of such behaviour, have, over many years, prescribed economic policies intended to 'manage' conspicuous consumption and the demand for status goods. Market realities and the need to address issues of increasing social and political concern have, in short, consistently overcome a longstanding reluctance to offer theoretical explanations of status consumption within the economic paradigm.

Prescriptions and policies relating to the management of conspicuous consumption are not new. In early societies, privileged élites looked to the law rather than to economics in order to suppress the luxury consumption of others: sumptuary laws, however, were often difficult to enforce and did little in real terms to diminish status-motivated consumption. After 1700, as the first consumer societies took shape in Europe, attempts were made to hold conspicuous consumption in check not by sumptuary legislation but by religious and moral exhortation to reject the evils of vanity and ostentatious display. John Rae ([1834] 1965 II, 265–99) believed that the long term answer did, indeed, lie with much improved moral and religious education, but, for the shorter term, believed that economic policies could be introduced in order to minimise the price paid for such vanity. First, taxes on pure luxuries needed to be steeply increased and the proceeds spent for the wider public good; second, domestic investment in luxury goods production should be heavily discouraged, prohibitive protectionist tariffs placed on imported luxuries and attempts at import substitution prevented; third, for those luxuries which nonetheless contained recognisable and significant utilitarian value, competition needed to be actively promoted, with a view to driving product prices down, so reducing their status value while at the same time making them more widely available to the general public.

By the middle of the nineteenth century, the religious and moral arguments against ostentatious economic display were beginning to weaken both in Europe and the United States. By the end of the century, the conspicuous consumption of goods and services, and its value to industry and commerce, was implicitly recognised if not universally condoned. Marshall (1907: 8–10), while holding to his view that excessive indulgence was morally indefensible, nevertheless recognised that the need for status and recognition among successful people was irresistible. His policy prescription was to mobilise public opinion against unproductive ostentatious expenditure while at the same time ensuring that a far greater status and prestige than hitherto be awarded to philanthropic expenditures which contributed to the greater public good (1907: 25–9). In this way, the expenditures of wealthy status-seekers could be channelled into productive ventures from which all members of society could benefit.

Subsequently, this policy met with some success, particularly in the United States where, between 1920 and 1931, some 350 personally financed foundations, agencies and charitable trusts were established (Mason 1981: 79).

The perception that conspicuous consumption was a 'problem' associated only with a minority of very rich status-seekers (as Marshall believed), had encouraged a belief that, in macroeconomic terms, it was an insignificant and largely trivial economic phenomenon which could safely be ignored. After 1945, however, as general living standards and levels of discretionary purchasing power rose, first in the United States and later in Europe, it became increasingly difficult to sustain any argument that conspicuous consumption was an economic *curiosum*. Preoccupations with status-seeking consumption and expenditure grew exponentially at all social and economic levels through the 1950s and 1960s and, by the 1970s, it was becoming clear that there were macroeconomic consequences associated with such behaviour which could not sensibly be ignored.

By the mid-1970s, Hirsch (1976) was arguing that, in modern affluent societies, 'positional economies', driven by social relationships and aspirations, were running parallel to the better understood 'material economies', centred on functional utility, production and productivity, which had traditionally been the concern of economic planners. More importantly, growth in the material economy not only generated increased wealth and prosperity but, in so doing, served also to intensify 'positional' competition between individuals for a higher place within prevailing social hierarchies. The two economies ultimately become competitive rather than complementary, as they make conflicting demands on the allocation of scarce resources (1976: 52–4), and the degree to which the positional economy is successful necessarily imposes a social limit on economic growth by diverting resources into satisfying social rather than economic needs.

Hirsch took a pessimistic view of such developments, arguing that policies were needed to suppress positional competition. He believed that societies needed to engineer changes in social ethics and to persuade individuals to put the social interest ahead of self-interest in their consumption behaviour (1976: 178–88). To others, however, more convinced that conspicuous consumption in pursuit of status gains and improved social standing was now irreversible, Hirsch's prescription appeared naive. Frank (1985: 249–50) believed it preferable to concede that consumer choice in this area could not be substantially altered through appeals and exhortations to be more socially responsible, advocating instead the introduction of a consumption tax to be levied on consumer purchases which imposed significant (negative) external effects on others. Congleton (1989: 185–7), in contrast, took a more benign view of the effects of conspicuous display, arguing that not all status-generating activity was undesirable; where it was deemed to be harmful, his (Marshallian) policy recommendation was to channel and redirect expenditures into more socially productive areas through the introduction and promotion of more generous tax conces- sions on philanthropic investments and expenditures. Finally, Ireland (1992: 12–17), concerned that preoccupations with status and prestige had relatively more damaging consequences for those with low incomes, looked at the possibility of introducing (unspecified) legislation designed to restrict or remove certain areas of status-seeking consumption, so reducing the number of opportunities to conspicuously consume.

Overall, the policy concerns relating to conspicuous consumption after 1980 reflected a growing recognition that such consumer behaviour needed to be acknowledged and treated as non-trivial. Against this, the wide variation in policy recommendations only served to emphasise a lack of consensus as to how such behaviour should be managed and con- trolled. In the event, few attempts at policy implementation have been undertaken and these have met with limited success.

The imposition of excise taxes on luxury goods has, over many years, been the preferred policy instrument against conspicuous consumption, and its widespread use is intended both to suppress excessive status- driven expenditures and to raise substantial revenues from those who persist in status-seeking through consumption. However, the arguments raised in favour of taxing 'positional' goods in order to suppress unac- ceptably high levels of conspicuous consumption and to promote greater 'material economy' growth were recently sufficient to persuade American legislators, historically opposed to consumption taxes, to attempt a greater level of selective luxury goods demand management. The Omnibus Budget Reconciliation Act of 1990 imposed a 10 percent excise tax on targeted categories of consumer goods (cars, boats, aircraft, jew- ellery and furs) where the retail price exceeded a given sum and the pur- chase could therefore be (subjectively) considered a luxury. In the event, the tax proved to be far from nondistortionary and merely succeeded in redirecting conspicuous consumption away from the tax-designated product categories and towards other goods of high status value. This outcome could have been avoided if the tax had been applied equally across a full range of status-linked consumption 'constellations' (Solomon and Buchanan 1991), rather than on a more limited selection of product categories. The tax, however, was not amended and the legislation was quickly repealed in 1993 (Mason 1998: 157–9).

In attempts to place a greater emphasis on philanthropic, status-con- ferring expenditure, there have also been moves both in Europe and the United States to introduce more generous tax concessions in order to promote higher levels of socially beneficial consumption. At the same time, given the historical failure of sumptuary laws, there is no prospect that prohibitive legislation (Ireland 1992) will be introduced, against the tide, to restrict, by statute, consumers' ability to conspicuously consume goods and services in pursuit of status and social standing. Overall, given the heightened consumer concerns and preoccupations with lifestyle, with image and with symbolic consumption, policy makers are still struggling to come to terms with the economic consequences of a form of consumption motivated only by considerations of status, identity and style.

7. Summary

Conspicuous consumption has always hovered at the edges of economic theory and thought – never in the mainstream but never wholly forgotten. For many years, it was considered to be a phenomenon so trivial in macroeconomic terms that it was not seen to merit serious discussion or analysis, a view which could be defended while such consumption was seen to be the preserve of a small, affluent, social and economic élite. From its origins as the indulgence of a privileged few, however, it has now become a major determinant of consumer demand in mass consumption societies, and a defining element of modern 'positional' economic activity. At the same time, this heightened importance has not brought about any significantly greater interest in status-seeking consumption within economics itself, an omission which must give cause for concern.

This reluctance to address consumer preoccupations with symbolism, status and prestige has many causes, but two factors predominate. First, a belief that any social processes determining consumer behaviour are the proper business not of economists but of other social scientists. Second, a desire within the discipline itself to secure recognition as an exact science, grounded in mathematics and econometrics, and capable of providing precise economic systems, models and measurements free from any 'psychological' baggage.

The macroeconomic consequences of today's consumer concerns with status, identity and style are now increasingly evident, and the need for appropriate policies and prescriptions relating to the management and control of 'positional' economic activity widely recognised. Economics will hopefully respond by recognising these new market realities and by adopting a more tolerant, inclusive, and interdisciplinary approach to the accommodation of status-seeking conspicuous consumption within a new consumer theory.

References

Bagwell, L. S. and Bernheim, B. D. (1996) 'Veblen effects in a theory of conspicuous consumption', *American Economic Review* 86: 349–73.
Barbon, Nicholas (1690) *Discourse of Trade*, London.

Basmann, R. L., Molina, D. J. and Slottje, D. J. (1985) Measuring Veblen Primary and Secondary Effects Utilizing the Fechner-Thurstone Direct Utility Function. Mimeo, Texas: A&M University.

Basmann, R. L., Molina, D. J. and Slottje, D. J. (1988) 'A note on measuring Veblen's theory of conspicuous consumption', *Review of Economics and Statistics* 70: 531–5.

Becker, Gary, S. (1974) 'A theory of social interaction', *Journal of Political Economy* 82: 1063–93.

Bentham, Jeremy [1801] (1954) 'The True Alarm', in W. Stark (ed.) *Jeremy Bentham's Economic Writings*, vol. 3. George Allen & Unwin, London.

Brady, Dorothy and Rose D. Friedman (1947) Savings and the income distribution. *Studies in Income and Wealth*, X. National Bureau of Economic Research, New York, 247–65.

Butel-Dumont, G. M. (1771) *Théorie du Luxe: ou traité dans lequel on entreprend d'établir que le luxe est un ressort non seulement utile, mais même indispensablement nécessaire à la prosperité des états*. Paris & London.

Clark, John Bates (1898) 'The future of economic theory', *Quarterly Journal of Economics* 13: 1–14.

Clark, J. M. (1918) 'Economics and modern psychology', *Journal of Political Economy* 26: 136–66.

Clower, Robert, W. (1951) 'Professor Duesenberry and traditional theory', *Review of Economic Studies* 19: 165–78.

Congleton, Roger, D. (1989) 'Efficient status-seeking externalities and the evolution of status games', *Journal of Economic Behavior and Organization* 11: 175–90.

Cournot, Augustin [1838] (1960) *Researches into the Mathematical Principles of the Theory of Wealth*, trans. W.T. Bacon, Hafner Publishing Co., London.

Creedy, John and Slottje, D.J. (1991) *Conspicuous Consumption in Australia*. Research Paper 307, June, University of Melbourne.

Cunynghame, Henry (1892) 'Some improvements in simple geometrical methods of treating exchange value, monopoly and rent', *Economic Journal* 2: 35–52.

Douglas, M. and Isherwood, B. (1978) *The World of Goods*. Penguin Books, London.

Downey, E. H. (1910) 'The futility of marginal utility', *Journal of Political Economy* 18: 253–68.

Duesenberry, James, S. (1949) *Income, Saving and the Theory of Consumer Behavior*. Harvard University Press, Cambridge, Mass.

Foley, Caroline, A. (1893) 'Fashion', *Economic Journal* 3: 458–74.

Frank, Robert, A. (1985) *Choosing the Right Pond: Human Behavior and the Quest for Status*. Oxford University Press, New York.

Friedman, Milton (1957) *A Theory of the Consumption Function*. Princeton University Press, Princeton.

Gaertner, Wulf (1973) 'A dynamic model of interdependent consumer behaviour', PhD thesis, University of Bonn.

Galbraith, J. K. (1958) *The Affluent Society*. Hamish Hamilton, London.

Hayakawa, H. and Venieris, Y. (1977) 'Consumer interdependence via reference groups', *Journal of Political Economy* 85(3): 599–615.

Hicks, J. R. (1946) *Value and Capital*. Clarendon Press, Oxford. [1st edn 1939].

Hicks, J. R. and Allen, R. G. D. (1934a) 'A reconsideration of the theory of value I', *Economica* 1: 53–76.

101

Hicks, J. R. and Allen, R. G. D. (1934b) 'A reconsideration of the theory of value II', *Economica* 1: 196–219.

Hirsch, Fred (1976) *Social Limits to Growth*. Harvard University Press, Cambridge, Mass.

Houthakker, H. S. (1961) 'The present state of consumption theory', *Econometrica* 29: 704–39.

Hume, David [1739] (1967) *A Treatise of Human Nature*. L.A. Selby-Bigge (ed.). Clarendon Press, Oxford [1st edn 1888].

Hume, David [1751] (1975) *Enquiries Concerning the Human Understanding and Concerning the Principles of Morals* (posthumous edition 1777). L.A. Selby-Bigge (ed.). Clarendon House, Oxford [1st edn 1894].

Hunt, Alan (1996) *Governance of the Consuming Passions: A History of Sumptuary Law*, Macmillan, London.

Ireland, Norman, J. (1992) 'On limiting the market for status symbols', Mimeo, University of Warwick.

Katona, George (1951) *Psychological Analysis of Economic Behavior*, McGraw Hill, New York.

Katona, George (1953) 'Rational behavior and economic behavior', *Psychological Review* September, 307–18.

Keynes, John Maynard (1936) *The General Theory of Employment, Interest and Money*, Macmillan, London.

Knight, Frank, H. (1925a) 'Fact and metaphysics in economic psychology', *American Economic Review* 15: 247–66.

Knight, Frank, H. (1925b) 'Economic psychology and the value problem', *Quarterly Journal of Economics* 39: 372–409.

Krelle, W. (1972) 'Dynamics of the utility function', *Zeitschrift fur Nationalekonomie* 32: 59–70.

Lancaster, Kelvin, J. (1966) 'A new approach to consumer theory', *Journal of Political Economy* 74: 132–57.

Lancaster, Kelvin, J. (1971) *Consumer Demand*. Columbia University Press, New York.

Leibenstein, Harvey (1950) 'Bandwagon, snob and Veblen effects in the theory of consumers' demand', *Quarterly Journal of Economics* 64: 183–207.

List, Friedrich [1841] (1974) *The National System of Political Economy*. Garland Publishing House, New York.

Locke, John (1692) *Some Considerations of the Lowering of Interest*, London.

Mandeville, Bernard [1714] (1966) *The Fable of the Bees: or, Private Vices, Publick Benefits*. F. B. Kaye (ed.). Clarendon Press, Oxford [1st edn 1924].

Marshall, Alfred (1890) *Principles of Economics*. Macmillan, London.

Marshall, Alfred (1907) 'The social possibilities of economic chivalry', *Economic Journal* 17: 7–29.

Mason, Roger (1981) *Conspicuous Consumption: A Study of Exceptional Consumer Behaviour*, St Martin's Press, New York.

Mason, Roger (1998) *The Economics of Conspicuous Consumption; Theory and Thought Since 1700*. Edward Elgar, Cheltenham.

Mill, John Stuart [1848] (1965) *Principles of Political Economy*. J.F. Robson (ed.). Toronto: Routledge and Keyan Paul.

Mitchell, Wesley, C. (1910) 'The rationality of economic activity II', *Journal of Political Economy* 18: 197–216.

Mitchell, Wesley, C. (1914) 'Human behavior and economics; a survey of recent literature', *Quarterly Journal of Economics* 29: 1–47.

Modigliani, Franco (1949) Fluctuations in the savings-income ratio; a problem in economic forecasting. *Studies in Income and Wealth* XI, National Bureau of Economic Research, New York, 371–431.

Modigliani, Franco (1975) 'The life cycle hypothesis of saving twenty years later', in M. Parkin (ed.) *Contemporary Issues in Economics*. Manchester University Press, Manchester, 2–36.

Modigliani, Franco and Richard, Blumberg (1954) 'Utility analysis and the consumption function: an interpretation of cross section data', in K. Kurihara (ed.) *Post Keynesian Economics*. Rutgers University Press, New Brunswick, 388–436.

Morgenstern, Oskar (1948) 'Demand theory reconsidered', *Quarterly Journal of Economics* 62: 165–201.

North, Sir Dudley (1691) *Discourses Upon Trade*. Thomas Basset at the George in Fleet Street, London.

Pigou, A. C. (1903) 'Some remarks on utility', *Economic Journal* 13: 58–68.

Pigou, A. C. (1910) 'Producers' and consumers' surplus', *Economic Journal* 20: 358–70.

Pigou, A. C. (1913) 'The interdependence of different sources of demand and supply in a market', *Economic Journal* 23: 19–24.

Pollak, Robert, A. (1970) 'Habit formation and dynamic demand functions', *Journal of Political Economy* 78: 745–63.

Pollak, Robert, A. (1976) 'Interdependent preferences', *American Economic Review* 66: 309–20.

Pollak, Robert, A. (1977) 'Price dependent preferences', *American Economic Review* 67: 64–75.

Pollak, Robert, A. (1978) 'Endogenous tastes in demand and welfare analysis', *American Economic Review* 68: 347–79.

Rae, John [1834] (1965) *Statement of Some New Principles on the Subject of Political Economy, Exposing the Fallacies of the System of Free Trade and of Some Other Doctrines maintained in the "Wealth of Nations"*, R. Warren James (ed.). Toronto: University of Toronto Press.

Roscher, Wilhelm [1854] (1878) *Principles of Political Economy*, trans. J.J. Lalor, New York: Henry Holt & Co.

Samuelson, Paul (1938) 'A note on the pure theory of consumer's behaviour', *Economica* 5: 61–71.

Samuelson, Paul (1947) *Foundations of Economic Analysis*, Oxford University Press, Oxford.

Schumpeter, Joseph (1909) 'On the concept of social value', *Quarterly Journal of Economics* 23: 213–32.

Senior, Nassau, W. [1836] (1863) *Outline of the Science of Political Economy*. Charles Griffin & Co., London.

Smith, Adam [1759] (1976) *Theory of Moral Sentiments*, D.D. Raphael and A.L. Macfie (eds). Clarendon Press, Oxford.

Smith, Adam [1776] (1976) *An Inquiry into the Nature and Causes of the Wealth of Nations*. R. H. Campbell and A.S. Skinner (eds). Clarendon Press, Oxford.

Solomon, Michael, R. and Buchanan, B. (1991) 'A role-theoretic approach to product symbolism: mapping a consumption constellation', *Journal of Business Research* 22: 95–109.

Stigler, George (1950) 'The development of utility theory', *Journal of Political Economy* 58 August & October. Reprinted in *Essays in the History of Economics*. University of Chicago Press, Chicago, 1965, 66–155.

Stigler, George and Gary, S. Becker (1977) 'De gustibus non est disputandum', *American Economic Review* 67: 76–90.

Veblen, Thorstein (1898) 'Why is economics not an evolutionary science?', *Quarterly Journal of Economics* 12: 373–97.

Veblen, Thorstein (1899a) 'The preconceptions of economic science I', *Quarterly Journal of Economics* 13: 121–50.

Veblen, Thorstein (1899b) 'The preconceptions of economic science II', *Quarterly Journal of Economics* 13: 396–426.

Veblen, Thorstein [1899c] (1957) *The Theory of the Leisure Class*, George Allen & Unwin, London.

Veblen, Thorstein (1900) 'The preconceptions of economic science III', *Quarterly Journal of Economics* 14: 240–69.

Veblen, Thorstein (1909) 'The limitations of marginal utility', *Journal of Political Economy* 17: 151–75.

7

THE ECONOMICS OF CRIMINAL PARTICIPATION

Radical subjectivist and
intersubjectivist critiques

Peter Wynarczyk

1. Introduction

This essay provides a critical examination of the economic approach to criminal participation embedded within the orthodox core of Chicago economics. Many of the key features of the economics of criminal participation are a reflection of its parent mainstream research tradition, including a narrow and mechanical model of *homo economicus* and rational choice largely removed from any societal context. Their shared assumptions of stable, fully-formed and independent preferences, along with ethical neutrality, results in the neglect of such factors as endogenous preferences, values and morality. Within such frameworks the notion of 'economic man' is seen as all encompassing with opportunistic rather than human action, detached from, and often disregarding of others. Such economic agents are presented as not only over-individualised but also under-socialised. This permits intersubjective distance to be established between agents and serves to reduce both the degree of potential connectedness and any gains from 'regarding of others' type co-operative strategies. In addition, the economics of criminal participation follows Chicago orthodoxy in neglecting the temporal and non-price dimensions of behaviour. Economic action is not only removed from (interpersonal) space but also (historical) time. This removes any threat of lock-in or costly errors from choosing which cannot be easily undone. Further, the Chicago focus upon price results in either the neglect of non-price entry barriers into crime or their incorporation under the guise of a price. Law establishes a set of prices (or penalties) which influence conduct; agents respond to these legal signals by engaging in crime when the net benefits from such activity outweigh those to be earned in the legal arena. We are all seen to be equally susceptible to criminal participation if the price is right and crime is presented as normal and not unlike work. Explanatory attention is directed at the role of changing constraints rather than changing preferences, with the key elements of rational choice – the preference, utility maximisation, and constraint hypotheses – serving to reinforce the emphasis upon changing external situational constraints (rewards and punishments) and supporting the economist's deterrence model of crime.

Although the economics of criminal participation has displayed both theoretical refinement and empirical success in its short history, it is difficult to deny that it remains decidedly over-simplified and increasingly conceptually jaded. In addition, its correspondence with reality is increasingly found wanting. Not only has there been a continued failure to *fully* account for such phenomena as the growth of crime experienced in the UK and elsewhere during the post-war period (mid-1950s to early 1990s), but further, there is an inability to explain why far more people are not engaged in criminal activity than currently, even though it would materially benefit them to do so. It neither can tell us why we have had so much crime recently nor why we should not be currently experiencing much more.

Given these problems of orthodoxy, and the methodological and ontological elements which underpin them, it may be appropriate to explore alternative perspectives drawn from within economics which contrast starkly with the mainstream model of criminal participation, outlined above, and in greater detail below (Section 2), in order to move toward a conceptually richer model of human agency that engages, rather than ignores, the temporal and interpersonal dimensions to behaviour. To that end, it will be argued that the economics of criminal participation provides an especially interesting window from which to view the contributions of radical subjectivists and intersubjectivists given their respective concerns with human action in historical time and the social dimensions of choosing and of recognition of mutual interests. The essay will broadly survey the radical subjectivist and intersubjectivist literature (Section 3) in order to highlight the shortcomings of orthodoxy and strengths of these alternatives.[1] What both radical subjectivists and intersubjectivist approaches offer is a model of human choice embedded within a historical and relational situation where potential susceptibility to criminal activity is neither equally shared by the population nor determined by price alone.

2. The economics of criminal participation: Criminals 'R' Us

2.1 Mapping the intellectual terrain: Locating the economics of criminal participation

The purpose of this section is to briefly locate the economics of criminal participation within its orthodox intellectual setting and then to provide a detailed examination of its key features. Figure 7.1 illustrates the main linkages connecting the specific domain of the economics of criminal participation with general Chicago economics.

The economics of criminal participation is a central element of the economics of crime which, in turn, is a subset of the modern approach to law and economics which applies the assumptions, principles and methodologies of neoclassical theory to the law and its institutions. It is dominated by the application of Chicago micro theory since the modern approach originated there with the founding of the *Journal of Law and Economics* in 1958, and the landmark contributions of Coase, Posner, and Becker, amongst others.[2] This Chicago brand of law and economics has largely taken precedence 'in the academic imagination' (Avio 1999: 511). Such has been the impact of the Chicago research tradition within mainstream economics that a sizeable proportion of Nobel Prizes have been awarded to its key exponents – Coase, Stigler and Becker are recipients who made notable contributions to the new law and economics research tradition. The Chicago research tradition has been remarkably successful in establishing not only the ontological and methodological guidelines for this particular field, but, increasingly, for economics as a whole.

Law is presented as a 'giant pricing machine' where legal sanctions or penalties are nothing more than an official method of pricing conduct.[3] It is a device for reallocating losses between contesting parties by providing an incentive structure to reduce harm and minimise social loss. Becker (1968), in his seminal contribution, viewed his analysis of crime as 'a generalization of the economists' analysis of external harm or diseconomies' and endeavoured to demonstrate that 'optimal policies to combat illegal behaviour are part of an optimal allocation of resources'.

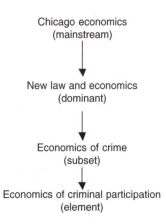

Figure 7.1 Main linkages connecting the specific domain of the economics of criminal participation with general Chicago economics.

The economics of crime perspective owes much to the Chicago-inspired work of Becker (1968) and Ehrlich (1973). Its main concerns are directed towards providing: (1) a rationale for criminal participation at the individual and aggregate level (the supply of offences); (2) policies to minimise the social losses from such activity; and (3) evaluations of the effectiveness of law enforcement agencies in combating crime. The present essay is primarily concerned with the matter of criminal participation, its conventional economic rationalisation in the literature, and radical subjectivist and intersubjectivist critiques.

2.2 Detailing the intellectual terrain: The key features of the economics of criminal participation

The economics of criminal participation utilises the time-allocation models of Becker and Ehrlich in order to characterise criminal actions as purposeful activity influenced by rewards and punishments. Becker (1968: 207) argued that 'entry into illegal activities can be explained by the same model of choice that economists use to explain entry into legal activities'; a point echoed in Ehrlich's (1973: 559) statement that 'offenders, as a group, respond to incentives in much the same way that those who engage in strictly legitimate activities do as a group'. More directly, such formulations largely ignore the moral dimension by implying that theft is a normal activity unconstrained by ethical considerations. Block and Heineke (1975) pointed to the presumed state of moral detachment with regard to the work-theft decision in the orthodox literature. They discuss *ethically neutral* individuals who find legal and illegal activity equally distasteful as work and 'probably most adequately represent the caricature of economic man' (1975: 322, n32). As Pyle (1995: 21, n1) has more recently acknowledged, 'Becker's formulation of the problem facing the individual ignores any moral qualms he or she might have about such activity'.

The general tenor of the argument is underpinned by the notion of the reasoning/calculating criminal who adopts the same cognitive strategies as are presumed for the rest of us when making decisions, namely rational choice based upon anticipated costs and benefits (see Cornish and Clarke 1986). To use a phrase I have coined elsewhere (see Wynarczyk 1993 and 1994–5) *criminals are us*; with an emphasis placed upon the similarities, rather than the differences, between individuals. The economics of crime tradition echoes the classical criminology of Beccaria and Bentham and was taken by Becker as representing the 'resurrection', 'modernization' and improvement of those pioneers.

The rational choice framework consists of three key assumptions: (1) the preference hypothesis; (2) the constraint hypothesis; and (3) the utility maximization hypothesis which serve to formalise a model of economic behaviour detached from any external context (apart from the necessary givens). It is a one-dimensional representation of human action that is far removed from the Scottish Enlightenment vision of Adam Smith and others.[4] The modern approach provides a thin concept of rationality exclusively identified with behaviour that maximizes the satisfaction of given preferences under given constraints. It will be argued that this concept of rational choice needs to be broadened out to allow us to look beyond, behind or beneath the givens. In particular, we need to take the problems of embeddedness and connectedness seriously. Individual action and choice take place within a given social context where such elements as personal biography and institutional structures play central roles in enabling or constraining purposeful behaviour.

Rational choice approaches have constantly been challenged throughout their history. Economic rationality is an elaboration and sophistication of Bentham's position that individuals are pleasure/pain calculators with its consequent conclusion that human life can be reduced to mere technical calculation. Hazlitt (1970), in his sparkling essay on Bentham, written one hundred and seventy years ago, set the tone in criticising an approach which reduced man to too logical a creature, enormously over-estimated the power of reason, and neglected the passions. For him, criminals were clearly not us but rather'a set of desperadoes, governed only by their passions'. Hazlitt believed, unlike Bentham and the modern Chicago crime tradition's formalisation of his approach, that we are *not* all equally susceptible to engagement in criminal activity. The truly telling point against Bentham (and the economic approach to criminal participation) remains the one raised four decades ago by Geis (1960: 57) who stated 'The problem of why certain persons pursue criminal patterns in their quest of happiness while others do not is not considered deeply by Bentham'.

Becker's economic approach to human behaviour combines the three assumptions of 'maximizing behaviour, market equilibrium, and stable preferences' (1976) and extends this model of *homo economicus* into other realms of human (and non-human behaviour). Such an approach has displayed both conceptual and empirical progress. Becker (1993: 402–3) has argued that the rational choice perspective offers both greater generality than its rivals and the potentiality for a unified approach to the social sciences. Of course, what undoubtedly helps to give this approach an imperialist thrust is the presentation of the allocation of time as a *timeless* fundamental economic problem and constraint (see Becker 1965).

When this economic approach is applied to criminal participation, attention is focused upon anticipated subjective costs and benefits or expected punishments and rewards. Legal sanctions are often viewed as the price for doing what is forbidden. They are the price of an offence captured in Becker's reference (1968: 195, n45) to a cartoon showing a police car carrying a sign which reads 'Speed limit 30 mph – $5 fine every mile over speed limit – pick out speed you can afford'. This focusing upon price is characteristic of Chicago and neoclassical economics in general. The orthodox approach to the economics of criminal participation maintains that we are all *potential* criminals – in the sense that it is simply a matter of price or the size of the indecent proposal. Cameron (1989: 32–3) succinctly argued that 'Anyone will, in this model, become a criminal if the price is right; if the prices cease to be right, people will cease being criminals'. This is because 'all individuals have ex ante criminal intentions' that may be transformed into 'ex post criminal acts' if the benefits of such action out-weigh the costs (leaving to one side the issue of attitudes to risk). This approach, by dwelling upon *homo economicus*, appears to either: (1) ignore what may be termed non-price entry barriers into crime, given the ten-dency within the literature to largely distance itself from any incorpora-tion of the moral dimension and other defined non-economic content or explanation within the analysis; or (2) maintain that the price variable cap-tures these, with its presumption that the more moral the person, *ceteris paribus*, the higher the entry price per given crime.

Regarding the first point, as Sen (1987) showed, modern economics has evolved by 'characterising human motivation in such spectacularly nar-row terms' that its neglect of the ethical dimension has served to impov-erish, rather than enrich, the analysis by its fixation on economic self-interest as the single ultimate human drive swamping all others. Actual human behaviour is far more complex and rich, being often guided or affected by moral and other non-economic considerations. The purely *homo economicus* fiction is sustained by its presentation of the indi-vidual as largely detached from, and disregarding of, all others. The inter-subjectivist challenge is largely devoted to undermining this central element of mainstream economics by emphasising the social dimensions of choice and recognition of mutual interests. With regard to the second point, Hausman and McPherson (1993: 685, n21) make reference to an anecdote about someone who attempted to bribe honest Abe Lincoln: 'Lincoln kept brushing him off genially and the briber kept increasing his price. When the price got very high, Lincoln clouted him. When asked why he suddenly got so aggressive, Lincoln responded – because you were getting close to my price!' There is a neglect of what Wilson (1985), and more recently Fukuyama (1995), have referred to as character and virtue, which leaves the economic model incomplete. Much of the failing of the conventional approach resides in its apparent inability to ade-quately recognise or make explicit the non-price elements that enter into human action.[5] There appears to be a refusal to address the moral issue directly and explicitly. As Ben-Ner and Putterman (2000) have recently made clear, economics remains largely unappreciative of human values other than the pursuit of self-interest.[6]

The real issue appears to relate to preferences and what underpins them – both economists and sociologists, at the intellectual margins and beyond, are increasingly aware of this. Coleman (1994: 178, n9) has correctly conceded that 'the real lacuna in rational choice theory lies... in explaining the origins of preferences'. Morality takes its place within an extended, richer and deepened preference structure generally rejected by an unsophisticated orthodoxy. There is a need to explore what Hirschman terms our metapreferences (i.e. our preferences for preferences), or to consider, as Sen (1979) has argued, the *rankings of preference rankings* to express our moral judgements'. Such deliberations take us beyond the over-simplified wanton preferences of conventional economic theory. Economists are extremely uncomfortable with focusing too much on preferences per se let alone delving behind them. When mainstream economists direct their attention to explanations of changes in behaviour they are primarily interested in constraints rather than preferences. It is usually assumed that such change has been induced by constraints and not preferences, given that the latter are presented as inherently stable and uniform. As Becker and Stigler (1977: 76) famously maintain, 'one may usefully treat tastes as stable over time and similar among people'. Becker (1976: 133) has also argued that 'no useful theory of the formation of tastes' is available in the social sciences. In stark contrast, traditional sociology displays greater partiality towards explanation via preferences rather than constraints (see Opp 1985: 234–6). It has been recognised by Vanberg (1994: 45–6) that orthodox economics has to make a choice – either completely reject the inclusion of the moral dimension or 'set aside the methodological objections against explanations in terms of preferences' – and that it generally follows Becker in explaining behaviour 'exclusively in terms of (income and price) constraints'. Coleman (1994: 168) appears aware of such limitations when he states that 'rational choice theory cannot explain individual breakdowns, or even change in preferences, but can explain system breakdown or change'. However, more economists are coming out in favour of taking preferences seriously. For instance, Peacock (1999) has recently conceded that more careful attention needs to be directed at preference formation and preference change *within* orthodoxy. This echoes the earlier argument of Aaron (1994) that economists need to surrender their predisposition toward treating 'values, habits, and social norms as given and beyond analysis and the reach of public policy'. We may find that attending to metapreferences may resolve the dilemma in the future by forming the bridge connecting conventional constraints and preferences.

The economics of criminal participation offers another alternative to the morality exclusion model outlined above which attempts to remove the degree of epistemic threat by reducing the moral dimension to a price. Several authors have recently suggested that morality acts as an entry barrier into criminal activity. They tend to take the view that incorporation of the moral dimension into the economic model is relatively straightforward – it affects the reservation wage for criminal work. Ehrlich (1996: 47) has argued that people's ethical values, or 'distaste for crime' will help set a threshold inhibiting entry into crime so that 'the net payoff must exceed some threshold level before an individual decides to engage in crime'. Likewise, Phillips (1993: 39) makes a similar point when he states that 'The reservation wage is a threshold affected by tastes and values. Hence, moral suasion may lead to a very high threshold, or reservation wage, for participating in an effort to obtain illegal gains'. The implication of this approach is that the more moral the person, *ceteris paribus*, the higher the net returns required from criminal participation in order to compensate for the loss of innocence and reputation, increased guilt, shame, etc. In addition, it suggests that the level of crime prevailing in society will be partly affected by moral standards and the current state of social capital, since changes in these factors will affect the crime reservation wage (with decline and depreciation of the former leading to a lowering of the latter). By introducing the moral element under the guise of price this approach to criminal participation suggests that people are honest only to the extent that they do not have economic incentives for being otherwise and that failure to engage in crime is merely a reflection of inadequate illegitimate returns. As Sen (1979: 99) neatly stated, orthodox economics maintains that 'people are honest only to the extent that they have economic incentives for being so'. Subsuming the moral dimension under the umbrella of price may appear logical and relatively easy from an economic perspective which emphasises price and income constraints but such a strategy could pose serious problems.

Taking entry and exit into crime seriously, as Cameron (1989) argues, means taking endogeneity of tastes and preferences seriously and leads to an examination of the learning process within a historical sequence rather than the naive static subjectivism of the orthodox approach with its presumed *a*temporal symmetry between entry and exit (and the consequent regaining of lost innocence). In addition, any meaningful discussion of social capital has to be placed within a given time–place framework which is path-dependent and hence makes manifest the inherent temporal weaknesses of mainstream economics. The reduction of morality to a price constraint means that all economic agents are assumed to consider the expected benefits and costs of each possible course of action including, where appropriate, selling their soul. As Vanberg (1994: 51–6) suggests, it may be rational for economic agents to adopt the strategy of 'a moral or co-operative *routine*' or habit whereby illegal options are *renounced* (even when they may result in specific optimal outcomes) on the understanding that acceptance of a shared morality limits choices which benefit all parties (by leading to a more efficient pattern of outcomes) over a prolonged period of time.

3. Radical subjectivist and intersubjectivist departures

There is a need to move beyond *homo economicus* and the failure to address social non-price barriers to crime. Agents, for very good reason, may place personal constraints on their own behaviour or accept societal constraints which prevent maximisation and incur economic costs. There is a need to take a wider view of the choice procedure to *include* 'one's commitments to values, one's beliefs, and one's desires' (Evensky 1992b: 31) and to recognise that these are 'shaped by social and personal contexts' (Shover and Honaker 1992: 291). Biography and background impact upon the choice decision and the opportunities that arise and are taken up. Choices are not made in isolation, removed from (historical) time or (interpersonal) space. As Ben-Ner and Putterman (2000: 40) make clear, values matter, and the *homo economicus* abstraction of orthodoxy is rejected for assuming 'away any possibility for social preferences, since it posits that people value their own consumption and leisure, and nothing else'.

3.1 (Austrian) radical subjectivist perceptions

On the radical subjectivist and intersubjectivist front, the Austrians provide a good starting point from which to challenge the Chicago model of economic behaviour. The Austrian position provides a middle-ground which rejects both the idea of the individual as a completely independent entity or as an agent who has no meaningful or purposeful choices to make. Mises' (1949) notion of *human action* serves to capture the essence of this Austrian fundamental by recognising the human element in the equation alongside that of action which matters and has the potentiality to make a difference, given it is not entirely predetermined. He took great pains to emphasise the fact that men are not only social beings and the products of given situational contexts but also the prime movers of change (see, for instance, Mises 1958: 159–160; 326). Mises was ahead of his time in recognising the link between the endogeneity of preferences and the social nature of man when he stated (1958: 22) that 'The immense majority of people take their valuations from the social environment into which they were born, in which they grew up, that moulded their personality and educated them'.[7] Steedman (1989) provided an early examination and illuminating discussion of intrinsically non-autonomous preferences and beliefs which gives due recognition of Mises' contribution. More recently, Bowles (1998), appears, somewhat unwittingly, to echo Mises in arguing that economists should surrender their axiom of exogenous preferences and the *homo economicus* fiction for a more realistic and conceptually rich model of human agency with tastes, preferences, values and commitments determined endogenously through processes of social interaction. This has consequences for both radical subjectivism and intersubjectivism.

A number of subjectivist-based criticisms can be levelled against the Chicago model in general and its application to criminal behaviour in particular. These would include the following elements: its failure to take subjectivism seriously; its neglect of historical time and path dependency; its overly end-state orientation based upon equilibrium rather than process; the doctrine of utilitarianism, and end-goal welfarist position which pervades its policy conclusions. Schmidtchen (1993) argues for incorporation of Austrian insights related to time, uncertainty, and subjectivism into the main body of law and economics. The Chicago approach is criticised for lacking any 'underlying concept of time' given its emphasis upon equilibrium (both partial and general), for failing to treat the law as sufficiently endogenous – with agents as lawmakers rather than law takers, for displaying 'an objectivist bias' at the core of its model of human agency (further bolstering equilibrium forces) by presuming that subjectivist beliefs and probabilities will match objectivist ones.

Cameron (1989) too makes a number of subjectivist points against the Chicago-inspired economics of crime that reflect genuinely Austrian concerns. The orthodox approach to the economics of crime is presented as 'methodologically misguided' on a number of serious counts; it embraces a general equilibrium model paying 'lip service' to the notion of subjective expectations by failing to take or measure agents' subjective expectations seriously and casting them in too objective and 'restrictively static' light. Much is seen to depend upon the orthodox commitment to a rational expectations framework which neglects where individuals, especially those who are considering being criminally active for the first time, get their expectations from. It ignores the formation of 'pre-crime expectations' and the irreversible distinction between such expectations and those learned from engaging in criminal activity, alongside neglect of the actual location of agents within the crime process and its particular networks. Such concerns echo Austrian concerns with regard to rational expectations. As I have recently argued elsewhere (Wynarczyk 1999), the Austrians reject the rational expectations, equilibrium-always framework in favour of a reasonable expectations perspective whereby individuals make best use of information subject to the various constraints of time, place and resources. They criticise the rational expectations approach for assuming that the subjective probabilities of economic agents match the objective probabilities without any recognition of the existence of differentiated, individual, personalised knowledge-information sets, and the problems posed by genuine uncertainty on expectations formation and correspondence. Rational expectations theorists are also guilty of conflating theoretical and entrepreneurial knowledge; of failing to distinguish between knowledge *of* and knowledge *within* by not separating the economist's knowledge from that of the economic agent. They assume that agents' subjective beliefs match the underlying objective reality, that such agents know and share the appropriate (true) economic model and apply it in the most proficient way, allowing equilibrium forces to be quickly re-established following any disturbances. The methodological and ontological underpinnings of the Chicago research tradition, and its reflection in the economics of crime subset in particular, cannot handle creative entrepreneurial endeavour in a non-ergodic (transmutable) reality whether in the legitimate or illegitimate arenas. This is a major weakness that prevents the orthodox literature of economics of crime from even addressing the simplest of entrepreneurial elements – criminal innovation as rule-breaking. Two of the great strengths of the Misesian brand of Austrian economics are its recognition of human action as purposeful activity, directed at making a difference by changing outcomes, alongside its extension of the creative and entrepreneurial element to all economic agents. As Simmel (1971: 4) so aptly put it 'Man, as something known, is made by nature and history; but man, as knower, makes nature and history'.

3.2 Intersubjectivist insights

Intersubjectivity pervades the economics of crime literature but remains largely unacknowledged by orthodoxy. As Fullbrook (1998: 726) makes clear, the intersubjectivists are engaged in recasting or reconceptualising *homo economicus* in order to highlight 'the view that consciousness is a *relation* which some forms of beings (e.g. human beings) have to other beings'. In addition to this concept of interdependency between individuals, the notion of human action directing behaviour comes very close to the Austrian, especially Misesian, argument that it is by necessity a disequilibrium phenomena since 'the incentive that impels a man to act is always some uneasiness' (Mises 1949: 13) or sense of lacking, as intersubjectivists would contend. The praxeological approach of Mises not only dismissed the alleged rationality of the Benthamite calculus but also the hedonism which motivated it. The purpose of action is not just the pursuit of happiness or material welfare but the goal of improvement, however defined, as perceived by the individual actor. Mises (1958) referred to the 'ceaseless striving to improve conditions' and the urge to remove uneasiness.

Swedberg (1994: 263) has suggested that game theory has played a key role in introducing intersubjectivity into mainstream economics 'by proposing a type of analysis in which each actor takes the decisions of the other actors into account'. Such a definition broadens the impact of intersubjectivity beyond mere demand, price and quantity issues alone and is particularly of interest in the area of law and economics. This has been recognised recently by Avio (1999: 520), who has perceptively suggested that 'An application of the intersubjective domain would seem particularly promising for law and morality, institutions which would be expected to have an intersubjective basis for their success insofar as that success depends upon the convergence of mutual behavioural expectations'. The desire for law and order and appropriate conduct depends upon whether others desire the same. Cooter has acknowledged the significance of game theory for the formal analysis of social norms and argued that an agent's informal enforcement of social norms depends upon reciprocal enforcement by others and the state; widespread commitment to social norms, reinforced by state enforcement, is seen as the greatest safeguard for law and order since 'successful state enforcement typically requires a close alignment of law with morality, so state officials enjoy informal support from private persons' (Cooter 2000). Likewise, Ormerod (1998: 28–46) has maintained, contrary to the conventional approach to the economics of crime, that agents are not only *not equally susceptible to crime* but that actual participation in crime depends upon the influence of social interaction; with a more law-abiding population likely to have less entrants into criminal activity than one where norms are eroding. An earlier contribution, but in similar vein, by Akerlof and Yellen (1993), showed how criminal participation was part of a *social* process, strongly influenced by community attitudes.

Economists are beginning to play closer attention to the matter of social norms. They are following the lead of the likes of James Coleman in applying a variant of the rational choice apparatus to the emergence of social norms as an internalised solution to an externality problem (see Frank 1992). In a similar vein Buchanan, (1991; 1994) has explored the economic origins of ethical constraints as not only self-imposed, singly or in concert with others, but also largely as a result of a desire to set constraints on the behaviour of others. Ethical norms are seen to provide important public domain benefits 'facilitating the achievement of mutually desired outcomes of social interaction' in situations where such behaviours are not directly tradeable. Such a view is based upon recognition of the interdependency between agents that lies beyond the traditional boundaries of economics and politics. Given that our economic wellbeing is seen to depend upon the behaviour of others it would be appropriate to support those social norms which serve to constrain behaviours which are opportunistic and disregarding of others. Buchanan is led to these conclusions by moving beyond the fixed, fully-blown, independent and dogmatic, preference postulate of mainstream economics.

Co-operative behaviour and 'regarding of others' type strategies which are widely shared within a community can generate outcomes which benefit all parties' interests even where there are short-run opportunity gains from breaking conventions. As Akerlof (1983) has shown, in his examination of 'value-changing experiences' where values are not fixed but a matter of choice, unlike in orthodox economics, 'honesty and co-operative behaviour pay off' in the long-run. *Even if they did not, there is always the likelihood that social beings get a 'taste' for moral behaviour which becomes its own reward (rather than a cost as in orthodoxy).* Human action often entails pursuing norms, underpinned by internal constraints, which incur economic opportunity costs under situations where the external sanctions, on their own, would fail to provide a credible threat. As Buchanan (1994: 63) states, 'Many of us do not steal, even if we should be certain that there is no possibility of discovery, apprehension, and punishment'. Frank's (1987) limited departure from the economist's standard application of rational choice, following his taking endogeneously determined tastes seriously, results in a model of *homo economicus* with a conscience. This recognises that 'people will often refrain from cheating not because they fear being caught, but because cheating simply makes them feel bad'. Conscience, preferences, commitments, beliefs, and values are all seen to have a powerful impact upon the choices that agents make (as do emotions, see Elster 1998). As Brennan (1996) and Rowthorn (1996) both suggest, orthodox economists need to more directly confront these matters and not seek to ignore or 'minimise' them or explain them away as simply manifestations of individual long-term self-interest.

4. Final reflections

The moral dimension impinges upon human behaviour, influences economic outcomes, and has implications for public policy. It is especially appropriate with regard to criminal participation. Field (1990: 35) recognised that 'The weakness of the pure economic theory of crime is that there are clearly many circumstances when people do not commit crimes which would materially benefit them'. People often sacrifice apparent material advantages by doing the right thing. This is a point constantly made in the socio-economic literature. Increasing attention is being focused upon the endogeneity of preferences and the need to go below the veneer of the wanton preferences of orthodoxy to an analysis of metapreferences, those values which underlie individual tastes (see Elster 1979: 77–86). This is a clear attack upon the orthodox citadel which discounts differences and changes in tastes (seen at best as reducible to differences in price constraints) – *de gustibus non est disputandum* (there is no arguing about tastes since they are postulated as stable and uniform) – this being the title of the famous paper by Becker and Stigler (1977) which reinforced the mainstream position on preferences and tastes as given and beyond analysis. Hirschman (1984) suggests replacing it with *de valoribus est disputandum* (the need to discuss differences and changes in values). There is a need to recognise that human behaviour is guided by more than price and income constraints. Biography and background matter, as they influence values and other metapreferences. Constitutional political economy has recognised that there are choices to be made about constraints and the fact that ethics serves to capture those explicitly non-tradeable or non-contractual elements located beyond market and political processes. People may voluntarily constrain their options, like Ulysses and the Sirens. There are basically two constraints on behaviour – internal and external. The economics of crime has concentrated on the latter and ignored the former. The external constraint is captured by legal sanctions whilst the internal sanction represents conscience or moral standards (Bidinotto 1995: 371–2). The middle ground of radical subjectivism and intersubjectivism recognises their interplay.

The orthodox economic argument in taking tastes as given is left with the single policy tool of price (legal sanctions) and it misses the opportunity to consider policy action directed at changing values. The growth in crime in the UK is more fully understandable in terms of both a decline in deterrence and a weakening of morality and social norms.[8] They have reinforced each other by lowering the price and non-price barriers into crime. The decline in deterrence appears less contestable than the alleged weakening of morality and the erosion of social norms. Across the political spectrum, however, attention is being increasingly focused, whether by ethical socialists or cultural conservatives, upon the dangers posed by an increasingly *individualising society*.[9] A renewed emphasis is being placed upon family, community, and active citizenship and its key attributes.[10] We appear to be witnessing an increasing moral deficit, especially among young males – who are most likely to engage in crime. The economics of crime literature with its emphasis upon 'criminals are us' similarities cannot adequately account for the gender and age differences in criminal participation rates or the wider role of biography and background in choice.

Policy needs to be directed toward both deterrence and the fortification of the social and moral rejection of crime. It is, however, much more difficult to change values in the short-run than legal sanctions. Although it has long been realised that there is something of a trade-off between legal sanctions and morality, the relationship may be seen as symbiotic. This trade-off was recognised by Edmund Burke when he argued that 'Society cannot exist unless a controlling power upon will and appetite be placed somewhere, and the less of it there is within, the more there must be without' (cited in Vanberg 1994: 41). The symbiotic relationship has recently been captured by Rowthorn's comment (1996: 22) that 'Morality can be seen as a kind of social capital, which requires the right combination of sanctions and personal autonomy to preserve it and help it grow'. As Vanberg (1994) rightly noted, the viability of morality as an efficient strategy depends upon the social enforcement of legal sanctions against rule violators. It is essential that legal sanctions have both credibility and legitimation. To its detriment, the orthodox approach to criminal participation has ignored this interplay between external and internal sanctions by largely neglecting the latter and remaining essentially blind to the role of non-price factors in explanations of human behaviour. Such failings can be overcome if the criticisms of the radical subjectivists and intersubjectivists are taken seriously by orthodox economics and there is a greater willingness to engage with ideas emanating from outside the neoclassical Chicago core.

Notes

1 This should not be taken as to deny the existence of other alternative perspectives from within economics or without; see Schmidtchen (1993) and Ellickson (1989).
2 For a detailed discussion see Medema (1997; 1998), Veljanovski (1990), and Hovenkamp (1995).
3 See, for instance, Posner (1992) and Cooter (1984). Rather revealingly, a key architect of the economics of criminal participation, Ehrlich (1977), has a section entitled 'deterrence variables as prices'.
4 The recent work of Evensky (1992a,b and 1993) has highlighted the alien nature of *homo economicus* for Smith: the invisible hand mechanism is premised on the assumption of ethical individuals thereby attached to the external world.
5 The problem posed by morality appears to be disposed of by assuming that such complications can be largely ignored on the grounds that they are of negligible influence, making no appreciable difference to the analysis, or remain stable and equally distributed in the population.
6 One remains somewhat sceptical of Peacock's (1999) recent suggestion that the moral dimension has been either 'sufficiently' recognised by economists or can *easily* be incorporated into the orthodox economic model.
7 A point conceded by Becker (1992: 336) without adequate consideration of its ramifications for the research tradition to which he belongs and has shaped.
8 Murray (1997) has recently reminded us that it became *both* much safer *and* more acceptable to participate in crime in Britain post 1955.
9 See the interesting work of that name by Ester, Halman and De Moor (eds) 1994.
10 It is perhaps surprising that Becker did not link together sufficiently his contributions on the economics of crime and of the family (see his 1981) and thereby directly address the issue of dysfunctional families and their impact on crime.

References

Aaron, H. J. (1994) 'Public Policy, Values, and Consciousness', *Journal of Economic Perspectives*, 8, 3: 3–21.
Akerlof, G. A. and Yellen, J. L. (1993) 'Gang Behaviour, Law Enforcement, and Community Values', Aaron, H. J., Mann, T. E. and Taylor, T. (eds) *Value and Public Policy*, Washington DC: Brookings Institution.
Akerlof, G. A. (1983) 'Loyalty Filters', *American Economic Review*, 73, 1: 54–63.
Avio, K. L. (1999) 'Habermasian Ethics and Institutional Law and Economics', *Kyklos*, 52, 4: 511–35.
Becker, G. S. (1965) 'A Theory of the Allocation of Time', *Economic Journal*, 75: 493–517.
Becker, G. S. (1968) 'Crime and Punishment: An Economic Approach', *Journal of Political Economy*, 74, 2: 169–217.

Becker, G. S. (1976) *The Economic Approach to Human Behaviour*, Chicago: University of Chicago Press.

Becker, G. S. (1981) *A Treatise on the Family*, London: Harvard University Press.

Becker, G. S. (1992) 'Habits, Addictions and Traditions', *Kyklos*, 45, 3: 327–46.

Becker, G. S. (1993) 'Nobel Lecture: The Economic Way of Looking at Behaviour', *Journal of Political Economy*, 101, 3: 385–409.

Becker, G. S. and Stigler, G. J. (1977) 'De Gustibus Non Est Disputandum', *American Economic Review*, 67, 2: 75–90.

Ben-Ner, A. and Putterman, L. (2000) 'Values matter', *World Economics*, 1, 1: 39–60.

Bidinotto, J. (1995) 'The "Root Causes" of Crime', *The Freeman*, 45, 6: 371–2.

Block, M. K. and Heineke, J. M. (1975) 'A labor Theoretic Analysis of the Criminal Choice', *American Economic Review*, 65, 3: 314–25.

Bowles, S. (1998) 'Endogenous Preferences: The Cultural Consequences of Markets and other Economic Institutions', *Journal of Economic Literature*, XXXVI: 75–111.

Brennan, G. (1996) 'The Economist's Approach to Ethics, A Late Twentieth Century View', in P. Groenewegen (ed.) *Economics and Ethics?*, London: Routledge.

Buchanan, J. M. (1991) *The Economics and the Ethics of Constitutional Order*, Michigan: University of Michigan Press.

Buchanan, J. M. (1994) 'We Should All Pay the Preacher: Economic Origins of Ethical Constraints', in J. M. Buchanan (ed.) *Ethics and Economic Progress*, Norman: University of Oklahoma Press.

Cameron, S. (1989) 'A Subjectivist Perspective on the Economics of Crime', in M. N. Rothbard and W. Block (ed.) *The Review of Austrian Economics*, Massachusetts: Lexington Books.

Coleman, J. S. (1994) 'A Rational Choice Perspective on Economic Sociology', in N. J. Smelser and R. Swedberg (eds) *The Handbook of Economic Sociology*, Princeton: Princeton University Press.

Cooter, R. D. (1984) 'Prices and Sanctions', *Columbia Law Review*.

Cooter, R. D. (2000) 'Law from Order: Economic Development and the Jurisprudence of Social Norms', in M. Olson and K. Kahkonen (eds) *A Not-So-Dismal Science*, Oxford: Oxford University Press.

Cornish, D. B. and Clarke, R. V. (eds) (1986) *The Reasoning Criminal*, New York: Springer-Verlag.

Ehrlich, I. (1973) 'Participation in Illegitimate Activities: A Theoretical and Empirical Investigation', *Journal of Political Economy*, 81, 3: 521–65.

Ehrlich, I. (1977) 'Capital Punishment and Deterrence: Some Further Thoughts and Additional Evidence', *Journal of Political Economy*, 85, 4: 741–88.

Ehrlich, I. (1996) 'Crime, Punishment, and the Market for Offences', *Journal of Economic Perspectives*, 10, 1: 43–67.

Ellickson, R. C. (1989) 'Bringing Culture and Human Frailty to Rational Actors: A Critique of Classical Law-and-Economics', *Chicago-Kent Law Review*, 65, 23–55.

Elster, J. (1979) *Ullysses and the Sirens*, London: Cambridge University Press.

Elster, J. (1998) 'Emotions and Economic Theory', *Journal of Economic Literature*, XXXVI: 47–74.

Ester, P., Halman, L. and De Moor (eds) (1994) *The Individualizing Society*, Tilburg: Tilburg University Press.

Evensky, J. (1992a) 'Ethics and the Classical Liberal Tradition in economics', *History of Political Economy*, 24, 1: 61–77.

Evensky, J. (1992b) 'The Role of Community Values in Modern Classical Liberal Economic Thought', *Scottish Journal of Political Economy*, 39, 1: 21–38.

Evensky, J. (1993) 'Adam Smith on the Human Foundation of a Successful Liberal Society', *History of Political Economy*, 25, 3: 395–412.

Field, S. (1990) *Trends in Crime and their Interpretation*, London: HMSO, Home Office Research Study no. 119.

Frank, R. H. (1987) 'If *Homo Economicus* Could Choose His Own Utility Function, Would He Want One With a Conscience?', *American Economic Review*, 77, 4: 593–607.

Frank, R. H. (1992) 'Melding Sociology and Economics: James Coleman's Foundations of Social Theory,' *Journal of Economic Literature*, XXX: 147–70.

Fukuyama, F. (1995) *Trust: The Social Virtues and the Creation of Prosperity*, London: Hamish Hamilton.

Fullbrook, E. (1998) 'Caroline Foley and the Theory of Intersubjective Demand', *Journal of Economic Issues*, XXXII, 3: 709–31.

Geis, G. (1960) 'Jeremy Bentham', in H. Mannheim (ed.) *Pioneers in Criminology*, London: Stevens and Sons.

Hausman, D. M. and McPherson, M. S. (1993) 'Taking Ethics Seriously: Economics and Contemporary Moral Philosophy', *Journal of Economic Literature*, XXXI: 671–731.

Hazlitt, W. (1970) *The Spirit of the Age*, London: Oxford University Press.

Hirschman, A. O. (1984) 'Against Parsimony: Three Easy Ways of Complicating Some Categories of Economic Discourse', *American Economic Review*, Papers and Proceedings 74, 2: 89–96.

Hovenkamp, H. (1995) 'Law and Economics in the United States: a brief historical survey', *Cambridge Journal of Economics*, 19, 2: 331–52.

Medema, S. G. (1997) 'The Trial of *Homo Economicus*: What Law and Economics Tells Us about the Development of Economic Imperialism', in J. B. Davis (ed.) *New Economics and Its History*, Durham: Duke University Press.

Medema, S. G. (1998) 'Wandering the Road from Pluralism to Posner: The Transformation of Law and Economics in the Twentieth Century', in M. S. Morgan and M Rutherford (eds) *From Interwar Pluralism to Postwar Neoclassicalism*, Durham: Duke University Press.

Mises von, L. (1949) *Human Action: a treatise on economics*, London: William Hodge.

Mises von, L. (1958) *Theory and History*, London: Jonathan Cape.

Murray, C. (1997) 'Sentenced to a crime wave' (5th January), 'The ruthless truth: prison works', (12th January), 'Loading the scales of justice', *The Sunday Times*.

Ormerod, P. (1998) *Butterfly Economics: A New General Theory of Social and Economic Behaviour*, London: Faber and Faber.

Opp, K. D. (1985) 'Sociology and Economic Man', *Journal of Institutional and Theoretical Economics*, 141, 2: 213–43.

Peacock, A. (1999) 'The Communitarian Attack on Economics', *Kyklos*, 52, 4: 497–510.

Phillips, L. (1993) 'Economic Perspectives on Criminality: An Eclectic View', in B. Forst (ed.) *The Socio-Economics of Crime and Justice*, New York: M. E. Sharpe.

Posner, R. A. (1992) *Economic Analysis of Law*, Boston: Little, Brown.

Pyle, D. J. (1995) *Cutting the Costs of Crime*, London: Institute of Economic Affairs, Hobart Paper 129.

Rowthorn, R. (1996) 'Ethics and Economics, An Economist's View', in P Groenewegen (ed.) *Economics and Ethics?*, London: Routledge.

Ruskin, J. (1985) *Unto This Last and Other Writings*, London: Penguin Books.

Schmidtchen, D. (1993) 'Time, Uncertainty, and Subjectivism: Giving More Body to Law and Economics', *International Review of Law and Economics*, 13: 61–84.

Sen, A. K. (1979) 'Rational Fools: A Critique of the Behavioural Foundations of Economic Theory', in F Hahn and M Hollis (eds) *Philosophy and Economic Theory*, Oxford: Oxford University Press.

Sen, A. K. (1987) *On Ethics and Economics*, Oxford: Basil Blackwell.

Shover, N. and Honaker, D. (1992) 'The Socially Bounded Decision Making of Persistent Property Offenders', *The Howard Journal*, 31, 4: 276–93.

Simmel, G. (1971) 'How is history possible?', in D N Levine (ed.) *On Individuality and Social Forms*, Chicago: University of Chicago Press.

Steedman, I. (1989) 'Economic theory and intrinsically non-autonomous preferences and beliefs', in *From Exploitation to Altruism*, Cambridge: Polity Press.

Swedberg, R. (1994) 'Markets as Social Structures', in N. J. Smelser and R. Swedberg (eds) *The Handbook of Economic Sociology*, Princeton: Princeton University Press.

Vanberg, V. J. (1994) *Rules and choice in economics*, London: Routledge.

Veljanovski, C. (1990) *The Economics of Law – An Introductory Text*, London: Institute of Economic Affairs, Hobart Paper 114.

Wilson, J. Q. (1985) 'The Rediscovery of Character: Private Virtue and Public Policy', *Public Interest*, Fall.

Wynarczyk, P. (1993) 'The Economics of Crime Perspective and Changing Family Structures: Some Preliminary Considerations', *East Midlands Economic Review*, 2, 2, 2: 21–32.

Wynarczyk, P. (1994–5) 'Criminals R Us', *Criminal Justice Matters*, 18: 17–18.

Wynarczyk, P. (1999) 'On Austrian-Post Keynesian Overlap: Just How Far is New York from Knoxville, Tennessee?', *Economic Issues*, 4, 2: 31–48.

8

'EVERYBODY IS TALKING ABOUT IT'

Intersubjectivity and the television industry

Shaun P. Hargreaves Heap

1. Introduction

A recent trailer on the BBC cut from one group of people to another using the now familiar jerky and speedy technique which is designed to capture even the most errant attention. The groups varied. Some were at work, some were at play, some were young, some were black, and so on; and taken together they probably represented a fair cross section of people and social settings. They shared one thing, however. They were all talking about what was happening in *Eastenders*, a BBC soap. The message was clear: if you want a social life, you had better watch *Eastenders*.

The BBC was trading explicitly on something that is well understood by broadcasters. People do not just watch something on television for the enjoyment it gives at the time, they also watch it because it is a conversational resource and conversation is central to social life. This is unsurprising as people like to make sense of their world, and talking to others is one way of doing this. However, as a result, the demand for particular television programmes is, in part, intersubjectively constituted: that is, it depends on a background of shared experiences and understandings which enable such conversations to occur. This in turn, has consequences for the demand for television programmes which is not always recognised. A person's demand for a programme depends positively on the number of other people consuming it.

I focus in the next section on this intersubjective influence because it is a potential source of market failure that has, typically, been overlooked by economists (e.g. see Davies 1999). I use the term market failure here in the usual economists' way to denote a case where the market produces an inefficient outcome in the sense that some rearrangement could produce

123

an improvement in at least some people's welfare without disadvantaging anyone. In Section 3, I consider whether the same intersubjective influence is likely to operate in other industries. I argue that, although demand in many industries similarly depends on the number of other relevant people who are expected to consume the product, the origin of this dependence is different to that found in television (and other media industries). This is important because the source of this dependence can affect whether there are grounds for public concern over the outcomes generated by the market (e.g. whether there is market failure). In other words, the presence of such demand interdependence may be ubiquitous, but it is not necessarily a cause for concern. This conclusion serves to highlight why it is important to develop a better understanding of the various ways in which demand is intersubjectively constituted as one needs to understand why demand is interdependent before one can judge whether such interdependence causes market failure. In Section 4, I return to the case of television where there are grounds for concern and consider what kinds of interventions might be appropriate to this neglected kind of failure.

2. The case of television

The conversational value of a television programme depends on the number of other relevant people who watch the programme for the simple reason that it is difficult to talk with someone about a programme unless they have seen it. So, the greater the number of viewers the larger the number of potential conversations one can have based on that programme. *Ceteris paribus*, this means that the demand for any television programme is likely to depend positively on the number of others wanting to see that programme. Two important effects follow. Demand is liable to get concentrated on a small number of programmes relative to underlying intrinsic preferences for programmes (that is, the preferences that exist independently of the number of other people watching a programme). This is one of the reasons why media markets, like television, have winner-take-all characteristics (see Field and Cook 1995 for a general analysis of these characteristics). In turn, the concentrating effect on demand makes the selection of programmes to watch involve solving a coordination game. These points can be seen most obviously in the simple case where there are two people and two possible programmes.

Suppose Bob prefers watching A to B in terms of the intrinsic merits of the programmes and this is represented in the usual numerical fashion by giving A a higher pay-off than B, say 2 and 1 respectively. Jill holds the reverse preferences with respect to the intrinsic merits of the programme: B is favoured over A and this is represented in the same numerical fashion. Further, suppose that the value of seeing a programme depends not only on its intrinsic merits but also on whether it is viewed by the other

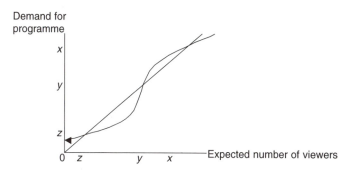

		Jill	
		A	B
Bob	A	4,3	2,1
	B	1,2	3,4

Figure 8.1 Programme choice.

Demand for programme

Figure 8.2 Demand for an individual programme.

person and so becomes a conversational resource. In particular, assume that the extrinsic, conversational value of the programme is given in this numerical scale by 2 when the programme is seen by both and by 0 when it is seen by only one. The choice of viewing for each is now represented by the game in Fig. 8.1.

There are two pure strategy Nash equilibria in this game: either both watch A or both watch B. Both are better off by selecting one or other of these equilibria than by being guided by their feelings with respect to the intrinsic merits of the programmes and so we should expect one or the other equilibrium to emerge.

In general, in the many person, many programme case, the demand for any individual programme will depend on the expected number of other viewers, as in Fig. 8.2. Again there are two potential (rational or consistent expectations) equilibria for this programme: either 'z' are expected to watch it and 'z' watch it, or 'x' are expected to watch it and 'x' do.[1] The question then is the same, which equilibrium is selected?

In both cases the answer seems bound up with what people expect others to do. In the general case of demand for an individual programme represented by Fig. 8.2 and where the programme is repeated, as in the case of Soaps, it seems natural to suppose that these expectations might be based on experience of actual numbers of viewers. If this is so, then the initial number of viewers will prove critical. If this number is less than 'y' then a bandwagon will roll against the programme until only a small number watch it; alternatively if the number is greater than 'y' then the bandwagon will roll in its favour.

125

This suggests that in the competition for viewers in the television market much effort will be devoted to gaining an initial audience when a programme is launched which will exceed whatever is the equivalent threshold to 'y'. For instance, there may be high expenditure on promotional activities. Likewise, the character of the programmes made could be affected. Although this is a matter for future research, it is possible to conjecture that programmes which are intrinsically more complex or novel and so less immediately accessible are less likely to attract a large initial audience than those which have a more straightforward or familiar and hence accessible content. If this is so, then one might expect a bias in programme content towards that which is familiar as compared with that which is new; and where something is new it will have a bias towards sensational content as the sensational will compensate in part for the novelty. In contemporary programming the sensational bias seems liable to cash in as more sex and violence. So, if these conjectures are right, competition in these television markets is liable to produce a bias in the content of programmes away from the novel towards the familiar and away from complex towards the sensational, like sex and violence, because these are the programme types which attract an immediate audience.

Of course, these are simply conjectures, but they are plausible enough to suggest that further research is required because these biases may be unfortunate from a welfare perspective on two grounds. First, some types of programmes will be underrepresented relative to people's underlying preferences. The innovative and the complex are my conjectures, but it is not difficult to see the general point. In my simple 2 programme, 2 person example, there seems no reason, as matters stand, for the pair to select A rather than B, and, over time, one might expect that Bob's preferred programme will be chosen as often as Jill's. But if some aspect of Jill's or Bob's intrinsic preferences connect differentially with the selection mechanism, then one person's preferences are likely to predominate over the other's. Or if some extraneous character of Jill or Bob connect differentially with the selection mechanism (as is typical in evolutionary game theoretic accounts), then the same asymmetry will obtain.

The bias in outcomes towards one person's preferences is plainly a matter of concern on grounds of equity. It is also potentially a source of inefficiency (and hence a cause of 'market failure' as defined earlier). Inefficiency can arise through a bias of this sort either when the individuals do not know well what they like or when preferences are not the exact mirror image of each other (as they currently are for Jill and Bob in Fig. 8.1). In the first case, this is because there is a potential welfare gain to both through the learning that comes from experiencing both programme types when neither is sure of their preferences. Equally, when the intensity of preference differs there could be an opportunity for improving both people's welfare through a periodic switch of programme type.

Suppose, for instance, there are diminishing returns to viewing the same programme type repeatedly, then there is likely to be scope for improving both people's welfare through a periodic switch that is accompanied by a side payment to the person who would otherwise temporarily lose out.

Second, in so far as programme content affects the nature of the conversations for which it is a resource, then this bias in programme content is liable to have further consequences. The discussion of people's behaviour in Soaps is but one way that we reflect on our own behaviour. Nevertheless, it is through such reflection that our preferences are subtly modified and, as a result, the bias towards particular kinds of preferences may have further effects on preference formation and change. One does not have to believe that violence on television encourages in any straightforward manner violent behaviour in the world to see the general point and it is a further cause for concern. Whether the concern surfaces here as a matter of market failure, as conventionally understood, is a moot point. Markets fail in efficiency terms when they do not satisfy people's preferences as well as they might and this seems to presume a given set of preferences. So, once preferences are rendered endogenous in this way, either a different way of talking about failure is required or a set of meta-preferences must exist in order to recreate the reference by which ideas of market failure can be reintroduced into the discussion. In some cases, for example those involving violence, there appear to be a commonly shared set of meta-preferences and so it probably makes sense to talk of a possible market failure. But this is not always the case.

I shall not say anything more here on how far the language of market failure can be stretched in this way to apply to this second kind of concern. Instead, I shall say something about how these concerns might be addressed in the final section of the paper. I turn next to whether similar worries may arise in other markets.[2]

3. How general is this?

It is tempting to think that this kind of demand interdependence may stretch well beyond the television industry. Film is obviously similar and so is the book industry because they have winner-take-all attributes for plausibly the same reason that they are used as a conversational resource. Furthermore, although economists do not typically conceive of consumption of other goods in this way, it is a commonplace observation from anthropology that goods are used conversationally. As Mary Douglas put it in her Radio 3 lectures,

> ... consumer choices should be seen as moral judgements about everything: about what a man is, about what a woman is, how a man ought to treat his aged parents, how much of a start he ought

to give to his children, how he expects to grow old – should he put aside something for his old age, or should he hope that something else will be done for him by other people? Has he got the kind of family obligations that stop him from migrating? Should he insure for his own funeral? .... Let us forget that commodities are good for eating and clothing and shelter (though, of course, that is the origin of their importance), and try instead to think that commodities are good for thinking. They can be treated as a non-verbal communication medium for the human creative faculty.

(Douglas 1977)

The thought that this phenomenon could be widespread is further reinforced by the way in which bandwagons roll in those consumer goods governed by fashion. However, there is a difference between watching a television programme or a film and wearing a pair of jeans in this respect which reflects the variety of intersubjective influences on action. The one is a resource that the individual can use to make a personal statement; the other is a statement and while the resource has to be shared to be valuable, statements are individual in nature even though they depend on a shared language. In this respect, the difference is exactly like the difference between needing to share a language in order to communicate and the making of individual statements using that language.

This is a fundamental difference even though it precludes neither people wanting to make rather similar statements through their consumption nor the phenomenon of bandwagons. Indeed, since the lexicon which gives meaning to consumption can shift, it is not surprising to find that some consumer markets are governed by bandwagons that look like those found in the television and film industries. The source of wanting to do the same here, though, is very different. The person who dresses in the same way as his or her peers is doing so because their clothing identifies them with their peer group and its values. In the same way, when an individual believes that acting in a particular way is honourable, he or she typically depends on this action being undertaken by others in similar circumstances and that they too will regard the action as a mark of honour. In both cases, the influence that others have on the individual's behaviour arises because an individual's evaluation or judgement of their behaviour often depends on an external standard for the simple psychological (but more complicated philosophical) reason that purely personal judgements have the capacity to be self-serving. The behaviour of a relevant group of others supplies that external standard. Thus, the influence that the behaviour of others has on an individual arises in these cases because the individual belongs to and wishes to express membership of a group that is defined in part by their shared beliefs over how to interpret actions.

In these cases, then, the positive influence of expectations on consumption decisions looks benign as compared with the earlier example. Demand is concentrated in much the same way as before but there are no underlying preferences that are compromised because the members of a group desire or need a common language for expressing their membership of the group. Furthermore, although membership of a group is important in preference formation, the choice of a language for expressing group membership does not appear to have any clear influence on this process. For instance, blue jeans and shell suits have acted as a type of uniform for two different groups in society and while their values were very different, it is difficult to see how an initial choice of apparel subsequently affected the values of those groups.

Some care is required here because there are further cases where other people's actions also form an external standard for judging individual action but where this influence has a notably different effect. For example, it is often remarked that journalists hunt in packs for the simple reason that an editor can sack a journalist but not all editors can sack all journalists. Thus, even the mildly risk averse journalist when facing an uncertain choice over what story to follow up may be guided away from his or her individual hunch towards what the average journalist is doing. Nor is this simply a consequence of the practical impossibility of sacking all journalists. The Anglo-Saxon legal tradition of torts appears to have a similar effect when judgements of liability turn on what was 'reasonable' to expect or do in some uncertain setting. This is because the practical legal understanding of what is 'reasonable' draws heavily on what is the average or common thing to do or believe in the circumstances (as in the famous reference to people on the Clapham omnibus). As a result, when there are a variety of views about the best course of action and the individual takes account of the possible legal liability associated with their action, there is a tendency to temper one's views in the direction of average opinion. The upshot is a condensing of action relative to the variety of underlying beliefs (see Hargreaves Heap 1989).

To summarise the argument of this section, it seems some care must be taken in distinguishing the various causes of demand or action interdependence. Sometimes this dependence narrows behaviour relative to preferences or beliefs and sometimes it does not, and it is only in the former cases that there seem likely to be grounds for concern.

4. Correcting market failures in the television industry

I return now to the problem of market failure in the television industry. To recap, there are two dimensions to the concern over the way that the intersubjective influence in broadcasting concentrates demand on a few programme types. One is a possible bias in this concentrating effect towards the familiar and sensational and the other relates to how this bias may affect preference formation. The possible influence of television programmes on 'public taste' has long been broadly recognised. For instance, there is often a watershed hour after which more sex and violence is permitted on the presumption that few children will watch programmes after that time. Likewise, the European Union has been concerned that the growth of North American programming will lead to the 'Americanisation' or 'cartoonisation' of European culture (e.g. see Tongue 1998). This aspect of concern has also become increasingly problematic because of the difficulty of defining in a plural society the standards for 'public taste'. Indeed, without such a standard, as I have mentioned before, it becomes difficult to talk of concern here in terms of even an expanded sense of market failure. In comparison, the bias towards the sensational and familiar relative to underlying preferences can be a clear example of market failure (as well as raising questions of equity) and it has *not* attracted attention. So, for both reasons, I focus on the bias aspect here. Before I consider what kind of remedies might be appropriate, it is perhaps useful to put this issue in some context.

The television industry has been heavily regulated in most countries until relatively recently. Regulatory regimes differed across countries but they commonly had the effect of muting competition in the industry to allow public service objectives to be pursued by the broadcasters. Typically, these public service objectives were couched in terms of the need to supply a diverse diet of programmes of high quality. Thus, one may suppose that they addressed, in some degree and albeit inadvertently, the problem of competition sketched in Section 2. However, in many countries, this regulatory regime is now breaking down. This is largely because the public debate has come to centre on the *market failure* reasons for public intervention (rather than any other public service mission) and the main perceived source of this kind of failure is the lack of competition which results from the scarcity of broadcasting space on the radio spectrum. Hence, with the advent of new technologies of cable and satellite combining with digital transmission to permit a genuine multi-channel world, the key source of market failure is seen to be in retreat. In turn, regulation has tended increasingly to become 'light touch'.

This process is perhaps most clearly demonstrated in the case of the UK. The Peacock (1986) Report established market failure as the key argument for public service broadcasting and looked forward to a multi-channel world where the forces of competition could be relied upon to regulate the industry. The pivotal position of market failure in the debate has been accepted by the subsequent reviews, including the most recent report on the funding of the BBC by the Davies (1999) Committee. Where the Davies (1999) Report differs from Peacock' (1986) wisdom is in its belief that market power may remain a problem in the broadcasting market with many channels. Hence, it is more inclined than its predecessor to see a continuing role for public service broadcasting.

The other interesting feature of the British history relates to accountability. As Public Choice theorists have famously argued, once the *prima facie* case for public intervention has been made, the issue of how to regulate still remains and, unless this is addressed, a market failure is as likely to be turned through public intervention into a government failure. The influence of this idea is easy to pick up in the UK. In the first place, the issue was finessed in broadcasting by the famous Reithian idea of a public interest which broadcasters had to serve (his dictum was that 'Few know what they want and fewer still what they need'). But as the suspicion grew that 'public interest' in this sense could as easily be used as a fig leaf behind which broadcasters pursued their own interests, governments struggled to find alternative ways of ensuring accountability. In this respect, broadcasting has been like other parts of the public sector; and it illustrates the same tendency: the movement towards gaining accountability through the injection of elements of the market. This was where the Peacock (1986) Committee had an immediate effect on policy through its recommendation to create greater competition among television producers through splitting production from broadcasting. In this respect, the BBC producer choice initiative preceded the more widely publicised internal markets of the National Health Service in Britain which turned many General Practitioners into the purchasers of specialist services on behalf of their patients from hospitals. Likewise, the BBC has increasingly set store in its ability to retain a large market share of viewing when arguing for the renewal of the licence fee. In other words, it has increasingly appealed to how well it does in the 'market' in order to justify how it spends the licence fee. In a similar fashion, the Davies (1999) Report uses the private sector as benchmark for the BBC when applauding the fall in production costs.

This brief contextual sketch is enough to underline the possible importance of the argument in Section 2. First, it supplies a further reason for market failure (and public intervention) that will continue *despite* the growth of competition in a multi-channel world. This means the question of public regulation and accountability will remain on the agenda (as the Davies Committee recognises, albeit for different reasons). Second, however, the argument casts some doubt on the direction that public policy has taken on this issue. The point is this: if an activity is publicly regulated because it is prone to market failure then extreme care needs to be exercised in using the market or quasi markets as a device for regulating and improving accountabilty of the public intervention. This is because the introduction of elements of the market into the publicly regulated activity could serve to recreate precisely the sources of market failure that public regulation was designed to offset. This may seem like an obvious point, but it has been surprisingly overlooked in the rush to embrace the market within the public sector (see Hargreaves Heap 2000, for more detail on this and the argument below on incentives).

The Davies (1999) Report offers one alternative. It recommends that the BBC should set public service criteria against which performance can be judged. However, there are well known problems with any payments by results system that arise because of the difficulty with specifying *exactly* what should be rewarded. Furthermore, such problems are likely to be significant in television broadcasting because, if the earlier analysis is correct, one of the market failures is a bias towards the familiar. Thus, public service broadcasting should encourage innovation. But how can one specify the kind of innovation that one would like in advance of the actual innovations occurring? It is, after all, in the nature of innovation that it produces something new. Indeed it is precisely because of such problems that governments often resort to market or quasi market solutions because their use avoids the difficulty of specifying exactly what outputs it will reward. Inevitably, then, the Davies (1999) approach will need supplementing and, if the problem of the market reintroducing the sources of market failure is to be avoided, then it will have to take some other form. I have a proposal that draws on the experience of other media industries and on the work of Brennan (1996).

The experience of other media industries is interesting because they have not been regulated in the same way as television. Some, like the newsprint industry, seem not to have been troubled by fears of the sort that I have been rehearsing. However, this is not surprising because reading different newspapers does not undermine their conversational value in the same way that viewing different soaps or films or reading different books does because different newspapers still deal in the same conversational commodity: the 'news'. The film and book industry have, however, been troubled by similar thoughts. For instance, there have been worries that the increasing commercialisation of the book industry following the collapse of the Net Book Agreement will undermine the ability of the publishers to use the profits from bestsellers to 'subsidise' new, innovative authors. Likewise, the film industry appears to be spending increasing proportionate sums on marketing (see Vogel 1998) and the time that a film is given to build an audience is apparently shrinking (see *Economist* 1997). In those industries there is typically a mixture of public intervention on a small scale through subsidy (which increasingly raises the same set of questions as television) and professional regulation. The professional regulation largely comes through awards and it is the possibility of reinforcing this kind of professional regulation through a different mechanism which I want to explore.

The problem of accountability that needs addressing is, at root, a question of how governments ensure that public sector workers do what the government wants rather than pursue their own interests. Much of the economics literature on this problem of agency has focussed, in the tradition of payments by results, on how to write contracts that will build in the incentives to produce this effect. Brennan (1996), however, argues that there is another way of tackling this problem which uses incentives in a different way.

Since potential workers are distinguished in part by their different interests, it might be possible to overcome the agency problem by hiring those workers whose own interests coincide more or less closely with the aims of the government. In other words, careful selection of workers in the first place could dispense with the need to monitor workers on the job because, with the right people in the job, their pursuit of their own interest would coincide with that of the government. The practicality of this solution, of course, depends on being able to select the 'right' workers and it is here that we need to think of incentives in a different way. We need to focus on how a remuneration package can be used to attract a particular kind of worker in the first place (and not just, as is more usually the case, on how it affects behaviour once the worker is in the job). Brennan's particular concern is with a related agency problem for academics with respect to research. His proposal is to pay academics a relatively low wage combined with an in-kind benefit which is valued highly by those who like to do research, but not by others. In this way, those who are naturally inclined to do research will be attracted to the job because the in-kind benefit can be set to compensate for the relatively low wage, whereas those who are not naturally attracted to research will be put off the job because the in-kind benefit offers no compensation for the relatively low wage. The logic is clear and the trick is to find an in-kind benefit which separates the pool of potential employees in the desired way. Brennan suggests that a research fund might do this in his case. Some thought is now necessary to see what analogous in-kind benefit for TV broadcasters could be combined with a relatively low wage to perform a similar selective function.

One possibility comes from drawing on the experience of such singular programmes as the *Morecombe and Wise comedy show*. The generally acknowledged highspot in that show's history came after the transfer from the ITV (the commercial, advertising-based channel) to the BBC; and the single most important change associated with that transfer was an increase in budgets which allowed much greater rehearsal time. Since it is not implausible to suppose that, quite generally, 'creativity' is costly, it is possible that a commitment to public service programmes having proportionately larger budgets than their private sector counterparts could serve as a suitable in-kind benefit. Plainly though, the idea needs developing as high budgets may also prove attractive to those who value other attributes like simple craftsmanship which may or may not bear any relation to the types of market failure that public service broadcasting needs to address.

Another candidate for an in-kind benefit for this purpose is a commitment to longer trial periods before a programme idea is dropped. Again this draws on the experience of another singular programme, the *Blackadder* series, and it connects directly with the worry that markets will be biased towards programmes that have an early success. The *Blackadder* series, of course, survived a close to disastrous first series to become one of the classics in the history of British comedy; and it is not implausible to suppose that those programme makers who naturally value making programmes with new and/or complex themes will be drawn to public service broadcasting if it has such a commitment because these types of programmes take a longer time to build an audience.

There is another side to the role of in-kind benefits which is worth mentioning very briefly. In effect, my proposal for regulating public service broadcasting can be located within a wider debate between what are sometimes called 'audit' and 'trust' modes of regulation. Payment by results and the introduction of a market are classic examples of an audit culture. In comparison, some organisations have little formal monitoring, eschew elaborate systems of reward and rely instead on 'trust' (e.g. see Fukuyama 1995). The motivational underpinning of audit cultures is unmysterious: it turns on the thought that we are instrumentally rational. We weigh the costs and benefits of each action and prefer that which best satisfies our preferences and the point of introducing something like payments by result is to alter the cost-benefit calculation in such a way that the person does what is desired.

The motivation that underpins 'trust' cultures is less clear (see Hollis 1998). One account, however, explains how people act in a trustworthy manner by reference to the idea of norm-governed behaviour. Norms supply public judgments on actions so that when people act in accordance with them they derive a sense of self esteem. The norm, so-to-speak, gives action symbolic properties and those symbolic properties are the building blocks for a person's sense of self-worth. Although, this is a very abbreviated account (see Taylor 1989, for something fuller) it makes interesting the question of how norms come into existence (that is, how actions acquire such publicly shared symbolic properties). This is a large and difficult question. Nevertheless, it is not implausible to suppose that the character of the in-kind benefits which were available to, say, public service broadcasters might influence any professional norms that might develop among public service broadcasters. In other words, my proposal for the introduction of in-kind benefits can be seen as part of a wider programme for turning parts of the public sector into a 'trust' rather than an audit organisation. The in-kind benefits both help select those who value what the in-kind benefits enable and they serve as a public statement of what is valued by that organisation.

5. Conclusion

The argument of this paper, to summarise it in a slightly different way, turns at crucial points on recognising that people like to reflect on what they do and these reflections have motivational force. It is this sort of reflection that explains in part the fascination with Soaps with which I started the paper. Likewise, my proposal for a new form of professional regulation has turned on the way that people derive a sense of self-esteem from norm guided behaviour. Putting the crux of the argument in this way also draws out the connection to the theme of the volume: self reflection often involves appeals to external standards and when all engage in such reflection, the standards are necessarily constituted intersubjectively.

This summary may help reveal what holds the essay together, but it does little to suggest what might be the concrete import of seeing these connections. I have tried to show why excavating the various intersubjective elements might be important through an example from the television industry where I trace an overlooked form of market failure and propose a novel remedy for combating it.

Notes

1 The precise shape of the demand function in Fig. 8.2 makes plain the possibility of two equilibria. In general there is no reason to suppose that it will be increasing at an increasing rate at first and then at a decreasing rate, crossing the 45 degree line twice. One can be confident about the latter, but there seems to be no compelling reason for supposing that this feature does not apply throughout. However, the same insights will apply when the function is in this manner increasing always at a decreasing rate. This may not be apparent at first because it may seem that such a function will either cross the 45 degree line once or not at all. In which case, there is either a stable equilibrium with positive viewers or there is not. However, the location of the function depends on the expected number of viewers of other programmes and these expectations are connected to expectations regarding the number of viewers of this individual programme. As a result, in a general equilibrium analysis, a change in expectations regarding viewers of this and other programmes will involve a shift in individual demand functions creating possibly either a stable equilibrium with a positive number of viewers or none at all as the function shifts below the 45 degree line. Hence, as before, there are likely to be more than one possible equilibrium for a programme and which is selected will depend critically on the evolution of people's expectations.

2 Jones(1984) is a useful source for a general discussion of the economics of conformism.

References

Brennan, G. (1996) 'Selection and the currency of reward' in R. Goodin (ed.) *The Theory of Institutional Design*, Cambridge: Cambridge University Press.

Davies, G. (1999) *The future funding of the BBC*. Report of the committee chaired by G. Davies, London: Department for Culture Media and Sport.

Douglas, M. (1977) 'Why do people want goods?', *The Listener* 8: 1977.

Economist (1997) 'The won and lost weekend', *Economist* 29: 123–4.

Field, R. and Cook, P. (1995) *The Winner-Take-All Society*, New York: Free Press.

Fukuyama, F. (1995) *Trust*, Harmondsworth: Penguin.

Hargreaves, Heap, S. (1989) 'Towards a post-Keynesian welfare economics', *Review of Political Economy* 1(2): 144–162.

Hargreaves, Heap, S. (2000) 'Forces of conservatism: how to incentivise the public sector', *New Economy* 7(2): 114–19.

Hollis, J. M. (1998) *Trust within Reason*, Cambridge: Cambridge University Press

Jones, S. (1984) *Economics of Conformism*, Oxford: Basil Blackwell.

Peacock, A. (1986) *Report of Committee on Financing the BBC*. (Chairman A. Peacock). London: HMSO (CMND 98824).

Taylor, C. (1989) *Sources of the Self*, Cambridge: Cambridge University Press.

Tongue, C. (1998) *Culture or Monoculture: the European audio visual challenge*, Office of Carole Tongue, MEP.

Vogel, H. (1998) *Entertainment Industry Economics*, Cambridge: Cambridge University Press.

Part II

INTERSUBJECTIVE STRUCTURES

9

MARKET, IMITATION AND TRADITION

Hayek vs Keynes

Jean-Pierre Dupuy

1. The logic of imitation

I will concentrate on Friedrich Hayek's notion of imitation which, like the concept of spontaneous social order, links him to the great tradition of the Scottish Enlightenment, the fertile soil from which political economy developed. I propose to compare Hayek and his celebrated adversary, Keynes, on this question of imitation. It is well known that the two economists were on opposite sides of the economic policy debate of the thirties over the respective roles of market dynamics and state intervention in the occurrence of disequilibria. Never to my knowledge has it occurred to anyone to compare their conceptions of the role of imitation in market functioning. It is not hard to understand why not. Hayek himself became aware of its importance only gradually, bringing it to the fore in his final book. As for Keynes, his remarks on the relations between imitation and rationality are found in his theory of financial speculation, a chapter of the *General Theory* that until recently was not taken seriously. The past several years, however, have seen an impressive blossoming of studies more or less directly inspired by Keynes's intuitions. The work of the French school of the 'economics of conventions' has a prominent place in this trend, and I will refer in particular to the research of André Orléan.

What seems to be a fundamental contradiction should strike any reader of Hayek from the outset. All through his writings, the Austrian economist marvels at that wonder of social self-regulation that is the market. It automatically finds the path of its equilibrium, and this equilibrium is an efficient social state. What gives the market its capacity for self-organisation? The answer lies in the negative feedback mechanisms that automatically go into play as soon as an agent departs from equilibrium behaviour. The penalty that he incurs (falling revenues, bankruptcy, etc.) obliges him either to quit the 'catallactic' game or to respect its rules.

Hayek bases himself precisely on the need to leave these mechanisms freedom of action in order to turn back against the partisans of social justice the accusation of conservatism often made against him. The State that intends, in the name of this ideal, to oppose the sanctions of the market, freezes accumulations of wealth and stabilises differences in income at the same time that it derails the economic engine.

Simultaneously, Hayek emphasises the role of imitation in market competition. Now, it is well known that imitation is eminently productive of *positive* feedback, a major source of dynamic instability. The vast majority of market theorists are oblivious to imitation. There are profound reasons for this. What is at stake here is both the conception of the modern individual and that of the social order. The independent and self-sufficient individual posited by economic theory is not supposed to be subject to the influence of his peers. The collective phenomena of which the market is the framework are not supposed to have anything in common with crowd phenomena and the contagion of sentiments and acts that characterise the latter. And yet, Hayek gives imitation a central role. To be sure, he is not alone: Smith and Keynes do the same. The company is not negligible: these are the finest economists of all time who see eye to eye on this point and give intersubjectivity a prominent function in social and economic dynamics. Nevertheless, the question remains: how can Hayek reconcile his unshakeable faith in the market's capacity for self-regulation and his acute perception of the importance of imitation? Indeed, the problem is much broader since it concerns not only his theory of the market, but also his theory of cultural evolution, which likewise associates competition, imitation and efficiency. In what follows, I will not always distinguish these two levels of analysis. The formal properties are essentially independent of the level. Moreover, for Hayek the market pursues the work of cultural evolution by other means.

In order to grasp clearly the nature of the problem that imitation poses for any theory of social self-regulation, consider the following elementary model. Two subjects A and B reciprocally imitate each other. The object of their mutual imitation is of indeterminate nature. But suppose that a rumour leads A to believe that B desires (seeks, wants to buy, places confidence in, hopes for, etc.) an object O. A now knows what he needs to desire (respectively: to seek, etc.): he then takes the initiative himself in such a way that his own action brings the object O to B's attention, and when B manifests in turn his interest in O, A has proof his initial hypothesis was correct. His representation, as implausible as it may have been *a priori*, has been *self-realised*. This phenomenon where an objectivity or exteriority emerges through the closure upon itself of a system of actions all imitating one another, gathers strength as the number of actions rises. The most absurd rumours can polarise a crowd unanimously upon the most unexpected object, everyone finding proof of its value in the eyes or gestures of all the others. The process unfolds in two stages: the first is a mirror game, specular or speculative, in which everyone watches for signs of the coveted knowledge in everyone else, until they all end up being propelled in the same direction; the second stage is the stabilisation of the object that has emerged – a stabilisation permitted by the fact that the arbitrariness inherent in the conditions of its genesis is forgotten. The unanimity that presided at its birth projects it for a time outside the system of actors, who, all looking in the direction that it indicates, stop searching for clues in one another's gaze.

This phenomenological description of the world of imitation can be sharpened and confirmed by mathematical modelling. A very active branch of formal economics is today exploring the role of intersubjectivity (under the more neutral name of 'interpersonal influences') in economic activity. We know enough about this subject, however, to appreciate how far removed this mimetic universe is from the ideal market. Contrary to what one might have thought *a priori*, and to what many authors have indeed thought, generalised imitation produces something rather than nothing. It creates self-reinforcing dynamics that converge so resolutely on their target that it is difficult to believe that this convergence is not the manifestation of an underlying necessity, in the manner of a mechanical or thermodynamic system returning invariably to its equilibrium state after straying from it under the effect of some perturbation. Yet, one sees that the concept of equilibrium, which the theory of the market imported from rational mechanics, is absolutely unsuited to characterise the 'attractors' of mimetic dynamics. Far from expressing an implicit order, they spring from the amplification of an initial disorder, and their appearance of pre-established harmony is a mere effect of unanimous polarisation. They are condensations of order and disorder. The mimetic dynamic seems to be guided by an end that pre-exists it – and that is how it is experienced from the inside – but it is in reality the dynamic itself that brings forth its own end. Perfectly arbitrary and indeterminate *a priori*, it acquires a quality of self-evidence as the vice of collective opinion tightens. If there is a social process that illustrates to the highest degree the notion of 'pure procedure' – even more than do economic exchange or the drawing of lots – it is the mimetic dynamic. There is no other way to determine its result than to let it proceed to its conclusion. It is a random procedure that takes on an aura of necessity.

In coming to an equilibrium, the economists' ideal market is supposed to reflect an external reality. The prices express objective, 'fundamental' values that synthesise information as diverse as the availability of techniques, the scarcity of resources or the preferences of consumers. The mimetic dynamic for its part is completely closed upon itself. The attractors that it generates are not in any relationship of correspondence with an external reality, they simply reflect a condition of internal consistency: the correspondence between *a priori* beliefs and *a posteriori* results. The mimetic attractors are self-realising representations.

Generalised imitation has the power to create worlds that are perfectly disconnected from reality: at once orderly, stable, and totally illusory. It is this 'mythopoetic' capacity that makes it so fascinating. If there are hidden truths somewhere to be discovered, one must not count on mimetic dynamics to disclose them. If it is real-world efficiency one is looking for, it is again better not to have to depend on them. Efficiency and the capacity to reveal hidden information: those are two properties that economists readily attribute to the ideal market. The distance between the latter and the mimetic process seems insuperable.

The clinical picture of the imitative logic is in its essentials already present at the stage of a very simple model in which the mimetic connections between agents are given and remain fixed throughout the whole process: the probability that a given agent imitates another given agent is a constant, possibly null (Orléan 1988).[1] Phenomenologically, we know that this hypothesis is too restrictive and that the mimetic dynamic has the ability to modify the structure of its own connections: one subject has all the more chances of being imitated by another given subject if he is already imitated by many other subjects. An opinion's power of attraction increases with the number of individuals who share it. One can see that if this is the case, the effects of mimetic polarisation are accentuated accordingly. It may seem, however, that such hypotheses depend too much on the irrationality of crowd phenomena. In fact, research in recent years has shown that they correspond to forms of behaviour that are individually rational. Several possibilities may be envisaged. There are cases where the personal advantage that an individual derives from joining the mass grows *objectively* with the size of the latter. This hypothesis is today a commonplace in the economic literature that deals with the choice of techniques (Arthur). As a technique spreads, more is learned about it and it develops and improves; the more users there are, the richer and more diversified the selection of products becomes; production costs diminish, and so does the risk of failure. In these conditions the competition between rival techniques displays features which distinguish it markedly from the 'perfect competition' of economists. The first is the multiplicity of 'equilibria' (the term is still used by historians of technology but, as we have seen, it is completely improper: it would be better to speak of 'attractors'). The 'selection' of one among them cannot be determined by deduction from the formal structure of the problem; it is the actual history of events, with its contingencies, fluctuations, and random turns, especially those affecting the system's first steps, which are responsible. One concept plays a crucial role here, that of 'path-dependence'. Fundamentally, it expresses the same idea as that of 'pure procedure'. We are poles away from Le Chatelier's principle, a thermodynamic reference still popular with theorists of the market who want to laud the latter's capacity to neutralise perturbations which affect it. The evolution of such a dynamic is highly unpredictable. There is obviously no reason for the selection that it accomplishes to be the most efficient one. If a certain technique is favoured by chance at the outset, it will benefit from a 'selective advantage' that it will maintain and amplify as the number of users grows. It may end up dominating the market even though another technique would have shown itself to be more advantageous for everyone if only chance had selected it from the start. Technological evolution thus has a strong propensity to get locked into undesirable paths from which it is harder and harder to remove it. Chance, selection, 'order through fluctuation', self-organising process: all of these terms used today by historians of technology define a theory of evolution that has only the remotest kinship with neo-Darwinism. The same troubling question thus recurs here in a new form: apart from his ideological biases or his possible lack of knowledge, what right has Hayek to ignore a type of evolutionary process that rests on imitation and mobilises the whole gamut of concepts that he himself champions? Is it simply that he would have been forced to give up the conclusion that cultural evolution has any kind of optimising function?

The foregoing hypothesis may seem too restrictive. In many cases, it is not true that the objective advantage derived from joining the mass increases with the size of latter. In the case of a culture or tradition in Hayek's sense, for example, one does not see why that should be the case. There exists, however, a more general reason to go with the majority: uncertainty. If one does not know what is good or what is true, it is rational to imitate others: there is a chance that they know, and by following their lead, one will benefit from their knowledge. Many economic models of what are called 'rational expectations' confirm and elaborate this intuition. If the imitated agents really do know what's what, the uninformed agents can accede to their knowledge, even if only indirectly through the intermediary of prices, whose role becomes that of disclosing hidden information (Grossman 1976). The rationality of speculative behaviour – the behaviour of the speculator, but also of those who take him as their model – rests on this mechanism. But what happens if the agents who serve as models are not themselves in possession of the coveted information? Or, a case at once subtler and perhaps more frequent, what if they know without being sure of their knowledge? They will themselves be encouraged to imitate those who imitate them. We have here, at a formal level, a general law of imitative logic: it inevitably leads to these mirror games and other dizzying *mises en abyme*. What remains to be understood is how or why Hayek seems to avoid them.

André Orléan has shown that the same models of rational expectations that serve to formalise the progressive unveiling of accurate information, if it exists, and the unanimous convergence of the agents on the optimal behaviour, can just as easily depict an effect of polarisation on *any* single arbitrary value when the agents, in the grip of uncertainty, seek a remedy in reciprocal imitation. Between the equilibrium and the self-realising representation, there is no *formal* difference. Yet, an abyss separates these two worlds as far as their meaning is concerned (Orléan 1986).

It cannot be emphasised too often – and Hayek is the first to do so – that in the face of the social world's complexity, imitation is the rational form of access to knowledge. But imitation is also, simultaneously, the source of all illusions – and this is the tragic side of the human social condition that Hayek does not want to see. A very simple model from André Orléan will suffice to illustrate this fundamental dilemma (Orléan 1990). A key variable of the social system under consideration (for example, the future value of a security) is assigned an objective uncertainty – of the 'meteorological' type. In a world where the representations were adequate to the external reality, the diversity of opinions concerning the value of this variable should correspond to the objective distribution of probabilities characterising it. However, each agent is able to base his opinion on two sources of information: his knowledge of the probabilities, but also observation of the distribution of opinions (such as it is reflected, for example, in the current market price of the security). Except in the case where he has absolute confidence in his apprehension of the objective probability, it would be irrational on the agent's part not to take into account the opinion of others: their opinion is based on observations that the agent has not directly made, but from which he may benefit indirectly by re-evaluating the probability (for example, using Bayes's formula) on the basis of existing opinions. The agent's reasons for proceeding in this manner are all the more sound in that he knows what we are in the process of demonstrating: namely that the very process of seeking information about a probability modifies it. If many opinions lean in a certain direction, they will pull the probability in the same direction. A key element in the agent's evaluation procedure is the relative confidence that he puts in his knowledge of objective factors compared to that which he places in the opinion of others. What we have just seen implies that this opinion will carry more weight the closer it is to unanimity. In these conditions, the distribution of opinions *evolves* in the course of time in *recursive* fashion: the evolutionary process perpetually feeds off its previous results, its determination is self-referentially closed. Question: can its limiting states be characterised? André Orléan has shown that there exists a critical value of the relative confidence that agents place in their knowledge of the objective probability such that, below this value, the distribution of opinions becomes totally disconnected from that objective probability. Average opinion becomes in a sense the principal cause of itself and it can converge on values that are stable but completely arbitrary. This collective narcissism is a source of aberrant behaviour even though it rests on individual strategies of information seeking and use that are, it should be emphasised, perfectly rational.

Most of the intuitions that guide these models come from Keynes. In his study of financial speculation (1936), Keynes, like Hayek, sees the fundamental role of imitation. In a situation of radical uncertainty, such as the one prevailing in a financial market in crisis, the only rational form of conduct is to imitate others. A first reason brings into play the cognitive mechanisms that André Orléan's model formalises: 'Knowing that our own individual judgement is worthless, we endeavour to fall back on the judgement of the rest of the world which is perhaps better informed. That is, we endeavour to conform with the behaviour of the majority or the average'. (1937). However, Keynes is sensitive to an aspect of imitation as a procedure for the discovery of information that Hayek obstinately ignores: its ambivalence. Take the case of an expert who, for his part, knows a given security's objective worth as a function of the probable dividends it will bring. Say that he observes its going rate to be seriously undervalued. Can he ignore the opinion of the ignorant? No, replies Keynes, for our expert cannot be assured that life's vicissitudes will not one day oblige him to liquidate his portfolio. And in that case it is at the market price that, *volens nolens*, he will have to do so: 'For it is not sensible to pay 25 for an investment of which you believe the prospective yield to justify a value of 30, if you also believe that the market will value it at 20 three months hence'. (1936: 155). It is too risky to depart from the majority evaluation. As Orléan (1986) remarks, 'One cannot be right against the crowd'. This second reason to resort to imitation puts the expert in the same boat as the ignorant. Note that it brings into play a mimetic rationality based on 'objective' considerations and not just 'cognitive' ones, to use the distinction we introduced earlier: an individual's interest is better served when he falls into line with the mass.

Hayek forgets all of this in his purely optimistic vision of the role of speculation. The speculator will only fulfil his social function as a seeker after accurate information if he is encouraged to do so. But he is only encouraged to do so if the market adopts, somewhat later of course, the same evaluations that he does. Suppose that the speculator judges a certain piece of information not to be relevant to the estimation of the 'underlying' or objective value of a security, but that he thinks the market, for its part, is going to consider it relevant. The information in question will be the basis for speculative behaviour. This is what André Orléan (1988b) has called the 'Reagan effect', with reference to the following anecdote. On a December day in 1987, President Reagan declared that, in his view, the dollar had fallen too low. No broker gave the least credence to the president's economic judgements. And yet, most of them bought dollars as soon as they heard the news. Irrational? No, because they expected that others would do the same, which would push up the price of the currency. Since these expectations were effectively fulfilled, we are justified in speaking of 'rational expectations', even though the movement of the market reflected no external reality.

It follows that the smart speculator is not the one who is the first to discern relevant information concerning the fundamentals of the market. Speculation becomes, in Keynes' words, 'the activity of forecasting the psychology of the market'. The smart speculator is the one who is able to 'guess better than the crowd how the crowd will behave'. (1936: 157–8). The speculator is like the snob: he wants to be the leader, the beacon of the masses; he is in their tow. Far from being the model imitated by all, he is the model of all the imitators. Result: the speculative market is like a crowd, Keynes (1937) writes, in which each 'is endeavouring to copy the others'.

I will now come back to my original question: how can Hayek avoid such cheerless conclusions, given that his social philosophy is based on a philosophy of mind in which imitation plays the starring role? Quite simple. Consider a universe where everybody imitates everybody else, with the exception of a single individual who imitates nobody. It is easy to demonstrate that this individual will become the keystone of the system in that everyone will end up imitating him and him alone (Orléan 1988). Let us make one more assumption: this individual imitates nobody because he knows he is right. Then we have an evolutionary process that acts as a very efficient discoverer and propagator of information. We encounter once more this troubling property of imitation that we have noted so many times, namely its ambivalence. It is efficient if the correct information is present somewhere and recognised as such, but otherwise it becomes a source of illusions and waste. The problem is that it is impossible from inside the system to know in which of the two cases one finds oneself. To overcome this undecidability, it is necessary to resort to an exteriority. When the evolving path arrives at 'truth' or 'efficiency', a buzzer must go off signalling 'look no further' – in other words, 'stop imitating'. The self-exteriorisation produced by generalised imitation will only manifest its optimising virtue within the framework of a genuine exteriority. Without an authentic transcendence to guide it, self-transcendence is liable to take a wrong turn and get thoroughly lost. If we are talking about the cultural evolution of humanity, the question is obviously what status to give to this transcendence and who may speak in its name. There is no way to avoid prophets here and the foremost prophet, of course, goes by the name of Hayek.

2. Dissolving contradictions in absolute knowledge

The exegetes and critics, even the most favourably disposed among them, have discovered in Hayek's writings what they believe to be major contradictions. We are now in a position to view these in a new light. To tell the truth, the contradictions vanish, but only to make way for what turns out to be a perfectly arbitrary act of faith.

Certain commentators see a contradiction at the very heart of the theory of cultural evolution. On the one hand, Hayek presents it as a self-organising process, unfolding beyond human consciousness and will; but he also asserts that the mechanism that selects the systems of abstract rules rests mainly on imitation. Does not imitation imply, on the part of the groups that imitate a tradition which originally is not their own, an awareness of the latter's superiority and a desire to adopt it for that reason? Are not this awareness and this desire the conditions for the efficiency of the evolutionary process? Hence the supposed contradiction (Manin 1983). If such were really Hayek's conception, his inconsistency would indeed be serious. For his entire philosophy of mind is opposed to this interpretation of imitation as the result of a conscious calculation and a deliberate choice. The imitation of rules of conduct is fundamentally blind: 'Most people can, after all, recognise and adapt themselves to several different patterns of conduct without being able to explain or describe them'. (1988: 78). The condition for the efficiency of cultural evolution is therefore not that those who imitate another tradition are aware of what they are doing. It is that those who, by chance, stumble onto the 'right' tradition stick with it and stop imitating others. It is thus not those who imitate, but those who do not imitate, who embody the consciousness of evolution. The problem is that this consciousness must come to them from the outside. The tragedy of the West, according to Hayek, is that having discovered the extended order of the market and the liberal principles that govern it, it was unable to recognise their superiority and immediately abandoned them in favour of the constructivist illusions. There is no contradiction; there is rather a very great consistency on Hayek's part in suggesting that the rejection of liberalism and the rise of interventionist governments are an 'error' that has spread by *contagion* (1944). Like Keynes, Hayek recognises here that generalised imitation can be the best or the worst of things. For it to be the best, it needs a guide on the outside to bring it to a halt once it has finally, if blindly, found the truth. One could not imagine a more depressing spectacle for Hayek than that of a progressive Western intellectual (Michel Foucault) seeking salvation from a Middle-Eastern theocracy; there was probably nothing crueller for him than the supposed current abandonment by American universities of the values of the West in favour of third-world or minority cultures. In the face of these renunciations, Hayek stubbornly asserted the necessity of defending liberty *dogmatically*.

Nearly all the commentators are alert to what seems to be the major contradiction in Hayek's social philosophy. I mean the status of the demonstration establishing the absolute superiority of the market. This demonstration rests in principle on the theory of cultural evolution. Only the abstract orders that pass through the filter of evolution can lay claim to the loftiest rank, whatever the criterion of the competition: efficiency, justice, liberty, utility, the reproduction and expansion of life, etc. In particular, never could the human mind or reason conceive of orders as complex as those selected by evolution. The problem is obviously that Hayek can hardly claim that the market has passed the test since all his work presents itself as a radical and, one wants to say, 'rational' critique of modern civilisation, guilty of letting itself be seduced by the sirens of constructivism. His critics therefore conclude that Hayek has to do one of two things. Either he should give up his theory of cultural evolution and found the superiority of the market on rationalist arguments, or else, if he maintains that theory, he needs to admit that the extended order of the market is not the best. This supposed contradiction, or at any rate this tension, colours the entirety of his output and gives it its peculiar tonality, a mélange of traditionalist conservatism and critical radicalism. On one hand, it is asserted that critical rationalism quickly reaches its limits, for it can only be exercised within a tradition that remains beyond criticism; on the other hand, condemnations are showered down upon contemporary civilisation in the name of an ideal of liberty which, as Hayek is the first to say, may have existed in thought but never in fact. John Gray rightly notes that the most diametrically opposite ideologies can find support in Hayek's writings: traditionalists who defend the existing social conventions and are prepared to sacrifice individual liberty to the 'bourgeois' values, transmitted by the family, of virtue, merit, honesty, morality, work, etc.; but also rationalist libertarians and 'anarcho-capitalists' who, not hesitating to wipe the slate clean of established moral values, promote a heroic ethic of individual autonomy and unbridled competition, where only success or failure count in the end, independently of any notion of merit or virtue. Conversely, criticism arrives from every camp. For example, such American neo-conservatives as Daniel Bell or Irving Kristol (1978) serve warning on Hayek: the liberal order that he promotes is founded on a moral capital of bourgeois values that its unlimited development tends to destroy irrecoverably.

Our analysis of the properties of generalised imitation allows us to dissolve this apparent contradiction. There is not, over here, an evolution that unfailingly finds by itself the right path, this right path turning out precisely to be *other* than that of the market; and, over there, Hayek who asserts the superiority of the market. Without the intervention of a knowledge that transcends it, there is no guarantee that cultural evolution based on imitation will converge towards a satisfactory order, and even less an optimal one. It is in the name of such transcendent knowledge that Hayek speaks, without of course being able to found this knowledge. Hayek was an 'engaged' intellectual who wrote books, gave lectures, mobilised his epigones on a world scale and organised them into powerful pressure groups: he sought to influence his contemporaries and, beyond them, the course of evolution. There is nothing here that is not perfectly consistent with a theory of evolution based precisely on reciprocal influences. But he could not, without imposture, speak in the name of evolution. Nor could he, without contradicting his philosophy of mind, speak in the name of mere human reason. There remains, of course, the vantage point of Absolute knowledge. It is understandable that an avowed anti-rationalist like Hayek hesitated to occupy this spot.

3. From the incentive system to the termite-colony market

Let us come to the question of social justice. We are now ready to see a contradiction, or at least a tension, in Hayek's celebrated criticism of this notion, which might go unnoticed by anyone who has not followed the road that we have here.

A first series of arguments advanced by Hayek can be found in Rawls as well. The *results* of the market are in themselves devoid of any moral value. They are ethically blind. All that is asked of the market is to be efficient. That entails letting it recompense everybody's activity, labour, efforts and strategic choices as it sees fit, if one may put it that way. Now, the remunerations and valuations effected by the market are utterly indifferent to the merit, moral worth, or needs of the agents. Take a hard-working doctor who is deserving and needy, but incompetent: he will be swept away by the competition. Is that unjust? Justice has nothing to do with it. The rules are the same for everyone; the process is anonymous, bereft of intention, without a subject. It is the intervention of a central authority acting as a protection against failure that would be immoral and destructive of freedom. Above all, it would break the engine that makes the market efficient by mucking up its system of penalties and rewards. The market gives to each not what he needs or deserves, but the equivalent of the services that he renders others. It encourages the subjects, even if unbeknownst to them, to step out of their subjectivity and to anticipate others and their needs. That is its own moral value.

For Hayek these arguments are so many blows struck against the notion of distributive justice. He pretends to believe that a theory of social justice is necessarily meritocratic and requires that everyone receive in accordance with his moral value or, possibly, his needs. The simple existence of the Rawlsian theory, of which Hayek is not unaware,[2] is enough to ruin this postulate.

In order to contrast it with what is to come, let us emphasise from this first series of arguments the following point: the market establishes a *visible* link between subjects' actions and the penalties or rewards they receive from it, but this link is not meritocratic. A policy of 'social justice' breaks this link and, distorting the system of incentives, destroys the beautiful efficiency of the economic machine. Egalitarianism, for example, renders subjects irresponsible: since they are assured of obtaining the same material advantages and the same esteem whatever they do, they have no incentive to make the effort to adopt the behaviours or to make the choices that are the most rational and, therefore, the most beneficial for everyone.

In the second series of arguments presented by Hayek, it is not only on the ethical plane that the results of the market are blind, it is also and above all on the cognitive plane. There is a lot of suffering in the market according to Hayek: people cannot find work or lose their job, firms go bankrupt, distributors are abandoned by long-time clients, speculators go for broke and lose everything, new products sink without a trace, researchers who toil long and hard discover nothing, etc. Now, these sanctions fall out of the blue like strokes of fate, unjustified, unpredictable, incomprehensible. The argument against a policy of 'social justice' is no longer that it unnecessarily upsets the incentive system since there clearly is no possibility of an incentive system here. It is that such a policy can only be blind itself for one does not dictate to a spontaneous order the results it must attain.

The foregoing argument is obviously founded on the thesis of *complexity*. Nobody can determine *a priori* the value of a job, an effort, or a product, for the market alone will decide and its verdicts cannot be anticipated. This argument in terms of 'pure procedure' demonstrates how far Hayek is from the neoclassical model of general economic equilibrium. The latter's 'non-complex' character is discernible in the fact that it is indifferent whether it is read 'bottom-up' or 'top-down'. In the first case, the thesis is that, the agents considering the prices as given and therefore known, their actions are automatically coordinated in an equilibrium, which is a (Pareto) optimum; in the second, the thesis is that any optimum can be reached in decentralised fashion, by communicating to the agents a set of adequate prices. That this is an 'anti-Hayekian' world is evident when one recalls the following delectable detail: not so long ago, in what is now a bygone era, one could still hear it affirmed that the best illustrations of the Walrasian model were the planned economies of the Eastern bloc. The central planner who communicates to the decentralised agents the values that will allow them to make their theoretically autonomous decisions had to solve, in order to calculate those values, an overall programme that gave him, not only the values, but also the decisions of the agents. What hypocrisy not to impose these decisions directly upon them! Hayek could only reject with horror this serfdom disguised as liberty.

Hayek's theory of market coordination has neither the clarity nor the precision of the Walrasian model, which has by now been totally axiomatised and formalised. Yet, one may assert that Hayek's theory refuses to give itself an ultimate level of explanation, whether it be that of individuals or that of the collectivity, because it insists on the *recursive* codetermination between the two levels. As a consequence, the agents do not have access to the collective knowledge represented by prices *before* these are established in the marketplace. Let us take an extreme example: a French worker suddenly learns that the value to the collectivity of his services and qualifications has become null at the moment that he is laid off, some multinational having decided to close the factory that employed him – the reason being that world economic conditions make it more profitable to set up shop in Singapore or Brazil. To be sure, in the world of perfect information that economists are fond of imagining, our man could have anticipated the process of factory migration and either migrated himself or trained for a new job. The complexity of the social process rules this out, Hayek declares. To make himself understood, he often uses terms like chance or good or bad luck rather than complexity. There is, however, a deep kinship between these categories. At this stage, it is not only merit or moral value that may receive blind retribution from the market; it is also effort, talent, skill, or studied strategic choices: no recompense is guaranteed in the face of the vicissitudes and contingencies of social life.

The right attitude is then – in a sort of *Gelassenheit* that is to the concern to 'repair social injustices' what laissez-faire is to the trial-and-error interventionism of the Welfare State – to abandon oneself to 'the blind forces of the social process'. To let oneself go in this way is the essence of liberty according to Hayek. It is also the condition for efficiency. The 'invisible hand' of the market takes on a very different meaning here from the one it has in the Walrasian model. We are no longer dealing with a spontaneously harmonious composition of behaviours that, even though they do not have the common interest for their object, remain nevertheless, at the individual level, guided by a spirit of calculation and a concern for rationality. What we have instead is the kind of self-organisation found in the termite colony – a termite colony, however, where imitation has supplanted instinct.[3] Individual behaviours that are blind succeed nonetheless in forming an efficient system thanks to a 'selection' that eliminates what must be eliminated. But, as we have analysed at length, there is no guarantee that the competitive *and* mimetic market will conduct itself in reasonable fashion if its self-exteriorisation is not in communication with a true exteriority, that of Absolute knowledge. Yet nothing, in what Hayek says, obviously, provides this guarantee.

The tension between the two series of arguments sometimes reaches a peak, when they are led to meet at the same point. The question of 'equal chances' is a fine example. Those who proclaim this slogan have in mind the sporting ideal of justice: may the best contender win! For the competition to be equitable, the 'initial' positions must be equalised, for example by a system of handicaps – 'setting the counters back to zero', in the elegant expression of French meritocrats. But in the 'continuous process' of social life, 'this initial position of any person will always be a result of preceding phases', Hayek (1976: 130; Nemo 1988: 239) remarks. If parents knew that their children's start in life would be independent of their own success because a central authority put everybody back on the same level by, among other things, abolishing inheritance, one of the most essential motors of market competition would be broken! Construed in this way, equality of chances also has totalitarian implications. As the enemy of efficiency and liberty, the equalisation of chances is truly a detestable ideal. Conclusion? 'We must resolve to consider the starting situation of each individual to be an "accident"', writes Philippe Nemo (1988: 239), commenting on this point in Hayek – and here is how the latter finishes the sentence we began to quote above: 'In a continuous process this initial position of any person will always be a result of preceding phases, and *therefore* be as much an undesigned fact and dependent on chance as the future development'. (1976: 130; emphasis added).

Here the tension is at its peak. On the one hand, as Nemo writes (1988: 239; emphasis added), 'these initial positions will be ... the fruit of previous efforts and *merits*, in particular within families'. We won't comment on 'merit', a slip which reveals that meritocracy dies hard. But on the other hand, one must ask of children to see in their initial position, and thus in the greater or lesser success of their parents – in the degree of effort and sacrifice that the parents invested in the children – a simple 'accident', a pure 'fluke'. That amounts, if not to a logical contradiction, then to an important psychological one. The incentive for parents to save on behalf of their children rests precisely on their hope that the latter will not treat the fruit of their labour as an 'unintended fact' or as manna falling arbitrarily from heaven. Here the argument of 'social complexity' does not hold: social inheritance or 'reproduction' is not realised anonymously at the abstract level of the 'great society', but in the most emotionally charged of face-to-face relationships, those in the family.

How could our author let his theoretical system get into such a fix? The market is in Hayek's view a source of great suffering for those who consent to live by its heroic morality. It is not difficult to understand why. According to the first line of argument, the supreme value of the market, which justifies all the sacrifices, is its efficiency, and this rests on a system of incentives whose principal signals are personal success and failure. To be sure, it is not their 'merit' or moral value that the agents put into play, but their ability to be useful to others. Those who fail receive the signal that others do not appreciate their enterprises, their efforts, their talents. They observe that others succeed and are encouraged to follow in their footsteps. The losers imitate the winners because they *envy* them.

Why are not people happy in the modern world? Because they envy one another. This answer which can be found in many analysts of modernity is also Hayek's. It is well, however, to reformulate this assertion in a more precise and nuanced manner. Envy as a *theme* is certainly present in the work of our author, but he quite obviously attributes only minor importance to it. Many are the notations that go as follows: some succeed, others fail even though they have expended just as much effort. Why? Perhaps because they are less gifted or less competent (first line of argument), perhaps because they had less luck (second line of argument). Be that as it may, the 'envy of those who have tried just as hard [as those who have succeeded], although fully understandable, works against the common interest'. (1988: 118). Hayek apparently belongs to that large set of authors who recognise the existence of envy, to be sure, but who do not take it very seriously. It is merely a 'nasty defect', as popular wisdom would have it, a benign affliction chiefly affecting children. Hayek adds: envy does not make for happiness, but happiness, after all, is but a rationalist philosopher's invention.

I claim on the contrary that it is the threat that envy poses for his system that leads Hayek to give the latter that bipolar and ultimately contradictory *structure* that I have analysed.[4] People suffer from envy in a competitive market, where only success and failure count (this is the market as a system of incentives). Failure signifying the incapacity to serve others adequately, it ought inevitably to entail the loss of others' esteem and, as a result, the loss of self-esteem: 'It is because there is a relationship between what I do and the esteem in which I am held that it is rational for me to seek to comport myself in the best way possible', writes Nemo (1988: 304). Hayek will seek a remedy for this threat in the most traditional of solutions: the appeal to an exteriority. It is the 'complexity' of the social which provides the requisite exteriority – or more precisely, as I have shown, it is the articulation between the self-exteriorising movement of the social and a genuine exteriority, that of Absolute knowledge (which pushes us over into the second conception of the market, that of the 'termite colony'). The following quotation from Hayek (1944: 106) is eloquent enough: 'Inequality is undoubtedly more readily borne, and affects the dignity of the person much less, if it is determined by impersonal forces than when it is due to design. In a competitive society it is no slight to a person, no offence to his dignity, to be told by any particular firm that it has no need for his services or that it cannot offer him a better job.... [T]he unemployment or the loss of income which will always affect some in any society is certainly less degrading if it is the result of misfortune and not deliberately imposed by authority'.

The problem is that this solution can only work on condition that everyone shares the philosopher's conviction, namely that they are dealing with a true exteriority, which is very doubtful. Nobody will abandon himself to these 'impersonal forces' if he has good reason to doubt that they will take the world in the right direction, or simply in a viable direction. But the 'extended order of the market' can easily get stuck in a dead end or even plunge into the abyss, as we have shown theoretically and as is proved by historical experience. Obviously, nobody can believe in the guarantee that Hayek's system requires in order that such misadventures be impossible: access to Absolute knowledge.

4. Market and tradition

To close this critical analysis, I would like to return to the question of tradition and to a closely related one, that of imitation. By placing imitation at the heart of his philosophy of mind, Hayek is led to make it play a central role, both in his theory of tradition, which is not unusual, and his theory of the market, which is much more so. The strength of his social philosophy is revealed here, but also its blindness. To put it somewhat schematically, Hayek's reconstruction of the cultural history of humanity falls into three stages. In the primitive phase, an instinctual morality is made up of solidarity and altruism, and animism and anthropomorphism dominate the conception of the world: every form of order is attributed to a design, a will. Then comes the invention of tradition and of the many human cultures. Spontaneous social orders deploy themselves and compete with one another; cultural evolution is off and running. It discovers that peculiar tradition constituted by the extended order of the market, founded on the abstract rules of liberalism. But, far from recognising its superiority, it abandons it in favour of constructivist and rationalist illusions: that is the modern phase, which represents a return to primitive anthropomorphism and a rejection of tradition.

Not only does this scenario involve certain naiveties (the irenic conception of primitive society); it is highly implausible and threatens the coherence of the evolutionist theory of culture. Hayek is certainly right to characterise modernity by the rejection of tradition. That is not very original, although one may dispute the notion that Descartes was responsible for this radical change with regard to tradition. But this is not the essential point. To restore coherence and plausibility to his scenario, it would be enough for Hayek to make two hypotheses: first, that the expansion of the market order is not unrelated to the break with tradition, since the market is anything but a tradition; second, that rationalist constructivism itself has profound affinities with the market. Hayek sometimes seems inclined to admit the second hypothesis – without being able to go very far in this direction, which makes the justification of liberalism in the terms of the theory of evolution extremely problematic. The idea is that the extension of the market to every realm of personal and social life generates an engineer's mentality, a spirit of calculation that tends to erode what are known as 'traditional' values. This criticism of the market, which one is not surprised to find in the neoconservative writings of Irving Kristol and Daniel Bell, sometimes meets with Hayek's approval. For example, *The Road to*

Serfdom tells us that the material advances made possible by liberalism have given men a 'new sense of power over their own fate, the belief in the unbounded possibilities of improving their own lot' (Hayek 1994: 17) and that as a consequence 'the very success of liberalism became the cause of its decline' (p.19).

Hayek is the furthest from the first hypothesis. It is essential to his system that the market be a tradition, springing from cultural evolution. This is to remain blind to the radical break separating the market order from the traditional order where imitation is concerned. In the traditional order, the models are so distant from those who imitate them that no rivalry can arise between them; in market society, on the contrary, the models are equals and competitors: one copies one's more fortunate rival and one is in rivalry with one's model.[5] Here Hayek does not measure up to his own model, Adam Smith. He does not see what the latter demonstrated: that this new regime of imitation gives rise to envy, and that this envy has highly ambivalent effects: it is on the one hand a cause of great suffering (the 'corruption of moral sentiments'), but on the other hand, it gives market society an unprecedented energy, a potentially unlimited force of expansion. Moreover, far from being a product of the 'constructivist illusion', the idea of social justice is inherent in the propensity of the modern individual always to put himself in the place of the other, to live permanently under the gaze of the other.

It is painful to have to imitate a rival who is successful. It means openly recognising what one would prefer to hide, from one's own eyes and those of the world: that one holds the other to be superior. In the world of business, and in the economy in general, it is nonetheless rational to act in this manner, as Keynes well saw, and Hayek himself in a lesser measure. Post-war world economic history provides a hundred examples of imitators become innovators in their turn. What is startling about the economy is that this truth is to be found in the public square. The reason for this doubtless lies in the market's remarkable capacity to transform envy into a source of creative energy, instead of letting it sink into resentment and impotent hatred.(Dumouchel and Dupuy 1979; Girard 1990). The same cannot be said for other areas of social life. Let us turn to those who are Hayek's *bêtes noires*: the 'intellectuals' (progressives, it goes without saying). In the area of culture, for example, the credo is: only what is new is interesting. Radical innovation, understood as creation *ex nihilo*, surpassing oneself rather than others, has the dual advantage of denying both imitation and competition. It takes a lot of naivete for Hayek to think that these intellectuals are nostalgic for the altruism and solidarity proper to primitive society. The rejection of competition typical of these 'critical demystifiers' springs from an excess, and not a lack, of competitive spirit.

The ambivalence of envy also manifests itself within the world of the economy. Despite the headlong flight forward that characterises it at every moment, it is no stranger to the torments of failure and resentment. Hayek at least deserves credit for recognising this, even if he does not see that the demand for social justice springs first from this suffering and not from what he terms the principal obstacle to the market: critical rationalism. We have studied the solution that he proposes: it is what is responsible for the tension that runs through his work, between an incentive-system market and a termite colony market. Since competitive imitation is the source of the evils, let us return to the traditional modality of imitation; let us make a tradition out of the market. The imitation of a transcendent model, in the manner of that of Jesus Christ, keeps people from taking each other as models and sinking into the torments of envy. The transcendence here is, however, only a self-transcendence that, in order to aspire to be a trustworthy guide, requires access to that genuine transcendence that is Absolute knowledge. Hayek's solution can only work if liberalism is made into a religion.

What has just been said about the market applies in the same manner to cultural evolution. Hayek wants to see in it nothing but a peaceable contest among traditions so that the best may win. It would be more consistent with his theory to present it as a war of religions. Hayek's philosophy of knowledge entails that people become attached to their tradition for reasons other than the benefits that they derive from it – benefits which they are incapable of measuring exactly. There is, therefore, a misrecognition on the part of the agents, that is, the individual counterpart of the opacity and complexity of the collective. Hence, the problem of the stability of tradition. It is rational for the agents to conform to tradition, but they do not know that. Only irrational motives can impel them to do so. For Hayek, it is religious, magical or mythical beliefs that fill this role (1988: 136). The animism and anthropomorphism of primitive thought, so criticised elsewhere, are at the source: what is the meaning of 'God' for a given society, asks Hayek, more Durkheimian than ever, if not the self-transcendence of the social that is not seen as such? (pp.139–140). In short, the role of religion in evolution is fundamental. The necessity for a *dogmatic* attachment to the principles of liberalism is but a particular instance. 'The only religions that have survived', Hayek notes, 'are those which support property and the family' (p.137).

But at the same time, as we saw, evolution can only fulfil its selective function effectively insofar as individuals and groups are ever willing to abandon one tradition for another, by siding with whichever ones muster the greatest numbers. Like the generalised market, which extends its action ten times more effectively, cultural evolution sets up a competition among ways of being, thinking and acting that are mutually fascinated by one another even while pretending to struggle jealously, 'dogmatically', to maintain their identity. One should, therefore, find at its level that same state of being torn between self and other that Smith called 'sympathy'

156

at the level of individuals. And that is indeed what one observes. A dominant culture that hates itself, and others, fascinated by it, that hate it while imitating it: there is no shortage of contemporary examples, which we could develop if we wished. Thus, as will have been understood, our criticism of Hayek does not bear on this point: to have placed competitive imitation at the heart of his system is his stroke of genius. The problem is that, a prisoner of his resolutely optimistic ideology, he remains blind to the irreducible ambivalence of this conflictual mimesis. Unless one gives the goddess Evolution a role equivalent to the one he attributes to the god of the Market, there is no guarantee, if the very idea has a meaning, that human history, with its sound and fury, will go spontaneously in the 'right direction'.

Hayek's *œuvre* doubtless constitutes the most grandiose attempt to found a theory of the good and just society on the contingence of human affairs and on social complexity. Its failure weighs heavily.

Notes

1 Under certain conditions, it is demonstrated that the imitative dynamic converges toward unanimity of the group. These conditions reflect the fact that there is an effective interdependence among all the agents; in other words, very few probabilities pij are null, pij being the probability that the agent i imitates the agent j.

2 In (1976, pp. xiii and 100), Hayek says he is in basic agreement with Rawls. In (1988), his position has changed radically: on p.74, he is able to write that a 'Rawlsian world could never have become civilised' because of the difference principle's 'repressing differentiation due to luck'. This new attitude is less surprising than the first one, but the wavering thus made manifest reveals that the Rawlsian theory poses a problem for Hayek.

3 In fact, imitation plays a role in the self-constitution of the termite colony, but the process is much more mechanical and therefore less reflexive than in a human society. See Deneubourg (1977); cited by Prigogine & Stengers (1984: 181).

4 The opposition that I employ here between envy as the apparent *theme* of a work, and the structuring but hidden *effect* of envy on a work, is analogous to the distinction made by René Girard (1986) between the victimage mechanism as theme and as structure.

5 This distinction corresponds to the one that René Girard (1965) establishes between 'external mediation' and 'internal mediation'.

References

Arthur, W. Brian (1988) 'Competing Technologies: An Overview', in R. Dosi et al. (ed.), *Technical Change and Economic Theory*, London: Pinter Publishers, 590–607.

Deneubourg, J.-L. (1977) 'Application de l'ordre par fluctuation à la description de certaines étapes de la construction du nid chez les termites', *Insectes sociaux* 24(2).

Dumouchel, Paul and Jean-Pierre, Dupuy (1979) *L'Enfer des choses*, Paris: Seuil.

Girard, René (1965) *Deceit, Desire, and the Novel*, Baltimore: Johns Hopkins University Press.

Girard, René (1986) *The Scapegoat*, Baltimore: John Hopkins University Press.

Girard, René (1990) 'Innovation and Repetition', *Substance* 62/63.

Grossman, S. (1976) 'On the Efficiency of Competitive Stock Markets where Traders Have Diverse Information', *The Journal of Finance* 21(2).

Hayek, F. (1944) *The Road to Serfdom*, Chicago: Chicago University Press.

Hayek, F. (1976) *Law, Legislation and Liberty*, vol. 2 'The Mirage of Social Justice', London: Routledge & Kegan Paul.

Hayek, F. (1988) *The Fatal Conceit: The Errors of Socialism*, Chicago: University of Chicago Press.

Keynes, J. M. (1936) *The General Theory of Employment, Interest and Money*, London: Macmillan.

Keynes, J. M. (1937) 'The General Theory of Employment', *Quarterly Journal of Economics* 51(2): 214.

Kristol, I. (1978) 'Capitalism, Socialism and Nihilism', in *Two Cheers for Capitalism*, New York: Basic Books, chap. 7.

Manin, Bernard (1983) 'F.A. Hayek et la question du libéralisme', *Revue française de science politique* 33(1).

Nemo, Philippe (1988) *La Société de droit selon F.A. Hayek*, Paris: Presses Universitaires de France.

Orléan, André (1986) 'Mimétisme et anticipations rationnelles: une perspective keynésienne', *Recherches économiques de Louvain* 52(1).

Orléan, André (1988) 'Money and Mimetic Speculation', in P. Dumouchel (ed.) *Violence and Truth*, Stanford University Press.

Orléan, André (1988b) 'L'autoréférence dans la théorie keynésienne de la spéculation', *Cahiers du CREA*, 11: 120–44.

Orléan, André (1990) 'Le role des influences interpersonnelles dans la détermination des cours boursiers', *Revue économique*, 5: 839–68.

Prigogine, Ilya and Isabelle Stengers (1984) *Order out of Chaos*, New York: Bantam.

10

RECONSTITUTIVE DOWNWARD CAUSATION

Social structure and the development of individual agency

Geoffrey M. Hodgson

The problem of agency and structure is one of the central problems of social science. The problem has ontological, epistemological and methodological dimensions. At the ontological level, it concerns the units of social and individual being. Is society more than the individuals that compose it? Or is there 'no such thing as society' other than an aggregation of individuals? Related, often familiar, questions arise concerning epistemology (knowledge) and methodology (explanation). In the present essay we are most concerned with questions of ontology as well as methodological questions of explanation.

On the one hand, some versions of Marxism, plus Durkheimian sociology, have been criticised for placing an excessive weight of explanation on the society, system or structure, to the neglect of the role of individual actor. On the other hand, versions of ontological and methodological individualism, especially in mainstream economics, have placed a one-sided emphasis on the individual, to the relative neglect of social structures.

A feature of the more extreme claims to a solution to this problem is that they do not, in fact, deliver what they promise. For example, Steven Lukes (1973) has shown that several prominent attempts to formulate and defend methodological individualism exhibit such a problem. While claiming to explain social phenomena exclusively in terms of individuals, it is openly admitted that individuals are themselves affected by structures. Any notion that individuals are socially determined must undermine any attempt to give the individual explanatory priority over social phenomena.

The reason for this is that a socially determined individual cannot provide the ultimate explanatory bedrock that methodological individualism requires. Once we admit that the individual is socially determined then we have an explanatory infinite regress, and neither individuals nor

159

institutions can be the final, explanatory term (Hodgson 1988; Nozick 1977). Hence, on closer inspection, many such accounts are not exclusively individualistic at all, as they admit that social explanations do not rely solely upon individuals. 'Thus the social phenomena have not really been eliminated; they have been swept under the carpet' (Lukes 1973: 121–2).

Likewise, 'methodological collectivist' explanations of social phenomena – solely in terms of structures or wholes – often ascribe a residual intentionality to organisations, classes or groups. To make such one-sided explanations in terms of structures, institutions or social classes 'work', the wholes have to be endowed with wills and purposes and treated in some ways as if they were individuals.

The problem of agency and structure is not soluble at the two extremes, where either individual or structure do most of the explanatory work. A complex articulation of the two elements is required. In the absence of simplistic solutions, there is now a fashionable tendency among some social theorists – particularly post-modernists and post-structuralists – to attempt to dismiss or transcend this issue. In response, Nicos Mouzelis (1995: 69–70) rightly assesses 'attempts to dismiss the agency–structure distinction … either by conflating the two notions, or by … deriving the one from the other' as leading to a theoretical impasse. Notably, many of these evasive attempts involve 'the reintroduction of the distinction by the back door … by keeping the logic of the agent–structure dichotomy while expressing it through a different terminology'. The solution to the agency–structure problem is not to pretend that it does not exist. Such strategies have notably ended up with the readmission of the problem in another form.

Debates over the relationship between structure and agency were much stimulated by the work of Anthony Giddens (1979; 1984). Giddens proposed an apparent solution to the problem that seemed to avoid the twin pitfalls of both methodological individualism and methodological collectivism. Giddens's 'structuration' approach will be summarised very briefly below. Among others, Giddens's work stimulated an important debate with critical realists such as Roy Bhaskar (1983) and Margaret Archer (1995). Again, some of the key issues will be summarised here.

While important positive moves were made in the 1980s and 1990s, it shall be argued here that the outcomes are not entirely satisfactory. In short, crucial problems remain concerning the nature of causality in the social realm and the causal relationship between individual intentions and actions, on the one hand, and structures and institutions, on the other.

This paper brings into the agency–structure debate the concept of 'downward causation', pioneered in psychology by Roger Sperry (1964; 1969; 1976; 1991) and taken up by Donald Campbell (1974) and others. A modified concept of 'reconstitutive downward causation' is proposed in this article.

1. Structuration theory and critical realism

An attraction of Giddens's 'structuration theory' is its proposal of an alternative to the extremes of both methodological individualism and methodological collectivism. Giddens argues that social theory should focus exclusively neither on any social totality, nor simply on the experiences or behaviours of individual actors. Instead, social theory should take its starting point as 'recursive social practice' and consider the ways in which such practices are sustained through time and space.

At the heart of his structuration theory is the notion of 'duality of structure'. For Giddens, the idea of a duality is contrasted with that of a dualism. The two elements of a dualism are regarded as mutually exclusive or separable. By contrast, crucial to the idea of a duality, is the notion that the parts are interdependent: each element may actually help to constitute the other. Giddens regarded agent and structure as a duality: where both human subjects and social structures are jointly constituted in and through recurrent practices, and where no element has ontological or analytical priority over the other.

In what respect does Giddens's structuration theory differ from the alternative perspective of social structure supplied by critical realism, principally by Bhaskar and Archer? At first sight, they seem to have much in common. Even in a critical engagement with Giddens, Bhaskar (1983: 85) wrote of their two theoretical conceptions as being 'very close'. However, the real differences in viewpoint had largely been obscured, because of the opposition, shared by both Bhaskar and Giddens, to the polar extremes of methodological individualism and methodological collectivism. It took Archer (1995: 14) to dramatise the crucial differences. She wrote:

> Unfortunately, because both realists and structurationists have both rejected the terms of the old debate between Individualism and Collectivism, there has been an over-hasty tendency to assume their mutual convergence and to lump them together as *an* alternative to the positions taken in the traditional debate. Instead the crucial point is that we are now confronted by two new and competing social ontologists.

The social ontology of critical realism differs from that of structuration theory in a number of respects. First, as Archer pointed out, a distinctive feature of Bhaskar's (1975; 1989a) natural and social ontology – as in the similar ontologies of predecessors such as Alfred Whitehead (1933), Arthur Koestler (1967), Mario Bunge (1973) and Donald Campbell (1974) – is its multi-layered character. Such a stratified ontology is essentially absent from structuration theory. What differentiates one layer from another is the existence of *emergent properties* at that level. The concept of emergence was defined by its originator, Conwy Lloyd Morgan, in the following terms:

> Briefly stated the hypothesis is that when certain items of 'stuff', say *o*, *p*, *q*, enter into some relational organization *R* in unity of 'substance,' the whole *R* (*o p q*) has some 'properties' which could not be deduced from prior knowledge of the properties of *o*, *p*, and *q* taken severally.
>
> (Morgan 1932, p. 253)

For example, we may treat human consciousness and agency as an emergent property of our complex neurosystem. Our consciousness is a higher layer of being, above the neurosystem. Consciousness depends upon our neurophysiology but it is not predictable from it, nor entirely explicable in its terms. At a further level below, the neurosystem depends on the substances of molecular biology, but it cannot be explained on the basis of molecules alone. In turn, molecular biology depends on the matter examined by chemistry and physics. Just as we may accept a layered ontology 'below' the human individual, we also have good reasons to accept the existence of layers 'above' human individuals. As a consequence, realists such as Archer, Bhaskar, Bunge and Whitehead have argued that social structures have emergent properties of their own. Although dependent upon both human individuals and the natural world, these properties are not found at the lower levels. Social properties are not reducible to individuals, nor explicable solely in individual terms.

Bhaskar makes extensive use of emergent properties in his work. In contrast, Giddens makes no significant or explicit use of the idea. A consequence of Giddens's rejection of emergent properties is not only the rejection of a higher and social levels of analysis with their own emergent properties, but also the analytical neglect of the natural and physical world as the essential substratum and context of human activity. The denial of emergent properties forces structuration theory to accept a *single* level of reality, with nothing (social or otherwise) 'above' it, or (natural or otherwise) 'below'. One consequence of this is the denudation of the concept of social structure. Another is the neglect of the natural and biological substratum of all human activity.

If structuration theory accepts a singular plane of being, then where is it? Giddens is quite explicit about this. For him, 'structure exists ... only in its instantiations of such [social] practices and as memory traces orienting the conduct of knowledgeable human agents' (Giddens 1984: 17). Symptomatically, the formulation is repeated: 'Structure exists only as memory traces, the organic basis of human knowledgeability, and as instantiated in action' (*op. cit.* p. 377). In his structuration theory, agency itself carries 'structural properties' as memory traces carried through time, and transmitted through practice from one agent to another.

In contrast, critical realism does not collapse the world into the mind of the actor. Both the social and the natural worlds retain an existence independently of our perceptions. Consequently, in contrast to structuration theory, critical realism explores more extensively the links between the social and the natural sciences. Bhaskar depicts reality as being much more than human knowledge and practice. Not only are there social structures that transcend individuals, but also social existence has enduring and indispensable natural substrata. Bhaskar openly accepts the dependence of the social upon the natural world, while denying that one is identical or reducible to the other.

The final contrast between structuration theory and critical realism concerns the historical priority and separate identity of structure over agency. For Bhaskar, but not for Giddens, human agents and structures are not different aspects of the same things or processes but, emphatically, *different things*. Bhaskar thus upheld the dualism of agency and structure that Giddens conflated into his singular, but Janus-faced, 'duality'. Bhaskar (1989a: 35) emphasises that it is important to distinguish

> categorically between people and societies, and correspondingly between human actions and changes in social structure ... For the properties possessed by social forms may be very different from those possessed by the individuals upon whose activity they depend.

Bhaskar's assertion is based on an insistence that emergent properties exist at the social level; there are properties of social structures that are not entirely reducible to individuals alone. For Bhaskar (1989b: 92) 'social structure and human agency are seen as existentially interdependent, but essentially distinct.'

There is a further reason for Bhaskar's conceptual separation of actor and structure. It is due to the fact that, for any particular actor, social structure *always exists prior to* his or her engagement with the world. As Bhaskar (1983: 85) writes: 'it is because the social structure is always *given*, from the perspective of intentional human agency, that I prefer to talk of reproduction and transformation rather than of structuration as Giddens does'. Elsewhere, Bhaskar (1989a: 36) elaborates the same theme:

> People do not create society. For it always pre-exists them and is a necessary condition for their activity. Rather, society must be regarded as an ensemble of structures, practices and conventions which individuals reproduce and transform, but which would not exist unless they did so. Society does not exist independently

of human activity (the error of reification). But it is not the product of it (the error of voluntarism).

As a result: 'People and society are not ... related "dialectically". They do not constitute two moments of the same process. Rather they refer to radically different kinds of thing' (Bhaskar 1989b: 76).

In recognising the temporal priority of structure, Bhaskar clearly takes his cue from Marx. In the 1850s, Marx (1973: 146) wrote that: 'Men make their own history, but not ... under circumstances they themselves have chosen but under the given and inherited circumstances with which they are directly confronted.' At the beginning of the twentieth century, in his *Rules of Sociological Method*, Durkheim (1982) made a similar point.

Following Marx, Durkheim and Bhaskar, Archer (1995: 72) wrote: 'This is the human condition, to be born into a social context (of language, beliefs and organization) which was not of our making'. She describes Giddens's structuration theory as involving a 'central conflation' because it conflates structure and agency into processes acting together at a single level. Giddens's duality of structure treats structure and agency as *inseparable*:

> Whilst this frees both from being an epiphenomenon of the other, it does so by holding them to be mutually constitutive ... although the implication of this is a rejection of both upwards and downwards conflation in social theorizing, its consequence is actually to introduce a new variant – central conflation – into social theory.
>
> (*op. cit.*, p. 61)

For Archer,

> the general principle of mutual constitution is entirely unobjectionable; what I resist is the representation of their bonding as contact adhesion such that structure and agency are effectively defined in terms of one another.
>
> (*op. cit.*, p. 87)

A problem for structurationists is that they 'deliberately turn their backs upon any autonomous features which could pertain independently to either "structure" or "agency"' (*op. cit.*, p. 97).

Archer, like Bhaskar, makes the concept of an *emergent property* central to her argument. An emergent property cannot be described or explained in terms of the powers and capacities of its components. Archer thus distinguishes between those activities of agents which are exercises of their own intrinsic powers, and those activities which are really powers which reside in social structures, but operate through the activities of human agents. She follows Bhaskar in taking the human agent and social structure as two separate layers of social reality, each with their own causal powers.

Archer thus exposes a major difficulty in structuration theory: it cannot incorporate historical time. Because it resists untying structure from action, it cannot recognise that structure and agency work on different time intervals. As individuals, we are born into a set of structures that are not of our making. Acting within them, they may be changed or sustained by our actions. We then bequeath them to others.

However, Archer does not conflate individual into structure, giving the latter the sole burden of explanation. Indeed, the reproduction of social structure depends upon the actions of the individuals involved. Her approach is based on two basic propositions: '(i) That structure necessarily pre-dates the action(s) leading to its reproduction or transformation; (ii) That structural elaboration necessarily post-dates the action sequences which give rise to it' (*op. cit.*, p. 15). She thus develops

> a theoretical approach which is capable of *linking* structure and agency rather than *sinking* one into the other. The central argument is that structure and agency can only be linked by examining the *interplay between them over time*, and without the proper incorporation of time the problem of structure and agency can never be satisfactorily resolved.
>
> (*op. cit.*, p. 65)

Let us now take stock of this engagement between critical realism and structuration theory. We have seen that structuration theorists and critical realists, along with many others, together agree on the following four propositions:

(α) *The dependence of social structures upon individuals.* Social structures would not exist if individuals ceased to exist. Individuals through their actions may create, confirm, reproduce, replicate, transform or destroy social structures, either intentionally or unintentionally.

(β) *Rejection of methodological individualism.* Nevertheless, social structures cannot be explained entirely in terms of individuals and their relations. They are not reducible, in an ontological or an explanatory sense, to individuals alone.

(γ) *The dependence of individuals upon social structures.* For their socialisation, survival and interaction, individuals depend upon social structures, and individual behaviour is affected profoundly by its socio-structural context.

(δ) *Rejection of methodological collectivism.* Nevertheless, individuals are not reducible to social structures, such as institutions. Such reductionist explanations are invalid. Individual behaviours cannot be explained entirely in terms of the social structures in which they are located.

As a result of these four propositions, we may accept that, in a strong but qualified sense, individuals and social structure are *mutually constitutive*. So far so good. There is agreement between the critical realists and the structurationists. Significantly, they both propose that the alternatives of methodological collectivism and methodological individualism do not exhaust all the possibilities open to the social theorist.

However, from then on, the structurationists and the critical realists part company. Archer argued that realist approaches like Bhaskar's saw human agency and social structure as two separate layers of social reality, each with their own causal powers. On the other hand, structurationists, like Giddens, denied the existence of autonomous properties at the level of actor or structure. Archer and Bhaskar thus elaborated some additional and necessary aspects of a social structure:

(ε) *The temporal priority of social structure over the individual.* Individual interactions with a social structure are engagements with something already made; in this sense, social structure pre-dates the individual. As individuals we do not make society: it is there in some form at our birth, bearing the marks of past practices of the former – even deceased – generations. This temporal cleavage establishes social structure and society as entities distinct from individuals (or mere aggregates of individuals), at least because of the structural legacy bequeathed by past actors, and separates structure and agency as distinct but interconnected objects of investigation.

(ζ) *The existence of emergent properties and causal powers at the structural level.* Social structures have emergent properties that are not themselves reducible to human thoughts or actions. These emergent properties are marked by the existence of separate and additional causal powers, although the causal power of structure is always mediated through, and dependent upon, human agency.

Crucially, propositions (ε) and (ζ) break the former symmetries between actor and structure found in propositions (α), (β), (γ) and (δ). The terminological symmetry between these terms is now disrupted.

2. Some remaining problems

From the above account, it can be seen how the social theory of actor and structure has made considerable headway in the 1980s and 1990s. However, some problems and gaps remain. In particular, the mechanisms by which structures affect actors need to be further explored and clarified.

For critical realists and others, the term 'social structure' refers to the 'rules, relationships, positions and the like' (Lawson 1997: 57) that help to make up social systems. A hallmark of critical realism is to add to the concept of social structure an ontological feature that is deemed to be common to structures in both the natural and the social realm. This is the notion that a structure displays causal powers and emergent properties (Archer 1995: 9, 174–5; Bhaskar 1989a: 20; Lawson 1997: 21). Examples given by critical realists of social structures include 'the economy, the state, the family, language' (Bhaskar 1989b: 4) and 'demographic structures' Archer (1995: 174–5).

Significantly, Archer (1995: 174–5) considers a demographic distribution as an example of a social structure. She claims that, like all structures, the age distribution of a population has causal powers and emergent properties. She argued (p. 174) that such a demographic structure has relational properties with 'the generative capacity to modify the powers of its constituents in fundamental ways and to exercise causal influences *sui generis*. This is the litmus test which differentiates between emergence on the one hand and aggregation and combination on the other.' Accordingly, 'a demographic structure ... can ... modify the powers of people to change it' by defining the size of the group of child-bearers necessary to transform that structure. Other powers can be curtailed or enhanced by such a structure. 'For example, with a top-heavy demographic structure, it is extremely difficult to introduce or sustain a generous pensions policy' (*ibid.*).

Putting this particular example of a structure to more uses than Archer would suggest, we first note that demography embraces a relatively weak type of structure, with rather restricted causal properties and emergent powers. This example of a structure combines both special and general properties. They are special in the sense that they are relatively thin.

Consider the nature of 'the powers of people to change' a demographic structure. If there were a policy to increase the proportion of young people in a population, then that would require a greater birth rate. Given a specific demographic target, the required birth rate would depend mathematically on the characteristics of the existing demographic structure. The further that the existing structure was from the higher target, the greater would be the birth rate required to reach the target in a given time. This is the sense in which Archer argues that a demographic structure has 'causal powers' over human agents.

One problem with this account of 'causal power' is that it seems to confuse power with the size of the mass that it would have to move. The 'power' of demographic structure over agents, in the sense explored by agents, is really the scale or mass of the problem that *other* (biological and social) powers (of fecundity and child rearing) are required to change. The causal power of a demographic structure does not necessarily nor directly affect the powers of human fecundity that are required to change that structure. The structural role of a demographic structure is thus a very weak and rather restrictive type of 'downward causation' – a term elaborated further below – from structure to agent. It is weak because it essentially concerns an impediment placed upon the agent and, in general, it does not change the character or constitution of the agent herself.

Consider a hypothetical and particular instance in which a stronger form of downward causation could emerge. If the demographic structure itself became a prominent and enduring topic of social discourse then it could promote and mould individual behaviours in a specific way. For example, it could be part of a culture and ideology of ethnic nationalism, exhorting young men and women to 'breed for the future of the nation'. Or we could use the opposite example of severe restrictions upon child-bearing, as in the recent history of Communist China. These restrictions were enforced both by legal sanction and by persuasion. Arguably, such explicit and widely rooted cultural discourses and practices can change the perceptions and goals of the population in a deeper sense than Archer was prepared to consider in her discussion of demography. Such cultures act upon behaviour as more than constraints: they can lead to changes in individual goals. In these particular cases, the downward causation of structure upon agent would result in a reconstitution of purposes and preferences, as well as behaviour. In terms affecting human action, it would not simply be 'downward causation' in the sense of an impediment or constraint imposed by structure upon agent. It would also be a *reconstitutive* downward causation, where the causal powers of structure help to bring about significant changes to some important attributes and dispositions of the agent.

3. Introducing reconstitutive downward causation

An idea that may be termed 'upward causation' is already widely accepted in the social and natural sciences: elements at a lower ontological level somehow affect those at a higher level. For example, viruses cause illnesses and individuals can change institutions. Upward causation can be reconstitutive, because lower-level changes may alter fundamentally a higher level structure. Individualist or biological reductionists accept and endorse the possibility of reconstitutive upward causation. Anti-reductionists endorse it too. However, such reductionists are obliged to deny the possibility of reconstitutive downward causation that is being proposed here. With reconstitutive downward causation it is impossible to take the parts as given and then explain the whole. This is because the whole, to some extent, reconstitutes the parts.

Some extreme versions of 'holism' are also reductionist in the sense that they attempt to explain the parts entirely in terms of the whole. For example, attempts are sometimes made to explain all social phenomena solely in terms of structures, institutions, culture or whatever. Such 'upwards' reductionism would have to deny reconstitutive upward causation but could accept reconstitutive downward causation. Critics of these renditions of holism rightly focus on their failure to accept reconstitutive upward causation.

The opposite term 'downward causation' in the context of a hierarchical ontology was coined by Campbell (1974) on the basis of earlier work on 'emergent causation' by Sperry (1964; 1969). A similar but limited concept appears in the work of Michael Polanyi (1967: 44–5). The notion of 'downward causation' was elaborated further by Sperry (1976; 1991), James Murphy (1994) and others.

In its literature, the notion of 'downward causation' has weak and strong forms. As an intermediate case, Campbell (1974: 180) sees it in terms of evolutionary laws acting on populations: 'all processes at the lower levels of a hierarchy are restrained by and act in conformity to the laws of the higher levels.' Here evolutionary processes help to reconstitute populations but not necessarily individuals. A stronger notion, which is here described as 'reconstitutive downward causation' involves both individuals and populations not only restrained, but also changed, as a result of causal powers associated with higher levels. Notably, Sperry (1991: 230–1) also suggests a strong interpretation of downward causation. He recognises, for example, that 'higher cultural and other acquired values have power to downwardly control the more immediate, inherent humanitarian traits.'

However, it is not enough to accept this possibility of reconstitutive downward causation. In each case the particular causal processes have to be explained. Crucially, the concept of reconstitutive downward causation does not rely on unexplained or mysterious types of cause or causality. As Sperry (1991: 230) rightly insists: 'the higher-level phenomena in exerting downward control do *not disrupt* or *intervene* in the causal relations of the downward-level component activity'. This could usefully be termed Sperry's Rule. It ensures that emergence, although it is associated with emergent causal powers at a higher level, does not generate multiple types or forms of causality at any single level. Causal monism is sustained at each level and in reality as a whole. Any emergent causes at higher levels exist by virtue of lower-level causal processes.

Adherence to Sperry's Rule excludes any version of methodological collectivism or holism where an attempt is made to explain individual dispositions or behaviour entirely in terms of institutions or other system-level characteristics. Instead, Sperry's Rule obliges us to explain particular human behaviour in terms of causal processes operating at the individual level, such as individual aspirations, dispositions or constraints. Where higher-level factors enter, it is in the more general explanation of the system-wide processes giving rise to those aspirations, dispositions or constraints. Similarly, Darwin's principle of evolution does not explain the origin of the features of a specific organism, but it does explain the general processes through which species evolve.

Accordingly, at the level of the human agent, there are no magical 'cultural' or 'economic' forces controlling individuals, other than those affecting the dispositions, thoughts and actions of individual human actors. People do not develop new preferences, wants or purposes because mysterious 'social forces' control them. What have to be examined are the social and psychological mechanisms leading to such changes of preference, disposition or mentality.

What does happen is that the framing, shifting and constraining capacities of social institutions give rise to new perceptions and dispositions within individuals. Upon new habits of thought and behaviour, new preferences and intentions emerge. Alfred Marshall (1949: 76) observed 'the development of new activities giving rise to new wants'. But we need to know how this happens. The institutional economist Thorstein Veblen (1899: 190, emphasis added) was more specific about the psychological mechanisms involved: 'The situation of today shapes the institutions of tomorrow through a selective, coercive process, *by acting upon men's habitual view of things'*.

The crucial point in the argument here is to recognise the significance of reconstitutive downward causation on *habits*, rather than merely on behaviour, intentions or preferences. Clearly, the definitional distinction between habit (as a propensity or disposition) and behaviour (or action) is essential to make sense of this statement. On the contrary, the meaning of habit adopted by Veblen, the pragmatist philosophers and instinct psychologists, was of an acquired propensity or disposition, which may or may not be actually expressed in current behaviour. Repeated behaviour is important in establishing a habit. But habit and behaviour are not the same.[1]

But a second point is also of vital significance. It is a central tenet of the pragmatist philosophical and psychological perspective to regard habit and instinct as foundational to the human personality. Reason, deliberation and calculation emerge only after specific habits have been laid down; their operation depends upon such habits. In turn, the development of habits depends upon prior instincts. Instincts, by definition, are inherited. Accordingly, reconstitutive downward causation upon instincts is not possible.[2]

In contrast, the ongoing acquisition and modification of habits is central to human existence: all action and reason depends upon prior habits. For example, much deliberative thought is dependent on, as well as being coloured by, language. In addition, to make sense of the world we have to acquire habits of classification and habitually associated meanings. To act in and adapt to the world, our complex nervous system has to be developed and rehearsed. It is now believed that these developments depend upon an evolutionary process within the brain, where neural connections are established, selected and reinforced (Edelman 1987). Be that as it may, the crucial point here is that all action and deliberation depend on prior habits that we acquire during our individual development. Hence habits have temporal and ontological primacy over intention and reason. This is a key point for the argument here and for institutional economics as a whole. As we have seen, reconstitutive downward causation works by creating and moulding habits. Habit is the crucial and hidden link in the causal chain.

Accordingly, as long as we can explain how institutional structures give rise to new or changed habits, then we have an acceptable mechanism of reconstitutive downward causation. In contrast, we cannot identify any causal mechanism that leads to the reconstitution of preferences by institutions acting directly upon them. Institutions may lead directly to changes in some intentions, but only by acting as non-reconstitutive influences or constraints. For example, we decide to drive within the speed limit because we see a police car on the motorway. The particular intention is explained in terms of the *existing* preference to avoid punishment. This explanation does not itself involve a reconstitutive process. Clearly, any attempt to explain changes in intentions through intentions alone must assume a *fixed* subset of (meta-)preferences behind the expedient changes of intention and action. In contrast, to provide a reconstitutive causal mechanism, we have to point to factors that are foundational to purposes, preferences and deliberation as a whole. This is where habits come in.

In this manner, it may be possible to overcome the dilemma between methodological individualism and methodological collectivism. By acting not directly on individual decisions, but on habitual dispositions, institutions exert downward causation without reducing individual agency to their effects.[3] Furthermore, upward causation, from individuals to institutions, is still possible, without assuming that the individual is given or immanently conceived.

Although critical realism has been shown to be an advance on rival theories in some respects, it can be criticised for not going far enough down this road. Critical realism shares a defect with much other social theory. It is simply assumed that all actions are motivated by reason. The causes of reason itself are neglected. There is no explanation of how reasons are caused.

In Bhaskar's work, this is taken to the point of inconsistency. Bhaskar (1975: 70–1) endorses an 'ubiquity determinism', meaning that each event is deemed to have a cause. On the other hand (a page or so later) he fails to pursue this universal principle. He writes somewhat vaguely of the 'self-determination' of the agent (Bhaskar 1975: 72). If every event has a cause, we are left wondering how reasons and states of mind are caused. Bhaskar does not cross this philosophical Rubicon; he does not point to an account of the cultural, psychological or physiological mechanisms that cause reasons themselves to emerge. In general, in Bhaskar's writing, there is a failure to sketch the possible causes of reasons and allusions are made to a vague and inconsistent notion of the 'self-determined' agent. There are two problems here. One is the failure to examine the causes behind reasons. The other is to assume, as an act of mere definition, that all action is motivated by reasons.

In contrast, an approach building on the earlier instinct–habit psychology of James, Dewey and others offers a way out of this dilemma. Instead of associating agency exclusively with reason, the mind is itself conceived as a layered entity, with different levels of consciousness and deliberation (Twomey 1998). All reason and deliberation makes use of previously acquired habits of categorisation, inference and calculation. The existence and role of these habits makes reconstitutive downward causation possible.

Institutions are social structures with the capacity for reconstitutive downward causation, acting upon ingrained habits of thought and action. The downward causation of institutional structure upon agents results in a reconstitution of purposes and preferences. Causal powers and constraints associated with institutional structures can encourage changes in thought and behaviour. In turn, upon these repeated acts, new habits of thought and behaviour emerge. It is not simply the individual behaviour that has been changed: there are also changes in habitual dispositions. In turn, these are associated with changed individual understandings, purposes and preferences. We now consider some of the processes involved in more detail.

4. Hidden mechanisms of persuasion

For example, the fable of 'sour grapes' speaks precisely of people declaring a change of preferences because of ambition frustrated by circumstances (Elster 1983). These circumstances could include structures or institutions. New habits would then arise, in accord with the changed preferences. The theory of cognitive dissonance (Festinger 1957) explains that when people are faced with a difficult choice between alternative courses of action their perception of the alternatives is adjusted to render one of them more acceptable. This is often done by imitating and acquiring the norms and perceptions of others (Hodgson 1988). This results in the transmission of habits of thought and behaviour from one person to another.

Another body of literature from psychology that can be reinterpreted in the terms proposed here is the empirical and theoretical work on obedience to authority (Kelman and Hamilton 1989; Milgram 1974). In particular, Herbert Kelman and his colleagues have proposed that obedience to authority can result from different processes. For example, it may be a direct effect of rewards for compliance or of punishments for non-compliance. Alternatively, it may result from a deeper identification with the values of those in authority. In the former case, reconstitutive downward causation will occur only if compliance eventually gives rise to habits of thought or behaviour consistent with obedience. In the latter case, to minimise unease and self-doubt, an original habit of deference to authority might be expanded into a reconstitutive acceptance of the norms and values of those in power.

In general, the causal processes of reconstitution discussed here are not mysterious 'social forces' but well-known psychological mechanisms of imitation, conformism, conditioning and cognition.

With the notion of *reconstitutive downward causation* in mind, we can begin to identify the special features of some structures that make them also institutions. In the above example, the demographic structure had to become an explicit and *widely accepted idea* and had to become tied up with widespread and commonly accepted *conceptions, habits* and *behaviours* before its downward causation became effective in reconstituting (instead of merely impeding or constraining) the agent (including a reconstitution of her purposes and preferences).

Bhaskar (1989a, b) and others rightly insist that beliefs are part of social reality. John Searle (1995) examines this further, explaining that the mental representations of an institution or its rules are partly constitutive of that institution, since an institution can only exist if people have specifically related beliefs and mental attitudes. On this basis, it is reasonable to assume that institutions, but not all social structures, are required by definition to have ideational representations. Institutions are simultaneously both structures 'outside' individuals and ideas 'inside' their heads. This does not, however, mean that institutions exist simply in the mind. It means that they depend upon subjective representations, as a necessary but not sufficient condition, as well as other, objective, circumstances. Recognition of the ideational facets of institutions is a partial safeguard against the mistake of reification. This error is to regard institutions or social structures as if they were just things, independent of social agency.

Going beyond the limited example of a demographic structure we can see more acutely the ways in which institutions form and shape individuals. For example, the institution of money imbues people with pecuniary habits of calculation and comparison. As another example, the institution of language is not simply the medium by which ideas are represented and communicated: it is also a means of shaping individual attitudes and ways of thought. Likewise, the institution of the family, and its associated practices and ideologies, can help to inculcate particular values and

173

purposes. Note that in all these cases institutions work upon individuals by spreading specific habits of thought and behaviour.

Accordingly, we regard an institution as a special type of social structure that: (a) involves codifiable rules of interpretation and behaviour, (b) that are widely followed and imitated in a social group, and (c) are being ingrained in habits of thought and conduct. Institutions are not merely a subclass of social structures. Institutions are the kind of structures that matter most in the social realm and make up the stuff of social life. They matter most because of their capacity to form and mould the capacities and behaviour of agents in fundamental ways, the manner of which we shall explore further below.

This capacity of institutions to change individuals in a fundamental sense is not only a key and long-lasting insight of institutional economics, but also, perhaps, its defining characteristic. Consider the following passages from the writings of leading institutional economists. Veblen (1899: 190–1) wrote:

> The situation of today shapes the institutions of tomorrow through a selective, coercive process, by acting upon men's habitual view of things, and so altering or fortifying a point of view or a mental attitude handed down from the past.

John Commons (1934: 73–4) likewise made it clear that,

> the individual with whom we are dealing is the Institutionalized Mind. Individuals begin as babies. They learn the custom of language, of cooperation with other individuals, of working towards common ends, of negotiations to eliminate conflicts of interest, of subordination to the working rules of the many concerns of which they are members. They meet each other ... prepared more or less by habit, induced by the pressure of custom ...

Wesley Mitchell (1937: 371), in his study of the evolution of money as an institution emphasised how it changed human mentality and nature:

> Now the money economy ... is in fact one of the most potent institutions in our whole culture. In sober truth it stamps its pattern upon wayward human nature, makes us all react in standard ways to the standard stimuli it offers, and affects our very ideals of what is good, beautiful and true.

This notion that the individual is not given, but can be reconstituted by institutions, pervades the tradition of 'old' institutionalism from its predecessors in the historical school to its successors today. Institutionalism is distinguished from both mainstream economics and the 'new institutional economics' precisely for the reason that it does not assume a given individual, with given purposes or preference functions. Instead of a bedrock of given individuals, presumed by the mainstream and 'new' institutional economics, the 'old' institutionalism holds to the idea of interactive and partially malleable agents, mutually entwined in a web of partially durable and self-reinforcing institutions (Hodgson 1988; 1993; 1998).

In sum, institutionalism in the tradition of Veblen, Commons and Mitchell concurs with propositions (α), (β), (γ) and (δ), which are also common to both structuration theory and critical realism. Institutionalism also concurs with propositions (ε) and (ζ) which are found in critical realism but not in structuration theory. But institutionalism goes further than critical realism by insisting on a seventh proposition. To be adequate in the social realm, the sixth proposition (ζ) – concerning the existence of emergent properties and causal powers at the structural level – must be supplemented by an additional proposition (η):

(η) The social structure stands above individuals in a hierarchical arrangement, and the causal powers associated with the higher level may not simply impede or constrain behaviour but may also affect and alter fundamental properties, powers and propensities of individuals. When an upper hierarchical level affects components at a lower level in this manner, this may be seen as a special and stronger case of 'downward causation' that we may term as *reconstitutive downward causation*. Those particular social structures that have the capacity for substantial, enduring and widespread reconstitutive downward causation upon individuals are termed *institutions*.

For contrast, it is useful to consider cases where downward causation is not reconstitutive. Such instances involve structures acting primarily as weights, deterrents or constraints upon human action. It may channel or redirect human behaviour, but if it is not reconstitutive then it does not change purposes or preference functions. Archer's discussion of a demographic structure illustrates a downward causation that is not necessarily reconstitutive. Something more than this is being emphasised here.

5. Some illustrations: Social power and learning

This matter has to do with social power. Bertrand Russell (1938: 35) noted that 'influence on opinion' was an important source of power over individuals, as well as by direct physical coercion and by punishments and rewards. Under the heading of 'influence on opinion' he included both propaganda and 'creating desired habits in others' by drill.

Lukes (1974) developed further the analysis of social power. He also considered the possibility that power may be exercised by 'coercion, influence, authority, force or manipulation' (p. 17) but these mechanisms do not necessarily involve changing individual preferences, purposes or values. For Lukes, the overemphasis on the coercive aspect of power ignores the way that it is often exercised more subtly, and often without overt conflict. Lukes (p. 23) thus wrote:

> To put the matter sharply, *A* may exercise power over *B* by getting him to do what he does not want to do, but he also exercises power over him by influencing, shaping or determining his very wants. Indeed, is it not the supreme exercise of power to get another or others to have the desires you want them to have – that is, to secure their compliance by controlling their thoughts and desires?

Consider an example. If a criminal desists from crime, simply because he or she fears the risk of apprehension and punishment, then behaviour is being changed through the force of constraint and deterrence. On the other hand, if a prison education programme persuades the criminal that wrongdoing is evil, and that there are better ways of earning a living, then the released criminal will desist from crime, even if the constraints and penalties are ineffective. The preferences and purposes of the criminal will have been changed through immersion in a culture of learning and self-improvement. New habits of thought would have emerged.

In mainstream economics, preference functions are not subject to reconstitutive downward causation. This is so even when an attempt is made to 'explain' tastes. Gary Becker's (1996) work on *Accounting for Tastes* makes an attempt to show that cultural and other influences can alter preferred outcomes. He does this by bringing cultural and other factors into the arguments of these functions. However, culture does not in fact alter the preference functions themselves. A problem with this analysis is that it cannot deal with the genuine evolution and fundamental development of the individual. It is a desperate attempt to make all explanations of social phenomena reducible to the given individual, but in doing so it has to make the individual preference function immutable. The preference function is already 'there', ready to deal with unpredictable and unknowable circumstances. For instance, it already 'knows' how to react to the technology and inventions of the coming decades. Miraculously, its parameter space already includes variables representing the ideas and commodities of the future. Mysteriously, it has already learned how to recognise them. The question is posed as to what does learning mean in such circumstances, when we already know essentially what is to be learned. Such a conception of learning must be sorely inadequate.

Learning is more than the discovery or reception of information: it is the reconstitution of individual capacities and preferences, tantamount to a change in individual personality. Today, we may not like Shakespeare, but after exposure to his work we may acquire a taste and understanding that may even alter our attitude to life. Learning *reconstitutes* the individual. Douglas Vickers (1995: 115) rightly identified this as a key 'difficulty that economic analysis has been reluctant to confront'. He stressed that with changing knowledge and learning 'the individual is himself, economically as well as epistemologically, a different individual'.

Learning typically takes place through and within social structures, and at least in this sense it is an important case of reconstitutive downward causation. Neoclassical economics has great difficulty accommodating the notion of learning because the very idea of 'rational learning' is problematic. It treats learning as the cumulative discovery of pre-existing 'blueprint' information, as stimulus and response, or as the Bayesian updating of subjective probability estimates in the light of incoming data. However, instead of the mere input of 'facts' to given individuals, learning is a developmental and reconstitutive process. Learning involves adaptation to changing circumstances, and such adaptations mean the reconstitution of the individuals involved. Institutions and cultures play a vital role in establishing the concepts and norms of the learning process (Hodgson 1988; 1999). Accordingly, the reconstitutive nature of learning is partly a matter of reconstitutive downward causation. To put it bluntly: if we are to accept fully the notion of learning into social theory then the concept of reconstitutive downward causation must also be sanctioned.

These subtle mechanisms of reconstitutive downward causation are far more widespread than the 'brainwashing' of individuals. Many economists, including Becker (1996: 225), mention 'brainwashing' as soon as any institutional influences on individuals are mooted. Typical of many economists, Becker recognises nothing in between 'brainwashing' on the one hand, and 'free choice' based on given preference functions, on the other. The truth is that most of social behaviour lies away from these two extremes. Learning is a case in point.

Methodologically, a significant implication of reconstitutive downward causation in a hierarchical ontology is that it gives additional reasons for ruling out any *exclusive* reliance on units at the lower level in any explanation of higher level phenomena. Although the existence of emergence properties is enough to prohibit such reductionism, reconstitutive downward causation redoubles this difficulty. In the social sciences, it undermines the notion of the individual as a primary and unalterable given. Accordingly, the possibility has to be considered that institutions, as well as individuals, have to be taken as units of analysis.

A further implication is that it means that universal approaches to the theorisation of economic or human behaviour – such as general equilibrium theory – may be challenged. Individuals are likely to be changed and constituted by their institutional environment and these institutions are often historically and locally specific. Accordingly, we are faced with the problem of developing a methodology and theory to encompass changing and historically specific objects of analysis (Hodgson, forthcoming).

6. Conclusion

One possible objection to this line of research would be to suggest that the assumption of agents with endogenously formed preference functions would be hopelessly complicated and intractable. Accordingly, it could be argued, it is necessarily to simplify matters and assume agents with preference functions that are exogenously given. To respond to this argument it is necessary to show what is possible within the framework discussed above. In some circumstances the assumption of malleable preferences may simplify matters rather than complicate them. It may be conjectured that the process of reconstitutive downward causation may provide a degree of durability and stability in institutional structure that is not explained adequately in standard models. The circular, positive feedback from institution to individuals and from individuals to institutions can help to enhance the durability of the institutional unit. What would then be theorised is the self-reinforcing institutional structure. Accordingly, within an institutional structure, it may be possible to show that malleable preferences lead to stable emergent properties. These properties may exist not despite, but because of, malleable preferences.

What is proposed here is a research agenda that takes both agents and structures into account, without reducing one to the other. In part, this approach is founded on a conception of the individual agent where habits are foundational for action and reason. The key concept of habit provides a mechanism through which structures can act upon individuals and help to reconstitute their natures and preferences. What is required now is to give this approach more theoretical and operational substance.

Notes

1 James (1890) and Dewey (1922) remain works with two of the best accounts of this concept of habit as a propensity.
2 However, 'downward causation' upon instincts, in the weaker sense of Campbell (1974), is possible, simply because instincts, like other human features, exist and evolve in consistency with higher level principles, such as the laws of evolution.
3 Behind some of the pretentious terminology, a similar insight and motive seems to lie with Bourdieu's (1990) concept of *habitus*.

References

Archer, Margaret S. (1995) *Realist Social Theory: The Morphogenetic Approach* (Cambridge: Cambridge University Press).
Becker, Gary S. (1996) *Accounting for Tastes* (Cambridge, MA: Harvard University Press).

Bhaskar, Roy (1975) *A Realist Theory of Science*, 1st edn. (Leeds: Leeds Books).

Bhaskar, Roy (1983) 'Beef, Structure and Place: Notes From a Critical Naturalist Perspective', *Journal for the Theory of Social Behaviour*, **13**, 81–95.

Bhaskar, Roy (1989a) *The Possibility of Naturalism: A Philosophic Critique of the Contemporary Human Sciences*, 2nd edn. (Brighton: Harvester).

Bhaskar, Roy (1989b) *Reclaiming Reality: A Critical Introduction to Contemporary Philosophy* (London: Verso).

Bourdieu, Pierre (1990) *The Logic of Practice*, trans. Richard Nice (Stanford and Cambridge: Stanford University Press and Polity Press).

Bunge, Mario A. (1973) *Method, Model and Matter* (Dordrecht, Holland: Reidel).

Campbell, Donald T. (1974) '"Downward Causation" in Hierarchically Organized Biological Systems', in Ayala, Francisco J. and Dobzhansky, Theodosius (eds) *Studies in the Philosophy of Biology* (London, Berkeley and Los Angeles: Macmillan and University of California Press), pp. 179–86.

Commons, John R. (1934) *Institutional Economics – Its Place in Political Economy* (New York: Macmillan).

Dewey, John (1922) *Human Nature and Conduct: An Introduction to Social Psychology*, 1st edn. (New York: Holt).

Dewey, John (1939) *Theory of Valuation* (Chicago: University of Chicago Press).

Durkheim, Emile (1982) *The Rules of Sociological Method*, translated from the French edition of 1901 by W. D. Halls with an introduction by Steven Lukes (London: Macmillan).

Edelman, Gerald M. (1987) *Neural Darwinism: The Theory of Neuronal Group Selection* (New York: Basic Books).

Elster, Jon (1983) *Sour Grapes: Studies in the Subversion of Rationality* (Cambridge: Cambridge University Press).

Festinger, Leon (1957) *A Theory of Cognitive Dissonance* (Stanford, CA: California University Press).

Giddens, Anthony (1976) *New Rules of Sociological Method* (London: Hutchinson).

Giddens, Anthony (1979) *Central Problems in Social Theory* (Berkeley and Los Angeles: University of California Press).

Giddens, Anthony (1984) *The Constitution of Society: Outline of the Theory of Structuration* (Cambridge: Polity Press).

Hodgson, Geoffrey M. (1988) *Economics and Institutions: A Manifesto for a Modern Institutional Economics* (Cambridge and Philadelphia: Polity Press and University of Pennsylvania Press).

Hodgson, Geoffrey M. (1993) 'Institutional economics: Surveying the "old" and the "new"', *Metroeconomica*, **44**(1), 1–28.

Hodgson, Geoffrey M. (1998) 'The Approach of Institutional Economics', *Journal of Economic Literature*, **36**(1), 166–92.

Hodgson, Geoffrey M. (1999) *Economics and Utopia: Why the Learning Economy is not the End of History* (London: Routledge).

Hodgson, Geoffrey M. (forthcoming) *How Economics Forgot History: The Problem of Historical Specificity in Social Science*.

James, William (1890) *The Principles of Psychology*, 1st edn. (New York: Holt).

Kelman, Herbert C. and Hamilton, V. Lee (1989) *Crimes of Obedience: Toward a Social Psychology of Authority and Responsibility* (New Haven: Yale University Press).

Koestler, Arthur (1967) *The Ghost in the Machine* (London: Hutchinson).

Lawson, Tony (1997) *Economics and Reality* (London: Routledge).

Lukes, Steven (1973) *Individualism* (Oxford: Basil Blackwell).

Lukes, Steven (1974) *Power: A Radical View* (London: Macmillan).

Marshall, Alfred (1949) *The Principles of Economics*, 8th (reset) edn (1st edn 1890) (London: Macmillan).

Marx, Karl (1973) *Surveys From Exile: Political Writings – Volume 2*, edited and introduced by David Fernbach (Harmondsworth: Penguin).

Milgram, Stanley (1974) *Obedience to Authority: An Experimental View* (New York and London: Harper and Row, and Tavistock).

Mitchell, Wesley C. (1937) *The Backward Art of Spending Money and Other Essays* (New York: McGraw-Hill).

Morgan, C. Lloyd (1932) 'C. Lloyd Morgan' in C. Murchison (ed.) *A History of Psychology in Autobiography, Volume 2* (New York: Russell and Russell), pp. 253–64.

Mouzelis, Nicos (1995) *Sociological Theory: What Went Wrong? Diagnosis and Remedies*, (London and New York: Routledge).

Murphy, James Bernard (1994) 'The Kinds of Order in Society', in P. Mirowski (ed.) *Natural Images in Economic Thought: Markets Read in Tooth and Claw*, (Cambridge and New York: Cambridge University Press), pp. 536–82.

Nozick, Robert (1977) 'On Austrian Methodology', *Synthese*, **36**, 353–92.

Polanyi, Michael (1967) *The Tacit Dimension* (London: Routledge and Kegan Paul).

Russell, Bertrand (1938) *Power: A New Social Analysis* (London: George Allen and Unwin).

Searle, John R. (1995) *The Construction of Social Reality* (London: Allen Lane).

Sperry, Roger W. (1964) *Problems Outstanding in the Evolution of Brain Function* (New York: American Museum of Natural History).

Sperry, Roger W. (1969) 'A Modified Concept of Consciousness', *Psychological Review*, **76**(6), 532–6.

Sperry, Roger W. (1976) 'Mental Phenomena as Causal Determinants in Brain Function', in G. G. Globus, G. Maxwell and J. Savodnik (eds) *Consciousness and the Brain: A Scientific and Philosophical Inquiry* (New York and London: Plenum), pp. 163–77.

Sperry, Roger W. (1991) 'In Defense of Mentalism and Emergent Interaction', *Journal of Mind and Behavior*, **12**(2), 221–46.

Twomey, Paul (1998) 'Reviving Veblenian Economic Psychology', *Cambridge Journal of Economics*, **22**(4), 433–48.

Veblen, Thorstein B. (1899) *The Theory of the Leisure Class: An Economic Study in the Evolution of Institutions* (New York: Macmillan).

Vickers, Douglas (1994) *Economics and the Antagonism of Time: Time, Uncertainty, and Choice in Economic Theory* (Ann Arbor: University of Michigan Press).

Whitehead, Alfred N. (1933) *Adventures of Ideas* (Cambridge: Cambridge University Press).

11

CONVENTIONS OF CO-ORDINATION AND THE FRAMING OF UNCERTAINTY

Laurent Thévenot

1. Introduction

Among the different social sciences (including economics), there is a large variety of models which account for human interaction. Three types of core assumptions are more or less explicitly formulated in each of these different approaches to interaction: the first type of hypothesis (H1) has to do with the *competence*, or the understanding with which social actors are endowed (their optimising rationality in the economic model); the second series of hypotheses (H2) identifies the set of relevant *objects* which, though they are exterior to the actors, are deeply involved in their inter-action (commodities, in the economic model); and the third set of hypotheses (H3) addresses the *mode of co-ordination* between the actors, i.e. the institutions, conventions, or rules of the game upon which the actors agree (mainly market competition in the mainstream economic model).

The first type of hypothesis is at the heart of economic theory and is reg-ularly brought to the fore. It leads to debates over the role of irrational behaviour, the detailed explanation of which is generally left to the other social sciences. The second type of hypothesis remains most often unspec-ified in mainstream economics, since the common identification of the list of commodities is generally considered as 'natural'. The third set of hypo-theses has only recently been commonly brought up in economics, many authors being interested in forms of co-ordination which differ from pure market exchange in the New Institutional Economics, in the Principal–Agent approach, or in the *Economie des conventions*.[1]

This essay deals with the tensions which occur in the economic model of action when it faces certain situations which we here will call critical because behaviour no longer follows a single mode of co-ordination that is universally applicable to everyone and in all kinds of circumstances such as market-coordination. In such critical situations, actors – and researchers who interpret their actions – are torn between incommensurable rationales. This multi-faceted choice and the possibility of taking into account a plurality of forms of co-ordination has the advantage of enabling us to see through the supposedly natural character of each form: it undermines the basis for the objective character of a unique form of co-ordination or, in other words, a common world. Recent developments in the economic literature increasingly deal with critical situations, and must therefore have recourse to concepts which are foreign to the explanatory framework of general market equilibrium, such as convention, commitment, trust, loyalty, solidarity, organisation, etc.

In this paper, I would like to mention some of the tensions bearing on the mainstream economic explanation of human action, as a result of the introduction of organisational, social, and institutional phenomena. Then, I will explore the conditions which must necessarily be met by a framework of analysis which aims at accounting for critical situations and yet intends to remain compatible with the economic analysis of market relations. I will, for that purpose, recall the main directions of a research programme that I have conducted with Luc Boltanski (Boltanski and Thévenot 1989; 1991) in order to elaborate such a framework of analysis.[2]

Briefly outlined, our approach is the following. We focus on the forms of evaluation that agents use to co-ordinate their actions. Primarily, we considered the most legitimate forms which govern highly general modes of co-ordination and which we called 'orders of worth' (Boltanski and Thévenot 1991; 1999). Market order of *worth* is viewed as one among a plurality of equally grounded modes of evaluation involved in the co-ordination of action. One finds in the literature different versions of pluralism which can help us to differentiate social actions and their motives. The sociology of Max Weber insisted upon the irreducible plurality of value-spheres and principles of legitimate domination (Weber 1978). Michael Walzer's *Spheres of Justice* (Walzer 1983) followed 'liberal theorists [who] preached and practiced an art of separation' (Walzer 1984: 315) while extending this pluralism to institutional spheres of shared understanding. This pluralist stance assumes that the many forms of justifiable action do not fall into any discernible hierarchy dominated by an overarching principle, and that there can be no uniquely permissible value ranking of the feasible options. Does this demise of Aristotelian ethics necessarily lead, as Alasdair MacIntyre suggested in *After Virtue* (1981), to interminable moral disputes among rival claims as long as moral rules are attached to *individual preferences*?

Turning away from the former kind of approach, we considered that the different forms of justification to which people refer when they have to co-ordinate distant actions with anonymous others, are not relative to people, as cultural values are, but are adjusted to the situation encountered. Our main purpose has been to characterise what constitutes a *justifiable* action, i.e. an action on which a specific form of co-ordination can be grounded because a general judgement is involved in the decision-making which leads to this action. Justifiable actions need to be adjusted to circumstances although they aim at going beyond contingencies and claim a general validity. We relate this classical tension between the rule and its application to the following question: how can justification be valid and co-ordination be effective if several underlying principles of justifiable action are available and each is supposed to be universally valid ?

The answer to this question requires a careful examination of the role of the relevant *objects* which, along with persons, are involved in this type of justifiable action. We consider that the justification of actions, and therefore the possibility of their co-ordination, presupposes the use of certain objects which will be coherent with each form of co-ordination – as, for instance, commodities in the market co-ordination. The actions we are interested in involve repertoires of objects which contribute to the justification and the co-ordination of the different possible types of behaviour. The fulfilment of expectations – which is the sign of a successful co-ordination – depends on the probative power of the objects effectively engaged in the action. As soon as we consider resources for action according to their capacity for establishing an equivalence with other situations, namely one's own future or others' actions, they bear a part of the *commitment* which is anchored in intention. Paraphrasing Michael Bratman, who illuminated the role played by the plans which 'allow us to extend the influence of present deliberation to the future' (Bratman 1987), I would emphasise that objects are qualified for this extension. Thus, in market transactions, the common identification of a list of commodities plays a crucial role in the possibility of market equilibrium. If one admits the existence of multiple forms of co-ordination, then one must also acknowledge a plurality of what we have called 'worlds' which are constituted by objects which are *relevant* for each of those forms.

The two previous arguments about the plurality of the forms of co-ordination (H3) and the role of objects (H2) suggest that we need to reformulate the hypotheses about rationality (H1). The uncertainty brought about by the plurality, on the one hand, and the necessity to identify a context of *relevant* objects for action before making any choice, on the other hand, both require a careful deliberation much in the sense of Simon's arguments about procedural rationality. An analytical framework allowing for an adaptation of action to contexts of such diverse natures implies significant changes in our way of addressing human action. It is to an outline of these changes that I now turn.

2. Critical situations for market agreement

As an introduction to the notion of critical situation, let us first consider an example, proposed by Oliver Williamson, of a situation that presents a conflict of justifications, and therefore, of possible modes of co-ordination. It clearly puts into play two different modes of evaluation of action that cannot be embraced simultaneously and makes clear the conflict that arises between the different guiding principles in particular circumstances.

Williamson describes the behaviour of an individual who considers giving his blood. His behaviour can take two different and, in fact, contradictory forms: either he donates his blood as a gesture of human *solidarity*, or he sells it on a market place, as any other type of commodity, in order to increase his *wealth*. According to Kenneth Arrow (1972), economists take for granted that the creation of a market, because it increases the possibilities for individual choice, is therefore always advantageous. However, the transformation of blood into a commodity goes against the altruism of the gift and destroys the donor's feeling of contentment which is based on a sense of solidarity and an inner persuasion of having contributed to the welfare of the community. Discussing this issue, Williamson adds a shrewd insight about the embarrassment of the spontaneous donor when the situation takes a critical turn given the confrontation of two good and yet incompatible reasons to act. He writes that a dual system is a cause of worry for the spontaneous donor who wonders if he is *generous* or else *naïve* (Williamson 1975: 38).

In order to show the problems posed by the necessity of a justification in a critical situation, let us place Williamson's insight in the larger framework of a confrontation between an actor and an interpreter – the latter either being present during the course of the action or elaborating a model to explain it – in a complex situation including two forms of justification allowing for two types of good reasons to act (see Table 11.1).

The first order of justification is *civic* (C) and is grounded on the notion of the common good constituted by collective solidarity. The second order is a *market* justification (M) based on the common good constituted by the possibility of a market agreement. The action of the 'actor' can be performed according to either one of these justifications (columns C and

Table 11.1 Figures of judgement in a complex situation

Interpreter	Actor	
	C(*civic*)	M(*market*)
C	sympathetic	greedy
M	naïve	realistic

M), but it can also be understood and evaluated by an 'interpreter' according to either one of these two forms (lines C and M). The two diagonal cells correspond to situations we will call 'natural' because both the actor and the interpreter agree upon the assumptions of the action. The off-diagonal cells, on the other hand, correspond to 'critical' situations in which the actor and the interpreter analyse the situation according to different forms of justification. When studying this table, we can also observe that Williamson only considers the case of the first column.

The first form of judgement of the spontaneous donor's action, generosity, is based on a principle of collective solidarity coherent with this action (case 1.1); the donor's worth is enhanced and his happiness grows in proportion. The second form of judgement leading to the qualification of naïveté, is grounded in an interpretation related to a market principle, quite different from the first one. Here the behaviour of the donor becomes unjustifiable (case 2.1). He is criticised for being naïve and his unworthy state – in terms of *market* worth – is held as the just consequence of his lack of attention to the opportunities for business.

In order to deal with action in a critical situation of this sort – two modes of justification of different natures being available at the same time – the solution proposed by Williamson is to introduce a new object, incorporated into consumers' preferences, the 'trading atmosphere'. Indeed he advises us to 'consider the process of exchange in itself – and not only the commodity (which is being exchanged) – as an object of value' (1975: 38). The presupposition for the action is thus reduced to the lower logic level of a commodity submitted to an exchange; the critical tension between different modes of action is thus dodged. However, the hypothetical optimisation encompassing these different atmospheres cannot be based on prices resulting from market transactions. Decision-making requires that another form of equivalence and evaluation be introduced in order to compare the two types of actions, leading to something like a deliberation upon the principle of action itself. Civic duties are ruled by evaluations which are other than monetary (1975: 44). Therefore, the hypothesis that the calculation remains unchanged and that there is a continuous shift from a 'market' to a 'civic' action, simply evades the difficulty illustrated by the previous example. It neglects the complexity of the situation brought about by the critical confrontation of these different modes of action, each grounded on radically opposed reasons for acting and forms of co-ordination.[3]

We have tried to demonstrate that, contrary to what is commonly admitted, the difference between the two good reasons for acting, illustrated by the donor's case, was not to be accounted for by a distinction between the individual and the collective, i.e. the individualistic and holistic frameworks of analysis. These two good reasons can both be part of the same construction which posits the possibility of a common valuation of action in relation to some sort of common good – the common good of market competition or the common good of civic general will. We have demonstrated elsewhere (Boltanski and Thévenot 1991) that these constructions follow the classical tradition, in political philosophy, of establishing the foundations of an order in the commonwealth. The common matrix at the basis of different positive social sciences (economic theory included) and, therefore, of competing explanations for human behaviour, can usefully be related to a common system of constraints regulating the forms of dispute and agreement to which the members of a society may have recourse.

3. The place of objects in the co-ordination of actions

A great part of the success of the theory of general equilibrium rests upon a co-ordination device which, given the mechanism of market prices, requires only little centralised information (Hayek 1945). However, as one moves away from a market situation – i.e. a situation corresponding to a competitive market with perfect information – the economist's view of the rationality of human beings (H1) becomes increasingly complex. For instance, we know that in a situation of imperfect information, expectations require a much higher capacity of calculation because they lead to infinite regressions whose convergence poses problems, both in terms of the expectations of the expectations of the opposite party and of the optimisation cost (Mongin and Walliser 1988). These speculations make the task of the theoretician much more complex and induce him to shift the burden of such complexity onto the capabilities of the actors. The economy of the market order, as suggested by the image of the invisible hand, is progressively reduced as the competence attributed to each human being comes closer to the science of the economist – the hand becoming more and more visible. As Kenneth Arrow observes, without these hypotheses (equilibrium, competition, and perfect market regulation), the very concept of rationality is threatened, because the perception of others, and particularly of their rationality, becomes an element of our own rationality (Arrow 1987: 25–6).

The problems encountered in trying to explain co-ordinated actions by taking into account only the first set of hypotheses (H1, which deals with the *competence* of the actors), should therefore induce us to explore the two supplementary hypotheses (H2, about the *objects*, and H3, about the *forms of co-ordination*).

As we have mentioned, the co-ordination between the actions of different particular persons facing different kinds of situations, presupposes the possibility of going beyond contingencies in order to reach an agreement on the *relevant* context for the action. Our approach to the issue of co-ordination led us to conceptualise the notion of *qualified* object.[4] The burden weighing on the anticipations of speculative actors becomes lighter as it is partially shifted onto the objects.

We highlighted the availability of several *forms of objectivity*, connected to the different modes of co-ordination of actions. One can easily recognise the role commodities play in the market co-ordination: they enable actions to be compared by providing a commonly accepted identification of objects external to the actors. Let us then now consider the objectivity of technical tools which differs from that of commodities, while still sustaining another mode of co-ordination. The standardised functionality of a technical tool actually supports common and reliable expectancies about the future. In fact, the efficiency of this type of object is based precisely on the fact that it is valid for the future since, as an *investment*, it perpetuates a function of production which co-ordinates productive actions. By establishing a time equivalency, industrial objects thus allow for the constitution of a form of co-ordination of actions which differs from that of the market co-ordination in so far as they constitute the basis for decisions which engage people's future, enable them to move through time, especially when an actor sees himself as linked to his counterpart in the future (Thévenot 1984). Without such objects it would simply be impossible to reason and to reach an understanding about the future.

By acknowledging the place of objects in co-ordination, we lessen the weight of the rationality constraint placed on people and partially shift it over to their environment and the context of action, a shift which is now considered closely in some current of cognitive science and artificial intelligence oriented towards 'situated cognition' or 'distributed cognition' (Conein, Dodier and Thévenot 1993; Conein and Thévenot 1997; Hutchins 1995; Lave 1986; Norman 1989; Norman and Draper 1986).[5] People's evaluation of the outcome of their action, i.e., the operations which they perform in order to adjust their behaviour, assume that the objects upon which they rely have an appropriate form. The notion of 'form investment' (Thévenot 1984) refers to the relationship between the objects upon which the actors rely and the co-ordination of their behaviour. The form is defined in terms of a capacity for time and space equivalency, and the yields on the form investment are the consequence of this generality which makes it possible for agreement to be grounded. The notion of form investment enables us to understand the implementation, particularly in the functioning of a firm, of conventional resources (rules, norms, trademarks, customs, etc.) which, though they are not exactly similar to tools, are clearly associated with a kind of efficiency, and which call for a redefinition of the function of production. The analysis in terms of form investments suggests that we recompose the roles attributed, in the economic model of action, to the three types of hypotheses dealing respectively with the rationality of the actors, the exteriority of the objective context of the actions, and their mode of co-ordination. The optimisation calculation (H1) requires that the elements which are extracted from the context and used as resources have an appropriate, objective form (H2).

This objectivity is a capacity for equivalence necessary for co-ordination both by a single actor over time and between different actors.

4. The evaluation of worth in legitimate modes of co-ordination

A justifiable action requires that the objects and rationale involved in the actions be general. It is based on a common presupposition which ensures the convergence of the series of 'why' and 'for what reasons'?. The strong hypothesis assuming that collective representations are simply shared must be rejected if we acknowledge the plurality of the principles capable of grounding an action. Our aim is thus to understand the composition of two hypotheses which are apparently difficult to reconcile: the possibility of grounding the co-ordination of actions on a common framework and the availability of a plurality of modes of co-ordination.

The analytical framework we proposed (Boltanski and Thévenot 1991) provides a model for reasonable action compatible with these two hypotheses. I will now introduce its major features while confronting it with a more classical economic presentation of rational action. I will, however, confine this presentation to a brief outline, highlighting only the definitions and hypotheses required to carry out the type of analysis that interests us here.

A major direction of this development, in the continuation of what has just been said about the adjustment of resources to action, consists of a more detailed explanation of the hypothesis (type H2) about the role of *objects* in the co-ordination of actions. These beings are good candidates to support co-ordination as long as they are resistant to the overflow of contingencies and idiosyncrasies. If we recognise several forms of generality, then we must face the possibility of several forms of objectivity. Objects are defined as germane things for action, as opposed to nameless scraps ('what-d'you-call-its') which cannot become reliable means. We therefore assume that objects are commonly identified and that they qualify for a certain form of co-ordination of the action. The *industrial* objectivity of the engineer, that of standard measures and statistical laws, which presupposes a certain stability and standardisation, has its place among other forms of objectivity. The *market* objectivity of commodities, though it belongs to another 'nature', is no less objective and determining for self-interested action: standardised mass-products are not adjusted to the 'market test', as is clearly shown by the critical tensions which nowadays come to bear upon this type of product when it has to face a competitive market place (Eymard-Duvernay 1986). We can infer the importance of this common identification of the objects from the consequences of its failure. Such is the case when the identity of the commodities becomes uncertain and when a doubt about their quality is introduced, thereby undermining the foundations of the market form of co-ordination (Orléan 1986). It is, indeed, the common identification of the objects which prevents the strategical manipulation of their identity.

Just as objects are important only insofar as they *qualify* for a certain form of co-ordination, so are people. Their qualification is required for them to be taken into account within a justification. However, we assume that people can be qualified in all the 'worlds', whereas objects are more easily attached to a single world.[6]

A justifiable action presupposes a qualification of things and people which orders them in an evaluative judgement. We designate by the term *worth* this common qualification which is scaled in degrees. To each degree of worth there corresponds a level of satisfaction for the actors who reach it, but also for the other actors, since co-ordination itself is possible because the measure of worth is common knowledge. Thus worth is related to a common or public good constituted by a given form of co-ordination.

A principle of worth establishes an order according to which agents place value on people and things in decision-making. However, all the orders available in complex societies are not legitimate, i.e. do not serve as common presuppositions ensuring the co-ordination of actions. We have linked the different legitimate orders that we encountered in empirical study of forms of co-ordination with different constructions of the city in political philosophy. We have brought to the fore a set of common properties upon which we have drawn a model of these legitimate orders of *worth* (Boltanski and Thévenot 1991).[7] Although they satisfy these common requirements, orders of worth are historically constructed. The list is not closed and we have studied the genesis of new worlds and new forms of worth, as the 'green' worth (Lafaye et Thévenot 1993; Thévenot, Moody and Lafaye 2000), the 'information' worth (Thévenot 1997) or the 'connectionist' worth (Boltanski and Chiapello 1999).

5. Natural uncertainty and critical uncertainty

Within the market co-ordination, the only objective things to be taken into account for rational action are the commodities. Their worth is commonly evaluated in terms of their prices, whereas the worth of persons is determined by their wealth, which demonstrates their capacity to engage in far-reaching market transactions. Natural relations are locked in budgetary constraints which link the person's resources with the price of commodities. More generally, each form of co-ordination enables actors to cope with a certain kind of uncertainty, that we shall call 'natural'. For instance, if the uncertainty about others' actions results from their purchasing desires, then the market principle makes it possible to overcome this natural uncertainty, thanks to the common identification of goods and to the common recognition of their prices.

The market test leads to a division between what can be evaluated in a market and what stems from contingencies and thus moves away from this form of worth. The notion of 'state of nature' belongs to the latter category since it designates a background noise which troubles exchanges. The treatment of these states of nature most coherent with market prerequisites was developed by Kenneth Arrow and consists in embodying, in the definition of commodities, all the circumstances of the exchange which are likely to influence the market transaction. This attempt to elim- inate the noise of contingencies without deviating from the market prin- ciple leads to a paradoxical stance, where one seeks to include what is contingent among the realm of what is objective. The impossibility of such an all encompassing explicative system that would thoroughly reduce contingencies is suggested by studies which take into account imperfect information as regards the states of nature. Thus Radner (1968) has demonstrated the market failure which arises when the structure of information, that is, the capacity to discriminate among the different states of nature, differs according to the agents. Contingencies lack the objectivity which, in the market world, is encapsulated in commodities.

In opposition to this *natural* uncertainty, there is a *critical* uncertainty which cannot be either reduced through the evaluation of worth, nor rejected as part of the noise of contingencies, but which casts doubt on the very nature of the action. Ruining the basis for co-ordination, this doubt may, however, lead to another form of worth.[8] The confrontation of several possible forms of worth brings about a critical questioning of the mode of co-ordination. In the case of the market world, a critical uncer- tainty is that which debilitates the common identification of commodities, their market objectivity. The uncertainty over the identity of goods is not located at the same logical level as the market uncertainty which is regulated by prices; it is more radical and denatures the market test.

The notion of 'adverse selection', as a case of asymmetrical information on the quality of a product, includes phenomena which involve this kind of uncertainty. If we give up the idea of a contingent market which would absorb exterior contingencies by the proliferation of goods, we must admit that some species of uncertainty have to do with the very *quality* of the commodity, with the hard core of its definition. This is the case with second-hand markets which, in the simple model proposed by Akerlof, may not be clear because buyers are not aware of the quality of goods – while sellers are – and thus estimate it on the average on the basis of their market price (Akerlof 1970). What is lacking is a detour by an *investment of form*, which is necessary for the constitution of market commodities, and the making of objects which are resistant to manipula- tion and interpretation (Thévenot 1984). The crisis of the second-hand market may be analysed as the encounter between two conflicting modes of identifying goods, i.e. natural objects supporting co-ordination.

The notion of 'moral hazard' points to a second type of situation characterised by asymmetrical information in which uncertainty is also critical. In such a situation, contingencies trouble the market exchange since they depend on the actions of certain agents who are thus confronted with the dilemma (said to be 'moral') of having to decide between being honest or manipulating what others take for noisy contingencies.

As one moves away from 'natural' situations, the relevant objects on which a justifiable action is based also change. The situation becomes disturbed, or, shall we say, 'denatured', because the parties involved do not agree any more on the nature of the reality test for the evaluation of the situation. The lack of objectivity leaves the way open for suspicion. Each one is then led to wonder what matters for the decisions of others and must pursue this interrogation by asking himself what others think of what he assumes about their action, etc. Addressing the convergence of this regression leads to the 'common knowledge' issue (Dupuy 1989). As Schelling has already noted, in a problem of 'tacit co-ordination', it is a question of co-ordinating expectations, 'of reading the same message in a common situation' (1980: 54). Justifiable actions are grounded on a common presumption we have made explicit in the model of worth, and fit situations where this 'common knowledge' is insured notably by the determination of objects (within the limits resulting from the plurality of worlds). Speculative regression about others' background knowledge is then forgone because of this common presumption and because of the support of the objects involved in the action.[9] Our analysis of the key role played by objects in the co-ordination of conduct is in line with Schelling's remarks on *salient* objects in the implementation of co-ordination equilibrium. The natural character of this salience (Schelling 1980: 58) must be relativized by the plurality of worlds.[10]

6. The critical tension between several worlds and the search for compromise

What are the consequences of this plurality of forms of co-ordination within a complex universe, as regards actors' competence or rationality (hypothesis H1)? In a complex society, each member experiences 'shifting involvement' (Hirschman 1982). He has the ability to adjust his action to situations involving different natures, to attune his conduct to various settings which shape how he acts. The same person can, successively, and even within a short period of time, engage in a market transaction which requires detachment from the objects and persons he is dealing with (*market* co-ordination), then rely on domestic loyalty and stick to ingrained local customs (*trust* co-ordination), before finally planning investments on the basis of technical tools designed for accurate forecasting (*industrial* co-ordination) A complex universe impels actors to make a responsive shift from one form of justification to another, thus preventing them from considering each world as a closed system of determinations (Stark 1996).

The extension of the scope of action from one world to two – a higher number of worlds does not significantly complicate the problem – entails a substantial modification of the framework which can no longer be reduced to the model of a unique worth we encountered in classics of political philosophy. The relation of one world to another is thus a critical relation of inversion, since what matters in one is reduced to nothing in the other and what is general becomes particular.[11] The critical situation in which beings belonging to several worlds are present opens up the possibility of criticism through an operation of revelation. This consists in abruptly swinging from the world of reference (A) to a different world (B), by calling attention to the importance of beings who are irrelevant within the first world (revelation in the sense of the showing off of a real worth). In a single movement, the beings which naturally mattered in A are denounced, from the point of view of B, as insignificant, and are thereby reduced to the state of noise (revelation in the sense of the exposure, the showing up of a false worth).

The operation of revelation is thus extremely radical and destabilising because it leads to a change of the *reality test*. The encounter between several worlds opens up the possibility of a crisis, since the very form of what is probable turns out to be doubtful and since several reality tests of different natures may be involved.

However, people can *compromise* to avoid such a crisis and go beyond the tension between two worlds, by aiming at a common good which would encompass both. What we mean by compromise is not a local arrangement of limited validity, which would only concern the persons who crafted it. It is an action subjected to more stringent constraints oriented towards justification. Such compromise setting is the stuff organisations are made of (Thévenot 2000b).

7. Conclusion: Rationality in a complex universe

In this text, I have sought to suggest the advantages to be gained from a systematic analysis of a plurality of general forms of co-ordination, each being based on the same requirements. Every form of justification, by its aspiration to universality, maintains a critical relation with the others. The analysis of these general forms of co-ordination contributes to understanding situations which are themselves critical, at the fringes of the market place, and which have been increasingly discussed in the economic literature. A form of co-ordination may be considered as a *constitutive convention*, as long as we admit that its conventional character only appears in a critical relation with another form. The reference to the qualified objects of a relevant world, in a reality test, halts strategic speculation. In order to see this world and its inner relations as conventional, instead of taking them as natural, it is necessary to escape from that world, to dismiss the objects which belong to it – which have a determining role in the foundation of a constitutive convention, as we have seen. It is the reference to another world which serves as a lever in this revelation; a theoretical framework which would only acknowledge one world could not account for this critical possibility.

In conclusion, I would like to mention some consequences of our analysis for the definition of the concept of rationality. I have mentioned before that optimising rationality must, when confronted with critical situations, be considerably burdened in order to continue performing its function, and that one may wonder whether the concept should not be profoundly modified. In such situations, it is patent that a critical uncertainty about the *relevant* context for action deeply disturbs the process of maximisation. In each of the worlds we have brought to light, the rationality of action is simple: the definition of benefits is clear, as is the evaluation of the elements which matter for having access to those benefits. The reality test which must be applied is unequivocal. The 'calculation' of benefits is considerably facilitated by the resources that each world makes available and which allow for it to be realised in practice. But the plurality of the worlds where the calculation can take place, the implementation of different forms of equivalence, requires a rationality of another order, relating to the classical notion of prudence. This presupposes that people will deliberate on what matters and search the objects which qualify for the justification of the decision. They need to take into account circumstances, that is, pick out, among what is only contingency from the point of view of one form of justification, elements which are pertinent in another nature.

Notes

1 The notion of 'convention' is at the centre of a recent trend in French social sciences which pervades both economic sociology and institutional economics and which is called as '*Economie des conventions*'. A series of books have developed this trend, attesting the dynamics of this growing intersection between economics and sociology: Salais et Thévenot 1986, Thévenot 1986, *Revue économique* 1989, Boltanski et Thévenot 1989, Boltanski et Thévenot 1991, Orléan 1994, Eymard-Duvernay et Marchal 1997, Storper and Salais 1997. For discussions oriented towards sociolgy, see: Dodier 1993, Wagner 1994; towards economics, see: Wilkinson 1997; towards political science and philosophy, see: Bénatouïl 1999, Wagner 1999; or more generally towards humanities and the social sciences, see: Dosse 1998.
2 For presentations in English, see: Thévenot 1995, Boltanski and Thévenot 1999; 2000.
3 Such is the meaning of the critical propositions of Amartya Sen, when he considers 'committed' behaviour connected with a civic form of worth. He

actually refers to the distinction made by Rousseau between the 'general will' and the 'common will', as the non-egotistical game in the dilemma of deer hunting equally inspired by Rousseau (Dupuy 1989). In order to account for these actions, he proposes 'a more complex preference structure including meta-ranking levels of order' (Sen 1977: 106, 109).

4 On this concept of 'qualification' and the way objects are crafted to qualify for different orders of worth, see: Thévenot 2000a.

5 One could parallel this orientation with the impact of the notion of 'embeddedness' in economic sociology (Granovetter 1985).

6 Bruno Latour has explored the rival hypothesis assuming that objects are also completely free from attachment (Latour 1984; 1987).

7 The development of this approach led us to craft the H3 type of hypothesis about the forms of co-ordination. The properties which we found to be shared by the different specifications of worth were the following:
(a1) a definition of a *common humanity* which enables the identification of human actors;
(a2) a *differentiation* assuming at least two possible states for the actors;
(a3) a *common dignity* endowing the actors with equal chances to reach all the states;
(a4) an *order* among the states which qualifies the actors (*worth*);
(a5) a *sacrifice or investment formula* linking together the benefits ensuing from a higher state of worth and the cost or sacrifice required to attain it;
(a6) a definition of the *common good* specifying the welfare associated with each state of worth, which posits that such a welfare, which increases with worth, benefits other actors.

8 Several classics have insisted upon this heterogeneous character of different forms of uncertainty. Knight (1971 [1921]) has outlined the difference between 'risk' and 'uncertainty', connected to the repetition or uniqueness of events. Keynes also tried to distinguish among probabilities according to different degrees of belief and Favereau has identified common points between the ideas Keynes developed in his *Treatise on Probabilities* (1921) and his considerations about short term and long term expectations, in the chapters 5 and 12 of his *General Theory of Employment* . . . (Keynes 1936). The connection between these two works is barely mentioned by the author himself – in a footnote in Chapter 12 referring to the notion of 'the weight of arguments' introduced in the Treatise on Probabilities. Favereau's work illuminates the connections between the Keynesian conception of the different forms of probability as incommensurable 'orders of similarity' (1921: 30, 39) and the 'possible-worlds semantics' (Favereau 1988). It points out that the distinction in Chapter 12 between two types of expectations – which also implies two types of uncertainties – according to the reversible character of the action, could be expressed in terms of different accessibility relations between possible worlds.

9 For example, in the case of an action whose generality concerns the future (the *industrial* form of co-ordination), technical tools can contribute to the co-ordination of actions. Schelling has mentioned a whole series of technical mechanisms sufficiently compelling to prevent manipulations and arrangements on the part of the persons involved, for example alarm systems which cannot even be controlled by their owners (1980: 38). Elster has developed this point while accounting for commitments which preclude market opportunism (Elster 1979).

10 Lewis' stress on the role of precedent, custom, familiarity, in the convergence of expectations (Lewis 1969: 36) can be understood in relation to the objectivity of the *domestic* order of worth and the justification by trust. But Schelling

also gives examples of saliency which involve the *inspiration* order of worth (Boltanski and Thévenot 1999): finding a clue may depend on imagination more than on logic; it may depend on accidental arrangement, aesthetic configuration (Schelling 1980: 58). The salient character of objects is thus relative to the inscription of action within one world.

11. The order of worth is an order of generality in which the greater encompasses the smaller, the latter being considered as the reduction of another form of worth. This relation of the greater to the smaller is somewhat similar to Dumont's 'encompassing of contraries' (1979: 397).

References

Akerlof, George (1970) 'The market for "lemons", quality uncertainty and the market mechanism', *Quarterly Journal of Economics*, 84: 488–500.

Arrow, Kenneth J. (1972) 'Gifts and exchanges', *Philosophy and Public Affairs*, 343–62.

Arrow, Kenneth J. (1987) 'De la rationalité -de l'individu et des autres- dans un système économique', *Revue française d'économie*, 2(1): 22–47.

Bénatouïl, Thomas (1999) 'A tale of two sociologies', *European Journal of Social Theory*, 2(3): 379–96.

Boltanski, Luc and Chiapello, Eve (1999) *Le nouvel esprit du capitalisme*, Paris: Gallimard.

Boltanski, Luc and Thévenot, Laurent (eds) (1989) *Justesse et justice dans le travail*, Paris: Presses Universitaires de France (Cahiers du Centre d'Etudes de l'Emploi 33).

Boltanski, Luc and Thévenot, Laurent (1991) *De la justification*, Paris: Gallimard.

Boltanski, Luc and Thévenot, Laurent (1999) 'The sociology of critical capacity', *European Journal of Social Theory*, 2(3): 359–77.

Boltanski, Luc and Thévenot, Laurent (2000) 'The reality of moral expectations: a sociology of situated judgment', *Philosophical Explorations*,

Bratman, Michael E. (1987) *Intention, Plan, and Practical Reason*, Cambridge: Harvard University Press.

Conein, Bernard, Dodier, Nicolas and Thévenot, Laurent (eds) (1993) *Les objets dans l'action*, Paris, (ed.) de l'Ecole des Hautes Etudes en Sciences Sociales (Raisons pratiques 4).

Conein, Bernard et Thévenot, Laurent (eds) (1997a) *Cognition et information en société*, Paris, Ed. de l'Ecole des Hautes Etudes en Sciences Sociales (Raisons pratiques 8).

Dodier, Nicolas (1993) 'Action as a combination of "common worlds"', *The Sociological Review*, 41(3): 556–71.

Dosse, François (1998) *Empire of meaning: the humanization of the social sciences*, Minneapolis: Univ. of Minnesota Press.

Dumont, Louis (1979) *Homo hierarchicus; le système des castes et ses implications*, Paris: Gallimard (1ere édit. 1966).

Dupuy, Jean-Pierre (1989) 'Convention et Common Knowledge', *Revue Économique*, 40(2): 361–70.

Elster, Jon (1979) *Ulysses and the sirens*, Cambridge-Paris, Cambridge University Press (ed.) de la Maison des sciences de l'homme.

Eymard-Duvernay, François (1986) 'La qualification des produits', in Salais Robert et Thévenot Laurent, (eds). *Le travail. Marchés, règles, conventions*. Paris, INSEE-Economica.

Eymard-Duvernay, François and Marchal, Emmanuelle, (1997) *Façons de recruter. Le jugement des compétences sur le marché du travail*, Paris: Centre d'Etudes de l'Emploi & ed. Metailié.

Favereau, Olivier (1988) 'Probability and uncertainty: "After All, Keynes was right"'. *Oeconomia*, 10: 133–67.

Granovetter, Mark (1985) 'Economic action and social structure; the problem of embededness', *American Journal of Sociology* 91(3): 481–510.

Hayek, Frederich A. von (1945) 'The use of knowledge in society', *The American Economic Review*, 35(4): 518–30.

Hirschman, Albert O. (1982) *Shifting involvments: private interest and public action*, Princeton: Princeton University Press.

Hutchins, Edward L. (1995) *Cognition in the Wild*, Cambridge: MIT Press.

Keynes, John Maynard (1921) *A treatise on probability*, London: MacMillan.

Keynes, John Maynard (1936) *The general theory of employment, interest and money*, London: Macmillan.

Knight, Frank H. (1971) *Risk, uncertainty and profit*, Chicago: University of Chicago Press (1st ed. 1921).

Lafaye, Claudette and Thévenot, Laurent (1993) 'Une justification écologique? Conflits dans l'aménagement de la nature': *Revue Française de Sociologie*, 34(4): 495–524.

Lamont, Michèle and Thévenot, Laurent (eds) (2000) *Rethinking Comparative Cultural Sociology: Repertoires of Evaluation in France and the United States*, Cambridge: Cambridge University Press.

Latour, Bruno (1984) *Irréduction*, Paris: Editions A.M. Métailié.

Latour, Bruno (1987) *Science in action*, Milton Keynes: Open University Press.

Lave, Jean (1988) *Cognition in practice*, Cambridge: Cambridge University Press.

Lewis, David (1969) *Convention: A Philosophical Study*, Cambridge: Harvard University Press.

MacIntyre, Alasdair (1981) *After Virtue: A Study in Moral Theory*, Notre Dame: University of Notre Dame Press.

Mongin, Philippe and Walliser, Bernard (1988) 'Infinite regressions in the optimizing theory of decision', in Munier Bertrand (ed.) *Risk, decision and rationality*, D. Reidel, 435–57.

Norman, Donald (1989) *The Design of Everyday Things*, New York: Doubleday (première édition 1988).

Norman, Donald and Draper, S.W. (eds) (1986) *User centered System Design. New Perspectives on Human-Computer Interaction*, Hillsdale, NJ, London: Lawrence Erlbaum.

Orléan, André (1986) 'Le rôle des conventions dans la logique monétaire', in Salais Robert et Thévenot Laurent, (eds). *Le travail. Marchés, règles, conventions*, Paris, INSEE-Economica, pp.219–38.

Orléan, André (ed.) (1994) *Analyse économique des conventions*, Paris: Presses Universitaires de France.

Radner, R. (1968) 'Competitive equilibrium under uncertainty', *Econometrica* 36: 31–58.

Revue économique (1989) 'L'économie des conventions', 40(2).

Salais, Robert and Thévenot, Laurent (eds) (1986) *Le travail. Marchés, règles, conventions*, Paris: INSEE-Economica.

Schelling, Thomas C. (1980) *The Strategy of Conflict*, Cambridge: Harvard University Press (1st ed. 1960).

Sen, Amartya K. (1977) 'Rational fools: a critique of the behavioral foundations of economic theory', *Philosophy and Public Affairs* 6: 317–44.

Stark, David (1996) 'Recombinant property in East European capitalism', *American Journal of Sociology*, 101(4): 993–1027.

Storper, Michael and Salais, Robert (1997) *Worlds of Production. The Action Frameworks of the Economy*, Cambridge MA: Harvard University Press.

Thévenot, Laurent (1984) 'Rules and implements: investment in forms', *Social Science Information* (23)1: 1–45.

Thévenot, Laurent (1986) *Conventions économiques*, Paris: Presses Universitaires de France (Cahiers du Centre d'Etudes de l'Emploi).

Thévenot, Laurent (1995) 'New Trends in French Social Sciences', *Culture*, 9(2): 1–7.

Thévenot, Laurent (1997) 'Un gouvernement par les normes; pratiques et politiques des formats d'information', in Conein Bernard et Thévenot Laurent (eds). *Cognition et information en société*, Paris, Ed. de l'Ecole des Hautes Etudes en Sciences Sociales (Raisons Pratiques 8): 205–241.

Thévenot, Laurent (2000a) 'Which road to follow? The moral complexity of an "equipped humanity"' in Law, John and Mol, Annemarie, *Complexities in Science, Technology and Medicine*. Duke University Press, Forthcoming.

Thévenot, Laurent (2000b) 'Organized complexity: conventions of coordination and the composition of economic arrangements', paper presented at the Stockholm Conference on Economic Sociology June 2–3.

Thévenot, Laurent, Moody, Michael and Lafaye, Claudette (2000) 'Forms of Valuing Nature: Arguments and Modes of Justification in French and American Environmental Disputes', in Lamont Michèle and Thévenot Laurent (eds), *Rethinking Comparative Cultural Sociology: Repertoires of Evaluation in France and the United States*, Cambridge: Cambridge University Press, 229–72.

Wagner, Peter (1994) 'Action, coordination, and institution in recent French debates', *The Journal of Political Philosophy*, 2(3): 270–89.

Wagner, Peter (1999) 'After *Justification*. Repertoires of evaluation and the sociology of modernity', *European Journal of Social Theory*, 2(3): 341–57.

Walzer, Michael (1983) *Spheres of Justice. A defense of Pluralism and Equality*. New York, Basic Books.

Walzer, Michael (1984) 'Liberalism and the Art of Separation', *Political Theory*, 12(3): 315–30.

Weber, Max (1978) *Economy and Society*, Berkeley: University of California Press (edited by G. Roth and C. Wittich).

Wilkinson, John (1997) 'A new paradigm for economic analysis?', *Economy and Society*, 26(3): 305–39.

Williamson, Oliver (1975) *Markets and Hierarchies: Analysis and Antitrust Implications. A Study in the Economics of Internal Organization*, New York: The Free Press.

12

INTERSUBJECTIVITY IN THE SOCIO-ECONOMIC WORLD

A critical realist perspective

Paul Lewis and Jochen Runde[1]

1. Introduction

Some of the most interesting recent contributions to the methodology of economics have focused on the ontological commitments of different economic theories and models, that is, on what those theories and models presuppose about the nature of the socio-economic world.[2] A number of research programmes have emerged that, although unified by a common concern with ontological issues, develop this interest in rather different ways. This essay compares and evaluates two variations on the general ontological theme: the project of critical realism in economics, most closely associated with the work of Tony Lawson (1997); and the phenomenological approach to the investigation of the socio-economic world, promoted in economic methodology by Edward Fullbrook (1997; 1998a) and employed in substantive economic theory by members of the French intersubjectivist school (Dupuy 1989; 1992; Orléan 1989).

The two approaches have much in common. Both argue that successful substantive research requires analytical tools that are tailored to suit the nature of the subject-matter under investigation. Both devote a great deal of attention to developing an abstract picture of the nature of the socio-economic world, which then forms the basis for their respective accounts of the methods appropriate for studying socio-economic life. And both conclude that the methods of mainstream economics are ill-suited to the social material to which they are applied.[3]

However, as Fullbrook (1998b) points out, there remain significant differences between critical realism and intersubjectivism, most notably in their accounts of socio-economic reality. Fullbrook makes two main points in this respect. First, he criticises the social ontology sponsored by critical realism for being 'incomplete' (Fullbrook 1998b: 434). In particular, he maintains that critical realism lacks a 'coherent and ontologically grounded model of the intersubjective agent,' the result of which is that its 'sketch of acting subjects and their interaction is simplistic'. Second, he argues that the remedy for these shortcomings lies in the conception of the economic actor developed by intersubjectivism (Fullbrook 1998b: 437). What follows is essentially a response to these two claims.

2. Intersubjectivity and the analysis of the socio-economic world

Fullbrook begins with the observation that ontological presuppositions are unavoidable in any sort of ordered thinking about the world, that any attempt to conceptualise socio-economic phenomena inevitably involves the adoption (if only implicitly) of some picture of the nature of the socio-economic being. In particular, so far as the metaphysical presuppositions of economics are concerned, he suggests that what is required is 'a well-drawn stereotype of the economic actor' (Fullbrook 1997: 68; 1998a: 725).

Fullbrook traces the lineage of *homo economicus* from Bentham and Mill through to John Locke, arguing that it is primarily to the influence of Locke that we owe the impoverished theory of human being to which mainstream economic theory currently subscribes (Fullbrook 1997: 69–77). Fullbrook criticises the Lockean model of man on two counts. First, he argues that Locke's empiricist philosophy gives rise to a mechanistic picture of human nature in which actors are portrayed as passive beings who are jolted into action purely at the behest of external forces. The possibility that human action may be a spontaneous, dynamic and open-ended enterprise involving 'original choice' is thereby excluded (Fullbrook 1998a: 712–4).

Fullbrook's second point concerns the *atomistic* conception of the economic actor inherited from Locke, according to which the properties of economic actors are fixed independently of any relations into which they might enter with each other. Fullbrook focuses on the fact that mainstream economics typically assumes that the preferences of the economic actor are constituted independently of the tastes and actions (the consumption, say) of all other economic actors. A corollary of this asocial specification of people's desires is the *additivity* of consumer demand. Just as Newtonian mechanics holds that the overall impact of a set of forces can be determined by the vector addition of the effects of those forces acting singly, so mainstream economics, with its socially impermeable Newtonian model of man, implies that market demand is also determined 'mechanically' as the simple summation of the individual demands of consumers taken in isolation (Fullbrook 1997: 71–7).

As Fullbrook sees it, the principal drawback of Lockean model of man is that its applicability is severely limited. To see why, note that Fullbrook subscribes to the methodological principle that, in order to be fruitful, an economic theory 'needs a set of preconceptions, especially an idea of ... *homo economicus*, which is not flagrantly incompatible with the empirical phenomena it intends to investigate' (Fullbrook 1997: 78). Specifically, Fullbrook argues that it is reasonable to assume that an individual's preferences are asocially determined only so long as he or she earns no more than a subsistence level of income. In such circumstances the satisfaction of basic biological needs is such an over-riding concern that it excludes all other influences on the actor's desires. However, as incomes rise above what is required to provide the bare necessities of life, there occurs a shift in the ontological basis of consumer demand, with the principal determinant of an individual's preferences becoming, not the atomistic or *intra*subjective dictates of subsistence, but a set of interpersonal or *inter*subjective influences deriving from the actor's regard for the opinions and actions of others (Fullbrook 1998b: 436; 1998a: 710–5). As Veblen put it:

> Ordinarily ... [the consumer's] motive is a wish to conform to established usage, to avoid unfavourable notice and comment, to live up to the accepted canons of decency in the kind, amount, and grade of goods consumed, as well as in the decorous employment of his time and effort
>
> (Veblen [1909] 1994: 71)

Where such interpersonal factors are important, so that the preferences of any one actor are influenced by the bundles of goods selected by other actors, individual demands combine 'chemically', implying that market demand is not simply the sum of the individual demands considered separately. The assumption that consumer demands are determined atomistically, then, holds good only for an extremely narrow subset of those circumstances upon which economic analysis might be brought to bear. And, when coupled with the methodological principle quoted above, the fact that an essential characteristic of the dominant class of demand phenomena, namely their dependence on intersubjective factors, is 'metaphysically excluded' from mainstream economic theory implies that the latter must resign itself to an 'ever-diminishing realm of applicability' (Fullbrook 1997: 81; 1998a: 715).

Fullbrook concludes that if economic analysis is to do justice to those aspects of life in which intersubjective dependencies between economic actors are important, the metaphysical basis of economic theory must be reformulated so as to admit an 'ontological account of intersubjectivity and a conceptualization of economic actors as open or non-atomistic systems' (Fullbrook 1998b: 436). He goes on to suggest that the requisite intellectual resources are to be found in the work of thinkers associated with (one strand of) the phenomenological tradition in philosophy, and Simone de Beauvoir in particular.

The origins of phenomenology lie in the work of the Austrian psychologist, Franz Bretano. Bretano's central claim is that human subjectivity or consciousness takes the form of a *relation* between a person (the subject) and a (real or imagined) object.[4] The implications that flow from this relational view of consciousness for our understanding of human nature in general, and of desire in particular, have been explored and developed by a number of thinkers, including Husserl, Heidegger and Sartre. But it is upon the interpretation provided by Simone de Beauvoir and her followers that Fullbrook relies most heavily. Of greatest significance here is that, if consciousness is a relation that requires objects for its existence, then it must continuously project itself towards the world in order to find them. It is this need for objects that provides the impetus for acts of consciousness in general and, more specifically, for (that aspect of consciousness connected with) human desire. Intersubjectivists argue that, in directing itself towards the objects of desire, a person's consciousness is often guided by his or her observations of other people. A person, perceiving an aspect of the life of some respected individual or group which is missing from his own life, becomes aware of this 'lack of being' (as de Beauvoir terms it), and so comes to desire the goods that can remedy it. In this way, the person's desires are influenced by (what he or she perceives to be) the desires of the individual or group chosen as a role model, so that desire becomes imitative or mimetic. Where people's basic needs have been satisfied, interpersonal interaction of the sort just described shapes most human desires.

The idea that, in its quest for objects, consciousness continuously projects itself toward the world gives rise to a picture of man as being inherently active and dynamic, as constantly searching out new role models which, once found, are used as reference points in the re-fashioning of his life. Furthermore, the mimetic aspects of this process imply that, rather than being autonomous or asocial, individual subjectivities are interdependent or intersubjective. As Fullbrook sees it, the broad significance of intersubjectivism's claim that a person's nature is influenced (but not determined) by his or her relations to and interaction with other people, is that it gives rise to a model of man that transcends the ontological extremes of individualism and holism (Fullbrook and Fullbrook 1998a; 1998b: 94–9). Fullbrook then goes on to argue, more specifically, that by providing a conception of the economic actor that recognises the interdependencies between people, the intersubjectivist approach furnishes social theorists with a metaphysics or set of categories that facilitates the analysis of mimetic processes underpinning intersubjective phenomena such as fashion and stockmarket prices. In this way, Fullbrook claims, intersubjectivism serves to bring a broader class of phenomena within the compass of economic analysis.

3. Critical realism and socio-economic reality

We now turn to the picture of socio-economic reality offered by critical realism. The fundamental metaphysical components of this picture are as follows. First, the socio-economic world comprises not only events and states of affairs (the actual) but also an 'underlying' and often unobservable reality of capacities, powers, structures and mechanisms that, once triggered or being otherwise in play, give rise to and govern events and states of affairs. These domains are held to be ontologically irreducible to one another. In the language of critical realism, the socio-economic world is *structured*. Second, most of the socio-economic world is *open* in the sense that the actual could have been other than it was. Third, the socio-economic reality is *intransitive*, by which is meant that, viewed as a possible object of enquiry, it pre-exists and therefore is not merely the construct of the investigations of social scientists.

The argument that underpins the critical realist metaphysics begins from the *ex posteriori* observation that there is a paucity of stable event regularities in the socio-economic world. (An event regularity is a pattern of the form, 'Whenever event or state of affairs x, then event or state of affairs y'.) (Lawson 1997: 70; 1998: 357). Systems in which such regularities obtain are described as *closed*, systems in which they are absent, *open*. The available evidence, namely the failure of generations of econometricians in finding much in the way of sharp and enduring event-regularities, suggests, then, that the socio-economic world is an open system. Critical realists contend that one explanation of this observation lies in people's (widely acknowledged) ability to choose which course of action they will follow. For, according to critical realism, the quintessence of choice is that a person could always have done other than he or she in fact did, implying that if, in circumstances x the person chose to do y, then (s)he could have chosen to undertake some other course of action not y. Conceived thus, the exercise of human agency renders intelligible the observed openness of the socio-economic world.

If a person's actions are indeed *chosen*, then it must be possible to give an account of them in terms of that person's beliefs and desires; that is, human action must be intentional (in the narrower, volitive sense of the word) under some description. Intentional agency is possible only if the actors in question have some idea about how to achieve their goals. The question is, whence comes the knowledge that informs people's attempts to pursue their objectives? The *ex posteriori* observation that the social world is an open system suggests that the objects of such knowledge are not predominantly (empirical) patterns of association between people's activities and the consequences thereof. Rather, according to critical realism, peoples' actions are guided by their understanding of (non-empirical) social rules and institutions. And it is to facilitate the conceptualisation of such objects of knowledge that the metaphysics to which critical realism subscribes includes the category of ontologically irreducible social structure (Lawson 1998: 357–60; Lewis and Runde 1999: 51–3; Runde 1993: 388–93).

Critical realists contend that the relationship between social structure and human agency can be understood adequately only if it is conceptualised as an inherently 'tensed' process in which, at any given moment in time, social structures and people stand in temporal relations of priority and posteriority towards one another.[5] To express the idea in terms familiar to (heterodox) economists, one might say that the interaction between structure and agency is an intrinsically historical process and as such must be thought of as occurring not in logical but in real historical time.[6]

The temporality of the structure–agency relationship becomes apparent once we recognise that all human activity takes place within the context provided by a set of *pre-existing* social structures. At any given moment of time socio-economic actors confront social structures that are pre-formed in the sense that they are the product, not of people's actions in the present, but of actions undertaken in the past. Most notably, everyone is born into a world of social structures that pre-existed them. These social structures are bequeathed 'ready made' to the current generation of actors, confronting them as an objective reality that is distinct from and irreducible to their subjective beliefs and actions. Hence, critical realists contend that pre-constituted social structure, inherited 'already formed' from the past, is ontologically distinct from the practices of actors in the present. Of course, the *continued* existence of social structures depends upon current human agency; indeed, it is this dependence that makes them *social*. However, this does not imply that social structures are merely the voluntaristic creation of individual human actors. Rather, because people constantly draw on pre-existing social structures in order to act, they must be understood as reproducing or transforming those structures, not as creating them *ex nihilo* (Archer 1995: 71–2, 137–41; Lawson 1997: 168–70).

According to critical realism, pre-existing social structures both facilitate and constrain current human agency. Cashing a cheque, for example, presupposes the existence of a banking system that makes possible this kind of activity. But the banking system also constrains it. A person who tries to cash a cheque that has not been written in accordance with the rules of the banking system is likely to find her efforts unsuccessful. Simply wishing that things were different, or acting as if they were, will not make it so. Of course, none of this is to say that human activity is fully determined by social structure. Like intersubjectivism, critical realism seeks to chart a course between voluntarism and determinism. For instance, while a person who wishes to pay by cheque will have to write out the cheque in the appropriate way, (s)he may always choose to use some other means of payment. In this way, the transformational model of socio-economic activity is well able to do justice to human agency. Critical realists also fully acknowledge that people may creatively devise new strategies for deploying (historically given) resources so as to achieve new goals.

We can see more clearly how the hand of the past comes to exert its influence on current socio-economic activity if we explore in greater detail the processes through which social structure and human agency are inter-connected. Two observations are especially significant in this respect. First, as critical realists see it, society is typically structured along hierar-chical lines in the sense that different people have different rights and obligations. For example, landlords are obliged to ensure that the accom-modation they provide meets certain safety standards, in return for which it is a landlord's prerogative to insist that tenants pay the rent on time and keep the property clean and tidy. Secondly, these rights and obligations typically exist independently of the particular individuals who happen to be landlords and tenants at any specific point in time. New tenants usually have the same rights and responsibilities as their predecessors. Critical realists maintain that these two observations can be rendered intelligible if it is recognised that social structure is constituted in large measure by a set of *positions*, each of which is associated with certain responsibilities and privileges. And it is through the occupancy of these positions by particular individuals – and more specifically via the condi-tioning of the subsequent behaviour of the incumbents by the rights, obligations and (as we shall see) interests which accompany the posi-tions – that social structure and agency are brought together.

Additional insight into the nature of social structure may be gleaned from the fact that the practices routinely followed by the occupants of such positions tend to be directed towards the occupants of other posi-tions. The rights of landlords, for example, are oriented towards, and defined in terms of, their interactions with tenants. Critical realists infer from this that social structure is highly *relational* in nature. More specifi-cally, they distinguish between two types of relation. Two entities are *externally* related if neither is constituted by the relationship in which it stands to the other. The association between two strangers who pass each other on the street is an example of an external relationship. In the case of *internal* relationships, however, the relata are what they are in virtue of the relationship in which they stand to each other. What it is to be a land-lord, say, is at least in part constituted by the relations which obtain between landlords and tenants. Critical realists contend that, while abstract ontological inquiry yields no *a priori* reason to suppose that one type of relation will be more prevalent than the other, observation of examples such as landlords and tenants, teachers and students, and bosses and workers reveals *ex posteriori* that social life does indeed appear to be highly internally related. Thus, like Fullbrook, critical realists reject the atomistic picture of society on which all social relations are external or contingent.

The picture that emerges from critical realism, then, is one in which society is portrayed as a nexus of often internally-related social positions, each of them accompanied by a corresponding set of rights and obligations and occupied by an individual actor. Significantly, each of these positions tends to be associated with various vested interests. These interests, like the social structures themselves, constitute an objective reality that endows the current cohort of people with reasons or incentives to follow particular courses of action (Lawson 1997: 264; 1999a: 47). Antecedent social structures also impact upon current activity because, at any particular moment in time, the material and cultural resources required to prosecute particular courses of action (wealth, power, status, expertise, access to credit and so on) are distributed unevenly between the various positions in the social structure as the result of actions undertaken in the past. Depending on their location in various social hierarchies, then, people are endowed with an historically given array of resources, which in turn constitutes an ontologically irreducible influence on their ability to further their interests in the future (Lawson 1997: 257).

Needless to say, critical realists stop short of a reductive materialism in which human subjectivity and action is no more than a reflection of pre-existent circumstances. While the pre-existing pattern of interests might dispose people to act in certain ways, it does not compel them to do so in a deterministic fashion; in many cases it may be such as to leave people with scope to choose from a variety of actions and, of course, people are often free to act against their interests if they wish to do so. Likewise, critical realists fully acknowledge that people may creatively devise new strategies for deploying (historically given) resources so as to achieve their desired goals.

Like Marx, then, critical realists subscribe to the view that 'people make their own history, but not just as they please; they do not make it in circumstances chosen by themselves, but under circumstances directly encountered, given and transmitted from the past'. Social events of interest must therefore be understood as the result of the interplay over time between (antecedent) social structure and (subsequent) human agency. Pre-existing social structures, the deposits or residue of actions undertaken in the past, constitute the environment in which current action takes place. As we have seen, these historically given structures condition (but do not determine) the behaviour of socio-economic actors in the present by laying down an initial distribution of resources and vested interests. And the (reproduced or transformed) set of social structures which emerges as the outcome of this process in turn forms the context in which the next round of social activities occurs.[7]

4. Intersubjectivism versus critical realism: An evaluation

Having outlined intersubjectivism and critical realism, it is now possible to compare and evaluate them. It will have become evident by now that proponents of critical realism would agree with the two points that Fullbrook raises against the mainstream conception of the economic actor. By maintaining first that people are able to choose the actions that they take and second that it is analytic to the notion of choice that one could always have done other than one in fact did in any particular situation, critical realists reject the behaviourist model of man to which orthodox economics is wedded. And, as we have seen, they also share Fullbrook's antipathy towards the atomistic view of man to which mainstream economics gives rise, preferring to regard human conduct as being influenced by the social context in which it takes place.

However, the critique of mainstream economics offered by critical realism is more general than that advanced by intersubjectivism and also differs from the latter in characterising the mainstream not in historical terms but rather in terms of its methodological commitments. The distinguishing feature of mainstream economics, critical realism suggests, is its commitment to deductivism. By deductivism is meant a mode of explanation or exposition that expresses or 'models' phenomena in terms of strict regularities between (sets of) actualities of the form, 'Whenever these conditions, then that outcome (or specific set or spread of outcomes)'.[8] The objection that critical realism raises against deductivism in the social sciences stems from the *ex posteriori* observation (mentioned earlier) that few such regularities have been uncovered in the social world. Given that the socio-economic world appears to be open, analysing aspects of it as closed systems invariably involves a distortion of the phenomena under investigation. For in order to achieve the kind of regularities required by deductivism, various 'closure' assumptions must be made in order to remove any possible sources of indeterminacy from the system under investigation (Lawson 1997: 76–81, 84–5, 98–103).

The two problems with the orthodox model of the economic actor identified by Fullbrook are a consequence of such closure assumptions. First, it is possible to deduce specific outcomes in economic models only if the choices of the hypothetical actors are determined by their preferences and the constraints they face. The standard models of consumer choice, which are designed to ensure that the decisions of economic actors produce 'single-exit' outcomes in any given situation, are a case in point.[9] A commitment to deductivism here does violence to the notion of choice since choice that is determined, as critical realists understand it, is no choice at all. Second, the deducibility of outcomes from given initial conditions also requires that the actions of the individual actors translate into a determinate outcome at the aggregate level. This requirement is met through the assumption of atomism, which ensures that individual actions combine additively to produce the overall outcome (Lawson 1997: 8–9, 38–9, 78–80, 98–9).

Thus, critical realism suggests that it is the constraints imposed by the dictates of deductivism that account for the behaviourism and atomism displayed by orthodox economics. The inability of deductivist models to incorporate either a meaningful degree of human choice or the internal-relationality of the socio-economic world, especially when viewed in conjunction with the *ex posteriori* observation that regularities displaying anything like the exactitude presupposed by deductivist models are scarcely to be found in the socio-economic realm, is taken by critical real-ists to indicate that the scope for applying such theories to social material is extremely limited (Lawson 1997: 19–20, 102; 1998: 364). Critical realists argue that it is possible to do justice to the noted features of socio-economic reality only if the deductivist mode of explanation is dropped and the crit-ical realist metaphysics and explanatory scheme is adopted in its place.

In arguing that economics requires a new metaphysics, critical realism arrives at a conclusion similar to that reached by Fullbrook. As we have seen, Fullbrook contends that the ontological presuppositions of orthodox economic theory imply that models developed within the orthodox framework cannot provide a satisfactory understanding of the (familiar and widely accepted) importance of interpersonal effects in socio-eco-nomic life. Only if an alternative metaphysical framework, which embod-ies a commitment to a more elaborate socio-economic ontology, is adopted will adequate theories of intersubjective phenomena (fashion, for instance) be forthcoming.

The question that then arises is how does the basic metaphysics of criti-cal realism compare with that sponsored by intersubjectivism. From the critical realist viewpoint, while the intersubjectivists have performed a valuable service in drawing attention to the importance of mimetic behav-iour, they run the risk of overemphasising the significance of interpersonal, intersubjective interaction in the socio-economic realm. The intersubjec-tivists argue that the basic building blocks of social reality are the relations between individual consciousnesses that arise as a result of people's regard for the opinions and actions of others. The problem is that, in bas-ing its account of the socio-economic world on the category of 'interper-sonal subject-object relations', intersubjectivism subscribes to a restricted metaphysics that leaves no conceptual space for historically given social structures.[10] We have seen that the latter are the product of actions under-taken in the past and therefore are relatively impersonal, being irreducible to human agency and interpersonal interaction in the present. As such, they cannot be satisfactorily accommodated by intersubjectivism.

Dupuy's (1989) analysis of conventional behaviour provides a good example of the point that we are making. We focus on this contribution, both because of its prominence and because it contains passages that, on the surface at least, would appear to indicate that it avoids the criticisms of intersubjectivism we have made above. Dupuy's paper is a wide-ranging one, but a dominant theme is the role of specular behaviour in different accounts of convention.[11] Having considered the role of specular behaviour in Keynes's famous beauty contest example, Dupuy (1989: 51; emphasis added) remarks that:

> Yet this is obviously not how the players in fact play the [beauty contest] game. The socio-cultural group is immersed in a history, a tradition, a particular world and a particular form of common sense. Each individual has an implicit, unformulated and tacit knowledge of this world, and although this knowledge is not explicit, it is constitutive of the individual's social being. *This common sense has been collectively created by individuals, but it nonetheless appears to them as if it were an objective reality wholly external to their own making and doing* ... The 'natural' way to play is clearly for each player to consult his or her common sense, making a judgement without engaging in any specular reference to what others might choose. *The others are still present in this agent's individual choice, but it is 'as if' their views had been crystallised into objects.* Mediation by means of common sense makes it possible to obtain with null specularity what logic thought only an infinite specularity could obtain.

The key issue that arises here concerns the identity and ontological status of the objects of common sense knowledge. Dupuy maintains that common sense encompasses actors' knowledge of the particular world they inhabit, including its history and traditions. He elaborates on this in the two italicised sentences, arguing that while the current generation of players may believe that common sense knowledge constitutes an objective reality that is external to their activities, it is in fact the creation of those same individuals. What this suggests is that, for Dupuy, the objects of common sense knowledge are ontologically reducible to the beliefs and actions of the current generation of actors. The trouble is that this sits rather uneasily with his claim that common sense knowledge includes a grasp of history and of traditions, for the latter, as the product of actions undertaken in the past, are irreducible to current agency and intersubjective interaction. The problem is that while Dupuy invokes the notions of 'history' and of 'tradition' the fact that the intersubjectivist metaphysics excludes the category of historically given social structure precludes him from doing justice to the way in which the residue of the past shapes current social interaction (in this case the way that pre-existing social structures facilitate human action in the face of uncertainty).

A more concrete illustration of the limitations of the metaphysical framework to which intersubjectivism subscribes can be had if we consider Dupuy's analysis of mimetic processes:

> Two subjects, A and B, reciprocally imitate themselves. The object of their mutual imitation is by hypothesis indeterminate. But suppose that a noise, a false rumour reaches A to the effect that B desires ... object O. From now on A knows what he should desire ... he makes the first move, indicating in this way to B the object O, and when B manifests in his turn his interest in O, A obtains proof that his initial hypothesis was correct
>
> (Dupuy, 1992, pp. 267–8; translated and quoted by Fullbrook, 1998a, pp. 727–8)

Note that in this model the social context in which the interaction between A and B takes place has been reduced simply and truistically to the current presence of other people. The result is that all influences on the behaviour of each actor except for (his or her beliefs about) the actions and desires of the other actor are excluded from models developed along the lines suggested by the intersubjectivists.[12] However, pre-existing impersonal social structures may well have a significant impact on a person's choice of role model and on his or her capacity to translate that choice of role model into action. For one thing, as we have seen above, it is a feature of the human condition that we are born into a social context which is not of our own making, involuntarily becoming members of a particular gender, race and class. And, while one would not want to claim that human subjectivity can be reduced to such factors, it seems clear enough that the circumstances into which people are born imbue in them a particular sense of themselves and thereby condition what they regard as desirable (Lawson 1997: 187–8; 1999a: 46). People's backgrounds, by determining the resources with which they are endowed, will also influence their ability successfully to pursue their desires. Similarly, an individual's location within the social hierarchy does a good deal to determine his or her ability to command status and prestige and thereby to act as a role model for others (Layder 1997: 44–5).

Lest this be thought to be an isolated example of the limitations of the intersubjectivists' metaphysics, let us consider finally de Beauvoir's analysis of the oppression of social groups. Having noted that de Beauvoir 'identifies the subject/object relation between consciousnesses as the ontological foundation and generative basis of many socially asymmetrical situations,' Fullbrook and Fullbrook 1998b: 107–8; also see p. 165) go on to outline her approach as follows:

> Members of oppressed groups tend to internalise subject groups' negative objectification of them. But the intersubjective worlds

conceived and described by Beauvoir which affect ethics extend much wider than this. Preconstituted spheres of intersubjectivity exist where one finds 'realities which resist consciousness and possess their own laws'. People are thrown into worlds of collective intentionality, wherein social habits and hierarchies have assigned values and meanings to various objects and groups of people. Beginning as a child, one 'emerges in a world filled with meanings which impose themselves'. Each value and each individual's values take on their meaning within these cultural fields of values. In this way, says Beauvoir, her 'situation is defined through its relation to the society to which I belong'. Collective intentionality even extends to specifying what kinds of characteristics do and do not count in defining and evaluating an individual. And, whatever the criteria, an individual is defined by herself and by others in relation to other individuals whose identities also are determined relative to others. We each exist, in part, as the ongoing product of this interdependence of subjectivities.

There is much in this passage with which critical realists would agree, most notably the idea that people are born or thrown into a context that pre-exists them and hence is not of their own making. However, the quotation also reveals that, like Dupuy, de Beauvoir and the Fullbrooks ultimately fail to exploit fully their intuition about the importance of the past. The problem arises because while they admit that current interaction is conditioned by meanings handed down from the past, they ignore the fact that the legacy of the past also encompasses material factors such as the distribution of vested interests and resources. The latter are (as we have seen) relatively impersonal and so cannot be reduced to intersubjectively agreed meanings. And because the influence of the past is not confined to, or analysable solely in terms of, 'preconstituted spheres of intersubjectivity' or 'collective intentionality', the perspective described in the above quotation excludes factors that may be of considerable importance. To see this, consider the following questions: Why do members of dominant groups wish to oppress other people? What factors influence who they choose to oppress? Why are they able to impose their preferred meanings on other groups? If it is indeed the case, as we believe, that such questions demand a consideration of the distribution of incentives and resources embodied in antecedent social structure, then it is difficult to see how they can be answered satisfactorily within a metaphysics which confines itself to intersubjectively agreed meanings (whether in the past or present). This suggests that if the intersubjectivists are to do justice to their insight that the hand of the past shapes current interpersonal interaction, their metaphysics must acknowledge the material aspects of objective, impersonal social structure as well as intersubjectively agreed meanings.

The fact that the metaphysics employed by the intersubjectivists does not extend beyond an ontology of human agency and interaction, then, would appear to deny them analytical purchase on a set of factors which are potentially of great explanatory significance. Thus, the limitations of the intersubjectivist metaphysics manifest themselves in the highly circumscribed set of explanatory possibilities to which it gives rise (Layder 1997: 190–202, 246–51). What is required instead is a more elaborate metaphysics that allows social scientists to conceptualise the relatively impersonal, social-structural influences on socio-economic life as well as the intersubjective (interpersonal) factors. And, as we have seen, it is just such a metaphysics that critical realism purports to provide.[13]

5. Conclusion

We are now in a position to assess the merits of Fullbrook's claims that critical realism lacks a satisfactory model of economic actors and that the solution to this problem is to be found in the work of the intersubjectivists. In addressing Fullbrook's argument, it is important to distinguish two distinct levels of analysis, namely abstract philosophical analysis (of the sort undertaken by critical realists) and concrete social scientific research (like that on which the intersubjectivists have embarked in developing their models of fashion and stock market behaviour). Critical realism operates at a higher level of abstraction than concrete research, using philosophical arguments to provide guidance about the sort of methods that are likely to prove productive in investigating the socio-economic world. More specifically, as we have seen, the objective of critical realism is to encourage researchers to develop (concrete) theories that acknowledge that the socio-economic world is structured, intransitive, open and at least in part holistic. In this way, it is argued, critical realism can help to underlabour for fruitful concrete socio-economic research (C. Lawson et al. 1996; Lawson 1997: 60–1; 1999b: 3, 14–5).

Intersubjectivism and critical realism share a good deal of common ground in this regard. They agree on the importance of adopting an explicit ontological orientation in economics and are united in their opposition to the atomism and behaviourism associated with the mainstream conception of economic man. Moreover, critical realists readily acknowledge the possibility that on occasions a particular causal factor may exert a dominant influence over the phenomenon being studied. And, by eschewing the asocial model of man to which orthodox economics subscribes, critical realism leaves conceptual space for the possibility that the dominant factor may be intersubjective in nature. In this sense, far from being incomplete owing to a failure to incorporate intersubjectivity, critical realism embraces the possibility that intersubjective factors such as mimetic behaviour may play an important role in socio-economic affairs.

211

However, according to critical realism, whether or not intersubjective influences are in fact important in any particular case cannot be determined in advance but can only be established *ex posteriori* through concrete research. The risk that intersubjectivism runs is that by concentrating so heavily on mimetic behaviour, it pre-judges the issue and thereby is in danger of offering a one-sided and so misleading analysis of the phenomenon under investigation. The critical realist metaphysics, on the other hand, leaves room for impersonal social structures as well as interpersonal interaction and is therefore able to accommodate intersubjective phenomena without running the risk of over-emphasising their significance by being committed to including them a priori.

What critical realism does *not* attempt to do is to undertake the work of substantive social scientific research. Critical realism does not purport to provide mechanical or algorithmic procedures for answering substantive questions about the socio-economic world (Lawson 1997: 191). Critical realism does not aim to provide concrete accounts of intersubjective phenomena such as fashion or stock market behaviour. Indeed, there may be a number of concrete accounts that incorporate such abstract features as the internally related nature of (much of) the socio-economic world and therefore are consistent with critical realism, and in and of itself critical realism does not differentiate between them. Hence, there is no specific model of mimetic behaviour that can be designated as *the* critical realist account. Rather, critical realists would argue that the models should be judged according to their capacity to explain a wide range of socio-economic phenomena of interest. And, to reiterate, such judgements are the prerogative of substantive social science, not of critical realism *per se* (Lawson 1999b: 14–5; 1999c: 3–6).

Herein lies the truth in Fullbrook's assessment of critical realism. The critical realist metaphysics (including its model of the socio-economic actor) is simplistic if 'simplicity' is understood in the non-pejorative sense of 'being pitched at a relatively high level of abstraction'. Critical realists are quite open and unabashed about this. However, if the criterion by which the level of sophistication of a metaphysics is judged is taken to be its capacity to draw attention to a wide range of (potentially explanatory significant) features of socio-economic reality that might otherwise go unheeded (such as pre-existing social structures), it can be seen that critical realism offers a rather sophisticated metaphysics.

Notes

1 We are grateful to Edward Fullbrook, Tony Lawson and participants in the Cambridge Workshop on Realism and Economics for helpful comments on earlier versions of this paper. Any remaining errors are the responsibility of the authors alone.

2 In this paper we use the term 'ontology' to refer to the nature of (what exists in) the world, that is, the nature of being. The closely related term 'metaphysics' will be taken to denote the set of (philosophical) categories in terms of which the ontology of the world is expressed and analysed (Harré 1988: 100; Butchvarov 1995: 489).

3 Lawson and Fullbrook employ different definitions of mainstream economics. Lawson reserves the term for all forms of formalist modelling in economics, which he associates with the use of what he calls a 'deductivist' explanatory/expositional format. Fullbrook, in contrast, seems to use the term to refer specifically to orthodox theorising of the standard general equilibrium variety (a special case of Lawson's definition).

4 This claim is known as 'the principle of intentionality': consciousness is always consciousness *of* something, that is, consciousness always intends an object. For Bretano, then, intentionality is the distinguishing mark of the mental, and 'intending' in the everyday, volitional sense of the word is a special case thereof.

5 The distinction between logical and real time is discussed in Shackle (1958) and O'Driscoll and Rizzo (1985).

6 This aspect of the critical realist argument has been developed most fully by Archer (1995, especially pp. 65–92, 154–8).

7 More extensive discussions of the critical realist metaphysics and of the explanatory framework to which it gives rise are to be found in Archer (1995: 165–344) and Lawson (1997: 157–227).

8 Many of the contributions of Neo-Ricardians, Post-Keynesians, analytical Marxists and members of the French intersubjectivist school are also deductivist by this definition and thus also fall into the critical realist category of the 'mainstream' (and are as open to its critique of deductivism as is orthodox economics).

9 Of course it is possible that actors could have done otherwise in orthodox models in which they choose an alternative from a set in which there is more than one that delivers maximal utility. But this possibility is usually excluded by assumption.

10 This diagnosis of the ontological commitments of intersubjectivism receives additional confirmation from an examination of the account of the relationship between social structure and human agency provided by Fullbrook and Fullbrook (1998a, b). According to the former, the difference between social structure and human agency is merely a matter of perspective, for the two are not (as critical realists maintain) ontologically distinct things but are simply two aspects of the same thing, namely people (Fullbrook and Fullbrook 1998a: 274). Social structure, on this view, is no more than a generalised aspect or feature of human behaviour and, as such, is ontologically reducible to the latter.

11 Specular behaviour is a manifestation of intersubjectivity that involves 'the capacity of the human mind to put itself in the place of another and "see" the world from this other party's point of view' (Dupuy 1989: 41).

12 The fact that either or both of the parties in the intersubjectivist model may be a 'group' does not resolve this problem because, as we have seen, on the intersubjectivists' definition, the 'group' is simply a collection of individuals, not (as critical realists would have it) an ontologically irreducible social structure (Fullbrook and Fullbrook 1998a: 276, 1998b: 96–8). For intersubjectivism, then, contrary to the critical realist claim that social structures possesses their own *sui generis* causal powers, the causal efficacy of the 'group' is reducible to the causal powers of its (current) members.

13 Nor does the claim that the methodology which flows from the intersubjectivist ontology is one in which 'social and economic phenomena may … be explained either in terms of individual human beings or in terms of

socio-economic wholes' (Fullbrook and Fullbrook 1998b: 98–9; emphasis added) identify a way of overcoming the limitations of intersubjectivism. Once again, the problem derives from the fact intersubjectivism elides the ontological distinction between social structure and human agency: because structure and agency are held to be two aspects of the same thing, social scientific explanations couched in terms of human agency and explanations framed in terms of social structure are held to be mutually exclusive. However, what the critical realist analysis presented earlier in this paper revealed is that satisfactory explanations of socio-economic phenomena require an account of the *interplay* over (historical) time between (antecedent) social structure and (subsequent) human agency, which in turn necessitates that structure and agency be ontologically separable. Once again, then, the failure to include the category of historically given, ontologically irreducible social structure within their metaphysics can be seen to vitiate the intersubjectivists' attempts to provide a satisfactory framework for the analysis of the socio-economic world.

References

Archer, M. S. (1995) *Realist Social Theory: The Morphogenetic Approach*, Cambridge: Cambridge University Press.

Butchvarov, P. (1995) '*Metaphysics*' in R. Audi (ed.) *The Cambridge Dictionary of Philosophy*, Cambridge: Cambridge University Press.

Dupuy, J.-P. (1989) 'Common Knowledge, Common Sense,' *Theory and Decision* **27**, 37–62.

Dupuy, J.-P. (1992) *Le Sacrifice et L'envie: Le Libéralisme aux Prises avec la Justice Sociale*, Paris: Calmann-Lévy.

Fullbrook, E. (1997) 'Post-Modernising *Homo Economicus*,' in S. Earnshaw (ed.) *Just Postmodernism*, Amsterdam: Rodopi.

Fullbrook, E. (1998a) 'Caroline Foley and the theory of Intersubjective Demand,' *Journal of Economic Issues* **32**, 709–31.

Fullbrook, E. and K. Fullbrook, (1998a) 'Simone de Beauvoir,' in S. Critchley and W.R. Schroeder (eds) *A Companion to Continental Philosophy*, Oxford: Blackwell.

Fullbrook, E. and K. Fulbrook, (1998b) 'Shifting the Mainstream: Lawson's Impetus,' *Atlantic Economic Journal* **26**, 431–40.

Fullbrook, E. (1998b) *Simone de Beauvoir: A Critical Introduction*, Cambridge: Polity Press.

Harré, H. R. (1988) *The Philosophies of Science*, Oxford: Oxford University Press.

Lawson, C., M. Peacock and S. Pratten (1996) 'Realism, Underlabouring and Institutions,' *Cambridge Journal of Economics* **20**, 137–51.

Lawson, T. (1997) *Economics and Reality*, London and New York: Routledge.

Lawson, T. (1998) 'Clarifying and Developing the *Economics and Reality* Project: Closed and Open Systems, Deductivism, Prediction, and Teaching,' *Review of Social Economy* **56**, 356–75.

Lawson, T. (1999a) 'Feminism, Realism and Universalism,' *Feminist Economics* **5**, 25–59.

Lawson, T. (1999b) 'Developments in *Economics as Realist Social Theory*,' in S. Fleetwood (ed.) *Critical Realism in Economics: Development and Debate*, London and New York: Routledge.

Lawson, T. (1999c) 'Connections and Distinctions: Post Keynesianism and critical realism,' *Journal of Post Keynesian Economics* **22**, 3–14.

Lawson, T. (1999d) 'What has Realism Got To Do With It? *Economics and Philosophy* **15**, 269–82.

Layder, D. (1997) *Modern Social Theory: Key Debates and New Directions*, London: UCL Press.

Lewis, P.A. and J.H. Runde (1999) 'A Critical Realist Perspective on Paul Davidson's Methodological Writings on – and Rhetorical Strategy for – post Keynesian Economics,' *Journal of Post Keynesian Economics* **22**, 35–56.

O'Driscoll, G.P. and M.J. Rizzo (1985) *The Economics of Time and Ignorance*, Oxford: Basil Blackwell.

Orléan, A. (1989) 'Mimetic Contagion and Speculative Bubbles,' *Theory and Decision* **27**, 63–92.

Runde, J.H. (1993) 'Paul Davidson and the Austrians: Reply to Davidson,' *Critical Review* **7**, 381–97.

Shackle, G.L.S. (1958) *Time in Economics*, Amsterdam: North-Holland Publishing Company.

Veblen, T.B. ([1909] 1994) 'The Limitations of Marginal Utility,' *Journal of Political Economy* **17**, 620–38. Reprinted in D.M. Hausman (ed.), *The Philosophy of Economics: An Anthology*, Cambridge: Cambridge University Press.

13

SOCIAL NETWORKS AND INFORMATION

Paul Ormerod

1. Introduction

The volumes in this series are linked by a common theme. As the frontispiece to the series proclaims: 'In contemporary economics the label 'theory' has been appropriated by a group that confines itself to largely asocial, ahistorical, mathematical 'modelling'. *Economics as Social Theory* thus reclaims the 'theory' label, offering a platform for alternative, rigorous, but broader and more critical conceptions of theorising.'

The mere existence of a general commonality of view does not, of course, guarantee that the particular offerings will meet with universal approval. Mao Tse Tung's injunction to let a thousand flowers bloom might indeed have been meant at its face value, neither more nor less, as an encouragement to diversity. But it has often been interpreted as a way of inducing the revelation of true opinions in order that heretical ones might be more easily identified and suppressed.

It must be said from the outset that this paper risks such dissolution in a suitable hail of fire and brimstone. For it does deal with mathematical modelling. In mitigation, before the scales are weighed and judgement passed, several points must be made.

Conventional economics pays very little attention to the ways in which individuals are linked together. The aim of this paper is to show three things. First, that this is an important omission from orthodox thinking. Second, that taking account of this in a systematic way can give powerful insights into social and economic issues. Third, that formal modelling is a useful way of doing this, which helps in the process of developing alternatives to orthodoxy.

An important assumption of orthodox economic theory is that all agents – individuals and firms, in everyday English – have access at all times to all available information. Further, it is assumed that the tastes and preferences of individuals, whilst they differ, are nevertheless fixed. Each individual acts in isolation, maximising, in the jargon, his or her

216

utility. The actions of others only impinge indirectly on the agent, via their impact on the set of prices which the individual faces.

The internal contradictions of this core model of economics have been explored rigorously by mathematical economists. I have described much of this work in both the *Death of Economics* and *Butterfly Economics*, and it is not my purpose to repeat this here.[1] Economists have responded to these problems in the past twenty years or so. A literature has grown in which individuals are assumed to have access to 'imperfect' information. The choice of phrase economists use to describe this theory is a telling one. For it implies that the world of free market theory is the 'perfect' one, the Platonic Idea towards which all actual economies must strive, and the messy world of reality is 'imperfect'. But even slight deviations from perfection in terms of the basic assumptions which are made can lead to outcomes and implications which are far removed from the world of perfect competition.

The first example in this paper illustrates exactly this concept, and the second deals with the importance of social networks in the process of how the unemployed find jobs. In both cases, the way in which economic agents are connected together for the exchange of information is of decisive importance for the outcome.

2. Market structures

The core world of economic theory consists of a very large number of small firms. No firm is of sufficient size to be able to exercise any control over the market for its product. An important implication of this is that companies are what is known as 'price takers'. In other words, each individual firm has to accept the market price for its product, and has no possibility of influencing it in any way.

In this make-believe world, firms can sell as much output as they choose to produce. There is no real incentive to increase production, because the forces of competition have eroded profit margins to a 'normal' level. However, if a firm decides to, say, double its output, it does so under very special conditions of production. In a sentence, the costs per unit of output never change regardless of whether a firm produces just one unit of output or a hundred million units. The cost per unit is always the same.

In the jargon, this assumption is called 'constant returns to scale'. If the inputs which the firm uses in the process of production are doubled in size, output is also doubled. In short, there are no particular advantages or disadvantages to being either big or small.

In reality, of course, this is far from being the case. The desirability of certain products depends almost entirely on the fact that they cannot be produced on a large scale. At one level, we might regard all red wine as being the same in the sense that each variety is a red, alcoholic drink made from grapes. This differentiates it sharply from other alcoholic drinks such as whisky, and non-alcoholic drinks such as milk. But only the most puritanical teetotaller can fail to be aware of the myriad of distinctions within the red wine market. For connoisseurs, the pleasure of drinking a *premier grand cru* Bordeaux would surely be diminished if the wine could be made on the same scale as, say, mass market fiery Algerian or Bulgarian red.

But more generally, there are great advantages to being big. Most markets are dominated by a few, very large firms. The costs of producing a unit of output, far from being constant, often fall as the amount which is produced grows. The decidedly Old Economy industry of car production illustrates this well. A dedicated and eccentric amateur could possibly manufacture his or her car from scratch in the back yard, though this would take a very great deal of time and hence cost. For mass production, a large and expensive plant is required. Once assembled, if the plant makes just one car per year, the costs of producing it are enormous. For, in addition to the small amount of additional labour costs needed to produce it, all the costs associated with building the plant fall on this one car. If two cars are made, the costs per car are already halved, as each car then shares the total costs. And so on and so on, until the limit of the capacity of the plant is reached. This state of affairs is known in economics as 'increasing returns to scale'. In other words, as the scale of output increases, the advantages of being able to produce more increase.

The car industry, indeed, contains the world's largest company, namely General Motors, with an annual value of sales of around $200 billion. But many other industries are dominated by a small number of firms. The various facets of the computer industry share this characteristic, with Microsoft being the best known example. The world of advertising might be thought to be immune from such trends, based as it is on the individual skills of the people employed rather than relying on huge amounts of investment with which to produce its output. In the cynical phrase, 'the assets walk out of the door at five o'clock every night'. But even here, where there is scope for lots of small businesses to survive by creating niches, the industry is dominated by a few large firms – J Walter Thompson, Publicis, Ogilvy and Mather and the like. Huge multinational companies often prefer to have their advertising accounts handled on a global scale by a single agency, and only the very biggest are capable of doing this.

In short, the typical market structure in the Western economies appears to be far removed from the world of perfect competition. Instead of many small firms, industries are dominated by a small number of very large ones. 'Oligopoly' rather than perfect competition is the empirical norm.

All these facts are well known. Indeed, they are an important reason why many students abandon the discipline of economics at an early stage. The world of economic theory seems remote from reality. This is a perfectly reasonable judgement to make. After all, many of the assumptions of conventional economics were made purely to make the maths tractable. When economic theory was first being formalised in the late nineteenth and early twentieth centuries, economists had to formulate their models in such a way that they yielded what are known as analytical solutions. In other words, the equations in the models could, in principle, be solved using a pencil and a sheet of paper. It might be difficult, but it was nevertheless feasible. In order to do this, the assumption of constant returns to scale was needed. Great economists, such as Alfred Marshall, who dominated the subject around the end of the nineteenth century, knew perfectly well that this was often not true. But it was the best which could be done at the time.

The closing years of the twentieth century have seen an explosion in computing power which enables more complex systems of equations to be solved for the first time. We need no longer rely on pencil and paper, but can obtain what are called numerical solutions – using the power of the computer to grind them out. The advantage of this is highly practical. More realistic models can be built.

How do economists justify the apparently glaring disparity between the oligopolistic structure of the real world with the perfectly competitive one of economic theory? There are two main defences. The first is the classic one of 'as if'. It may seem – indeed it may even be the case – that many industries are dominated by just few firms. But competitive pressures are such that it is 'as if' there were a large number of small firms in these industries. To be fair, this argument has a certain amount of validity. Car companies, despite their enormous size, are feeling the pinch as car ownership amongst Western households approaches saturation levels, at least as far as first cars are concerned. It is becoming more and more difficult for them to increase prices. A newcomer like Microsoft, which it was in the 1980s, can enter a market characterised for many years by the towering presence of IBM.

Yet, with the best will in the world, it *is* hard to imagine that these industries are essentially the same as the theoretical world of perfect competition. Certainly, there are many able free market economists who would long to receive the sorts of consultancy fees available to those hired in the various anti-trust actions brought against Microsoft by the US authorities. But despite the huge potential supply, the price – the fees – of those who were chosen were not eroded to a perfectly competitive level.

The second argument used by economists is not even as good as the first. Confronted by the very many examples of oligopoly, there is a general waving of hands, and a murmuring about how this arises because of increasing returns. In some way, it is the real world which is seen as the aberration. Perfect competition is the ideal norm, and all other forms of market structure are a deviation from it.

Using the power of computers, we can set up models which demonstrate that this is *not* the case.[2] Almost all of the assumptions of the perfect competition model can be retained. But relaxing just two of them, in other words, making the model more realistic, leads to an outcome in which oligopoly and not perfect competition is the norm – exactly as we observe in reality.

The basic model may still seem unrealistic, but that in itself is not a criticism. All models must by definition be approximations to reality. But the purpose of this model is to show that we do not need to invoke increasing returns to bring about situations in which oligopoly is the norm. Of course, increasing returns actually do exist, and exist pervasively. So in this important sense the model is deliberately *un*realistic. It illustrates an important aspect of the *process* of how a competitive structure evolves into an oligopolistic one.[3]

We start with a large number of firms operating under conditions of constant returns to scale. Just as in conventional theory, the product produced by each of these firms is identical. We might imagine these firms as being small companies which supply, say, the motor vehicle industry. More precisely, these are firms which supply firms which themselves supply the likes of Ford and General Motors. They manufacture, for example, bits of metal which are used to make bits of gearboxes. We need to think of this kind of situation, in which companies are supplying fairly standard industrial parts to other companies, in order to make the assumption that their products are identical at all realistic. In many markets, firms make a great deal of effort to convince people that their product is different from that of other companies even when it is essentially the same. Air travel, for example, consists of transporting people long distances in metal tubes at high speed. The speed is its key advantage over other forms of travel. Travelling, say, from London to New York, it does not matter which airline is chosen in terms of getting there much faster than by ship. Yet, airlines spend huge amounts to convince customers that they are different from each other, efforts which by and large are successful.

One of the variations we make in our assumptions from those of conventional theory is that the companies making the product are not identical to each other. They make the same thing, but with different levels of costs. We can rule out differences in the costs of transporting the product to the buyer by imaging these companies to be part of a geographic cluster, so both the buyers and the sellers are close to each other. In areas with large car plants, myriads of small and medium sized firms have developed over the years in the same places, each supplying component parts into the final product. This also rules out differences in labour costs in the area where production takes place. Cost differences arise because they produce with varying degrees of efficiency. This could arise for many reasons, for example, from the existence of different vintages of the capital stock needed to produce the commodity. Once again translating from economic jargon into English, this means that some of the firms use older and less efficient machines than others.

An enormous amount of empirical work demonstrates that firms in the same industry do differ, often substantially, in efficiency. This is a source of embarrassment, for two reasons. First, it is often hard to explain exactly why companies do differ. The marvellous concept of 'X-efficiency' has been invoked to account for differences. To a cynic, this could very well mean 'we don't know how to explain this phenomenon, but, like Rumplestiltskin, now we have given our ignorance a name we feel much better about it'. However, being charitable we could think of X-efficiency as arising from different qualities of management. All firms could have identical capital stocks, labour costs and so on, but management efficiency might vary across the firms. For our model to operate, we only require that firms differ with respect to a single factor.

The second difficulty is more profound for orthodox economics. Competition is meant to involve the survival of the fittest. Everyone is forced either to drive costs down to those of the most efficient producer, or to go out of business. For, by definition, the price of the product cannot be affected by individual firms and so higher costs cannot be passed on as higher prices. Yet, in the real world, inefficiencies can persist for very long periods of time. Study after study, government report after government report have shown, for example, that whilst the very best firms in the UK are as good as any in the world, a large proportion of British business transparently is not.

This leads into the second difference in the assumptions of our model from those of the perfectly competitive world of conventional theory. There is a large number of producers and we assume that there is an equally large number of buyers. Each of the producers is making the identical product at its own price, which differs from that of every other firm. But, and this is the second difference in assumptions, there are substantial costs of acquiring information about these prices. One practical reason for this might well be the fact that the Managing Director of the firm you have always bought from is your cousin, or your golf partner, or a member of your Masonic Lodge. There would be non-monetary social costs associated with buying from someone else.

In a more realistic setting, in which firms are geographically dispersed for example, information may be costly to acquire for many reasons. One of the advantages of the Web is that it enables businesses buying from other businesses – B2B – to acquire quotes from around the world very cheaply. Yet, paradoxically, this apparent enhancement of competition may trigger a process which leads to more and more oligopolistic market structures.

Suppose, in our imaginary world, that each buyer only gets a quote from a single supplier, and buys one unit of output from this seller at the quoted price. We have an equal number of buyers and sellers, and we assume that the buyers are connected to the sellers at random. There are no other connections in the model. An important practical example of this latter feature would be to specify a network of connections between the sellers, across which information about their prices could be transmitted, so that collectively they might exercise some control over the market price. Of course, active collusion on these lines is illegal in many countries, but there are many ways and means of signalling such information. In consumer markets it is very easy. Prices are visible for all to see, so companies can perfectly legally all charge the same price without any suggestion of collusion. In business to business markets it is a little harder, and anti-trust cases often turn on whether or not companies can be judged to have taken part in price-fixing agreements, explicit or otherwise.

We can now examine the effect of reducing the cost to buyers of acquiring information in this market. We have set the simple rules of the game, as it were, and can observe how it unfolds. We start off with, say 100 buyers, each connected at random to a single one out of 100 sellers, so that buyer number 53 might be connected to seller number 34 and so on. Because of the way the connections are specified, some sellers will not be connected to any buyer initially. In other words, they make no sales. The precise number will differ each time the game is played, but usually between 30 and 40 out of the 100 sellers will find themselves in this position. We can introduce rules about how long such sellers can remain in the game, or we can think of them as potential rather than actual participants. To keep the rules as simple as possible, we choose the latter. Firms which make no sales do not go out of business, but are able to quote and price and produce subsequently if they are asked to do so by a buyer.

Apart from the firms with no sales, most of the sellers will start by being connected to just one buyer, so they produce one unit of output. A small number will be connected to two buyers, an even smaller number to three, and very occasionally, if we play the game lots of times, we will start with some sellers having four or five buyers. But in general, at the start of the game, the sellers are all producing broadly similar amounts of output.

The game now moves onto the next step. This time, each buyer is connected to two sellers. One of these is the previous selection, and the new one is chosen at random. We can think of this happening because the cost of acquiring information has fallen. For the same amount of cost and effort involved in dealing with one seller, buyers can now contact two. Each buyer ruthlessly selects the lowest price. There is no difference in the quality of the product, whether actual or merely perceived, which will promote buyer loyalty to the previous seller. And buyers switch supplier even if the difference in price between them is tiny. We can add features such as allowing suppliers to make a one-off reduction in their price if they would otherwise lose a sale, but this makes no difference to the eventual outcome.

At each subsequent step of the model, an additional connection between each buyer and the group of sellers is added. With each step, The extra connections can be interpreted as further reductions in the cost of obtaining information. One point to notice is that this is subject to diminishing returns. The first additional connection doubles the amount of information obtained from one quote to two, the next increases it by fifty percent, from two to three, and so on in ever diminishing proportions.

The buyer obtains a price from the previous firm with which he or she did business, and a number of other quotes chosen at random. Just as before, the lowest price is chosen without sentiment. Low-cost sellers will begin to obtain more and more of the total market. Eventually, of course, all buyers will be connected to all sellers. When this happens in our game, everyone will choose the lowest price seller. The competitive circumstances in which the game began will evolve into a monopoly, with just one seller.

As it stands, the game is a simple one, but it nevertheless informs about the process of how an apparent increase in the degree of competition eventually leads to less rather than more competition. Figure 13.1 plots a typical solution of the game showing the number of active sellers – those firms making sales in the current period – and the number of connections from each buyer.

To begin with, in this particular outcome of the game, we have just over 60 sellers active in the first step – those which are connected to a buyer. The most interesting point about Fig. 13.1 is that the number of active sellers falls away initially very rapidly as the number of connections

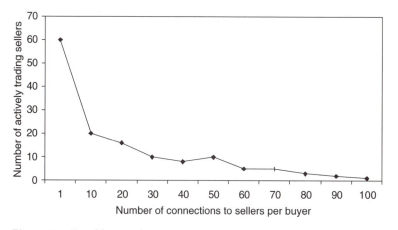

Figure 13.1 Equilibrium distribution of active sellers.

increases. Further, the size of those which remain active begins to vary substantially. In the above example, with just 10 (out of a possible 100) connections from each buyer, the number of active sellers falls from over 60 to 20. The largest seller is now producing 0 units of output and the smallest (ignoring those not able to sell anything at all) just one. This is qualitatively very similar to the sort of market structure which we observe in many real world markets.

The model, or game as we have been calling it, can be made more realistic. For example, we can specify networks on which the sellers are connected, as mentioned above, and allow price collusion to emerge once sellers on the same network acquire more than a certain percentage share of the total market.

But, even in a very simple form, this illustrates how markets in which firms are producing a very standardised product can evolve into oligopolies. By definition, in this model, firms produce under constant returns, so we do not need to invoke increasing returns to get this result. Further, all firms produce an identical product, thereby eliminating the scope for creating partial monopolies or oligopolies by product differentiation, another reason often put forward to account for the market structures which we actually see. The only departure we require from the orthodox theory of perfect competition is that firms differ in their efficiency, a pervasive feature of reality. As the costs of acquiring information fall and the number of connections rises, perfect competition gives way to oligopoly. The ideal outcome of economic theory, with many small firms producing under identical circumstances, should be seen as the particular rather than the general case. Unless *all* of the theoretical conditions required are met, oligopoly and not perfect competition is the standard outcome towards which markets evolve.

3. Unemployment[4]

A familiar and depressing feature of the developed economies is the way in which high pockets of unemployment can persist in certain areas even when the overall demand for labour is high. In the South of England at the end of the year 2000, for example, there is effectively full employment. In many areas the unemployment rate is less than 1 per cent, a rate not seen since the Golden Years of the 1950s and 1960s. Yet, in particular localities, often in close geographical proximity to very prosperous places, the unemployment rate is in double figures.

In part, this is due to the low skills and educational attainments of people in these neighbourhoods, but the phenomenon can be seen at an even more local level, comparing employment outcomes for residents of neighbouring housing estates or schemes, or often within individual schemes themselves. Despite broadly similar skills – human capital as economists like to describe it – some people on the estates appear to find it easy to get a job whilst others struggle and remain unemployed.

A key way in which people find jobs is through personal contacts. Mark Granovetter, the American sociologist who did seminal work in this area in the 1970s, reported, for example, that over 60 per cent of professional and managerial workers in the US obtained their jobs through personal contacts. The same phenomenon occurs much lower down the jobs hierarchy. The infamous British Old Boys' Network was often invoked as a reason why Etonians or Harrovians found themselves in top jobs, but the same sort of thing happens at all levels of the jobs market.

For example, in a University of Essex paper in 1999, Carmel Hannan reported the results of a detailed statistical study of micro-data held in the British Household Panel study, examining the impact of both traditional economic explanations of exit from unemployment such as the level of human capital of the individual, and the social network hypothesis. This latter is found to be very important. Pamela Meadows, former chief economist at the UK's Department of Employment, wrote in 2000 that 'The use of friends, relatives and social contacts as a means of getting jobs remains very important to young people and is attractive to employers. However, this works to the disadvantage of those who are outside these networks, because their parents and friends are unemployed, because they have lost contact with their family or because they have a bad reputation or criminal record'. She went on to point out that a key reason for this is the attitude of employers: 'informal methods work in a variety of ways. There are traditional introductions by fathers, uncles, brothers and family friends, who essentially take the role of sponsor to the young person, and provide some guarantee of his worth to the employer. This has always been an important route into work for young men and it remains surprisingly strong…. From the point of view of the employer, the grapevine is seen as less risky than recruiting in the open market, because it includes an element of social control'.

This section of the chapter sets out a highly stylised model of unemployment and job search. The aim is to focus explicitly on the nature of the social network which connects agents in the model, and on the implications for unemployment of different degrees of connectedness of social networks.

We set up a model in which unemployment can persist only because of a failure of the social network to inform individuals about job opportunities. It must be stressed that we are not suggesting that this is the only reason why unemployment exists. But to the extent that a lack of information about job vacancies might be a cause of unemployment, we quantify the influence on this type of social network by which individuals are connected and information exchanged between them.

An important result which emerges is that, even when jobs are being created, high rates of unemployment can emerge in social networks which are only weakly connected. And as noted above, we do observe high pockets of unemployment even in the face of a strong demand for labour. Abstract though the model is, it points clearly to the kinds of policies which are needed in order to deal with this problem.

We have a model populated by a largish number of individuals. We might think of it as representing a housing estate or other local area. At any point in time, the actors in the model are either unemployed or employed. In other words, the focus is on people of working age. In the most straightforward version, the assumption is made that everyone is identical. Patently, this is not true, but as an approximation of the sorts of skills and qualifications which might be found in a rundown inner city housing block, for example, or in one of the massive estates which surround certain British and French cities, it is not completely unreasonable.

In this model, job losses and the creation of new jobs takes place at random. In other words, the motivations of firms in reducing/expanding employment are not considered in this model, and neither is the overall economic climate in which firms operate. We could imagine a situation in which the economy as a whole is close to full employment. Even in these conditions, job losses still occur, but are balanced out by job creation. And from the perspective of the low skill inhabitants of a housing scheme, the job gains and losses in nearby companies is essentially a random process. There is little which they feel they can do to influence the outcome. They are unlikely, for example, to be able to borrow large amounts of venture capital to create the new Microsoft.

In our artifical world, if a job vacancy arises and a person hears about it, he or she will apply for the job and be hired with certainty. We can make this more realistic by giving individuals their own probabilities both of applying and of being accepted by the employer. But the simpler version illustrates the same principles.

To complete the model, or the rules of the game, we need to specify how it evolves. As with the competition model in Section 2, the action takes place in consecutive steps. Imagine, to begin with, that everyone is out of work. As it happens, the eventual outcome is the same no matter how people start off, but the details of demonstrating this need not concern us here. In the first step of the model, two things happen. First, someone is chosen at random from the population. If already unemployed, he or she remains unemployed. But if the person has a job, it is deemed to be lost and the person becomes unemployed.

The second part is a bit more complicated. Another random selection is made from the people in the model. If the person chosen is unemployed, he or she is offered a job and takes it. But if the person is already employed, the process does not stop there. The job offer is passed on to those people on the individual's social network. In other words, to friends, family or neighbours – to whomever the person is likely to tell the news about a job being available. From this group, anyone who is unemployed takes up the job.[5] This is exactly the process described above in empirical accounts of an important way in which actual labour markets work. The network both informs people about job vacancies, and helps them secure them when they apply. The model then moves on to the next step. For completeness, if everyone on the network is employed, the job offer disappears from this group completely. It is not carried over to the next period. This seems quite realistic: a firm has a vacancy and asks some of its workers if they know anyone who would be suited. If they do not, the company will start looking elsewhere.

The process then continues, step by step, and the mixture of employed to unemployed in the group of people in the model evolves. By experiment, examining many different solutions of the model on the computer, we can judge when this split between the employed and unemployed settles down. At every step there may, of course, be a change, but these eventually become small, and a constant proportion emerges.

The relative size of the employed and unemployed groups which the model generates depends crucially upon how we specify the social network. We can judge the eventual outcome by reference to the two extremes. First of all, suppose we have a very gregarious, integrated community in which everyone knows everyone else and tells them about job offers. Of course, no actual group is ever like this. But with the professional groups examined by Granovetter which we discussed above, well over half the people obtained jobs through personal contacts. The outcome of the game in this situation is easy to see. In the first step, someone is bound to be offered a job because everyone is unemployed. In the second step, even if by chance this same person is selected to be offered the new job, he or she will tell everyone else, and so the job will be filled. Every time someone in work is told of a new job offer, everyone else in the population is told about it. So, eventually, everyone ends up employed.

The other extreme is a very disjointed, anomic group in which people keep to themselves and do not communicate directly with anyone else. In many ways, this is the model of free market economics. No one passes on job offers to anyone else and operates as a completely selfish individual. The outcome in this case is that the unemployment rate settles down at 50 per cent of the population: half find work, but the other half do not. It takes about a page of straightforward algebra to demonstrate this result, and it could be described in words. But this would be a lengthy diversion. The intuitive interpretation of this is that at any step of the model, anyone who is chosen has a 50/50 chance of being made unemployed (the first part of each step), or of being offered a job (the second part). If we allow the model to run for a sufficient number of steps to give everyone the chance of being chosen in each part, this is the overall split which will emerge in the population.

Imagine we have 100 people in our model. In the two cases examined above, any particular individual has a social network with either 100 or 0 connections. In the first one, everyone is connected to everyone else, and passes information on. In the second, no one has any connections to anyone else. And the unemployment rate is either zero or 50 per cent, depending on which network we specify.

What happens when we have a different number of connections per individual? How rapidly does the unemployment rate fall with the number of connections, with the closeness of the social networks? Here, we usually do need the computer to obtain the result. There are many different ways in which people can be connected, and there is a whole branch of mathematics – graph theory – which deals with this sort of situation. The precise results do depend on the exact geometry of the connections, but the most important influence on the outcome of our model is how many connections, on average, does each individual have.

Figure 13.2 illustrates how the eventual rate of unemployment which emerges depends upon the density of the social network, on how well connected and integrated people are.[6]

The interesting feature of the figure is that only a very small number of connections in a social network are needed to make a dramatic difference to the outcome. With each person being willing to pass on information to

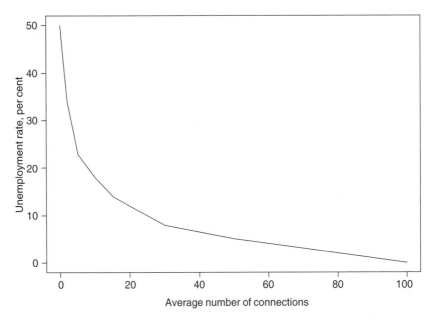

Figure 13.2 Unemployment rate and average number of people on each person's social network.

just five others, out of a possible one hundred, the unemployment rate falls by just over a half. This suggests that policies which succeed in increasing the flow of information about the availability of jobs in socially isolated communities can have a strong impact upon the rate of unemployment (provided, of course, that jobs are actually available). But in more integrated social groups, the return to such polices is much lower.

4. Conclusion

For most of the social sciences, the idea that individuals operate within society, and that their behaviour is affected directly by the way in which people are integrated, is a fundamental aspect of the discipline. In contrast, in standard economics, people operate in isolation, as autonomous individuals. The behaviour of any one person only affects others indirectly, in as much as it might change the set of relative prices which people face. Economics has been able to offer many insights into how the world works. But in order to do so, simplifying assumptions had to be made which precluded direct interaction between individuals. Many modern economists appear to have lost sight of the fact that the great, early formalisers of economic theory knew perfectly well that they were making assumptions which were dramatic simplifications of reality. But given the tools they had available, this had to be done.

Modern computing power enables more realistic assumptions to be made about how people behave, and the consequences of these assumptions analysed. The concept of formal modelling is not to everyone's taste, but the two examples above illustrate the potential of what can be done.

In the first, most of the assumptions of the ideal, perfectly competitive world of economic theory are retained. But simply by allowing firms to differ in their efficiency levels and then increasing the flow of information between them, we show that the prevailing market structure which emerges will be one of oligopoly, with markets dominated by a few large firms. This is the norm and not the deviation.

In the second, we offer an account of how high unemployment rates can persist in local areas even when the overall demand for labour is high. In disjointed communities, where the flow of information between individuals is low, unemployment can remain high even when jobs are being created. People simply do not get to hear about them in time.

Ultimately, it is only by making use of the insights of the other social sciences, and incorporating them in formal models such as these, that the economics community will be persuaded to move away from what has become a narrow and scientifically restrictive perspective.

Notes

1 Readers interested in the formal details should go to Roy Radner's brilliant paper 'Competitive Equilibrium under Uncertainty'. Published in *Econometrica*, a world class journal, as long ago as 1968, this single paper completely undermines the theoretical basis of orthodox economics.

2 The first example in the chapter can, in its simplest form set out here, actually be solved analytically. But this soon ceases to be the case when even slightly more complex and realistic assumptions are made.

3 My colleagues at Volterra, Craig Mounfield, Bridget Rosewell and Laurence Smith are all actively involved in this ongoing research.

4 An expanded version of this section is given in a paper I presented with Laurence Smith to the Tenth World Congress of Social Economics held at the University of Cambridge, August 2000.

5 If more than one person on the relevant network is unemployed, one of these is selected at random to take the job.

6 The particular topology used to specify the network is a k-nearest neighbours one, where the agents are placed at random in 2-dimensional Euclidean space and each is connected to its k nearest.

14

DISPOSITIONS, SOCIAL STRUCTURES AND ECONOMIC PRACTICES

Towards a new economic sociology

Frédéric Lebaron

1. Introduction

Several recent publications testify to a kind of revival of economic sociology in France. This follows an international movement born in the 1980s, originating, to a great extent, in the United States, as evidenced by the publication in 1994 of the *Handbook of Economic Sociology* by Neil Smelser and Richard Swedberg (Smelser and Swedberg 1994). Some journals, such as *Actes de la Recherche en Sciences Sociales, Génèses, Regards Sociologiques, La Revue Française de Sociologie, Cahiers Internationaux de Sociologie, La Revue du MAUSS*, have also, in the last few years, dedicated a number of issues to economics, examined from a sociological or ethnological point of view. Various books dealing with the history of economic sociology have accompanied a renewed interest in Durkheimian sociologists who contributed extensively in laying the foundations in this field during the first half of the twentieth century – principally Simiand, Halbwachs and Mauss – even though their following has remained limited, at least within this discipline (see, in particular, Gislain and Steiner 1995). Several French sociologists are turning more and more towards economic sociology, as is indicated by the recent research carried out by Pierre Bourdieu in the economic field or, with substantially different theoretical approaches, the research of Michel Callon – recent co-ordinator of a collective book on the social construction of the market (Callon 1998) – as well as that of Bruno Latour and Luc Boltanski (see Heilbron 1999; Steiner 1999). The success, among the 'quantitativist' sociologists, in the United States and in France, of the methods of network analysis contribute to the revival of interest in a better sociological understanding of the real conditions of the emergence of economic action, and of the socially constructed functioning of organisations and markets.

This revival bears witness to the persistent difficulties facing neo-classical theory in justifying its fundamental presuppositions, such as the primacy of rational calculation in individual action, and the self-regulating role of the market in the functioning of economies. The significant interest, in France, given to the 'heterodox' schools of thought, such as the theory of regulation and the economy of conventions, can be analysed as an indication of a persistent internal critique targeting some of the over-simplistic and unreliable postulates of the dominating theory. Some specialists in microeconomics and mathematical economics no longer attempt to hide their deep dissatisfaction with a discipline which, nevertheless, is perceived as being self-confident and domineering. (Guerrien 1996; see in particular page 326). Similarly to what happened at the end of the nineteenth century (Gislain and Steiner 1995), the sociological reconstruction of the economic sciences is being undertaken at a time of crisis in the prevalent theory of economics.

Another reason – parallel to the one mentioned above – for this revival of economic sociology probably lies in the aggravation of the social damage caused by the changes in the world's economic system, following its neo-liberal change of direction under the pressure of the big international organisations and transnational firms. The calling into question of the social norms which were set up, with difficulty, for a large part of the population, between the end of the nineteenth century and the 1970s, resulted in the worsening of living conditions for much of the population and in the emergence of an intellectual, as well as social, critique of the many undesirable effects of a market economy which knew almost no limits. The return of economic sociology into the world of scientific issues thus expresses a kind of civic awareness of the responsibility of sociologists, as producers of knowledge questioning the over-confident truths of the economic theory whose temporal dominance is greater than ever.

2. The social conditions of calculation and economic action

At the centre of this recent revival, the research carried out by Pierre Bourdieu on the economic field holds an original place. Indeed, economics has had a significant importance for him for a long time and most probably has been one of his oldest and deepest theoretical preoccupations, even though he might have privileged other subjects in the past (the education system, the dominating classes, the fields of cultural production …). During his first years of research in Algeria (for a synthesis, see Bourdieu 1977), Bourdieu pondered the relations between transformations of the economic system and social dispositions, particularly as regards time, which he has always considered a blind spot in neoclassical economics. The integration of the Algerian economy into the world's capitalist system occurred so quickly and brutally, that there was no time for the economic *habitus* of the indigenous population to adapt to the new *cosmos* of the market economy. The rational *habitus* associated with the capitalist system is a product of history, not a natural phenomenon, but nevertheless an essential element of the functioning of the capitalist economic order. So are all the institutions, considered as obvious frameworks of the economic action, which are the products of the long history of capitalism (firms, accounting, banks, the stock exchange, etc).

In a similar way, Bourdieu's reflection on what he called the 'causality of the probable' (Bourdieu 1974) fed on a direct confrontation with the *homo-oeconomicus* model, which represented an attractive framework for the interpretation of inequalities – between the social classes as regards the education system – whereby the choices of studies differed according to groups and individuals. Bourdieu shifted the object of the theory of action, and turned from rational calculation and prediction to the genesis and the *social* conditions of calculation and prediction. The latter seem to be immersed in a fabric of collective beliefs depending, first of all, on the agents' social position and path incorporated in their *habitus*.

These are the dispositions – acquired and to a great extent unconscious – which make it possible to make all types of 'decisions' of an economic nature. The relation between these acquired dispositions and a certain state of the social world (defined by a number of indications of what is to 'be done' and what 'should not be done', of what is 'good' and 'bad', 'true' or 'false', etc.) is at the heart of economic practice; the latter appears, from then on, to be the result of an almost physical *adjustment* rather than of a simple calculation, even though, *ex-post*, one might mistake the 'model of reality' with the 'reality of the model', and find, in the statistical regularities, the apparent consequences of purely rational choices.

Thus, the sociological theory of the economic action appears not as an alternative to the economic theory, but as a broader and deeper approach made possible by the rational critical de-construction of some presuppositions. The 'individual' is separated from his body as the receptacle of an experience which is indissociably individual and collective. The 'choice' is isolated from the social context in which it is produced, and, above all, from anything about the choice which is the product of acquired dispositions, and therefore does not truly depend on a choice. Lastly, 'rationality' is separated from the social genesis of economic systems where it is defined, and, more precisely, from the relation between the economic systems and the dispositions of the agents determining their functioning.

This programme of research, which was formulated mainly in the 1960s, informed a great number of empirical works in the following decades. They include, above all, Abdelmalek Sayad's research, which followed the studies made in Algeria, in which he mentions the social conditions of the flows of migration which turn the 'migrants' into agents who, moved from one national space to another, are defined by the complex relation between their position (dominated) in the immigration space, and the dispositions associated with their social origin in the emigration space. (Sayad 1991). But this programme can also be associated with the research which, through an 'analysis of taste', has made it possible to define the systems of preference associated with different social groups and paths (Bourdieu 1979). The *Distinction* can thus be understood as the systematic product of the empirical exploration of the systems of preference associated with the occupation of some positions in the social space. By thinking of the social reality as being essentially relational, Bourdieu describes tastes, not as facts which 'one does not discuss' (an expression used by the neoclassical economist Gary Becker) but as determining elements of the consumption and cultural practices which only make sense in the complex relation they have with each other. It does not make sense to talk about a 'working class taste' or 'popular taste' or 'bourgeois taste' or an individual's tastes in isolation, because any system of taste is continually being redefined by the logic of exposure and distinction.[1]

Another field of research has made it possible to verify the validity of a systematic analysis of economic dispositions: the sociology of labour which, in the 1970s, was revived by issues inspired by books written about Algeria, but dealing with new subjects (as far as this kind of questioning is concerned at least) such as the behaviour of 'young workers' in the context of the rise of unemployment and the crisis of the traditional labour movement. At the end of the 1970s, Michel Pialoux offered, in an article which has become a milestone (Pialoux 1979), an original interpretation of the development of temporary work among the working-class youth. The development of short-term work and the rise of unemployment do not lead to the 'social explosion' announced by the political and media prophets. This is due, above all, to the fact that the new systems of integration in the world of labour are adapted to a certain kind of social disposition. The children of working class families – many of whom were immigrants with little or no education – are nowadays better educated and prefer to multiply their experiences at the frontiers of the world of labour rather than 'ending up' in the working class, employed in factories, as their parents were. Their attitude could be interpreted as a refusal to reproduce, for themselves, working-class living conditions. This refusal is made possible thanks to the new possibilities offered by the systems of education and employment. The last two decades, since the publication of various books inspired by this analysis, have confirmed the strength – both 'integrating' (from the point of view of the capitalist economic system) and 'dis-integrating' (socially) – of unemployment and short-term work for the people arriving on the labour market. Associated with dominant values such as mobility, change, individual experience, promotion opportunities and etc., the new jobs offered and the new conditions of access to the working conditions make it possible to maintain in a weak position an army of industrial reservists of a new type – often women (Maruani 1996) – which is generally fragmented, powerless and facing disgraceful conditions and individual suffering. These new types of 'integration journeys' also correspond to new, more subtle forms of domination, whose impact can be worse on a collective level because they create disillusionment, individual despair and an inability to act collectively (see the two issues of *Actes de la Recherche en Sciences Sociales* dedicated to the 'new forms of domination at work', numbers 116 and 117). The crisis of the 'traditional' labour movement, which is studied in the collective book *La Misère du monde* ('Déclins', pp. 317–595, in Bourdieu 1993), testifies to its inability to alter the forms of organisation and action when faced with the new realities, leading them to fall back on the most traditional segments of the labour world.

3. Social structures and fields

At the beginning of the 1970s, Pierre Bourdieu proposed a critique of the 'interactionist' model of action, through his re-reading of the religious sociology of Max Weber (Bourdieu 1971). Even though the study of the functioning of the religious fields requires an analysis of the relations between preachers and prophets, between prophets and theologians, etc. – as Weber indicated – one must not consider these relations as simple interactions, but as structural relations, determined by the occupations of different positions in one social space (and therefore by the different possession of several kinds of capital). This criticism is also at the heart of his idea of economic sociology. His critique is addressed, for instance, to the 'new sociologists of sciences' who question, because of the weight of local interactions and historical contexts, the Mertonian model which they consider too general and idealistic, without offering any real alternative (Bourdieu 1994). The sociologists who question the concept of *homo oeconomicus*, using the argument of integration of individuals in the social structures, do so generally by starting from an idea of action which is strictly interactionist, and which ignores the existence of structures underlying interactions, defined by the distribution (specific to each field) of different types of capital. It is this concept which influences, for example, the analyses in terms of 'networks', which have almost become the 'mainstream' of the American, and therefore of the world's, economic sociology (see W. W. Powell and L. S. Smith-Doerr, 'Networks and Economic Life' in N. J. Smelser and R. Swedberg 1994). Yet, Bourdieu does not question the role of the 'networks' or social capital in the functioning of the economic field. According to him, economic practices are, above all, dependent on the position and the strategies of the agents situated in specific, structured and constraining social microcosms, that is, in 'fields'. The economic *illusio*, the advantage gained from playing the economic game, is the product of the particular investment made in this field, which is both a field of struggle and a field of forces (Bourdieu 1994). The social capital that economic agents possess and use is itself determined by their position in a particular field, the economic field (Bourdieu 1997).

The economic field can be described as a field of forces, where the goal of the participants is to impose their rules of the game on the others, and not just to be better at this game whose rules are already defined. The domination of a company in the economic field consists not only in controlling an important part of the market, or in higher benefits, but also in the ability to impose on others its own definition of the game and in taking advantage, economically as well as symbolically, of a position of domination, linked to the possession of various forms of capital. The specifically symbolic dimension (and not only 'monetary' or 'financial') of domination in an economic field, whatever it is, expresses itself through the work which aims to perpetuate the differences between the dominant company and the others, who, whatever they do, have to acknowledge that the company in question is the point of reference and that they are forced to position themselves, actively or passively, in relation to that company (Bourdieu 1997: 57). If the economic field is the place where the real constraints conditioning economic decision-making are exerted, as Bourdieu illustrates with the example of the housing market (Bourdieu 1990; 2000), then it depends on struggles which occur in the world of economic policies. Indeed, it is in a politico-bureaucratic field that some of the rules of the game (including law) which determine the result of economic struggles are defined. Thus, the housing market is not separable from an incentive policy whose genesis was the object of a process of social and political construction by some bureaucratic and political dominating agents.[2] Moreover, each company appears as a field where the aim is to elaborate a strategy within a wider economic universe and to reconvert forms of capital according to the exchange rates determined by the structural dynamic of the field. The strategies of the economic units are, in fact, the product of the combination of their positions in the field and of the dispositions of different agents who contribute to the definition of their strategies. The economic *habitus*, linked to the positions occupied, enters into the specific social struggles which occur in the economic field.

The 'structural' sociological economy, which arises, is inconsistent with 'individualistic' philosophy and with an 'interactionist' philosophy of the action. Instead, it has an affinity with the heuristic usage of the correspondence analysis, and, more particularly, of the analysis of multiple correspondences, in which Bourdieu finds a starting point for the formalisation of the theory of the fields (Bourdieu 1997: 52). This formalisation is geometrical (Rouanet and Le Roux 1993). The agents who contend within one field can be represented by points in a Euclidean, multidimensional space. Each agent is associated with a number of properties defined by their structural relations. The distances between the agents are determined in each analysis of the correspondences, and therefore in the implicit theoretical model on which it is based, by the efficient proprieties characterising the agents: the position and the path in the field, the origin and the social and educational path, etc. The analysis of the correspondences makes it possible to summarise the positions on principal axes and to highlight (by projecting them on these axes) the objective relations between the space of the positions and the space of the different agents' positioning.

4. The reactivation of the Durkheimian project

Even though Pierre Bourdieu's first works on economic sociology can be qualified as 'Weberian', because of their insistence on the process of rationalisation, which is characteristic of capitalism (which, by the way, in the context of the liberation war in Algeria, distinguished him from the 'Marxist' or 'developmentalist' analyses of many economists and sociologists), it is the reference to Durkheim and to the Durkheimian school which imposed itself forcefully in the 1990s. In 1993, with *La Misère du Monde* (Bourdieu 1993), Pierre Bourdieu and his team proposed a first sociological assessment of the economic policies of liberal inspiration carried out in France since the end of the 1970s; this assessment is strongly reminiscent of that of Durkheimian sociologists at the beginning of the twentieth century. The withdrawal of the state from a number of sectors and areas resulted in an increase of social suffering among the agents who were the most underprivileged economically and culturally (with the development of the 'misery of conditions') and simultaneously, of the suffering affecting 'The State nobility', teachers, social workers, paramedical workers, junior civil servants ('the misery of position'). Because their social means and prestige were decreasing, they were confronted with consequences which were more and more anomic of a mode of development originating from the reconstructions of the economic field and from the inflections of the political field, but which also benefited from the connivance between the dominating forces of the media world, and the intellectual field (see Bourdieu 1996). It is in such a context that Pierre Bourdieu, with the publications of the *Liber-raisons d'agir* Editions, whose creation followed the social movement of December 1995, became, in the second half of the 1990s, the principal representative of the committed sociology which he has always defended as the logical consequence of the position of autonomous researchers in the social sciences (see Duval *et al.* 1998). The research on the evolutions of the American society carried out, among others, by Loic Wacquant (Wacquant, 'De l'Amérique comme utopie à l'envers', in Bourdieu (dir.), 1993: 169–79), confirms the hypothesis that the movement of deregulation is accompanied, when it is taken to an extreme, by the setting up of a new mode of 'crisis' management (crisis originating from social insecurity) with the choice of a systematic 'law and order policy' and the almost exponential increase of the number of prisoners originating from the stigmatised groups (first of all black youth). This embryo of a social state (compared, for instance, to that of Northern Europe) tends to be replaced by an over-developed penal state which allows for the 'normal' functioning of a market economy from which a number of the most basic social norms have sometimes disappeared. Unless a social European State, capable of imposing itself as a pole of social stability and security in a world facing the American domination, is created, European societies, in their diversity, will be facing a historical choice, since the model of the penal state tends to accompany a tendency towards a neo-liberal adaptation to the rules of international trading (see issues 121/122 and 124 of *Actes de la Recherche en Sciences Sociales*, dedicated in 1998 to the 'tricks of the imperialist reasoning' and to 'from a social to a penal state', also see Bourdieu 1998).

With 'Durkheimian' inspiration, Pierre Bourdieu's project puts forward the idea of an economic sociology which integrates, in the economy, the social costs and factors which neoclassical theory, as well as national finance, tend to exclude from their object by a dubious and tendentious choice of methods and constructed objects. This 'mutilated' science is also in the wrong when, in the name of a high degree of mathematical sophistication which would take it closer to natural sciences, it denies the socially constructed, and therefore partly arbitrary, character of the economic institutions, like that of 'consumption', for example, which is the product of a specifically political endeavour of the institution, as Pinto indicated (1992), or the market which, in some extreme cases, appears as the product of an effort aimed at making the economic theory exist in the social reality (Garcia 1986). Refusing to admit that economic facts are 'matters of opinion' (as Durkheim used to say), this 'science' abstains from any reflective position, and thus from considering itself as an element of a larger process of social construction of the economic reality. And yet, several empirical works make it possible to display the role of economists in the neo-liberal revolution (Dezalay and Garth 1998; Dixon 1998), and, helped by the sociology of the scientific field, to characterise the economic discipline as a strongly 'heteronomous' world, affected by dominant forces, whether they be economical, administrative or political, contrary to the image it has of itself (Lebaron 1997; 2000).

A Durkheimian inspiration is found in the conception of a social reality where the classification systems (the divisions into 'classes' to start with) play a central role, because, as products of the social structures, they are also producers of the structures of the perception of the social world (Boltanski 1982; Bourdieu 1984). Such a conception, which is both structuralist and constructivist, can be applied to the economic world because it allows one to think of the process of construction of the economic reality as the product of objective structures and regularities (for instance, the transformations of the 'production system' which distort the structure of the economic field by favouring the fall and rise of some sectors, firms and social groups, etc.), but also as the schemes and operations of classification they are then subjected to (including, by the organisational activity of the State and of international organisations which consider some objects, such as inflation or the money supply, as economic objects, by giving them the authority associated with their official nature). This kind of economic sociology extends over a very wide spectrum of problems and objects, which ranges from the positive analysis of social regularities that underlie the ordinary functioning of the economy, in conformity with the positivist and critical project of François Simiand (see for instance Simiand 1932), to the more introspective and constructivist analysis of the world of agents who are struggling to impose a certain vision of economic reality and make the economy a world of well-founded beliefs.

Notes

1 Thus one can see that *marketing* feeds on some of the results and instruments of analysis developed in the framework of such a programme of 'analysis of taste'. Driven at once by both the desire to adjust the offer to the existing systems of preference and by the necessity to create future tastes, the professionals of marketing redefine the social categories into more or less reliable schemata.
2 In a similar way, in another world, the history of the state control of the family is the product of structural transformations in the bureaucratic–political field, as was shown by Remi Lenoir (Lenoir 1992).

References

Boltanski, L. (1982) *Les cadres. La formation d'un groupe social*, Paris: Minuit.
Bourdieu, P. (1971) 'Genèse et structure du champ religieux', *Revue française de sociologie* 12 (3): 295–334.
Bourdieu, P. (1974) 'Avenir de classe et causalité du probable', *Revue française de sociologie* 15 (1): 3–42.
Bourdieu, P. (1977) *Algérie 60. Structures économiques et structures temporelles*, Paris: Minuit.
Bourdieu, P. (1979) *La distinction. Critique sociale du jugement*, Paris: Minuit.
Bourdieu, P. (1984) 'Espace social et genèse des classes', *Actes de la recherche en sciences sociales* 52 / 53: 3–14.
Bourdieu, P., Bouhedja, S., Christin, R. and Givry, C. (1990) 'Un placement de père de famille. La maison individuelle : spécificité du produit et logique du champ de reproduction', *Actes de la recherche en sciences sociales* 81–82: 6–33.

Bourdieu, P. (dir.) (1993) *La misère du monde*, Paris: Seuil.

Bourdieu, P. (1994) *Raisons pratiques*, Paris: Seuil.

Bourdieu, P. (1996) *Sur la télévision*, Paris: Liber/Raisons d'agir.

Bourdieu, P. (1997) 'Le champ économique', *Actes de la recherche en sciences sociales* 119: 48–65.

Bourdieu, P. (1998) *Contre-feux. Propos pour servir à la résistance contre l'invasion néolibérale*, Paris: Liber/Raisons d'agir.

Bourdieu, P. (2000) *Les structures sociales de l'économie*, Paris: Seuil.

Callon, M. (ed.) (1998) *The Laws of the Markets*, Oxford: Blackwell.

Dezalay, Y. and Garth, B. (1998) 'Le 'Washington consensus'. Contribution à une sociologie de l'hégémonie du néolibéralisme', *Actes de la recherche en sciences sociales* 121/122: 3–22.

Dixon, K. (1998) *Les évangélistes du marché. Les intellectuels britanniques et le néolibéralisme*, Paris: Liber/Raisons d'agir.

Duval, J., Gaubert, C., Lebaron, F., Marchetti, D. and Pavis, F. (1998) *Le 'décembre' des intellectuels français*, Paris: Liber/Raisons d'agir.

Garcia, M.-F. (1986) 'La construction sociale d'un marché parfait: le marché aux cadrans de Fontaines-en-Sologne', *Actes de la recherche en sciences sociales* 65: 2–13.

Gislain, J.-J. and Steiner, P. (1995) *La sociologie économique. 1890–1920*, Paris: PUF.

Guerrien, B. (1996) *Dictionnaire d'analyse économique. Microéconomie, macroéconomie, théorie des jeux, etc.*, Paris: La Découverte.

Heilbron, J. (1999) 'Economic sociology in France', *Economic Sociology. European Electronic Newsletter*, vol I, 1.

Lebaron, F. (1997) 'La dénégation du pouvoir. Le champ des économistes français au milieu des années 1990', *Actes de la recherche en sciences sociales* 119: 3–26.

Lebaron, F. (2000) *La croyance économique. Les économistes entre science et politique*, Paris: Seuil.

Lenoir, R. (1992) 'L'Etat et la construction sociale de la famille', *Actes de la recherche en sciences sociales*, 91/92: 20–37.

Maruani, M. (1996) 'L'emploi féminin à l'ombre du chômage', *Actes de la recherche en sciences sociales*, 115: 48–57.

Pialoux, M. (1979) 'Jeunes sans avenir et travail intérimaire', *Actes de la recherche en sciences sociales*, 26–27: 19–47.

Pinto, L. (1992) 'La gestion d'un label politique : la consommation', *Actes de la recherche en sciences sociales*, 91/92: 3–19.

Rouanet, H. and Le Roux, B. (1993) *Analyse des données multidimensionnelles*, Paris: Dunod.

Sayad, A. (1991) *L'immigration ou les paradoxes de l'altérité*, Bruxelles: De Boeck, préface de Pierre Bourdieu.

Simiand, F. (1932) *Le salaire, l'évolution sociale et la monnaie. Essai de théorie expérimentale du salaire*, Paris: Alcan.

Smelser, N. J. and Swedberg, R. (eds) (1994) *The Handbook of economic sociology*, Princeton: Princeton University Press/Russell Sage Foundation.

Steiner, P. (1999) *La sociologie économique*, Paris: La Découverte.

15

ADAM SMITH'S SYMPATHY

Towards a normative economics

S. Abu Turab Rizvi

1. Introduction

Normative economics is not a thriving field. Among its problems is a paralysis in the face of number of oppositions, between which it is hard to choose. These dilemmas include selfishness vs. altruism, interpersonal comparability vs. interpersonal incomparability, laissez faire vs. interventionism and individual vs. society. These dilemmas seem to be so deep-seated that it is hard to make progress. We only see clashing views. In this chapter, I argue that while these oppositions refer to entities and problems that are real enough, they need to be considered within a framework that is broad enough to allow progress. To move ahead in at least a preliminary way, I will appeal to Adam Smith's normative theory in the *Theory of Moral Sentiments*. Since this text and its approach may seem far from the usual normative work that economists undertake, I begin with a discussion of the problems of the normative theories that recently have been influential in economics and in social thought more generally. It may then be clearer why reaching as far back as Adam Smith may be helpful in understanding many normative matters.[1] In addition, it may also become clearer what features of theories are impediments to progress and what features a good normative theory ought to have.

2. Problematic theories

Several significant and popular approaches to normative matters are determinedly inconclusive (Nussbaum 1994). In one group of authors, who may be styled as *deconstructionist* or *postmodernist*, the following sorts of arguments are seen. Since any interpretation or argument can be countered with a contradictory one, and there is no transcendental authority to judge between them, the arguments are effectively of equal weight. We must therefore refrain from any judgment. This argument, advanced by Derrida in *Spurs* (1979), is acknowledged by him to be true of his own text. Criticism and judgment not being possible, we are left with an irresolvable free play of back and forth.[2] A variant of this view is put forward by Stanley Fish (1989: 215–46). Fish also points out that there are no universal normative standards (Fish 1989: 221–2; 226–31; 235–9; 241–2). But he says that it is nevertheless possible to reach decisions by simply following professional expertise. Professional expertise, not being based on standards, is an exercise of power and gives us a way to act (Fish 1989: 242–3). Thus, Fish differs from Derrida in offering power rather than pure play as the motive force in normative matters, but both agree that normative judgments are impossible; both, too, turn this critique onto their own works. In a later book, Fish concludes, "All I have to recommend is the game, which, since it doesn't need my recommendations, will proceed on its way undeterred and unimproved by anything I have to say" (Fish 1994: 307, cited in Nussbaum 1994: 727). The game is a game of politics and power solely, not of reason or argument or feeling.

Such ideas have had a considerable impact on economics, particularly development economics. The idea that there are rational bases for criticizing normative stances has been taken to be peculiarly Western, and one that violates the integrity of other cultures (Marglin 1990a, b). This has been taken to mean that what happens in other cultures, no matter how unfair or gruesome some practices may seem, cannot be criticized by members of other cultures, particularly Western ones. To do so would be to appeal to transcendental standards that are unavailable, and as we have seen, Derrida and Fish argue that we cannot but refrain from judgment, and any such judgment is but an expression of play or of power.[3] The conclusion then seems to be, leave things alone.

What is unusual is that this is the same conclusion reached by a very different set of authors, the *neoclassical economists* (Nussbaum 1994). They still take the positive/normative distinction very seriously while acknowledging interrelations among the two. When discussing positive economics, these economists firmly believe that judgment based on the results of the hypothesis of individual utility maximization is possible, but in normative matters we are left with subjective preferences alone, and *de gustibus non est disputandum.*[4] As Milton Friedman wrote concerning differences in basic values, these are "differences about which men can ultimately only fight" (1953: 5). Thus in both the postmodernist-deconstructionist view and the neoclassical view, normative matters are not resolvable by appeal to reason or other mechanisms, save that aspects of play or power may resolve them to some degree. Both approaches are present in the writing of Herrnstein Smith (1988), who again argues that disagreement, lack of standards and radical subjectivity make normative evaluation impossible, but adds that normative discourse ought itself to be seen as a market (Herrnstein Smith 1988: 30, 98–102). This conclusion also bears kinship to come-whatever-may outcomes of play or power.

There is yet another possibility for trying to reach a standard of normative evaluation based on the given subjective preferences of individuals. This is to try to aggregate them into a social preference for a group or society, as in social choice theory. Yet, while the needs and desires of individuals are no doubt important, this attempt runs into well-known problems. Arrow's theorem and related results demonstrate that – even if plausible and mild conditions are imposed on this aggregation process – an overall ordering cannot be obtained (Arrow 1951). He showed that there is no consistent method of ordering a set of alternatives that follows reasonable restrictions on the method of aggregation. Arrow's theorem, though fifty years old, is very robust and a long history of attempts to reach around its problems has met with little success (Sen 1985). Thus, whatever regularities we might discern in normative stances of groups or societies cannot be understood in this manner. But since there is no theory of the aggregate realm, weaker, individual-based, notions of welfare such as Pareto optimality remain paramount. And according to these, as in the two theorems of welfare economics, competitive equilibrium and Pareto optimality go hand in hand (Debreu 1959). So, whatever theory there is tends to support a laissez-faire approach towards markets and, by theoretical omission, towards groups as well. That is to say, issues of group conflict and reconciliation cannot be addressed in this manner nor can they be conceptualized easily, so their reality is ignored. Given these problems with the state of the normative theory that has made its way into economics, a fresh approach seems to be in order; it should at least be considered. But what is it that normative theory ought to address?

3. Two-tiered preferences

When we deal with normative issues – with what ought to be chosen or preferred – we need to assume that preferences have two tiers. Suppose an individual is deciding how she ought to choose. She is not now choosing with a single or given set of preferences; if she were, she would know already how to choose. Instead, based on her normative faculties, she is deciding whether to choose in one manner or another. That is, her normative faculties are a set of preferences with which she will decide among sets of preferences that concern the immediate objects of choice. She thus has two-tiered preferences. This two-tiered process will be ongoing, as normative faculties may continue to inform lower-level preferences. Because of this likelihood, using two-tiered preferences to consider normative matters implies a dynamic process unfolding through time. As such, it deals non-trivially with normative choice and deliberation.

This is the only way to proceed in normative matters. Consider the alternatives. We might suppose that preferences are given to individuals as in traditional neoclassical theory. But immediately we can see why the neoclassical approach to normative economics is far wide of the mark. Nothing in normative economics based on neoclassical theory can be about how individuals ought to behave. Individual preferences are taken as data by that theory – for welfare economics. The goal is then to come up with a preference ordering for a society or group using the data of individual preferences; or to otherwise make some statement about the functioning of the economy as a whole (as in the Arrovian theory discussed above). Thus, traditional welfare economics is about the entire economic system or the aggregate realm. It is of no consequence for an individual trying to figure out how to choose.

Another possibility is to think that the normative behavior of an individual comes pre-determined by the group the individual belongs to. There are several problems (other than those already identified) for this approach. First, this approach could only describe a very traditional society where individual behavior was inculcated by group norms (Levine 1999: 241–3). In this case, many authors, such as Benhabib (1995), have argued that what group theorists describe as monolithic cultures are in fact not very uniform. Thus, it is inaccurate (or far too incomplete) to speak of traditional Indian culture since India contains within it different genders, religions, classes, languages, regions, levels of Westernization, struggles and so on. Any one individual living in India feels the power of the value systems these different aspects may promote or suggest. Thus, some Western commentators speak inconsistently of their own societies as multicultural and of non-Western societies as unicultural. It would be more correct to say that individuals in what are described as traditional cultures have many sorts of preferences to choose from; and if there is more than one set of preferences to choose from, they need a higher-order set of preferences to decide among them. Second, and more importantly, the group-determination of individual normative preferences does not accord with what we think of as individual autonomy and self-determination. For that, individuals themselves, out of the myriad influences around them, must decide what is best. So for a normative theory that respects individuals, we again need second-order preferences. Thus, while groups and group solidarity are important phenomena, a much more subtle approach than group-determination of individuals is needed.

4. Smith's impartial spectator

At this point, it is instructive to turn to Adam Smith's normative theory. A key tenet of it is that when people are in society, they have feelings about their feelings; for consider the contrary:

> Were it possible that a human creature could grow up to man-hood in some solitary place, without any communication with his own species, he could no more think of his own character, of the propriety or demerit of his own sentiments and conduct, of the beauty or deformity of his own mind, than of the beauty or defor-mity of his own face. All these are objects which he cannot easily see, which naturally he does not look at, and with regard to which he is provided with no mirror which can present them to his view. Bring him into society, and he is immediately provided with the mirror which he wanted before.
>
> (TMS III.1.4)

In modern terms, Smith is arguing that people have "second-order desires" that allow them to reflect on the propriety or impropriety of their "first-order desires." This is what Harry Frankfurt also argued in his essay, "Freedom of the Will and the Concept of a Person" (1971). Persons, he said, have the special capacity for reflective self-evaluation. This idea gives the normative-positive distinction a twist, since the preferences needed for positive economics may themselves be formed by normative second-order desires (see Rizvi 2001, who also discusses multi-order preferences).

So Smith indicates the constitutive importance of second-order desires for a normative approach to a person, for "the propriety or demerit of his own sentiments and conduct." He is quite explicit:

> When I endeavour to examine my own conduct, when I endeav-our to pass sentence upon it, and either to approve or condemn it, it is evident that, in all such cases, I divide myself, as it were, into two persons; and that I, the examiner and judge, represent a different character from that other I, the person whose conduct is examined into and judged of. The first is the spectator, whose sentiments with regard to my own conduct I endeavour to enter into, by placing myself in his situation, and by considering how it would appear to me, when seen from that particular point of view. The second is the agent, the person whom I properly call myself, and of whose conduct, under the character of a spectator, I was endeavouring to form some opinion. The first is the judge; the second the person judged of. But that the judge should, in every respect, be the same with the person judged of, is as impos-sible, as that the cause should, in every respect, be the same with the effect.
>
> (TMS III.2.6)

By this means, Smith refers to his concept of the impartial spectator, to what is for people "the tribunal of their own consciences, to that of the supposed impartial and well-informed spectator, to that of the man within the breast, the great judge and arbiter of their conduct" (TMS III.3.32).

Where does the impartial spectator come from? Such a spectator would provide the normative faculties that we need for a normative theory. Smith says that society provides the mirror by which we can examine our own preferences. Specifically, the impartial spectator is the distillation of those who have had influence upon us, "what in the twentieth century, George Herbert Mead would call the 'generalized other,' and Mikhail Bakhtin, 'the superaddressee'" (Todorov 1996: 8).

5. Self-interest and altruism

Smith's concepts help to deal with some of the problems that have dogged normative theory. The first concerns the nature of human beings; is it selfish or benevolent? Economic theories often rely on self-interest as the only motivating factor, in which case they are at a loss to explain altruistic behavior. The lacunae include explanations of why people bother to vote, why they leave tips (gratuities) for strangers, and why they do not bargain ruthlessly. Theories purporting to explain these phenomena are met with great acclaim. But the converse assumption, of assuming that we are always benevolent, is also problematic. More recently, as in evolutionary economics, different types of actors are posited, some selfish, some benevolent. Then the population composition of these types changes in response to changes in the environment.

An episode illustrating this sort of confusion occurred when standard bargaining results based on self-interested play were not confirmed in experiments using the ultimatum bargaining game (see Rizvi forthcoming). Some authors argued that the assumption of self-interested preferences may have been wrong, with participants "playing fair" (Camerer and Thaler 1985; Thaler 1988; 1992). This precipitated a debate between those assuming strict self-interest and those assuming a norm of fairness. Neither side had decisive arguments. The fairness doctrine itself had problems in experiments since the strictness with which experimental subjects played fair varied with successive plays of the game (Ochs and Roth 1989; Bolton 1985). These debates fueled the rise of evolutionary-type reasoning, in which there is a multiplicity of player types (e.g. own-gain maximizers and those preferring equality). Samuelson (1995) concludes that the response to this situation was "to abandon the model of rational players optimizing against stable preferences" of whatever sort. "The result has been the development of evolutionary game theory."

But none of these views is as compelling as the consideration that a person can act *both* with self-interest and with benevolence (along with many other motives as well). This is seen in Smith's view in TMS, which neither inclines primarily to altruism, nor to selfishness. This is because the impartial spectator modifies the extreme expression of those and other traits. Thus, the arguments between those who conceive of people as being selfish, or alternatively as altruistic, miss the important point that people can be both and are typically both. For Smith, the check that the impartial spectator puts on excessive self-interest is real and universal:

> When the happiness or misery of others depends in any respect upon our conduct, we dare not, as self-love might suggest to us, prefer the interest of one to that of many. The man within imme-diately calls to us, that we value ourselves too much and other people too little, and that, by doing so, we render ourselves the proper object of the contempt and indignation of our brethren. Neither is this sentiment confined to men of extraordinary mag-nanimity and virtue.
>
> (TMS III.3.5)

Thus, it is not that we are originally benevolent (or, for that matter, self-ish) that explains our behavior but instead the urgings of our conscience, which are the distillations of the influences upon us. Smith acknowledges that we have and ought to have an interest in self-preservation and self-advancement, but that this is not without limit and is also subject to the impartial spectator's consideration:

> Every man is, no doubt, by nature, first and principally recom-mended to his own care; and as he is fitter to take care of himself than of any other person, it is fit and right that it should be so...[Yet] If he would act so as that the impartial spectator may enter into the principles of his conduct, which is what of all things he has the greatest desire to do, he must, upon this, as upon all other occasions, humble the arrogance of his self-love, and bring it down to something which other men can go along with.
>
> (TMS II.2.1)

6. Imagination and sympathy

A second conundrum illuminated by Smith's theory regards interper-sonal comparability. Dobb lamented the "neo-Paretian vogue for denying the possibility of inter-personal comparisons of mental states, hence of utility or welfare, and for purging normative economics of considerations concerning income-distribution" (Dobb 1973: 213). In neoclassical eco-nomics, then, interpersonal comparability has long been denied. Smith's view of the relations between individuals, and the formation of normative concern, is typically realistic and convincing. He is careful to say "we have no immediate experience of what other men feel" (TMS I.1.1.2); thus he acknowledges the fact of the lack of direct access to others' feelings. We are all radically separate physically. Yet, this does not end the matter as it does in modern neoclassical theory. For, because of this lack of immediate experience, "we can form no idea of the manner in which they are affected, but by conceiving what we ourselves should feel in the like situation" (TMS I.1.1.2). Thus the mistake of those who see incomparability of sensations as an impediment to normative theory is that they base their theory of comparability on sensation and not on imagination. For Smith, the senses "never did, and never can, carry us beyond our own person, and it is by the imagination only that we can form any conception of" what others feel (TMS I.1.1.2). And he suggests that all of us have the capacity and inclination to feel what others feel. His opening sentences in *The Theory of Moral Sentiments* are:

> How selfish soever man may be supposed, there are evidently some principles in his nature, which interest him in the fortune of others, and render their happiness necessary to him, though he derives nothing from it except the pleasure of seeing it.
>
> (TMS I.1.1.1)

Apart from the objection that if we enjoy such an apparently "selfless" pleasure, we are nevertheless being selfish (which is the objection that every motivation is selfish), we can see that Smith supposes that everyone has the inclination, however imperfect, to be interested in others. This feeling Smith calls *sympathy*, and he does not restrict sympathy to commiseration with misery. Rather, in his usage, sympathy means "our fellow-feeling with any passion whatever" (TMS I.1.1.5). But Smith's idea is not that we sympathize with feelings as such, but that we enter imaginatively into someone else's situation: "sympathy, therefore, does not arise so much from the view of the passion, as from that of the situation that excites it" (TMS I.1.1.10). Thus Smith's view is not that we crudely feel what others feel (it is not just empathy shallowly understood, a mere nodding of the head), but that in many cases we will want to understand the perspective and situation of others more deeply, using our understanding, judgment, insight and feelings. And when we do so, we may not always agree with how someone else feels. This allows us to judge the responses of others, to see if their reactions are appropriate to the situation. Thus, Smith's framework allows for normative judgment of others. As always, Smith sticks close to how we behave in everyday life, as opposed to how many proceed in systematic philosophizing; and his observations therefore ring true.

Smith observes that we may sympathize with situations that we could never be in, or be in again, or are not in currently. Thus, we may sympathize with the dead, with infants or with the insane. Men may sympathize with women as they have labor pains. From this fact, that we sympathize quite readily with others in situations that we could never be in, we can conclude that sympathy cannot be (at least exclusively) selfish; that sympathetic feelings cannot only be feelings evoked as we imagine ourselves to be in those situations. Thus, sympathy concerns not how we would feel in particular situations, but how we imaginatively reconstruct how others feel in their situations.

Smith's theory of sympathy is truly normative. He illustrates it by using literary examples and many compelling examples from ordinary life. These examples recall our own intuitions and reinforce normative tendencies within us. Because of his call for the use of imagination for normative understanding, we see immediately the importance to normative development of interventions by family members, teachers, friends, to careful attention to situations written about in literature and seen in the arts generally, to careful and reflective introspection, and to many sorts of education broadly considered. (As is discussed below, these influences are never all positive, and every realistic normative theory has to consider negative emotions and, indeed, normative failures and catastrophes.) Once the givenness of preferences is broached, and preference formation is seen as having two tiers and being ongoing, attention can properly be paid to the formation of normative preferences.

Thus far, we can see that Smith's approach to the intersubjectivity of feelings is two-fold. From one perspective, individuals adopt feelings and actions as if they are being viewed by a generalized other, an impartial spectator. From another, individuals possess a broadly defined sympathy, so that they can feel and understand the situations of others. By these concepts, Smith is able to bypass and render understandable the progress beyond the oppositions of selfishness / altruism and interpersonal comparability / incomparability.

7. Individuals and groups

A third conundrum that has thwarted the development of normative theory and perplexed many might well be illuminated by Smith's theory. This is the tension between emphasizing individuals on the one hand, and emphasizing groups or society on the other. I have already given examples of both approaches. In neoclassical economics (and most of the formal theory of behavior generally) individuals have a subjectivity of a narrow sort. We have seen that they are unable to carry on normative deliberation because they are supposed to have given preferences, rather than having to choose among preferences. More generally, referring to positive as well as normative theory, Pareto is famous for saying that "The individual can disappear, provided he leaves us [a] photograph of his tastes" (Pareto 1906: 120). Given that in the continuum characterization of perfect competition, agents are likened to points on a line (Aumann 1964),

Pareto's statement is prophetic. Thus, all of the structure of neoclassical theory is remarkably uninterested in individuals, even if it is methodologically individualist. We have already seen that many theories of groups give short shrift to the individual's subjectivity as well. The individual is only of interest as far as he or she conforms to group norms, and there is little scope for self-determination (Levine 1999).

Smith's theory improves on these portrayals in a way that is truly intersubjective and that allows for theories of individual development and of group formation. As far as groups are concerned, Smith has a number of interesting observations (Griswold 1999: 96–104). While his theory is that each of us has the ability and inclination to sympathize with the situation of others, this ability is attenuated in important ways. He begins, as we saw, with the fact of our separateness, one from each other. He acknowledges that sympathy is stronger among certain groups, such as families (TMS VI.2.1.7). More importantly, sympathy, in many cases, requires the proper use of imaginative understanding of the situation of others. What if this is lacking with regard to certain groups of people? Indeed, many would deny (though not Smith) that sympathy is possible between individuals of groups differently situated. And since sympathy requires the active use of imagination, it requires an act of good faith to undertake it. Thus, given the imperfectness of sympathetic imagination, we can see how sympathy could be stronger between members of groups than between groups, and therefore how groups as normative entities with common feelings and sets of assessments could arise. Indeed, many – especially and quite naturally those who have studied ethnic, racial and gender conflict, and violence generally – have argued that the process of individual development is not only particularly susceptible to attraction to group identities but and also to group-based hostility (Volkan 1988). Thus, with the possibility of groups and the problems they pose, the possibilities for reconciliation and sympathetic understanding seem to be placed in doubt. Just as in the Hobbesian origins of the individualistic doctrine, there was a war of all against all, with group theory many have tended to expect nothing but conflict.[5]

But to me, that this juncture arises in considering Smith's theory, seems to be a strength rather than a weakness. For we would want to have a normative theory that was supple enough to account for normative flaws and problems as well as normative progress and understanding. Thus, a good normative understanding does not ignore real problems. Thus, we can understand why divisions between genders, races, ethnicities, nationalities, religions, and so on, often proceed by a process of what Erikson (1966) called "pseudo-speciation," whereby it is asserted that members of different groups do not share the same humanity. What is important in Smith's theory is that, with its account of sympathy and of the impartial spectator, it provides a basis for making progress on the problems. He argues from everyday experience that sympathetic understanding, while it may be difficult to achieve, is quite possible between people. Thus, the task of normative theory in facing problems between groups is to provide understanding of the nature of this impulse towards pseudo-speciation so that the problems arising from it can be faced and dealt with (Volkan 1988).

8. The reality of the normative

An objection may be made to the impartial spectator account. In what sense are its dictates "real"? Why do they bear the respect of the agent? These questions have a number of replies (Griswold 1999: 364–6). Smith's theory is a secular one. He does not seek the ultimate bedrock of normative recommendations in a spiritual being or some other such oracle or revelation. Nor do many authors do so today. With his emphasis on the social aspects of normative evaluation, we can see that normative influences are made by society.[6] Recall that he asserts that we would have no normative intuitions outside of society. But to say that our normative intuitions are our own products does not mean that they are not compelling. Otherwise, the only compelling normative imperatives would be God-given ones, or things that were compelled under threat of force. Norms, institutions, the evaluations of peers, patterns of upbringing, are all very real even if they are ultimately "constructed." This is also a good thing for those who do not agree with some prevalent normative thinking, for they can see that this can be altered.

Indeed, that norms are "constructed" in this fashion allows for progress in resolving disputes when there are apparent conflicts between advocates of different normative stances (Taylor 1993). What is most corrosive to this sort of progress is the assertion that norms are externally given (by God, culture, biology, etc.) and therefore not debatable or malleable. The reason that normative intuitions are deeply held even though they are constructed is that they are truly intersubjective. We do not have the freedom – the impartial spectator does not allow us – to change our moral intutions willy-nilly. There are institutions, practices, deep-seated influences that operate on us, whose recommendations we have internalized. But we always are dealing with more than one level of preference in normative matters. Therefore, it is always possible for change in normative outlooks to occur since the higher-order preference pattern that deals with choice among outlooks is always there.

Notes

1 There has been a burgeoning of important literature on Adam Smith. This includes the putting to rest by Werhane (1991) of the myth that by the image of the invisible hand Smith meant to advocate laissez faire; Brown's (1994) examination of the Adam Smith problem, the relation between the Smith of *The Theory of Moral Sentiments* (TMS) and the Smith of the *Wealth of Nations* (I refer

in this chapter exclusively to TMS); the contribution of Smith's work to the enlightenment project of social betterment written by Griswold (1999) on which I have relied; and a much-needed modern biography of Smith by Ross (1995).

2 As Nussbaum points out, Derrida seems to have revised his views to include more traditional ethical arguments (Derrida 1988), but his earlier position is the one that has been influential.

3 For further analysis of this position, see Nussbaum (1995).

4 This is the title of the article by Stigler and Becker (1977).

5 On this point, see the illuminating discussion by Todorov (1996) of the illusory universality of the neo-Hegelian master-slave dialectic that has swept over social theory.

6 Todorov (1996) writes that Smith is in a tradition of writers who consider the social to be *necessary* for a proper theory of the individual. For most theories, the social is an add-on to the theory of the individual; if one can theorize the social that is good; if not, theorizing can still go forward.

References

Arrow, Kenneth J. (1951) *Individual Choice and Social Values*, New York: Wiley.

Aumann, Robert J. (1964) "Markets with a continuum of traders", *Econometrica*, 32: 39–50.

Benhabib, Seyla (1995) "Cultural Complexity, Moral Interdependence, and the Global Dialogical Community." In *Women, Culture and Development*, edited by Martha Nussbaum and Jonathan Glover, pp. 235–59. Oxford: Clarendon Press.

Bolton, Gary E. (1991) "A Comparative Model of Bargaining: Theory and Evidence," *American Economic Review*, 81: 1096–136.

Brown, Vivienne (1994) *Adam Smith's Discourse: Canonicity, Commerce and Conscience*, London: Routledge.

Camerer, Colin and Richard H. Thaler (1985) "Anomalies: Ultimatums, Dictators and Manners," *Journal of Economic Perspectives*, 9: 209–20.

Debreu, Gérard (1959) *The Theory of Value*, New Haven: Yale University Press.

Derrida, Jacques (1979) *Spurs: Nietzsche's Styles = Eperons: Les styles de Nietzsche*. Trans. Barbara Harlow (French and English on facing pages). Chicago: University of Chicago Press.

Derrida, Jacques (1988) "The Politics of Friendship," *Journal of Philosophy*, 75: 632–45.

Dobb, Maurice (1973) *Theories of Value and Distribution Since Adam Smith*, Cambridge: Cambridge University Press.

Erikson, E. H. (1966) Ontogeny of ritualization. In *Psychoanalysis: A General Psychology*, edited by R. Loewenstein, pp. 601–21. New York: International Universities Press.

Fish, Stanley (1989) "Anti-Professionalism." In *Doing What Comes Naturally: Change, Rhetoric, and the Practice of Theory in Literary and Legal Studies*, edited by Stanley Fish. Durham, NC: Duke University Press.

Fish, Stanley (1994) *There's No Such Thing as Free Speech ... And It's a Good Thing Too.* New York: Oxford University Press.

Frankfurt, Harry (1971) "Freedom of the Will and the Concept of a Person," *Journal of Philosophy*, 68: 5–20.

Friedman, Milton (1953) *Essays in Positive Economics*, Chicago: University of Chicago Press.

Griswold, Charles (1999) *Adam Smith and the Virtues of Enlightenment*, Cambridge: Cambridge University Press.

Herrnstein Smith, Barbara (1988) *Contigencies of Value: Alternative Perspectives for Critical Theory*, Cambridge: Harvard University Press.

Levine, David P. (1999) "Creativity and Change," *American Behavioral Scientist*, 43: 225–44.

Lifton, Robert J. (1993) *The Protean Self*, New York: Basic Books.

Marglin, S. (1990a) "Losing Touch: The Cultural Conditions of Worker Accommodation and Resistance." In *Dominating Knowledge: Development, Culture, and Resistance* edited by F. A. Marglin and S. A. Marglin, pp. 217–82. Oxford: Clarendon Press.

Marglin, S. (1990b) "Towards the Decolonization of the Mind." In *Dominating Knowledge: Development, Culture, and Resistance* edited by F. A. Marglin and S. A. Marglin, pp. 1–28. Oxford: Clarendon Press.

Nussbaum, Martha C. (1994) "Skepticism about practical reason in literature and the law," *Harvard Law Review*, 107: 714–44.

Nussbaum, Martha C. (1995) "Human Capabilities, Female Human Beings." In *Women, Culture and Development*, edited by Martha Nussbaum and Jonathan Glover, pp. 61–104. Oxford: Clarendon Press.

Ochs, J. and A. E. Roth (1989) "An Experimental Study of Sequential Bargaining," *American Economic Review*, 79: 355–84.

Pareto, Vilfredo (1906) *Manual of Political Economy* (reprint edition, 1969). New York: Augustus M. Kelley.

Rizvi, S. Abu Turab Rizvi (2001) "Preference Formation and the Axioms of Choice." *Review of Political Economy*, 13: 141–59.

Rizvi, S. Abu Turab (forthcoming) "Rationality, Evolution and Games." In *Strategic Rationality in Economics*, edited by Marina Colonna and Andrea Salanti. Oxford: Oxford University Press.

Ross, Ian Simpson. (1995) *The Life of Adam Smith*, Oxford: Clarendon Press.

Samuelson, L. (1995). "Bounded Rationality and Game Theory," *Quarterly Review of Economics and Finance* (Special Issue), 36: 17–35.

Sen, Amartya K. (1985) "Social Choice and Justice: A Review Article," *Journal of Economic Literature*, 23: 1764–76.

Smith, Adam (1982) *The Theory Of Moral Sentiments*, edited by D. D. Raphael and A. L. Macfie. Indianapolis: Liberty Fund.

Stigler, George J. and Becker, Gary S. (1977) "De Gustibus Non Est Disputandum," *American Economic Review*, 67: 76–90.

Taylor, C. (1993) "Explanation and Practical Reason." In *The Quality of Life*, edited by Martha Nussbaum and Amartya Sen, pp. 208–31. New York: Oxford University Press.

Thaler, R. H. (1988) "Anomalies: The Ultimatum Game." *Journal of Economic Perspectives*, 2: 195–206.

Thaler, R. H. (1992) *The Winner's Curse*, Princeton: Princeton University Press.

Todorov, T. (1996) "Living Along Together." *New Literary History*, 27: 1–14.

Volkan, V. (1988) *The Need to Have Enemies and Allies: From Clinical Practice to International Relationships*, Northvale, NJ: Jason Aronson.

Werhane, P. (1991) *Adam Smith and his Legacy for Modern Capitalism*, New York: Oxford University Press.

16

THE THEORY OF CONVENTIONS AND A NEW THEORY OF THE FIRM

Thierry Levy

A new approach to economics emerged in France in the 1980s known variously as "Intersubjectivist Economics" and "the Economics of Conventions". Led by Jean-Pierre Dupuy and André Orléan from the Ecole Polytechnique in Paris, and by Laurent Thévenot from the Ecole des Hautes Etudes en Sciences Sociales (EHESS), this group presented their research-agenda in a special issue of the *Revue Economique* devoted to *"l'économie des conventions"* (March 1989). Their work has been introduced to the English-speaking world by P. Wagner (1994) and Edward Fullbrook (1996; 1997; 1998).

The economics of conventions has, as its goal, the inclusion of cognitive interactions between individuals within economic analysis. Its metaphysical position lies between holism and methodological individualism. It has been described as a sophisticated individualism based on a non-atomistic *homo-oeconomicus* (Fullbrook 1997), so as to underline the fact that the metaphysical position of this group differs radically from the neoclassical mainstream. Like neoclassicists, conventionalists believe that "only persons are actors" (*Revue Economique* 1989: 143). But they also believe that various conventions, including social beliefs and institutions, transcend the individual, shaping and constraining his or her behavior, and thereby invalidate analysis that treats economic agents as isolated maximizers. The position taken by this group insists that conventions "must be apprehended twice: as resulting from individual actions and as constraining subjects" (*Revue Economique* 1989: 143, *op. cit.*).

This approach has been applied to a number of diverse economic fields, including the dynamics of financial markets (Orléan 1990; 1992), the theory of value (Levy 1994), monetary theory (Aglietta and Orléan 1982), the theory of consumer demand (Fullbrook 1996; 1998), the theory of the firm (Biencourt, Favereau and Eymard-Duvernay 1994; Levy 1995) and other more specific fields, such as, for example, technical change (Dalle 1995), the economics of education, development economics (Favereau 1995), and entrepreneurship (Verstraete 1999). The chapter in this book by Laurent Thévenot offers an illustration of this approach. This essay applies the theory of conventions to the problem of quality control within organizations. Although quality evaluation and quality production problems are central dimensions of business and economic reality, standard economic theory is incapable of analyzing them effectively because of their intersubjectivist and cognitive aspects.

In General Equilibrium Theory (GET), quality is not really considered, because goods are supposed to be homogeneous. In its developed versions, neoclassical theory analyzes quality problems exclusively in terms of signaling. Firms are supposed to emit signals which reveal the quality of their products. But quality itself is not analyzed *per se*. Instead, it is considered as an exogenous variable, so that its production within the organization is not theorized. This results partly from the fact that the concept of the firm is restricted to the idea of the entrepreneur, and partly because the consumer is supposed to correctly interpret the signals emitted by firms. These assumptions are very restrictive and help to explain the wide and widening gulf that exists between business reality and orthodox economic theory.

French conventions theory suggests a new framework for analyzing firms. Under the concept of conventions, individuals in a firm are seen as intersubjective interfaces between themselves, their firm and the market. Notions of quality are then analyzed as both intersubjective and group specific. This results in different evaluations of quality, not only between an organization and its market, but also between groups within an organization. And if quality depends on multiple conventions of evaluation, then economic efficiency requires that a firm both identify those conventions and the relationships between them.

This paper divides into two principal sections and some concluding remarks. First, I will present a brief review of the neoclassical economics of quality, which will focus on the limitations of traditional analysis. Next, the case will be made for the theory of the economics of conventions as a more relevant and effective alternative for analyzing quality problems. Finally, broader possibilities for developing a theory of the firm on the basis of the theory of conventions will be noted.

1. The limitations of the neo-classical approach for analyzing the economics of quality

1.1 Quasi ignorance of quality problems

Neoclassical economics never tires of saying that it is individualistic and centered on the subject. This claim, however, appears paradoxical given that, in GET, the central analytical apparatus of neoclassicism, prices are the only interface between markets and firms. Economic agents (both firms and consumers) are considered merely as price-takers, who adjust their behavior to the market price, which is supposed to be a perfect reflection of the state of supply and demand. Furthermore, this theory, through its assumption of product homogeneity, excludes consideration of the quality of products. The introduction of quality dimensions into the analysis requires a theory that admits product differentiation.

The now traditional solution for introducing quality into the neoclassical analysis was developed by Lancaster (1966). But it introduces quality considerations only in a very limited and artificial way. The "consumer", rather than making his or her choices with regard to products, is presumed to study the *characteristics* of the products. With each exchange object he or she, says the theory, associates a series of qualitative and usually conceptually vague properties (such as sturdiness, safety, lightness, tastiness, etc.) which he or she estimates quantitatively. A consumer attributes a given intensity to each characteristic of a consumer good, and, by this means, is able to appreciate its relative quality. He or she then compares the characteristics of the goods on the market with his or her platonic ideals of those qualities, and ranks the different characteristics, associating with each intensity of each characteristic a certain degree of utility. The implicit assumption running through this analysis is that utility belongs to the product's innumerable separate characteristics rather than to the product as a whole.

This approach is broadly consistent with economics' standard axiomatic of rational choice. The consumer's calculations, already presumed to be infinitely complex, are merely deemed to be even more so. He or she, claims Lancaster's strictly *a priori* theory, chooses by maximizing utility, taking into account the given prices and product's characteristics (which the theory treats as objective), and, of course, the consumer's tastes and expectations about these characteristics.

This theory does not, however, consider how the firm comes to produce the different characteristics and in differing intensities in the first place. Nor does it explain how the consumer interprets and analyses them effectively. Instead, the consumer is merely presumed to have the cognitive capacity to do so. Furthermore, the characteristics and intensities he or she identifies are supposed to be incontestable, the implicit supposition being that firms do not cheat or mislead when it comes to their products' characteristics.

So Lancaster's world, like that of neoclassicism of which it is a part, is one where inter-individual interfaces in the market are extremely limited, and where consumer choice is humanly and conceptually unproblematic. Choice is assumed to be informed by unlimited information and infinite powers of calculation. And judging a product's quality is without problems for consumers.

But, as everyone knows, this choice situation has little relevance to humans and markets of the real world. It is not only the happy unreality of Lancaster's reworking of the neoclassical model of consumer choice that leads one to ask if it is not more an exercise in escapism and ideological mischief than a contribution to human understanding. It also fails completely to explain how it is that, in a given market, a particular set of preferred characteristics comes to be socially dominant. Neoclassical resorts to "aggregation processes" and models based on a "representative consumer" merely and blatantly beg the question. The cognitive and social processes, for example, that have led German consumers to be more sensitive than French consumers to environmental characteristics of products are not taken into account. These kinds of considerations, however, form part of the research agenda of the economics of conventions.

1.2 Getting past the neoclassical axioms

Like a barrier reef, the basic axioms of neoclassical economic theory stand in the way of exploring the reality of quality. But as soon as the myth of the objective observation of quality by the consumer is rejected, exploration of this domain starts to become possible. This is illustrated by Akerlof's famous article (1970), "The Market for Lemons". Beginning from the position that quality is not directly observable by the consumer, he analyzes quality in terms of information asymmetry.

Akerlof underlined the difficulty for a seller on revealing the quality of his product, and, of course, the consumer's reciprocal difficulty in evaluating the objective quality of the product concerned. Once it is admitted that several quality levels exist, (two levels in Akerlof's model: a used car can be good or defective), an inefficient market is possible. Since the buyer of a used car cannot tell the difference between a good and a defective car (a lemon), both good and defective used cars sell for the same price. When this is the case, owners of good used cars are likely to find the equilibrium price of a used car so low that they are not motivated to offer many of their cars for sale. On the other hand, defective used cars may constitute a large number of the used cars offered for sale, and this makes potential buyers even more inclined to offer relatively low prices for used cars. In this situation, where the seller knows whether a car is good or defective, but the buyer does not, it is difficult for exchanges to occur.

Akerlof's simple example shows how taking the heterogeneity of quality levels (even when there are only two) of products into account is problematic for economics' neoclassical mainstream. Faced with the situation described above, sellers of used cars try, in various ways, to signal to buyers that their cars are good, and buyers look for these signals. Looking at how this signaling works in practice, the reputation of the seller may be particularly interesting to the buyer. Still looking at the practical reality, one thinks of the existence of laws which are supposed to indemnify the buyer against hidden faults. These are two examples of ways that consumers try to guard against buying defective products, and neither is consistent with neoclassical explanation.

Neoclassical economists tried to solve this conceptual problem through a generalization of signaling theories, following the well-known model of Spence (1973) about employees' effort. As I will demonstrate, when applied to the quality of products, signaling theories resolve the paradoxical consequences of information asymmetry and hypothetically allow trade to occur. But they do little to resolve the inability of the neoclassical approach to explore the interface between market and organization and to provide a conceptual foundation for quality economics.

In signaling theories, unlike in GET, prices are not the only interfaces in the marketplace. But while other factors, such as advertising, are also considered, the subjects themselves are not. Intersubjectivity, in other words, remains out of bounds in the analysis. For this reason, I will argue, the neoclassical approach, even with the addition of signaling theory, permits only a narrow and superficial analysis of quality problems.

1.3 Products' quality and the theories of signaling

The most natural position for the neoclassical mainstream is to consider price as a quality-signal. Wolinsky (1983) proposed a signification model in which the consumer regards the price of the good as a signal of its quality. In this model, the consumer associates a given, expected quality level with a given price. And *a priori*, the higher the price is, the higher the expected quality level. The model is quite simple and does not require a description of the internal functioning of the firm producing the product. The firm is described in the same way as in standard microeconomics. The consumer considers existing firms and their prices (p) as signals of quality (d) which he compares to the quality level he associates with the given ($q(p)$). Then, the consumer decides if he is ready to pay the given price (p) for obtaining the associated quality-level. Of course, if the consumer realizes that, contrary to the signal (d), the quality is inferior to the one he expects for the given price, he will decide not to buy the product. This behavior is a credible threat which incites the firm to produce the quality-level the consumer expects. In this context, Wolinsky shows that the equilibrium price exceeds marginal cost. The difference is a measure of the quality premium which rewards the firm. But as is evident, it supposes that the consumer is perfectly informed. He is supposed to know the firm's cost functions and the amount of the price premium which guarantees quality. The assumption of these rational expectations is very constraining. The relevance of such models to known economic realities is, at best, extremely limited.

Models which consider advertising as a quality signal are more realistic. Advertising is there for the consumer to observe, and in some cases may inform him. A model of quality signaling based on advertising and inspired by the work of Nelson (1970; 1974) has been developed by Kihlstrom and Riordman (1984). They consider a market for a new product in which firms advertise to inform the consumer about the new product's existence. Considering two possible quality levels for the firm (L: Low, and H: High), the authors show that, under specific conditions, advertising may be an efficient signal of quality which then allows trade to occur. The conditions are the following:

- Advertising costs must be high enough to dissuade a firm producing a L product from launching an advertising campaign that will persuade the consumer it produces a H product.
- But at the same time, advertising costs must not be so high as to dissuade firms producing H products from advertising to inform the consumer of this.

But if the second condition does not hold, then the advertising signal will not be effective. And although it is conceptually possible to combine price-signaling and advertising-signaling, as suggested by Milgrom and Roberts (1986), this does not alter the main limitations or the metaphysical aspects of this approach. In all these models, quality is still described as an *exogenous* phenomenon which, when taken into account, disrupts the market because of the information asymmetry it creates between producer and consumer. This information asymmetry invalidates the axioms of perfect competition. And the signaling systems which are supposed to resolve the problem are efficient if and only if agents are perfectly rational and have infinite capacities of calculation and especially the ability to realize rational expectations. The consumer must, for example, be able to interpret a high price as a signal of high quality. And he must be able to detect any misleading signals. And the only thing that should dissuade firms from emitting misleading signals is care for their reputation.

1.4 Towards the integration of cognitive and intersubjectivist aspects

Some neoclassicists are well aware of these problems and have tried to address them within the confines of their metaphysical commitments. One original and yet neoclassical model is that offered by Shapiro (1983) which argues that neither prices nor advertising are effective signals which convince the consumer to purchase a product. Instead a cognitive object, reputation, is what attracts consumers. This is one of the attempts to integrate cognitive aspects in the neoclassical analysis of quality. As Shapiro (1983: 660) suggests, the consumer gets an idea of the product's quality and then contributes to building the firm's reputation when he tries the product. Therefore, the entrepreneur, who is the sole representative of the firm and its product quality, is encouraged to offer attractive launch prices (that is, prices which are lower than costs). As soon as the firm becomes known, the consumer is again sensitive to the price signal, and the entrepreneur then asks for a quality-premium (high price) in return for quality and the reputation of the firm. Here, reputation is exogenous and supposed to be common knowledge. All the consumers in the model share the same perception of the firm's reputation. However, one knows that, in reality, reputation is generally only valid in a given geographic and sociological network and may be contested by both individuals and groups. Furthermore, in Shapiro's approach, reputation is based only on market aspects (the prices), which is contrary to the reality in which inter-individual trust, reference to tradition, or sensitivity to the mode of manufacturing are often the foundations of reputation. The theory of conventions offers a conceptual framework to integrate these crucial aspects.

In the most sophisticated and probably the most ambitious neoclassical work dealing with quality, namely "the economics of quality" (De Vany and Saving 1983), another aspect of intersubjectivity is evoked for analyzing product quality phenomena. In this model, each consumer knows, for each firm, both the product's price and the firm's production capacity. The consumer has only to collect information about the number of other consumers wanting to buy the product. The object of this information collecting is to minimize the "Full Price" (P) the consumer has to pay, that is: the price of the product (p) plus the cost generated by the waiting time for obtaining the product (W). The "Full Price" is $P = W + p$, and of course $P > p$; the price is known and given for the consumer. Optimization minimizes W, a positive function of time (v) and of quantity produced (q) and a negative function of the maximum production capacity (S).

The authors present $1/W$ as if it were an indicator of quality. The idea is that the product's quality is inversely proportional to the waiting time. But, in truth, $1/W$, rather than being an indicator of a product's quality, is an indicator of service quality.[1] The higher the firm's production capacity, the faster you are satisfied.

This model suggests that the notion of quality is not limited to the appreciation of a product characteristics but also is affected by the service which accompanies the product. Because it includes production capacity as a partial determinant of demand, this model has an interesting aspect: in it, an individual's assessment of quality is affected by the action of others. An otherwise desirable product associated with a low production capacity would lead to a low individual quality evaluation if the resulting waiting time is high. As a consequence, we can think of De Vany and Saving's consumers as preferring to be the first users of a given new product. Quality evaluation is then tainted with reference to others, exactly as Caroline Foley argued, before Veblen, at the end of the nineteenth century (Foley 1893; Fullbrook 1998). Quality evaluation is actually deeply influenced by the *social proclivities* of the consumer such as "love of distinction", "imitation" etc. (Beincourt 1994; Foley 1893). De Vany and Saving's model suggests this idea, but only to a very limited extent describes the way the consumer regards other consumers. Nevertheless, it implies that maximizing is not the only optimal behavior in situations of information asymmetry. Imitation can be efficient too. This model's position regarding quality is analogous to the position of neoclassical analyses of "rational bubbles in financial markets". (Orléan, 1989b) With regard to the phenomena of financial bubbles, theorists acknowledged that imitation could be a rational strategy. But in so doing they were contradicting the neoclassical axiomatic which Orléan (1989b) described as an "objectivist" approach because "the only freedom of the economic subject is to adapt himself to objective constraints" (*op. cit.*, p. 154). Traditional consumer theory generally seeks to explain and predict the behavior of economic agents only from the point of view of predetermined preferences and external technological constraints. It also, as the neoclassical quality models illustrate, implies that "added complexity is always matched by commensurably more sophisticated decision strategies on part of the typical agent". (Leifonhufvud 1992: 9) As we saw with De Vany and Saving's model, introducing a small proportion of intersubjectivity into the neoclassical framework supposes an even higher cognitive capacity from the agent. That he or she is supposed to be able to collect and process so much information is, to say the least, unrealistic. In fact, beyond a certain point, the increasing of complexity causes agents to simplify their strategies and use routines or conventions that "may involve ignoring potentially relevant information that a more competent agent would always utilize to optimize" (Leifonhufvud, *op. cit.*). In other words, to analyze quality effectively it is necessary to "enlarge the notion of rationality" and "to give a place in our analysis for social and cognitive phenomena" (Orléan 1989a: 269), and to admit limited rationality and imitation.

1.5 Which rationality and which theory for apprehending the notion of quality?

It is time to sum up the lessons of this overview of the neoclassical models which have made some gestures towards dealing with the notion of quality.

Except in GET, where quality is not considered, quality is always analyzed as an exogenous variable. In these theories, the entrepreneur's choice of one or another level of quality is treated as unproblematic. His production system is presumed to be very flexible. Of course, this is an utopian view which results from a simplistic representation of the firm. As previously explained, the firm is treated as a Black Box, with the entrepreneur as its efficient representative agent. The neoclassical approach to quality is a demand oriented one, whereas a complete economics of quality should focus not only on the demand aspects but also on the quality production aspects. The analysis of quality also requires a theory of the firm that describes the firm as a collectivity of intermeshed individuals and groups.

Focusing on the demand aspect of quality, the neoclassical approach considers that the main characteristic of quality is that the consumer is unable to observe it directly. He is consequently obliged to observe signals that firms emit in order to make judgments regarding quality. But, as I have mentioned earlier, the consumer has other possibilities for escaping from the information asymmetry dilemma which confronts him. He may have recourse to the advice of friends, in which case his reasoning is not based on traditional maximization, but on a logic of trust. A similar logic may operate between buyers and sellers. Buying can be considered, then, as instigating a relation. A signal of quality would be the durability of the relation which is founded on trust. This observation is very common in the business world. But conceptually, it is necessary to create a model of the human interface between the buyer and the firm. This is exactly what standard theory lacks. As it has been noted, this approach is an objectivist one. The market relation between buyers and firms is limited to objects like prices, advertising, and abstract reputations with no subject-interface, no intersubjectivity. This reveals that the neoclassical approach is wrongly called a subjectivist approach.

All this also implies that the neoclassical paradigm of rationality is ill-suited for analyzing market situations. In the neoclassical model, dealing with quality evaluation, the consumer is asked to anticipate the behavior of the sellers. He, especially, has to discern if the entrepreneur emitting a signal is trustworthy or opportunistic. In this case, instrumental rationality (that is, where everything is the result of an optimizing process), which constitutes one of the axioms of neoclassical theories, is not sufficient. The neoclassical models outlined earlier can only continue with this axiom at the high cost of making further assumptions about the cognitive capacities of the agent. Once it is admitted that consumers' cognitive capacity is limited, one has to refer to a new paradigm of rationality called "Cognitive Rationality" (Orléan 1989b) which, in fact, corresponds to the two models of Jürgen Habermas (*The Ethics of Debate*). These are models of *strategic rationality* and of *communicational rationality*. I am opposing these two models to the model of *instrumental rationality*.

Strategic rationality describes behavior through which a subject wishes to achieve an objective, taking into account either the cooperation or the opposition of at least one other person. Acquiring the cooperation of the other or winning a struggle against the other supposes a strategic calculation. It is the typical framework of game theory.

Communicational rationality operates when several individuals agree on facts and moral norms of judgment and when this agreement leads them to a shared commitment. This is the typical paradigm of the economics of conventions. It is this which I now propose as a relevant theoretical framework for analyzing the notion of quality and for an intersubjectivist theory of the firm.

2. The French theory of conventions and quality evaluations

Conventionalist authors, seeking to indicate the meaning of "convention", often refer to Lewis (1969) and to Schelling (1977). They suggest that a convention is a mode of coordination that emerges in a group or in a society in order to allow the collective resolution of problems in which uncertainty and limited rationality make decisions difficult. But these references can be very misleading, because convention would be then assimilated to "institution" in the sense of game theory (Schotter 1981; 1983). The theory of conventions would then be located only in the field of *strategic rationality* which is much too restrictive. True, like institutions, conventions are supposed to transcend the individual. But a convention is more than an "institution". It has an additional dimension. Conventions theory has to be located in the field of *communicational rationality in the sense that the social norms, i.e. conventions, used to resolve problems of indecision may be discussed and deliberately modified by the individuals using them.* To the usual sense of the institutions of game theory, conventionalists add the fact that a convention is both a guide for action and an individual collective system of legitimating the actions, that, consequently, can be submitted to critical testing and to interrogation. (Gomez 1996: 186). Contrary to the universal ambitions of game theory (where an institution is a general social solution for a given kind of game), conventions theory holds that two identical situations in two different groups can be solved with very different conventions. And, of course, conventions may evolve (Boyer and Orléan 1991; 1994). According to Jürgen Habermas, the choice of and the evolution of conventions are the result of a generic *discussion*. The result of the implicit discussion is that "*a convention is a system of reciprocal expectations about the behavior of the other*" (Salais 1989).

Thus defined, conventions simultaneously permit collective action and common evaluation of reality. One can perceive here how convention theory makes it possible to unite the consideration of production and the evaluation of quality. According to Boltanski and Thévenot (1987), subjects use six different generic and alternative modes of coordination and of evaluation that the authors call *metaphysical worlds, natures,* or "*cités*" (cities). These are: "*la cité marchande*" (the market city) in which the individuals

263

agree on the basis of market principles, for example price; "*la cité de Dieu*" (God's city) in which the agreement amongst the individuals would be founded on grace and divine inspiration; "*la cité du renom*" (the city of fame) in which the objects and the subjects are appreciated according to others' opinions; "*la cité civique*" (the civic city) in which the agreement about evaluation and action comes from the fact that the individuals are sensitive to the collective welfare; "*la cité domestique*" (the domestic city) in which the individuals agree by referring to tradition; and "*la cité industrielle*" (the industrial city) in which agreement would be founded on objective data (for example, this can be technical and measurable). Each of these metaphysical worlds corresponds to a particular paradigm of moral and political philosophy. For instance, "*la cité de Dieu*" refers to the writings of St. Augustine; "*la cité marchande*" to Adam Smith; "*la cité domestique*" to Boosuet and "*la cité industrielle*" to the writings of Saint Simon.

In this model there exists, therefore, "a plurality of possible justifications of action" (Thévenot 1989: 148). Thus, analyzing firms and the notion of quality from a conventionalist perspective involves describing the intersubjective relations inside the firm (the firm is a place of conventions and conflicts); the intersubjectivity among firms (firms look at each other to elaborate their quality policy); and how this interfaces with the consumer's evaluations of quality. As was mentioned above, neoclassical economics only and very limitedly focuses on this last aspect, which will now be analyzed in terms of conventions of quality.

2.1 Quality conventions

Based on Thévenot and Boltanski's conceptual analysis, there are three distinctively different sorts of conventions applied to quality evaluation (by the consumer) which have been elaborated by Eymard-Duvernay (1989). They are conventions of *qualité domestique, qualité industrielle* and *qualité marchande*. As in the neoclassical theory of price-signaling, in the market city (*cité marchande*), quality is associated with a product's price and its other quantitative aspects, such as delays. But, in the world, quality may be appreciated with reference to the traditions of the producer (e.g. "this company was founded in 1912"). Other consumers will refer to the industrial world and will apprehend quality with respect to technical standards they expect for the product. When a firm performs product tests and advertises the results, it is making an appeal to this kind of consumer evaluation. In ways such as these, quality evaluation under the economics of conventions is not at all limited to those market aspects covered by neoclassical analysis.

Furthermore, this approach recognizes that conflicts in quality evaluation naturally emerge in markets. Different groups of consumers (and different producers) may, in decisions, refer to different quality conventions.

Firms have to take this into account. Further, evaluations of the quality of products that are made within the firm may differ between its members just as they may differ too from the consumer's evaluation. When these tensions occur, it is particularly apposite, in seeking an explanation of the market process, to appeal to the interface of actors, including members of the firm, who try to reconcile external and internal evaluations of quality. Under this approach, quality evaluation is a much more complex process than that considered by neoclassical theory. The economics of conventions goes inside "the Black Box".

2.2 Going inside and outside the Black Box: Internal and external evaluations of quality and the interface-actors' role

Traditionally, a firm's sales employees are considered as interface-actors between the firm and the market. Their role is not only to convince the buyer to choose the firm's products, but also to collect information about consumer desires so that the firm adapts its products to demand. In fact, the sales person collects information about the external modes of quality evaluation and, working with an evolving list of selling points, tries to make this external evaluation evolve in the firm's interest.

New management approaches to quality, such as those offered by Malcolm Baldridge and in European Foundation for Quality Management's publications, suggest that all the actors in a firm are concerned with this mission. The switchboard operator as well as the bookkeeper are supposed to be attentive to the client. And when they are relating to a client, they are supposed to be conscious that they represent the firm. Lack of interest in the client can be prejudicial to the reputation of the firm. Reputation, in this prospect, cannot be considered as an exogenous element, as in Shapiro's model. Instead, it clearly appears as a social construct of the firm. Furthermore, each member of the firm participates in its construction. For instance, in a commodities carriage firm, the lorry driver carries a large responsibility towards the client. A manager questioned by Biencourt and Favereau (1994) said: "The lorry driver has got the client in his hands." The way he looks and dresses and his comportment will eventually have an influence on the client's evaluation of quality. Of course, this influence will depend on the quality conventions of the client. It will be very strong if the client is influenced by the domestic quality convention. On the other hand, the client will not be sensitive to these details if the convention of market quality is the primary framework of values by which she judges.

In opposition to the neoclassical approach, the theory of conventions assumes that there are many individualistic and cognitive interfaces in markets and organizations. But the interface-actor is, in some circumstances, in a difficult position. He sometimes has to manage tensions between external quality conventions and the internal conventions which are used to produce a particular quality and to evaluate its success. Tensions arise when a change occurs in the market or in the firm. Thévenot (1991) argues that the tension is resolved by what he calls an accommodation process. For example, when a firm is bought by another it can provoke a cultural shock. The shock may be serious, requiring an accommodation between opposing conventions. Thévenot considers the case of the famous French pastry-making firm, Lenôtre. Henri Talaszka was the company's executive director when it was bought by the international group, Accor. Thévenot analyzes the change in terms of tensions between different conventions. Lenôtre was a traditional firm with small-scale production and with internal conventions compatible with the domestic convention. But after acquiring Lenôtre, the Accor staff wanted to "rationalize" the organization with respect to a mix of industrial and market conventions. Confirmed in his position, Talaszka had to broker an accommodation between these different conventions and serve as an interface between them.

In another firm observed by Eymard-Duvernay (1994), the redevelopment of a product line for a new market led to serious tension regarding quality. This firm was producing equipment for military aeronautics. Its concept of quality was based on the rigorous standards consistent with the industrial quality convention of its client. But when the firm decided to adopt a strategy of diversification and started producing equipment for the commercial air travel industry, it had to face a different market situation, where different economies were in force. It asked its employees to be sensitive to the price constraints they faced in this market and where technical quality norms were more flexible. Some of the employees were shocked, because they regarded the change as a deterioration in quality. But what, in fact, was being asked for was a change in the firm's *concept* of quality to one that fitted its new external market. This example gives another illustration of how quality is a social construct and how this can make it imperative for a firm's management to cope with different apprehensions of its activities.

In order to achieve an accommodation between quality conventions and internal conventions, firms and consumers sometimes require external experts, such as consultants, laboratories, and consumer groups who test the products, etc. But the quality evaluation of one expert may conflict with those of others. As Gomez (1994) suggests, these varying views can be used to co-produce judgments about quality. Table 16.1, like the

Table 16.1 Co-production process for quality

Internal convention	Quality conventions	
	Industrial market city	Domestic and fame's city
Industrial-Market	1. Standard quality model	3. Liberal quality model
Civic-Domestic	2. Home quality model	4. Service quality model

foregoing discussion, illustrates this co-production process and reveals how much this view of the process of the production of quality differs from that presented in neoclassical theories. Instead, it suggests the conventionalist position that, "quality is the expression of a confluence between the internal and the external." Quality phenomena reveal that both broad socio-economic quality conventions (which result from the collective preferences of the consumers and are partly imposed on the firm) and a firm's internal conventions contribute to decisions about quality. (Gomez 1994: 216). Quality production and quality control by the firm consist of finding ways to make the external quality conventions and the internal conventions[2] correspond. And, of course, there are several solutions to this problem.

2.3 The interface management

Following Gomez (1994), it is possible to schematize these quality relations in a tabular grid. Suppose that only two quality conventions exist. The first one corresponds to a mix of the values of the market city and the industrial city, with buyers attentive to objective data such as prices, delivery time, delays and technical requirements. The second convention combines the views of the city of fame and of the domestic city, in which the buyer values the quality and length of the relation she has with the seller.

By attending to one or the other of these market situations, the firm can opt for multiple internal strategies. Consider, for example, two *effort conventions*. The first one focuses on the individualization of effort. Interface roles and all individual success or progress will be individually rewarded (perhaps with a system of individual bonuses and promotions). This strategy corresponds to a mix of the views of the industrial and market cities. The second convention focuses on team spirit and corresponds more to a civic and domestic outlook. Four quality development models result from the combination of these internal and external conventions. (See Table 16.1)

When the industrial market conventions pertain, the management can proceed by selecting one of two models. In the Standard Quality model, the external quality conventions and the internal conventions are close. Calculation and objectivity with regard to the evaluations are crucial, and quality is analyzed in quantitative terms, both for the client and for the firm's members. This model works with respect to very severe norms and objectives. Optimization and operations research are used to develop quality. Neoclassical theory is relatively efficient for describing this model.

But the firm can and may develop another answer to the given quality convention. In the Home Quality model, the internal convention is complex. There may be a great number of collective rules inside the firm. The idealization of this model corresponds to the Japanese school of quality (K. Ishikawa) which envisages a harmonious firm dedicated to the client's service.

When the consumer is sensitive to the product's and the firm's reputation, the two quality models available for the firm's management to choose are the Liberal Quality model and the Service Quality model. The first appears appropriate and often characteristic of consultancy firms, and small computer and software companies. Performance evaluations within the firm are individualized but nevertheless reputation is collective and important. Here, the management finds a balance between an internal and positive judgment and the necessity to assure that each member of the firm contributes as required to its reputation. At the opposite extreme, the Service Quality model represents the primacy of the collective. One thinks here of private clinics and of American law firms.

Despite its simplicity,[3] this model emphasizes the fact that the firm's quality position results from the complex interaction of internal and external conventions. Developing the effective interfaces amongst them requires the ability to identify the operative conventions in each case.

3. Concluding remarks

A gap often exists between the rationales which individuals, when questioned, give for their actions and the conventions that they actually used in reaching their decisions. (Argyris and Schön 1981). Consequently, identifying the operative conventions is problematic. J.C. Moisdon (1988), an operational research consultant working in France, frequently observed that when he intervened in organizations, there was a serious divergence between the prescriptions of his model at the end of his intervention and subsequent practice. He concluded that this discrepancy came from the fact that his consultative brief, which was formulated by the top management and which was intended to frame his enquiry, was not consistent with the realities of the firm's collective performance and needs. The conventions which the management presumed for the firm were, in fact, often not the operative ones. Hence, Moisdon came to treat his brief as part of the diagnostic model he constructed, particularly as possible evidence of discrepancies and tensions between the operative conventions at different levels and divisions in the organization. Through interviews with individual actors he was able to identify the conventions that were in fact in force at different points in the firm.

Recognition of different quality conventions also serve as the conscious basis of company decisions. As illustrations, consider a pair of cases, both regarding quality and both concerning the externalization (or not) of services. The first involves the French firm Novotel and the cleaning of its premises. It had contracted out its cleaning on grounds of cost. Subsequently, however, without any change in the cost situation, it reversed this decision because clients expressed dissatisfaction with the externally provided service. In the conventions theory of quality, this reversal is intelligible. Novotel reversed it decision because it shifted its operative conventions from that of the market to the industrial and domestic cities. On the other hand, consider a strategically important quality decision reached by the tire producer, Michelin. Its decision to externalize its design and planning activities is incomprehensible without the conventions concept. Michelin is a very hierarchical firm, and it recognized that the general conventions of the firm (a mix of domestic, industrial and market cities) were incompatible with the known conventions of innovative and creative design teams (a mix of domestic, civic and God's cities).

This paper's considerations of the problem of quality suggest the possibility of a theory of the firm which views the subject as the interface between the market and the organization. But the application of the theory of conventions to theorizing the firm could have relevance far beyond the problem of quality. I will offer a brief example. It concerns the currently fashionable field in Business Studies of Entrepreneurship, where the relevance of the conventions approach is rather obvious. Although in neoclassical theory, the entrepreneur is thought of as central, in fact, the theory, in the main, assimilates him/her to the firm. Just as the objectivist context of neoclassical theory evaporates the problem of quality, so its exclusion of intersubjectivity precludes recognition, analysis, and understanding of the entrepreneurial function. Even in transaction costs theory the entrepreneur's function is limited to acting as a stand-in for the price system in seeking optimal resource allocation in the firm. Like quality, the entrepreneur is treated, paradoxically, as exogenous to the firm, as someone who comes along after its creation. The conventionalist theory of entrepreneurship, on the other hand, would consider the entrepreneur as an actor who tries to convince others (employees, partners, suppliers, etc.) to agree with her on a project and on common modes of evaluation and of action. In other words, she would be the one who would try to establish "a convention of effort" (Gomez 1996: 227). In such a theory the entrepreneur would be regarded as existing and performing her role in this context of *intersubjectivity*. Indeed, without the intersubjective context, there is no entrepreneurship.

Notes

1 Biencort (1994) has shown that considering $1/W$ as a direct indicator of a products' quality can be counter-intuitive. For some products like cinema, restaurants, the size of the queue may be a positive signal of quality. If you have no information about the reputation of two similarly priced restaurants and if one

is full and the other is empty, you may conclude that the former offers the higher quality.

2 In order to underline that the internal convention is the basis for determining which form of quality will be produced, Gomez calls it "effort convention". In what follows, I will adopt his terminology.

3 In reality, more than two quality conventions and more than two internal conventions should be considered. A plurality of quality models would ensue. And of course, the interaction amongst internal actors and quality conventions should be better explained. Overall, in the present development, the firms were defining their strategy looking at the quality conventions. This is only one level of intersubjectivity integration. As it was discussed in a previous work (Levy, 1995) and following White (1981), firms also look at each other to define their strategy and especially to determine their quality position. *"Markets are tangible cliques of firms watching each other. Pressure from the buyer side creates a mirror in which the producers see themselves, not consumers."* (White, *op. cit.*, p. 543). One can think that when discussing with a client, the interface-actor learns about his modes of quality evaluation but also about the quality performances of the other firms that the consumer evaluates too.

References

Aglietta, M. and Orléan, A. (1982) *La violence de la monnaie*, PUF, Paris.

Akerloff, G. (1970) "The Market for Lemons: Quality uncertainty and the Market mechanisms." *Quarterly Journal of Economics* 89: 488–500.

Argyris, C. and D. Schön (1974) *Theory in practice*, Jossey Bass, San Francisco.

Biencourt, Olivier (1994) "Economie de la Qualité: du signal à la convention," Paper presented at the seminar ROME (Rules, Organizations, Markets, Enterprises), Paris.

Biencourt, Olivier, and Olivier Favereau (1994) "Concurrence par la qualité et viabilité d'un marché: le cas du transport routier," Report for the Commissariat Général au Plan, May, Paris.

Biencourt, Olivier, Favereau, Olivier and Eymard-Duvernay, François (1994) "Economics should define the firm prior to the market, not the other way around," Paper presented at the annual Congress of the *Society for the Advancement of Socio-Economics* (SASE). Paris.

Boyer, R. and Orléan, A. (1991) "Les transformations des conventions salariales. Entre Théorie et histoire," *Revue Economique* 42(2): 233–72.

Boyer, R. and Orléan, A. (1994) "Why are institutional transitions so difficult ?" in A. Orléan (ed.): *"L'Analyse des conventions économiques,"* PUF, Paris.

Boltanski, L. and Thévenot, L. (1987) *"Les Economies de la grandeur,"* Cahiers du Centre d'Etudes de l'Emploi, PUF, Paris.

Dalle, Jean-Michel (1995) "Dynamiques d'adoption, coordination et diversité: la diffusion des standards technologiques", *Revue Economique* 46(4): 1081–98.

De Vany, A. and Saving, T. (1983) "The Economics of Quality," *Journal of Political Economy* 91(6) 979–1000.

Eymard-Duvernay, François (1989) "Conventions de qualité et formes de coordination" (Definitions of quality and forms of organization), *Revue Economique* 40(2).

Eymard-Duvernay, François (1994) "Coordination par l'entreprise et qualité des biens" (Firm's coordination and goods' quality), in A. Orléan (ed.) "*L'Analyse des conventions économiques*," PUF, Paris.

Favereau, Olivier (1995) "Développement et Economie des conventions," in P. Hugon (ed) "*L'Afrique des incertitudes*," PUF, Paris.

Foley, Cavoline A. (1893) "Fashion," *Economic Journal* 3: 458–74.

Fullbrook, Edward (1996) "The Metaphysics of Consumer Desire and the French Intersubjectivists," *International Advances in Economic Research* 2: 287–94.

Fullbrook, Edward (1997) "Post-modernizing *homo-oeconomicus*," in S. Earnshaw (ed.) *Just Post-modernism*, edited by Steven Earnshaw, pp. 67–87, Rodopi Press, Amsterdam & Atlanta.

Fullbrook, Edward (1998) "Caroline Foley and the Theory of Intersubjective Demand." *Journal of Economic Issues* 32(3).

Gomez, P. Y. (1994) *Qualité et Théorie des conventions* (Quality and conventions theory), Economica, Paris.

Gomez, P. Y. (1996) *Le gouvernement de l'entreprise. (Modèles économiques de l'entreprise et pratique de Gestion).* [Firm's governance], InterEditions, Paris.

Kihlstrom, R. and Riordan M. (1984) "Advertising as a Signal," *Journal of Political Economy* 92(3): 427–50.

Lancaster, K. J. (1966) "A New Approach to Consumer-Theory," *Journal of Political Economy* 74: 132–57.

Leijonhufvud, A. (1992) "Towards a not too-rational macroeconomics," Working-Paper no. 1, Center for Computable Economics, UCLA.

Levy, Thierry (1994) "Measurement Economics, Value Theory and the Social Function of Money", *Atlantic Economic Society Best Paper Proceedings* 4(2): 11–18.

Levy, Thierry (1995) "An Intersubjectivist Economic Approach and the theory of Firm's dynamic", *Archives of Economic History* 6(1): 35–62.

Lewis, D. K. (1969) *Conventions: a philosophical study*, Harvard University Press, Cambridge (Mass.).

Milgrom, P. and Roberts, J. (1986) "Price and Advertising signals of Product Quality," *Journal of Political Economy* 94(4): 796–821.

Moisdon, J. C. (1998) "Vers des modélisations apprenantes" (Towards learning models) *Sciences de Gestion*, no. 25.

Nelson, R. (1970) "Information and consumer behavior," *Journal of Political Economy*, 78: 311–29.

Nelson, R. (1974) "Advertising as information," *Journal of Political Economy* 81(4): 729–54.

Orléan, André (1989a) "Pour une approche cognitive des conventions économiques," (Towards a cognitive approach to economic conventions), *Revue Economique* 40(2): 241–72.

Orléan, André (1989b) "La crise du paradigme walrasien," (The walrasian paradigm in crisis), *Cahiers du CREA*, Ecole Polytechnique, Paris no. 13, September: 147–66.

Orléan, André (1990) "Le rôle des influences interpersonnelles dans la formation des cours boursiers," *Revue Economique* 5: 839–68.

Orléan, André (1992) "Contagion des opinions et fonctionnement des marchés financiers" (Contagion of opinions in Financial Markets), *Revue Economique* 4: 685–98.

Salais, Robert (1989) "L'analyse économique des conventions de travail" (The Economic analysis of labor conventions), *Revue Economique* 40(2): 199–240.

Schelling, Thomas C. (1977) *The Strategy of Conflict*, Oxford University Press.

Schotter, Andrew (1981) *The Economic Theory of Social Institutions*, Cambridge University Press, New York.

Schotter, Andrew (1983) "Why take a game theoretical approach to economics?" *Economie Appliquée* 36: 673–95.

Shapiro, C. (1983) "Premiums for High Quality products as Returns to Reputation," *Quaterly Journal of Economics* 98: 659–80.

Spence, M. (1973) "Job Market Signalling," *Quaterly Journal of Economics* 87: 355–74.

Thevenot, L. (1989) "Equilibre et rationalité dans un univers complexe," (Equilibrium and rationality in a complex universe), *Revue Economique* 40(2): 147–97.

Thevenot, L. (1991) "L'Economie des conventions à l'épreuve de l'innovation," (Conventions Economics and Innovation), Paper for the symposium "Cultures, Structures et Innovation," French Ministère de la Recherche et de la Technologie, Ecole Polytechnique, miméo, Paris.

Verstraete, Thierry (1999) *"Entrepreneuriat, Connaître l'entrepreneur, comprendre ses actes,"* (Entrepreneurship; knowing the entrepreneur; understanding his actions) L'Harmattan, Paris.

Wagner, P. (1994) "Action, Coordination and Institution in Recent French Debates," *The Journal of Political Philosophy* 3: 270–89.

White, H. (1981) "Where do markets come from?" *American Journal of Sociology* 87(3): 517–47.

Wolinsky, A. (1983) "Prices as signals of product quality," *Review of Economic Studies* 50: 647–56.

17

AN INTERSUBJECTIVE THEORY OF VALUE

Edward Fullbrook

1. Introduction

The subjective theory of value holds that the *quantitative order* variously called "exchange-value", "market-value" and "money-value" is analyzable into *intra*subjective preferences and ratios of exchange between pairs of commodities. This paper will demonstrate:

1   that this presumed reducibility is logically impredicative;
2   that exchange-value is conditional upon and describes a broad *inter*subjective space;
3   that the structure of exchange-value is boolean rather than euclidean;
4   that this boolean structure, rather than the maximizing behavior of individual agents, accounts in the main for downward sloping demand curves; and
5   that some well-known paradoxes that appeared in twentieth-century economic theory were due to applying euclidean and intrasubjective assumptions to intersubjective boolean reality.

2. The nature of the beast

Length, time, mass, angular distance, probability, temperature and other measurement orders are characterized by various properties which together constitute a *structure*. These properties are open to description by elementary abstract algebra. That the metrical properties of these measurement orders – for example, mass, temperature and probability – diverge widely stands as common knowledge. So too does the fact that the Einsteinian revolution centered upon a reassessment of the metrics of fundamental orders of physical measurement. Previously, all physicists had assumed that lengths and masses could, in principle, be combined indefinitely in a manner analogous to arithmetical operations on the set of real numbers. In economics a similar euclidean assumption structures the conception of market or exchange value. As with one's everyday perceptions of the physical world, economists take this euclidean assumption so much for granted that usually it escapes mention. In theoretically fundamental texts, however, one does find this, *the* most central structural hypothesis of economic theory, explicitly stated. Debreu, for example, launches his *Theory of Value* by noting that his analysis is "organized around the concept of a price system or, more generally, of a value function defined on the commodity space," and whose euclidean structures he makes explicit in the course of the work (ix).[1] More profound, however, is what Debreu fails to do. His demonstration of a euclidean structure extends only to his *concept* of "exchange-value". Regarding exchange-value itself, that is, whether his concept correctly describes it, he offers no evidence.

Debreu's choice, and that of economics generally, to disregard the possibility that one's most basic presuppositions might not correspond to reality, is, as noted, part of a once venerable tradition. Its greatest champion was Kant. In *The Critique of Pure Reason* he argued that it is possible to know some of reality's basic structures *a priori,* and he used everyday euclidean notions of space and time as his central example. History, however, is cruel to *a priorism,* and never more so than to Kant's celebrated pronouncements on space and time. But, as evidenced by the acclaim attached to Debreu's and similar essays, economics has not yet escaped from subjective idealism as a way of thinking. Economists, with exceptions, do not permit empiricism to come between them and their basic concepts.

Yet, that is what I propose to do with respect to "exchange-value". The parallel between the distinction that the following passage from Bertrand Russell describes and the one that this paper is going to pursue is fairly exact.

> 'Geometry', as we now know, is a name covering two different studies. On the one hand, there is pure geometry, which deduces consequences from axioms, without inquiring whether the axioms are 'true'; this contains nothing that does not follow from logic, and is not 'synthetic'... On the other hand, there is geometry as a branch of physics, as it appears, for example, in the general theory of relativity; this is an empirical science, in which the axioms are inferred from measurements, and are found to differ from Euclid's. [688]

Economists, like physicists of an earlier age, share the general human weakness of presuming that the world's deep structures resemble surface appearances. For economics this means believing that everyday, commonsense understanding suffices for comprehending exchange-value's structure. Leaving this most fundamental of questions in the realm of pre-science or commonsense also gives the presumed answer the epistemological certainty demanded by economics' theoretical heritage. Neoclassical value theory defines both general and partial equilibrium as a relation between market supply and demand functions, and it defines these functions as summations of individual supply and demand schedules. The postulation of these summations requires the assumption of *additivity*, the key feature of the euclidean structure. Additivity, however, "is only valid if the demand functions of the various individuals are independent of each other." (Morgenstern 1948: 175) Independence means no *intersubjective effects*, that is, that each agent's demand, rather than being affected by the demands of other agents, is purely *intra*subjective. It is only in this special case that, by definition, the neoclassical theory of value pertains. This requirement of additivity, especially of demands, locks neoclassicalism and economics generally into presuming that exchange-value is euclidean. Recognition of the importance of intersubjective supply and demand phenomena in determining market outcomes frees economics from this traditional presumption, thereby making psychologically possible an empirical and critical inquiry into the structure of exchange-value. This paper seeks to initiate this project.

3. The structure and methodology of this paper

The argument develops in three stages. The first entertains a few fundamental questions about the minimum requirements for the establishment of exchange-value as a quantitative order. Tradition says exchange-value is, like weight and probability, a relational property – not one that holds for commodities individually as do mass and extension for physical objects. But what exactly are the terms of the exchange-value relation? And how many are required for its existence? The accepted view that exchange-value is reducible to a relation between market agents and two commodities will be tested for logical coherence. The second and main stage of the argument considers what various commonly observed market phenomena imply about the structure of exchange-value. Is this empirical knowledge consistent with the view that exchange-value is euclidean, and, if not, is it possible to identify its real structure? The third stages considers the broad implications of the results of stages one and two, and shows that several major theoretical anomalies that surfaced in the twentieth century result from economics' misunderstandings of the structure of exchange-value.

Four aspects of this paper's methodology need foregrounding. First, the analysis is purely *synchronic*. Time, including the hypothetical instantaneous time of equilibrium analysis, does not figure.

Second and more important, the method is *retroduction* (Lawson 1997). Economists accustomed only to working with the deductive method – as described by Russell above – will be predisposed to read this paper inside-out, making it appear that I have indulged in a bizarre selection of axioms to produce a whimsical Escher-like landscape. But such an error is easily avoided by grasping one crucial point. *This paper's logical inferences proceed from the level of observable phenomena back to the level of underlying structures or "axioms" in Russell's second sense of the word.* The goal is to discover, not the properties of an axiom system, but rather those of a particular real-life system of intersubjective relations, the market price system. In lieu of economics' traditional axioms, the argument begins on the basis of a presumption of possibility, namely, that, just as the objective character of lightning is not exhausted by its visual appearance, so it is unlikely that the structure of exchange-value reveals itself fully in the situation of everyday market exchange. Given the long hegemony of *a priorism* in this field, little, in fact, is known about the metrical structure of exchange-value. This paper will show that its structure is more highly defined than previously thought.

Third, *structure*'s explanatory significance must be clarified. As noted above, structure plays a foundational role in neoclassical explanation. But because neoclassicism's euclidean assumption performs its function unnoticed, it has been possible to foster the myth that neoclassical conclusions have been reached solely on the basis of axiomatic generalizations about individual behavior. If inquiry reveals that exchange-value is not euclidean, then the theorizing of value must begin afresh. A logical starting place would be the possibility that some of the facts explained by neoclassical axiomatics, (i.e. by "a set of postulated behavioural regularities") are, in reality, determined *directly* by exchange-value's non-euclidean structure. (Lawson 1997: 102)

Fourth, as previously noted, the belief that exchange-value is euclidean is folkloric. This paper breaks with that tradition, taking the question of exchange-value's structure out of the realm of folklore and into the realm of science. This means looking for and at evidence as to exchange-value's structure. Doing so requires a bit of very elementary abstract algebra. Its use here, however, will be kept to a minimum and paralleled with verbal explanations. Only once, and then very briefly, will the mathematics lift slightly above this basic level. Here, as elsewhere, the abstract account will be matched by a verbal one.

4. Testing the notion of comparative exchange-value for logical coherence

Physics' classical concepts of length and mass emerge from comparative concepts, pairs of empirically defined relations, one equivalence, the other precedence, which have been shown to hold between pairs of objects.[2] Can exchange-value also be identified as originating with or shown to be reducible to a set of relations between a pair of objects, in other words, to a concept of comparative exchange-value? The following passage from Alfred Marshall identifies exchange-value as, like mass and length, based on a comparative concept, one holding between pairs of commodities.

> The value, that is the exchange value, of one thing in terms of another at any place and time, is the amount of that second thing which can be got there and then in exchange for the first. Thus the term value is relative, and *expresses the relation between two things* at a particular place and time.
> [emphasis added] [*Principles* 1920: 61]

To give it every possible chance, I want to formulate this notion of comparative exchange-value more precisely before seeing if it holds up to logical analysis. Thus:

> For pairs of commodities, there is the exchange-value of each commodity *relative to the other*, in the sense that quantities of the two commodities are said to be equal in value if they exchange for each other and to change in value if there is a change in the pair's market-clearing exchange ratio.

This reformulation, as well as Marshall's sentence, appears coherent. But the twentieth century discovered that the logical relations of statements are not always what they appear to be. So I am going to test the stated notion of comparative exchange-value against the general principle that, between any two magnitudes of the same empirical order, an equality relation either holds or does not. Consider two commodities X and Y, and whose units are x and y. Let a, b, and σ be rational positive numbers.

Assume that the initial market-clearing ratio of $ax : by$ changes to $ax : \sigma by$. Then, according to the concept of comparative exchange-value, the exchange-values of quantities of X relative to Y have changed. Any two quantities of the same order are either equal or not equal. Therefore, the exchange-value of σby relative to X at the new exchange ratio is either equal or not equal to the exchange value of by at the old exchange ratio.

First assume that it is equal. Then, because at the old ratio the exchange-values of ax and by were equal and at the new ratio the exchange-values of ax and σby are equal, it follows that the exchange-value of ax is unchanged. This contradicts the assumption that the exchange-values of quantities of X relative to Y have changed, and so one must conclude that this case cannot obtain.

Assume the other possibility: the exchange-value of σby at the new exchange ratio is not equal to the exchange-value of by at the old exchange ratio. If, relative to X, by and σby are not equal in exchange-value, then by the concept of comparative exchange-value they do not exchange for the same number of units of X. However, by assumption they do exchange for the same number of units of X. Therefore, this case also cannot obtain. And this exhausts the logical possibilities.

The concept of comparative exchange-value generates paradoxes because it is circular. It defines a commodity's exchange-value in terms of the exchange-value of a second commodity whose exchange-value is defined in terms of the exchange-value of the first. In technical terms, this constitutes "vicious circularity" which renders the definition impredicative.

This simple but unexpected outcome of the test for logical coherence shows that, as a quantitative order, exchange-value has unexpected properties. Already the euclidean presumption appears farfetched. The initial result also bears directly on this collection's theme. Whereas the traditional but impredicative notion of exchange-value reduced to the field of two atomistic agents – two independent subjectivities – making an exchange, we now know that the minimal field for existence of exchange-value must be larger. It is premature to ponder what this might mean. Doing so now would risk perplexity. First we must pursue other possibilities for analysis and hope that with further results all will become clear.

5. False resemblances

Confusions, like the one unearthed in the previous section, come easily when thinking about exchange-value because in two respects it bears a false similarity to familiar physical magnitudes. First, the notion of exchange-value as a relation between two commodities exhibits a superficial resemblance to comparative concepts of mass and length. These physical concepts, however, are not predicated as relations between individual masses and lengths. It is only their measurement numbers that are conceived in this way. Instead, Newtonian physics predicates mass and extension as properties possessed by bodies independently of their relations to other bodies. This independence saves concepts of comparative length and mass from impredicativeness. (Carnap 1966: 51–61)

Second, and related to the first, although exchange-value numbers are expressed on a ratio scale like mass and length numbers, they are generated in a profoundly different manner. Physical measurement numbers refer to physical phenomena, called concrete quantities, which have been found to have a structure isomorphic to the system of units and numbers (abstract quantities) by which they are represented. A cardinal point is that these concrete physical quantities do not come into being as the result of humankind's invention of processes of numerically representing them. If a means of numerically representing the weight of your body had never been invented, you would experience its weight all the same. The existence of the properties of extension and mass are independent of the processes by which they are measured or compared. In contrast, the quantitative order of exchange-value does not exist independently of the process which assigns exchange-value numbers. Without market exchange there is no exchange or market value. Market exchange, in other words, is the process by which the exchange-value order, not just the numbers which describe it, comes into being.

The fact that the process that determines concrete exchange-values also assigns numbers to represent them invites conflation of concrete exchange-values and exchange-value numbers. The latter, stripped of their units, belong to R, the set of positive reals which defines a euclidean space. Thus, the conflation of concrete and abstract exchange-values leads smoothly to the unsupported conclusion that a "price space" is a euclidean space. (Debreu 1986: 1261)

It is on the basis of this presumed "fit of the mathematical form to the economic content" (Debreu 1986: 1259) that the whole neoclassical edifice, not just general equilibrium theory, has been constructed. At every point it presumes – through the convenience of its conflation – that a system of exchange or market values has the same structural properties, i.e. euclidean, as do the numbers that represent them. But this subconscious presumption, the most fundamental *hypothesis* of neoclassicalism, is easily tested when the conflation between concrete and abstract quantities is avoided.

6. Test procedure

"How many snowballs would be required to heat an oven?" (Duhem 1905: 112) This joke, credited to Diderot, illustrates three verities of quantitative science: profound structural differences exist between various quantitative orders; their structures may diverge radically from that of ordinary arithmetic; and, most importantly, the structures of empirical quantitative orders are autonomous *vis à vis* human will and imagination.

In a more positive vein, but to a similar purpose, Bertrand Russell identified the principle by which science applies mathematics to empirical phenomena. "Whenever two sets of terms have mutual relations of the same type, the same form of deduction will apply to both." (Russell 1937: 7) Application of arithmetical addition to mass, length and time are familiar examples. Yet, in such cases, where one set of terms is logical or mathematical and the other set is not, the existence of a homomorphism between the two sets is, as Diderot's jest illustrates, a purely empirical matter. It presumes the discovery of a set of extra-mathematical relations which repeated testing, not a set of axioms, shows to be structurally analogous to the arithmetical ones of $=$, $<$, $>$ and $+$.

Monetarized markets assign to each set of commodities exchanged a denominate number describing a property – the "exchange-value" or "market-value" – of that set. It is, therefore, although unorthodox, eminently sensible to examine those exchanges as measurement operations. But the rarity of this approach and its false resemblance to demand theory's axiomatic method, makes it wise to begin by outlining and illustrating, even at the risk of laboring the obvious, the general empirical principles involved.[2] For this purpose I will consider in some detail the procedures, and the logic behind them, for measurement of mass.

A loaded scales in level balance defines operationally a symmetrical, transitive and reflexive relation $=_m$ between a pair of masses. This physical relation, $=_m$, is an archetypal *empirical* equivalence relation. Similarly, a scales out of level balance defines the asymmetrical, transitive, and irreflexive precedence relations lighter than $<_m$ and heavier than $>_m$. I am particularly concerned with the property, or absence of, additivity, and with the fact that physics attributes this property to mass, not on the basis of any axiom or axiom set, but rather on the basis of the results of empirical operations. It is only after equivalence and precedence relations and a numerical scale have been developed and tested for a domain of objects that it becomes possible to *test* for additivity. This property, it must be emphasized, never holds absolutely for elements of a measurement order. Instead, additivity holds *only* relative to some particular mode of combination. Lengths, for example, are additive only when combined end-to-end in a straight line perpendicular to the axis of gravity. With the measurement of mass, the combining operation is merely the joint positioning of two objects in a pan of a scales and weighing them as a single object. In general, where $\bigcirc$ denotes an empirical combining operation and p the measurement number assigned to the object in the parenthesis, the additivity condition may be stated:

$$p(a \bigcirc b) = p(a) + p(b).$$

For mass, this condition is interpreted as follows. One puts object a on one of the pans of a scales which then is brought into balance with standard weights whose mass number m is observed. Object a is then replaced with object b and its mass is noted. Then the two objects are placed together on the scale, this being the combining operation for mass $\oplus$, and the measurement number of the combined mass is determined. From experience, one predicts that the mass number of a and b combined will be the arithmetical sum of the mass numbers of a and b weighed separately, i.e.

$$m(a \oplus b) = m(a) + m(b).$$

With respect to the equivalence and precedence relations $=_m$, $<_m$ and $>_m$ and the operation of combining masses in the pans of a scales, the physical order of mass satisfies not only the additivity condition, but also a set of conditions structurally analogous to those satisfied by arithmetical addition in the set of positive real numbers R^+. *Arithmetical addition* $+$ together with the arithmetical relations $=$, $<$ and $>$ satisfy the following conditions for any elements x, y, z of R^+:

A1 $x + (y + z) = (x + y) + z$ (associativity)
A2 $x + y = y + x$ (commutativity)
A3 $z + x = z + y$ implies $x = y$ (cancellation property of $+$ with respect to $=$)
A4 $(z + x) < (z + y)$ implies $x < y$ (cancellation property of $+$ with respect to $<$)
A5 $(x + y) > x$ (monoticity)
A6 For any x and y there exists an integer n such that $nx > y$ (Archimedean property).

Where $=_p$, $<_p$ and $>_p$ denote unspecified empirical equivalence and precedence relations for a property P, $\bigcirc$ an unspecified empirical combining operation, and a, b, c are elements of the set S of all objects possessed of the property P, then the empirical conditions corresponding to A1–A6 are as follows:

P1 $a \bigcirc (b \bigcirc c) =_p (a \bigcirc b) \bigcirc c$
P2 $a \bigcirc b =_p b \bigcirc a$
P3 $c \bigcirc a =_p c \bigcirc b$ implies $a =_p b$
P4 $c \bigcirc a <_p c \bigcirc b$ implies $a <_p b$
P5 $a \bigcirc b >_p a$
P6 For any a such that $a =_p a_1 =_p a_2 =_p \cdots =_p a_n$ and any b there is a nth power $a \bigcirc a \bigcirc \cdots \bigcirc a$ of a, written na, such that $na >_p b$.

It is important to note that the conditions P1–P6 refer to relations holding between empirical objects, not between measurement numbers describing those objects. But where an empirical order such as mass has been metricated – that is, where an easily reproducible object or process possessing the property has been chosen as a standard for defining a unit of that property – conditions corresponding to P1–P6 can be expressed in terms of measurement numbers and *arithmetical*, rather than empirical, relations. The P' list that follows includes as $P'3$ the basic *additivity condition* noted above. Thus, where p denotes the measurement number assigned to the object in the parenthesis, we have:

P'1 $p(a \bigcirc (b \bigcirc c)) = p(a \bigcirc b) \bigcirc c$
P'2 $p(a \bigcirc b) = p(b \bigcirc a)$
P'3 $p(a \bigcirc b) = p(a) + p(b)$
P'4 $p(c \bigcirc a) = p(c \bigcirc b)$ implies $p(a) = p(b)$
P'5 $p(c \bigcirc a) < p(c \bigcirc b)$ implies $p(a) < p(b)$

281

P'6 $p(a \bigcirc b) > p(a)$

P'7   For any a such that $p(a) = p(a_1) = p(a_2) = \cdots = p(a_n)$ and any b there is a nth power $a \bigcirc a \bigcirc \cdots \bigcirc a$ of a, written na, such that $p(na) > p(b)$.

We will use these P' conditions to guide the inquiry into the structural characteristics of exchange-value. Each P' condition generates a question to ask about exchange-value: Does exchange-value satisfy condition P'x, and if not what corresponding condition does it satisfy? To answer these questions requires that various aspects of exchange-value noted in the introduction are examined *from the structural point of view*. These include market exchange as a measurement operation, downward sloping demand curves, inelastic demand, exchange-value units and, eventually, monetary inflation. In this way the investigation reveals a set of structural properties of exchange-value paralleling the P' conditions. This method of proceeding also has the advantage of placing the concrete structural properties of exchange-value in direct comparison to a structure, P'1–P'7, made commonplace through length and weight measurement. First the operational basis of exchange-value measurement must be explained.

7. Exchange-value as a measurement phenomenon

Everyday usage fails to differentiate between quantities of *things* and quantities of *measurement*. In science, however, the distinction between these two kinds of denominate numbers is fundamental. By definition, numbers of count have reference only to particular classes of objects. This property severely limits the scientific significance of count numbers, even when their units are based on measurable properties, for example, a pound of butter. Instead, it is the quantification of *properties* common to many classes of objects (for example, mass, length, time and exchange-value) which enables the generation of quantitative laws and of theoretical structures which transcend Aristotelian categories.

Just as mass and extension are properties common to all physical objects, so exchange-value is a property of all economic objects. It is on this basis that exchange-value must be judged a measurement order. But it is an extremely curious one, because the process of exchange-value measurement, that is, market exchange, is an integral and central part of economics' object of inquiry. Nevertheless, exchange-value, like the fundamental measurement orders of classical physics, is operationally defined in terms of a combining operation, a measurement object, an equivalence relation and a pair of precedence relations. Each of these elements of exchange-value measurement needs examination.

In a time period T, various categories of goods are exchanged for money in markets. In each of these markets, the placement in period T of multiple units of a good for exchange constitutes the empirical combining operation $\odot$ for the measurement of exchange-value, just as the simultaneous placement of multiple objects on a scales for weighing defines the combining operation $\oplus$ for the measurement of mass. Physical objects combined under $\oplus$ for weighing constitute the "object mass"; similarly, the units of a commodity X combined under $\odot$ constitute X's *market exchange or measurement set* for period T.

The market conditions of equilibrium and disequilibrium serve as equivalence and precedence relations for the measurement of exchange-value. A market which clears and is in equilibrium defines an exchange-value equivalence relation $=_e$ such that the exchange-value of the quantity of a good exchanged equals the exchange-value of the quantity of money exchanged for it. This relation parallels the equivalence relation used in weighing. When a loading of a scales results in a level equilibrium, the object mass is said to be equal to the combined mass of the mass standards ("weights") placed in the opposite pan. Markets which do not clear, like scales which do not balance, also identify quantitative relations. Excess supply or excess demand in a market defines an exchange-value precedent relation $<_e$ or $>_e$ such that the exchange-value of the commodity's market exchange set is less than or greater than the exchange-value of the money for which it was traded.

Still another parallel exists between mass and exchange-value measurement. In market trading, as in weighing, equilibrium is reached through trial and error. The initial price set for a commodity may or may not result in a market equilibrium, just as the initial number of units of standard mass placed in one pan may or may not result in an equilibrium of the scales.

As with the measurement of mass, the conditions of associativity and commutativity appear to hold for exchange-value by definition. Thus, where e denotes the exchange-value number, i.e. market-value, assigned to the homogeneous commodity set in parentheses:

E1 $e(a \odot (b \odot c)) = e((a \odot b) \odot c)$
E2 $e(a \odot b) = e(b \odot a).$

8. The law of demand as a law of negative non-additivity

Despite the structural similarities between the measuring of mass and the measuring of exchange-value, the numerical results of the two sets of operations are structurally dissimilar. This disparity becomes obvious once the negative slope of commodity demand curves is interpreted in terms of the additivity condition. If exchange-values were additive relative to their measurement combining operation, then all demand curves would be horizontal. A demand curve's slope means that as additional units of the commodity are placed on the market for exchange, $\odot$, their exchange-value is not additive. Moreover, the fact that a demand curve slopes downward means that exchange-value is negatively non-additive in the following sense. On the basis of experiential knowledge of market exchange, one can predict: for a given demand, that the exchange-value of homogeneous commodity sets a and b combined into one market exchange set will be less than the arithmetical sum of the exchange-values of a and b if they are exchanged separately in different periods.

Thus, where e denotes the exchange-value number assigned to the market exchange set of commodity X in the parenthesis:

E3 $e(a \odot b) < e(a) + e(b)$.

9. Inelastic demand

This section continues with the deployment of the properties P'1–P'7, which describe the structure of metricated empirical orders analogous to arithmetical addition in R^+, as heuristic devices for identifying the structural properties of exchange-value. I wish to discover how the phenomenon of inelastic demand relates to the properties

P'4 $p(c \bigcirc a) = p(c \bigcirc b)$ implies $p(a) = p(b)$
P'5 $p(c \bigcirc a) < p(c \bigcirc b)$ implies $p(a) < p(b)$
P'6 $p(a \bigcirc b) < p(a)$.

The previous section showed how the inverse relation between price and quantity demanded means that, over the operation of market exchange, exchange-value is non-additive. Inelastic demand identifies a situation in which exchange-value is not only non-additive, but "negatively" so, in the sense that increasing the size of the market exchange set *decreases* its exchange-value. This condition generates relations which violate conditions P'4–P'6.

I begin by considering P'6, because the inconsistency of inelastic demand with this property is self-evident. Interpreted in terms of exchange-value, inelasticity of demand means that beyond a certain size, the larger a commodity's market exchange set, the less its market-value and vice versa. Formally, when the demand for a commodity is inelastic or unitary and the sets in parentheses are market exchange sets of the commodity, we have:

$e(a \odot b) \leq e(a)$,

which is contrary to P'6. On the other hand, when the demand for the commodity is elastic:

$e(a \odot b) > e(a)$.

Therefore the following relation characterizes exchange-value:

E6 $e(a \odot b) >, =$ or $< e(a)$.

Inelastic demand's inconsistency with conditions P'4 and P'5 *vis à vis* exchange-value and the operation of market exchange is only slightly less obvious. It is illustrated, in Figs. 17.1 and 17.2, by a curve which I will call a "total exchange-value curve". It plots changes in a commodity's market exchange set's size to changes in that set's exchange-value. In other words, the total exchange-value curve shows how, as the number of units of a commodity traded in a period of time changes, the market value of that total changes.

In Figs. 17.1 and 17.2 *a*, *b*, and *c* stand for quantities (or sets) of the market's commodity, whereas the quantities in parentheses stand for *market exchange sets*, that is the total quantity of the commodity exchanged in period *T*. Figure 17.1 shows that the market exchange sets of $(c \odot a)$ and $(c \odot b)$ have the same exchange-value, but that the exchange-value of the market exchange set (*a*) is less than the exchange-value of that of (*b*). This violates condition P'4. Instead of P'4, the following relation characterizes, exchange-value:

E4 $e(c \odot a) = e(c \odot b)$ does not imply $e(a) = e(b)$.

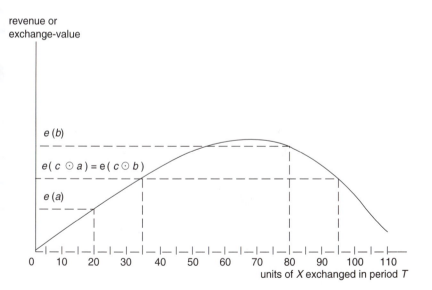

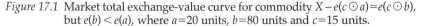

Figure 17.1 Market total exchange-value curve for commodity $X - e(c \odot a) = e(c \odot b)$, but $e(b) < e(a)$, where $a=20$ units, $b=80$ units and $c=15$ units.

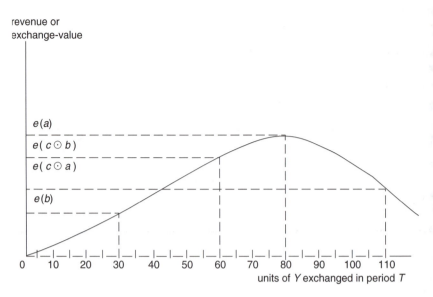

Figure 17.2 Market total exchange-value curve for commodity $Y - e(c \odot a) < e(c \odot b)$, but $e(a) > (e(b))$, where $a=80$ units, $b=30$ units and $c=30$ units.

Figure 17.2 shows that the market-value of the market exchange set of $(c \odot a)$ is less than that of $(c \odot b)$, despite the fact that the exchange-value of (a) is greater than that of (b). This violates condition P′5. Instead of P′5, the following relation characterizes exchange-value:

E5 $e(c \odot a) < e(c \odot b)$ does not imply $e(a) < e(b)$.

Thus, the existence of inelastic demand means that the conditions P′4, P′5 and P′6 do not hold for exchange-value.

10. The commensurability problem with units of account

A ratio scale representation of a quantitatively structured property P, such as mass or exchange-value, is constructed with a unit of the property defined on the basis of some object or process characterized by P and called the standard. (Campbell 1928; Carnap 1966; Ellis 1966; Feather 1959; Hempel 1952; Krantz 1971) But given the creation of such a scale, there still remains the empirical question of that scale's range of magnitude relative to that of the property to whose measurement it is applied. Existence of a ratio scale representation system across a property's full range of magnitudes, a "complete" as opposed to only a "partial" scale, means it is possible in principle to *combine* enough copies of the standard to make it P-commensurable, $=_{p}$, with every object in the domain.

286

(Hempel 1952: 62–8) This corresponds to a weak version of the Archimedean conditions A6 and P6 and P'7 of Section 2.

When working with real models, economics concerns itself tangentially with the process of constructing a system of representation, including a scale, for exchange-value. Without money, it is necessary to adopt a commodity as a numeraire; and, regarding such designations, Pigou (1917) summed up what has remained the traditional wisdom regarding exchange-value's satisfaction of an Archimedean condition. In "The Value of Money" Pigou declared, "the value of any combination of commodities in general can be cited in terms of any single commodity." This "Pigou Hypothesis" may be stated formally for the aggregate endowment Γ as follows:

> For any A and Γ there is potentially a nth power of a $\odot a \odot \ldots \odot a$ of a, written na, such that $na \geq_e \Gamma$.

where "a" is the standard unit of a commodity A and $\geq_e$ means equal or greater than in exchange-value.

Further thought, however, shows that not only is Pigou's hypothesis false, but also that there is no single commodity and only one combination of commodities in terms of which the value of the aggregate endowment can be cited. (Fullbrook 1992) The argument by which this result is reached is disconcertingly simple. Just as a physical object only has weight in a gravitational field, so too a good only has exchange-value in the context of a system of markets, with its "forces" of supply and demand. If a good's exchange-value were equal to the exchange-value of the aggregate endowment, then it would be the only good in the endowment, in which case there would be no demand, no exchanges, no market and no exchange-value. A similar contradiction arises when it is assumed that the equilibrium exchange-value of a quantity of a good is more than half the value of the aggregate endowment. This structural attribute of exchange-value may be expressed formally as follows, where, as above, Γ indicates the aggregate endowment and "a" the standard unit of a commodity A.

E7.   For any Γ there is no A such that there is a nth power of $a \odot a \odot \cdots \odot a$ of a, written na, such that the exchange-value of na is more than half the exchange-value of Γ.

A corollary of E7 is that for any commodity there must be a quantity beyond which its demand ceases to be elastic, or, from this paper's point of view, beyond which the exchange-value of the commodity's market exchange set does not increase.

This obstacle to a full representation of exchange-value in a real economy can be overcome if and only if the aggregate endowment Γ is adopted as the standard of exchange-value (Fullbrook 1992). Under such a system, exchange-values would be represented as proportionate *parts of the whole exchange-value,* in the same way that probabilities are conceived and expressed as fractional parts of a certainty or of the universal event. These peculiarities of representing exchange-value in a real economy are further indications of exchange-value's idiosyncratic structure.

11. Monetary inflation

Monetary inflation may be commonplace, but as a *measurement* phenomenon it is eccentric. (Fullbrook 1992; 1993) Consider mass. Increasing the number of standard weights used in weighing operations does not decrease the mass of those weights. Likewise, increasing the number of standard rods used in measuring length does not change the length of any of those rods. But increasing the quantity of money exchanged, that is, the number of standards of exchange-value used in measuring the exchange-value of the component sets of the aggregate endowment – not only decreases the exchange-value of existing money tokens, it also decreases each one's value by the same proportion. This shows that, in still another way, exchange-value has a structure radically different from mass, length and arithmetical addition.

Consider, further, the case of mass. The property of mass is understood as a function of micromasses, whose existences are independent of the larger mass in which they are grouped. A body's mass is the totality of the masses of that body's parts, and its mass will increase if more parts are added to it. With quantitative properties of this type, each magnitude is *the aggregate of its parts,* the direction of determination running from the micro to the macro level.

But quantitative properties are not always of this type. Probability provides a relevant example. Certainty not only defines an upper bound for magnitudes of probability, but also serves as a whole in relation to which the probabilities of events in the probability space are conceived as parts. In other words, certainty, or the certain event, provides a *unique* standard of measurement for probability, with all other probabilities in the space being defined as parts of that "whole" probability. In this sense, just as the existence of a mass is based on a sum of its parts relation, an event's probability is based on a *part of a whole* relation.

As a means of gaining insight into the structure of exchange-value and its relation to token money, consider the case of an uniform probability space, such as drawing from a deck of cards. Under the concept of probability, each card in the deck shares equally in the "whole" probability, that is, the certainty that when a card from a deck is drawn one of the n cards in the deck will be drawn. Changing the number of cards in the deck changes each card's probability of being drawn, but does not change the probability of the certain event. Furthermore, despite the increase in the number of elementary events, and the change in every card's probability of being drawn, the sum of their probabilities remains equal to the probability of the certain event, and each card's probability remains equal to every other card's probability. A formally identical set of relations holds for the exchange-value of money. It is generally agreed that an increase or decrease in the number of units of money exchanged for the aggregate endowment Γ, although altering the exchange-value of every unit of money, and thereby changing the scale on which exchange-values are represented, does not change the exchange-value of Γ, nor disturb the equality between the exchange-value of MV and the exchange-value of Γ, nor eliminate the exchange-value equivalency between all the individual money tokens. These relations are loaded with structural significance, and so need to be added to the list of exchange-value's structural properties. Where m is a unit or standard token of money, n is the numeric of MV (i.e. $nm = \mathrm{MV}$), Γ is the aggregate endowment, each of whose elements is exchanged only once, and all markets clear, the following relations describe operational aspects of exchange-value measurement.

E8   The exchange-value of Γ is constant for all magnitudes of MV.
E9   For any (numerical) value of MV, $\mathrm{MV} =_e \Gamma$.
E10   Where $nm = \mathrm{MV}$, for any value of n, $m =_e \mathrm{MV}/n$.

We need to consider further these relations.

Token money affords a unique analytical opportunity, because with it the usual order of dependency between use-value and exchange-value is reversed. Token money has use-value only because it has exchange-value.[3] This reversal provides a case where the exchange-values of a homogenous set of objects are determined independently of multifarious use-value considerations. For this reason, token money offers a much clearer view of the structure of exchange-value than the one had from looking at the exchange-value of other commodities.

Of special interest are the properties of the relations by which the market system causes definite magnitudes of exchange-value to become associated with (i.e. become a property of) the individual money tokens. Most of all, it is important to note the direction of determination. Is the exchange-value of MV determined by the number and the exchange-value of the individual money tokens composing MV, that is, a micro-explanation, or is the exchange-value of the individual tokens determined by the number of parts into which the exchange-value of MV is divided, that is, a macro-explanation? If the market exchange process assigns an exchange-value directly to the standard money unit, then the exchange-value of MV would be *directly* proportional to MV. But if the primary assignment of exchange-value is to the total quantity of money exchanged, whatever its magnitude, then the exchange-value of the money unit would be *inversely* proportional to MV. The existence of inflation, as described above, shows that it is the latter process which characterizes exchange-value and money. The exchange-value of the total quantity of money exchanged equals that of the goods for which it exchanges, or, in an economy where all markets clear, the exchange-value of the aggregate endowment of goods (E9). This means that it is the aggregate endowment that acts as *the primary standard of exchange-value* (E8), with the exchange-value of each of the individual token-money units being determined as *equal parts* of the aggregate endowment's exchange-value (E10).

This inverse relation between the quantity of money and the exchange-value of its units corresponds to the negative non-additive law derived earlier with respect to the exchange-value of commodities (E3). But here, with the exchange-value of money, is a very special or pure case of this law, pure in the sense that it is characterized by a fully specified and invariant function – the rarest of all phenomena in the social sciences. Other things remaining unchanged, a percentage change x in the quantity of money exchanged decreases the exchange-value of a unit of money by $1/(1+x)$. In other words, for a given Γ, a money unit's elasticity of exchange-value with respect to quantity of money exchanged is unitary, that is, a constant.

This section has used the empirical phenomenon of inflation to reveal the structure of the economic process by which token money comes to have the property of exchange-value. If, as with most quantitative orders, the determination of magnitude proceeded from the part to the whole, then an increase in the quantity of money exchanged would not only increase the exchange-value of MV, but would also leave the exchange-value of the individual tokens unchanged. In such a world, monetary inflation would be impossible. Instead, other things being equal, increasing MV affects the exchange-value of individual tokens in the same way as increasing the number of elementary events in an equiprobable probability space affects each of those events' probability.

12. Summary of structural properties of exchange-value discovered

This paper's results thus far spring from two simple but novel analytical manoeuvres: raising the question "What is the structure of exchange-value?" and undertaking an analysis of the market system as a measurement system. This dual strategy affords a fresh analytical point of view on a much observed and often analyzed set of phenomena. Old verities and celebrated results may be scrutinized and further examined within the context of this new but complementary analytical framework. Thus, the law of demand (in the empirical sense of an observed regularity), is now interpreted as a law of negative non-additivity of exchange-value. Likewise, from relations expressed in the equation of exchange, a fully specified law of negative non-additivity of exchange-value has been derived for money. Because of the failure to look at price and quantity phenomena from the measurement and structural angles, these non-additivity laws, despite their simplicity, have not previously entered into economic thought.

The measurement/structural approach also raised questions about the representation of exchange-value, questions whose answers have not been backed previously by analysis. In considering this set of questions, it has been found that the commensurability condition in a real economy is satisfiable only if exchange-values are represented as fractional parts of the whole exchange-value, that is, the exchange-value of the aggregate endowment. Furthermore, it also is the aggregate endowment's exchange-value which serves as the primary standard of exchange-value in a monetary economy, with the exchange-value of the individual money units depending on *the number of parts into which the whole exchange-value is divided*.

There follows a list of the structural properties of exchange-value as a measurement order discovered thus far.

E1 $e(a \odot (b \odot c)) = e((a \odot b) \odot c)$.

E2 $e(a \odot b) = e(b \odot a)$.

E3 $e(a \odot b) < e(a) + e(b)$.

E4 $e(c \odot a) = e(c \odot b)$ does not imply $e(a) = e(b)$.

E5 $e(c \odot a) < e(c \odot b)$ does not imply $e(a) < e(b)$.

E6 $e(a \odot b) >, =$ or $< e(a)$.

E7 For any Γ there is no A such that there is a nth power of $a \odot a \odot \cdots \odot a$ of a, written na, such that the exchange-value of na is more than half the exchange-value of Γ.

E8 The exchange-value of Γ is constant for all magnitudes of MV.

E9 For any (numerical) value of MV, $MV =_e \Gamma$.

E10 Where $nm = MV$, for any value of n, $m =_e MV/n$.

13. Exchange-value as a boolean algebra

The analysis of Sections 7 and 8 entail certain scientifically curious requirements and possibilities for the numerical representation of exchange-value. Expressions E8–E10 show that the exchange-value of money, the operational standard, is related to the primary standard in an idiosyncratic but highly structured way. Under the terms of the convention of monetary exchange, MV's exchange-value is identically equal to Γ's, meaning that changes in MV change the exchange-value of MV's units and not the exchange-value of MV itself. Under these relations, the exchange-values of the units of money are *equal parts of the given whole exchange-value*, that is, the exchange-value of Γ. Analysis also has shown that the commensurability condition can be satisfied for exchange-value metrication, be it a monetary or a real economy, only by using Γ, the aggregate endowment, as the primary measurement standard. This is a situation completely at odds with the physical measurement orders of mass, length and time, where, vis à vis the commensurability condition, there exist an infinite number of possible primary standards for metrication. Since, for these orders, the choice of standard is ultimately arbitrary, so too is the size of the unit. Therefore, these orders can be metricated at best on a ratio scale, meaning that their measurement numbers are unique only up to a similarity transformation. But exchange-value, since for a given aggregate endowment there is only one possible primary standard, may, like probability, be metricated on an absolute scale, that is, represented as fractional parts of the exchange-value of its singular standard. Such exchange-value numbers would be unique up to an identity transformation. The fact that exchange-value invariably has been represented on a ratio scale is irrelevant to the present inquiry. What is important is that analysis has shown that in principle those ratio scale representations can be converted to absolute ones by dividing them by MV.

Quantities of money and quantities of commodities exchanged can be interpreted as *money exchange sets and commodity exchange sets*. The special sets corresponding to MV and the set of all units of all commodities exchanged in period T will be termed the *money exchange space* or Γ_M and the *commodity exchange space* or Γ, respectively. This yields $P(M_\Gamma)$ and $P(\Gamma)$, the power sets of M_Γ and Γ, which, each being a set of all subsets of a given set, are boolean algebras. Because, as shown above by E8, E9 and E10, the exchange-value of M_Γ is always uniquely determined by Γ such that $M_\Gamma =_e \Gamma$, the exchange-value of money can be uniquely represented as parts of *the whole exchange-value*, i.e. as parts of the exchange-value of Γ. Furthermore, since all of the elements (units of money) comprising M_Γ are interexchangeable, i.e. of equal exchange-value, M_Γ is a *uniform or equivaluable* exchange space. It follows that where,

$$M_\Gamma = \{m_1, m_2, \ldots, m_n\}$$

and a money exchange set A is formed of g money units, that $e(A)$, the exchange-value of A, is g/n parts of the whole exchange-value $e(\Gamma)$. For every commodity exchange set, monetary exchange also identifies a money exchange set of equal exchange-value. Thus, when MV or the cardinal of M_Γ is known, it is possible to satisfy the following conditions.

D1   With every element A of $P(M_\Gamma)$ and every element A of $P(\Gamma)$, it is possible to associate a non-negative number $e'(A)$, the *absolute exchange-value* of A, such that $0 \le e'(A) \le 1$.

D2 $e'(M_\Gamma) = e(\Gamma) = 1$.

D3   If A and B are mutually exclusive subsets of M_Γ or of Γ, i.e. if $A \cap B = \varnothing$, then $e'(A \cup B) = e'(A) + e'(B)$.

D4   For every $e'(A)$, where A is a subset of M_Γ or of Γ, there is an element $e'(A')$ such that $e'(A) + e'(A') = e'(M_\Gamma) = e'(\Gamma) = 1$.

Condition D1 specifies a set $E_{M\Gamma}$ or E_Γ of absolute exchange-value numbers for $P(M_\Gamma)$ or for $P(\Gamma)$ respectively. *Conditions D1–4 determine that $E_{M\Gamma}$ and E_Γ are boolean algebras.* (See Appendix for the axioms of boolean algebra.)

Under the boolean hypothesis, increasing or decreasing the size of a commodity's exchange set assumes a theoretical significance which *transcends the individual commodity market.* Any change in the size of a single market exchange set means that the commodity exchange-space Γ also changes. If Γ_1 was the original exchange space and A_1 was the ath commodity's market exchange set, then, after $A_1 \odot A_2$, the new exchange space is $\Gamma_2 = \Gamma_1 \cup A_2$. *This represents a change in the standard of exchange-value.* Consequently, the exchange-values of the elements of $P(\Gamma_1)$ and $P(\Gamma_2)$ are not *strictly* comparable. The algebraic analysis of value identifies every exchange-value as a part of a whole exchange-value, and $e(A_1)$ and $e(A_1 \odot A_2)$ represent exchange-values which are parts of two different wholes. This attribute of being defined only relative to a particular universal set, which is the ultimate basis of the index number problem, is a peculiarity of the boolean structure. This relativity property manifests itself in other boolean fields. For example, for every set of statements there is a different statement calculus, and the probability numbers of events belonging to different event spaces are not combinable by arithmetical addition.

14. Applications

This section considers the relevance of the foregoing results to a pair of theoretical problems which have resisted solution. Both anomalies appeared when analysis began from a non-zero degree of aggregation.

14.1 The homogeneity problem

After the appearance of *The General Theory* (1936), efforts were made to overcome the micro/macro split that had always been the fault-line of economic analysis. These attempts centred on the integration of money into the general equilibrium model. But these efforts at synthesis revealed an antinomy that was potentially as undermining to existing economic theory as the results of the Michelson–Morley experiment had been to classical physics. The impasse centred on the so-called "homogeneity postulate". Whereas the n equations for excess demands in the commodity markets were homogeneous of degree zero in money prices, the one equation for the excess demand for money was homogeneous of degree one in money prices and the quantity of money, an apparent contradiction where the excess demand for money is taken to be identically equal to an excess supply of commodities. (Fullbrook 1992; 1993; 1994; Patinkin 1956)

Seen through the lens of this paper's structural analysis, the homogeneity difference in the monetarized general equilibrium model, far from being a problem, is precisely what is predicted. This difference arises, according to the new approach, because the money demand equation introduces a quantitative order with a different structure from that of the ratio scale of money prices. In other words, the monetarized model of GET brings directly into play the boolean structure of exchange-value. Exactly how this introduction takes place needs examination.

When the *exchange-values* of quantities of money are considered at the micro level, i.e. the exchange-values of subsets of M_Γ, they exhibit the same structural properties as the n quantitative orders of the n commodities. In other words, if M_1, M_2, and M_3 are disjoint subsets of M_Γ – as, for example, three ten-dollar bills in one's wallet – then their exchange-values are combinable according to the conditions A1–5, as are also the probabilities of independent events belonging to the same event space. But when the exchange-value of money is considered at the *macro* level, as is the case when a change in M_Γ is entertained, then the analysis is brought up against exchange-value's boolean structure, especially its universal set which acts as an upper bound, thereby imposing the degree-one homogeneity on the demand for units of money.

Instead of a structural crack to be papered over, the apparent contradiction thrown up by the attempt to integrate money into the general equilibrium paradigm may be viewed as the thin end of a heuristic wedge. Further research, one suspects, will reveal that exchange-value's boolean structure is integrally tied up with the micro/macro "paradoxes" revealed by Keynes, and which, half a century on, even after the brilliant analyses of Clower and Leijonhufvud, remain largely intellectually intractable.

14.2 The Fisher–Becker curio

Gary Becker (1962; 1971) showed that from the existence of budget constraints alone it follows that a *market* demand curve must slope downward, whether consumer behavior is rational or not. By beginning his analysis at the level of the market, rather than at the level of the individual, Becker shows that there exists a macro budgetary effect which entails "the basic demand relations". (Becker 1971: 11) In other words, scarcity of funds is a condition for negative sloping market demand curves, and rational consumer behavior is not a necessary condition. In fact, Becker showed that the whole of the subjective side of demand theory is otiose when it comes to the deduction of the general inverse relation between price and quantity demanded at the market level.

Becker's result needed an explanation which would integrate it into a larger theoretical edifice, but none was forthcoming. Without this theoretical grounding, Becker's "scarcity principle" remained an anomaly and, therefore, survives today only as a curious and obscure footnote to economics, with students continuing to be taught that the downward slope of the market demand curve is due to intrasubjective factors.

But Gary Becker was not the first to point out the budget effect, that is, "the effect of a change in prices on the distribution of opportunities." (Becker 1962: 6). With a different emphasis and at a higher level of aggregation, Irving Fisher noticed and expounded on the same macro dimension of *relative* prices forty years earlier. In *The Purchasing Power of Money*, Fisher writes:

> if one commodity rises in price (without any change in the quantity of it or of other things bought and sold, and without any change in the volume of circulating medium or in the velocity of circulation), then other commodities must *fall* in price. The increased money expended for this commodity will be taken from other purchases. (1920: 178)

Note that here Fisher is not considering the absolute level of prices, which he assumes is constant, but rather relative prices and how at the macro level there exists an interdependency between them. Fisher realized, in a way that Becker did not, that his discovery posed a major paradox for economics. (1920: 180) Furthermore, because Fisher carries the analysis to a higher level of aggregation, he comes much closer than Becker to discovering the boolean structure of exchange-value. His nearness to this elementary truth becomes apparent when two terms of his foregoing passage are translated into the terminology of the present paper. Substituting "exchange-value per unit" for Fisher's "price" and "measured exchange-value" for his "money expended" yields the followings statement:

> If one commodity rises in exchange-value per unit (without any change in the quantity of it or of other things bought and sold, and without any change in the volume of circulating medium or in the velocity of circulation), then other commodities must *fall* in exchange-value per unit. The increased measured exchange-value for this commodity will be taken from [the exchange-value of] other purchases.

Thus translated, Fisher's passage captures "the part of the whole" relation which, as for probability, is one dimension of exchange-value. It captures also the fact that, despite all the concrete individuality that goes into exchange-value's making, the exchange-value of every unit of every commodity is irreducibly and fundamentally a SOCIAL relation that extends as far as the economy in which the exchange of the unit takes place.

What Fisher could not do was explain how the micro and macro levels of "causation" were linked. His insight, like Mendel's discoveries concerning heredity, lacked a contemporaneous means of explanation. Abstract algebra was little known, and without this set of tools *the boolean structure* which links exchange-value's two levels of "causation" could not be identified.[4]

15. Conclusion

Quantitative orders possess structures. This paper has investigated the structure of exchange-value and found that it is an unsuitable subject for ideological or metaphysical purists. Market forms of economic value are reducible neither to wholes nor to relations between atoms. Because of its boolean structure, to increase the probability of one event decreases the probability of another and vice versa. Likewise for exchange-value. Every exchange-value in a money economy exists only as an integral and inter-dependent *part* of an intersubjective system of other exchange-values. For entrenched intellectual positions, these results have obvious negative implications. But in closing I prefer to emphasize their possible positive importance for understanding two significant current problems.

One is the need to bring ecological considerations into economic deci-sion-making. Disclosure of the boolean structure of exchange-value means that attempts to intellectually come to grips with the problem by placing money-values on ecosystems and other mega ("trans-boolean") entities are, like basing engineering calculations on speeds in excess of the speed of light, radically misplaced and counter-productive. Many ecolog-ical economists have suspected as much, but found it difficult to argue against the euclidean commonsense of neoclassicists.

The second problem is the redistribution of income and wealth from the poor and middle-classes to the rich and super-rich now taking place both intra- and internationally at a rate and on a scale unprecedented in human history. No adequate theory exists to explain and thereby to enable us to curtail, stop or reverse this radical change in the human condition. Of course it has something to do with globalization. But why should global-ization have this redistributive effect? And how can the process be managed so that human will controls the direction and magnitude of the redistribution? This paper provides a theoretical framework in which to think about the problem.

Globalization means that all monetary exchanges are pulled into one giant system of exchange-value. Nothing much may have changed nationally, but the market-value of commodity X no longer exists prima-rily in relation to the other commodities of that country. Instead each per-son's economic assets are valued by a *different system* than before, by a global system that brings new forces into play.

The boolean structure of exchange-value means that the neoclassical dichotomy between value and distribution theory is spurious. For a cen-tury economists have taught themselves and others to think of value and distribution separately. This doctrine stands in the way of understanding globalization. The present analysis has shown that ultimately value and its distribution are, as earlier thinkers intuited, merely different ways of looking at the same thing. To explain one is to explain the other. To explain why any commodity or any person's day of work is worth so many dollars or euros or yen is to explain why the world's income and wealth are distributed the way they are.

Appendix: Axioms of a boolean algebra

A boolean algebra is a 6-tuple $[B, \cup, \cap, ', 0, 1]$, where B is a set, $\cup$ and $\cap$ are binary operations in B, $'$ is a binary relation in B having B as its domain, 0 and 1 are distinct elements of B, and for all a, b, and c belonging to B the following axioms are satisfied.

1 Each operation is associative
  $a \cup (b \cup c) = (a \cup b) \cup c$ and $a \cap (b \cap c) = (a \cap b) \cap c$.
2 Each operation is commutative
  $a \cup b = b \cup a$ and $a \cap b = b \cap a$.
3 Each operation distributes over the other
  $a \cup (b \cap c) = (a \cup b) \cap (a \cup c)$ and $a \cap (b \cup c) = (a \cap b) \cup (a \cap c)$.
4 For all a in B,
  $a \cup 0 = a$ and $a \cap 1 = a$.
5 For each a in B there exists a $'$-related element a' such that
  $a \cup a' = 1$ and $a \cap a' = 0$.

Notes

1 Likewise, Arrow and Debreu's famous proof of the existence of an equilibrium in a competitive economy proceeds on the basis of the assumption that the system of prices is an euclidean space. [Arrow and Debreu 1983]
2 For a very accessible account of these fundamentals see Carnap 1966: 51–124.
3 The demand for token money is a pure case of the type of market situation analyzed by the French Intersubjectivists. See Dupuy 1989; Levy 1991; 1994; Orléan 1990; 1992; and most especially 1998. See also Fullbrook 1994b; 1996b.
4 This boolean structure, with its internal relations, is consistent with Hodgson's reconstitutive downward causation, where "it is impossible to take the parts as given and then explain the whole," because the whole to some extent shapes its parts. [See Hodgson's essay in this volume. (p. 168)]

References

Arrow, Kenneth J. and Gerard, Debreu (1983) [1954] "Existence of an Equilibrium for a Competitive Economy", *Collected Papers of Kenneth J. Arrow*, vol. 2. Cambridge, Massachusetts: Belknap, pp. 58–91.
Becker, Gary S. (1962) "Irrational Behavior and Economic Theory", *The Journal of Political Economy* 70(1): 1–13.

Becker, G.S. (1971) *Economic Theory*, New York: Knopf.

Campbell, Norman Robert (1928) *An Account of the Principles of Measurement and Calculation*, London: Longman's, Green and Co.

Carnap, Rudolf (1966) *Philosophical Foundations of Physics: An Introduction to the Philosophy of Science*, New York: Basic Books.

Clower, R. W. (1965) "The Keynesian Counter-revolution: a theoretical appraisal", in F. H. Hahn and F. Brechling (eds) *The Theory of Interest Rates*, London: Macmillan.

Clower, R. W. (1967) "A Reconsideration of the Microfoundations of Monetary Theory", *The Economic Journal* 6: 1–9.

Debrev, Gerard (1986) 'Theoretical Models: Mathematical Form and Economic Content", *Econometricz* 54(6): 1259–70.

Duhem, Pierre (1977) *The Aim and Structure of Physical Theory*, (1905), New York: Atheneum.

Dupuy, Jean-Pierre (1989) "Convention et common knowledge", *Revue économique* 2: 361–400.

Ellis, Brian (1966) *Basic Concepts of Measurement*, Cambridge: Cambridge University Press.

Feather, Norman (1959) *Mass, Length and Time*, Edinburgh: Edinburgh University Press.

Fisher, Irving (1920) *The Purchasing Power of Money: Its determination and Relation to Credit, Interest and Crises*, New York: Macmillan.

Fullbrook, Edward (1992) "Some Surprises (Mostly Good) Regarding the Representation of Value", *Atlantic Economic Society Best Papers Proceedings* 2(2): 13–7.

Fullbrook, E. (1993) "Logic and Abstract Units of Account", *Atlantic Economic Society Best Papers Proceedings* 3(2): 2–6.

Fullbrook, E. (1994a) "Rabbit or Duck: An Introduction to Measurement Economics", presented to the American Economic Association, Boston, Mass., January.

Fullbrook E. (1994b) "Nominal Versus Real Values: A Nominal Distinction", *Atlantic Economic Society Best Papers Proceedings* 4(1): 11–8.
Reprinted in *Archives of Economic History* 5(2) 1994, pp. 165–74.

Fullbrook, E. (1996a) "Consumer Metaphysics: The Neoclassicalists Versus The Intersubjectivists", *Archives of Economic History* 3(1): 165–74.

Fullbrook, E. (1996b) "The Metaphysics of Consumer Desire and the French Intersubjectivists", *International Advances In Economic Research* 2(3): 289–94.

Hempel, Carl G. (1952) *Fundamentals of Concept Formation in Empirical Science*, Chicago: University of Chicago.

Krantz, D. H., *et al.* (1971) *Foundations of Measurement*, vol. 1, Cambridge, Mass.: Massachusetts Institute of Technology.

Lawson, Tony (1997) *Economics and Reality*, London: Routledge.

Leijonhufvud, Axel (1968) *On Keynesian Economics and the Economics of Keynes*, London: Oxford University Press.

Levy, Thierry (1991) *Conventions et foundements de l'échange marchand et de la monnaie*, Paris: Paris-IX-Dauphine University.

Levy, Thierry (1994) "Measurement Economics, Value Theory and the Social Function of Money", *Atlantic Economic Society Best Paper Proceedings* 4(2): 11–8.

Marshall, Alfred (1938) *Principles of Economics*, London: Macmillan.

Morgenstern, Oskar (1948) "Demand Theory Reconsidered", *Quarterly Journal of Economics* 62(1): 165–201.

Orléan, André (1990) "Le role des influences interpersonnelles dans la formation des cours boursieers." *Revue économique* No. 5, septembre.

Orléan, André (1992) "Contagion des opinions et founctionnement des marchés financiers", *Revue économique* No. 4, julliet: 685–98.

Orléan, André (1998) "La monnaie autoréférentielle: réflexions sur les évolutions monétaries contemporaines", *La Monnaie Souveraine*, eds. Michel Aglietta and André Orléan, Paris: Editions Odile Jacob.

Patinkin, Don (1956) *Money, Interest and Prices: An Integration of Monetary and Value Theory*, Evanston, Ill.: Row Peterson.

Pigou, A. C. (1917) "The Value of Money", *The Quarterly Journal of Economics* 32: 38–65.

Russell, Bertrand (1937) *The Principles of Mathematics*, 2nd edn London.

NAME INDEX

300

SUBJECT INDEX